All for the Regiment

CIVIL WAR AMERICA

Gary W. Gallagher, editor

ALL FOR THE REGIMENT
The Army of the Ohio, 1861-1862

GERALD J. PROKOPOWICZ

The University of North Carolina Press • Chapel Hill and London

Manufactured in the United States of America

Designed by Heidi Perov

Set in Bembo with Birch Display

by Keystone Typesetting, Inc.

The paper in this book meets the guidelines for permanence
and durability of the Committee on Production Guidelines for
Book Longevity of the Council on Library Resources.

Library of Congress Cataloging-in-Publication Data

Prokopowicz, Gerald J.

All for the regiment : the Army of the Ohio, 1861–1862 /
Gerald J. Prokopowicz.

p. cm. — (Civil War America)

Includes bibliographical references and index.

ISBN 0-8078-2626-x (alk. paper)

1. United States. Army of the Ohio. 2. United States—
History—Civil War, 1861–1865—Regimental histories.

3. United States—History—Civil War, 1861–1865—
Campaigns. 4. Kentucky—History—Civil War, 1861–1865—
Campaigns. 5. Tennessee—History—Civil War, 1861–1865—
Campaigns. I. Title. II. Series.

E470.4.P76 2001

973.7'471—dc21   00-051230

05 04 03 02 01   5 4 3 2 1

For Emily

Contents

Illustrations

Acknowledgments

On a wintry day in November 1967, while returning to Detroit from a family vacation in Washington, D.C., my father detoured our Ford station wagon off of the highway to the visitors' center at the Antietam National Battlefield Site. I am not sure why we stopped there; no one in the family had any particular interest in the Civil War. There were few other people on the battlefield that day, but as we drove along the Sunken Road and looked across the bare fields to the Dunker Church, I sensed that there were plenty of ghosts present. When we left late in the afternoon, the rest of the family knew a little bit more about the battle than they had that morning, but I was changed. My imagination had been taken prisoner by the men who had fought there, a capture ratified a month later by a Christmas present of toy soldiers in blue and gray plastic, many of whom have survived to this day. For their boundless gifts of inspiration, encouragement, and love, as well as for the toy soldiers, my parents are first in the long line of people who made this book possible.

Of the many fine teachers I have known, three mentors gave much more of their time than I deserved to encourage my interest in history generally and the Civil War in particular: Mike Bartnikowski at Henry Ford Middle School in Highland Park, Michigan; John Shy at the University of Michigan; and David Herbert Donald at Harvard University. To Professor Donald I owe a particular debt for his extraordinary patience in directing the dissertation from which this book developed.

I am also grateful to Ernest May of Harvard University, codirector of my dissertation, and to my graduate school colleagues, in particular Fran McDonnell, who advanced the progress of this book as much through the camaraderie of the Friday morning basketball games as through their comments and ideas regarding this work. Professors Donald and May, Gary Gallagher, Michael Fellman, Robert J. Brugger, and Scott M. Bushnell all read the manuscript with care and offered valuable suggestions and corrections.

The editorial team at the University of North Carolina Press, including Lewis Bateman (now at Cambridge University Press), David Perry, and Paula Wald, have been models of professionalism and sources of sound advice. Copyeditor Stevie Champion did an outstanding job of removing errors and fixing inconsistencies; the imperfections that remain are mine alone.

The staffs of all the libraries mentioned in the notes were courteous and helpful, with special thanks due to the staffs at Stones River National Battlefield, Shiloh National Military Park, Perryville State Historic Site, and the Civil War Institute at Gettysburg College. This book would not have been possible without the generous support of a fellowship from the U.S. Army Center for Military History and the encouragement and friendship of its former director, Brigadier General Harold Nelson (retired). The Charles Warren Center at Harvard University also provided much-appreciated financial assistance. No institution was more vital to me over the past seven years than The Lincoln Museum of Fort Wayne, Indiana, as a place of productive and rewarding employment, as well as for its outstanding research collection. I am glad to have this chance to express my appreciation to Joan Flinspach, president and chief executive officer, and to all of my colleagues at the museum for their support.

My deepest gratitude is to my wife Emily and my daughters Caroline and Maria.

All for the Regiment

Introduction

In July 1862 at St. Clairsville, Ohio, a group of young men answered Abraham Lincoln's call for three hundred thousand more Union soldiers by joining Company B of the 98th Ohio Volunteer Infantry Regiment. One of them, John Patton, recalled the month of his enlistment as one of "the dark hours of the Civil War," a time when Northerners were discouraged by the failure of the Peninsula campaign in the East and disappointed by the inactivity that had followed the costly victory at Shiloh in the West. The government urgently needed new blood to reinvigorate its war effort and halt the tide of Southern success, especially after rebel forces went on the offensive in Kentucky and Maryland. Regiments like the raw 98th Ohio were rushed to the front after receiving no more than a week or two of training. On August 29, 1862, Patton and his comrades found themselves near Richmond, Kentucky, listening to the sound of enemy artillery for the first time. The guns were being fired by veteran Confederate troops led by Edmund Kirby Smith, who on the following day attacked two brigades of newly raised Yankee regiments and routed them.

The 98th Ohio, which had remained in reserve during the battle, was ordered to cover the retreat of the demoralized Union army. As he stumbled north through the drought-parched Kentucky countryside, Patton saw men so thirsty that "some of them drank of the thick muddy water [that] ran along the turnpike gutter" and others so tired that they fell asleep by the roadside "but a few feet from the passing wagon wheels." The morale of the Federal troops fell still further as they approached Lexington, where citizens flew Confederate flags in celebration of the recent Union defeat. At one point the men of the 98th Ohio were ordered into battle formation to hold off the pursuing rebels, who were expected to catch up at any moment. When the teamsters who were driving the regiment's wagons saw the troops preparing for a fight, they fled in terror. "They come rushing on us like panic stricken cattle," Patton wrote, and broke through a stone wall before disappearing into the distance, headed for Louisville or perhaps Cincinnati. But no rebels came, and eventually Patton and his tired comrades made beds for themselves on the ground, where they spent an uneasy night.[1]

The retreat resumed the next day. During a brief halt, the men of Company B discovered that they had inadvertently left their unit's flag behind. Captain Mitchell, the company's commander, called for volunteers to retrieve the standard, and two came forward. When they retraced their steps to the place where the company had slept the previous night, however, they found the area occupied by enemy soldiers. Rather than abandon their quest, they boldly walked into the camp, unchallenged by sentries, and began to look for the flag. They found it just where it had been left, picked it up, and completed their daring mission by bringing the treasured banner back to the regiment before nightfall. The retreat continued.

This book is a history of the field army in which John Patton served, the first Army of the Ohio, from its origins in the early months of the war through its final battle at Perryville in October 1862.[2] It tells the story of the creation of the army and how it fared in several critical campaigns,[3] a story that amid the recent flood of Civil War scholarship has somehow escaped the telling. No general history of the army has been written since the nineteenth century, an omission that has become all the more glaring as students of the war have increasingly appreciated the importance of events west of the Appalachians.[4]

More important, the history of the Army of the Ohio illustrates how that institution developed certain social and organizational characteristics that were typical of all Civil War armies, characteristics that made those armies incapable of destroying one another on the battlefield. In most of the war's major engagements, the forces of both sides emerged bloodied and temporarily disorganized (the victor little less so than the vanquished) but still able to function, confounding the participants' widely held expectation that their battles would be as short, intense, and decisive as Napoleon's defeat at Waterloo in 1815. With the exception of John Bell Hood's ill-fed, outnumbered, outgeneraled Army of Tennessee, which disintegrated after the Battle of Nashville in 1864, no Civil War field army suffered a truly decisive battlefield defeat.

Many Civil War historians have found it difficult to abandon the paradigm of Waterloo and have spilled enormous quantities of ink to explain why battle after battle deviated from the supposed norm of Napoleonic decisiveness.[5]

Beginning with the writings of veterans in the years immediately following the war and continuing through the middle of the twentieth century, most military narratives employed the "drum and trumpet" style, portraying battles as competitions between individual generals who clenched cigars in their teeth as they leaned over lantern-lit maps in their tents on the eve of the contest, then bravely led their troops to victory, waving their swords heroically while riding on foaming steeds through the bloody fray. Rank-and-file soldiers rarely appear as individuals in these accounts; instead, anthropomorphized regiments and brigades collectively display human qualities like bravery, patriotism, and fear, sharing the stage with their leaders as the main characters of the story. The outcomes of battles in these stories are typically attributed to some combination of the shortcomings of the losing general (who unaccountably fails to seize the opportunity just as decisive victory lies within his grasp) and the tenacity of the winning side's regiments, which again and again rally miraculously at the last possible moment to stave off defeat. For the war's veterans, these narratives helped them come to terms with their experiences by recasting their memories of the chaos of battle into forms that seemed more rational and controlled. Since the passing of the veterans, such stories have provided vicarious thrills to generations of Civil War buffs.

As satisfying as it may be to blame defeat on the extraordinary incompetence of Joseph Hooker or Braxton Bragg, or to praise the Stonewall Brigade or the 20th Maine for exceptional gallantry, the use of such remarkable phenomena to explain recurring results is unpersuasive as analysis. Extraordinary events that occur again and again are, by definition, no longer extraordinary. Recognizing this, historians seeking to explain the pattern of indecisive battle between 1861 and 1865 have for the last fifty years generally attributed it to changes in technology and doctrine. Since the end of World War II (a war in which technological developments played a dominant role), historians have focused on the impact of the rifled musket, the standard infantry weapon of the Civil War. The rifled musket had a range several times greater than that of the smoothbore musket of Napoleon's day, which meant that a defender could load and fire many times, instead of only once or twice, in the time it took an enemy to charge through his field of fire. It was this capability, the argument goes, that rendered the mass infantry assault and the mounted cavalry charge obsolete, making it impossible for an attacking army to achieve decisive battlefield success.[6]

There are, however, several problems with this explanation. First, the fact that most major battles did not have decisive results conceals that within each battle there were numerous local actions in which attacking forces won clear, tactically decisive victories over defending troops, driving them from their positions and inflicting substantial losses. In many of the war's smaller battles, the victorious force retained enough cohesion to pursue and harass the defeated enemy, as the Confederates did to John Patton's regiment after the battle at Richmond, Kentucky. Inconclusive results were not characteristic of all Civil War battles, only those that swelled to encompass whole armies. Second, smoothbore muskets remained more common than rifles until late 1862, at least in the western theater. Third, where rifles were available, the heavy woods and rolling terrain found on most battlefields restricted the troops' ability to employ their weapons at long distances, so that much of the fighting took place at close ranges that made the new technology irrelevant. Finally, if long-range muzzle-loading rifles made decisive battle impossible, how did the Prussian army of the 1860s and 1870s manage to inflict devastating battlefield defeats on a series of enemies armed with weapons that were as good or better than those of the Union and the Confederacy?

The reason that the Army of the Ohio (and by extension other Civil War armies) fought as it did in 1861–62 was not because of the will of its leaders or the capabilities of its weaponry, but because of the way in which it was recruited, trained, and organized. Assembled out of a collection of independent and fiercely clannish companies and regiments, the Army of the Ohio resembled a strong but ponderous beast whose component units could absorb enormous punishment on the battlefield without breaking, but which lacked the agility to execute the maneuvers necessary to destroy its enemies.

The story of John Patton's company flag makes the case in miniature. The men of the 98th Ohio lacked training and experience in August 1862, and it is unlikely that many of them were even aware of the name of the field army to which they had just been assigned (which was at that moment the Army of Kentucky, a short-lived organization that was absorbed into the larger Army of the Ohio six days after its inception). But they had already developed such powerful bonds within their company and regiment that the men of Company B were willing to put their lives at extreme risk rather than lose the symbol of their solidarity, the company flag. Stories like this, of soldiers risking and often losing their lives in trying to save their company or regimental flags, are common in the history of the war, and they offer a significant insight into how the war was fought.

The soldiers' loyalty centered on the smallest units to which they belonged, the company and especially the regiment. Consider that most people belong to many organizations at any given moment. If in 1860 one of the men who was to serve in the Army of the Ohio had been asked, "What are you?" he might have answered "a Democrat," "a Hoosier," "a Methodist," "a McGillicudy," "a Mason," "a farmer," "ein Turner," and so on. By his answer, he would have indicated that he primarily identified himself with his family, political party, church, social club, commercial enterprise, or other organization. When that same person volunteered to fight in 1861, he became part of a new set of organizations. He was a member of the infantry, cavalry, or artillery. He belonged to the Army of the Ohio, the Army of the Potomac, or one of several other field armies. Within his army, he belonged to a particular corps, division, brigade, regiment, and company. Of all those options, if simply asked to name the unit to which he belonged, the typical soldier would name his regiment. The regiment, more than any other unit, was a self-aware community, held together by bonds based on common geographic, social, cultural, or economic identities, strengthened by months of training and campaigning as a unit. Organizational loyalty and cohesion at the regimental level was thus extraordinarily strong.[7]

In contrast, bonds of organizational identification and loyalty rarely extended throughout larger units. Frequent reorganization and sheer size meant that brigades, divisions, corps, and armies did not have the permanence or human scale that might have allowed such bonds to develop. The complexity of these larger units made battlefield management difficult for the few professionally trained soldiers available and almost impossible for the many volunteer officers on whom the armies relied. Unlike their component regiments, larger units were readily disrupted by combat and almost incapable of performing complex offensive maneuvers.

Students of Civil War battles have long recognized the primary place of the regiment in the hearts and minds of Civil War soldiers. E. B. Long wrote in 1971, "Perhaps in no other war was the 'esprit' of the regiment more vital or apparent than in the Civil War."[8] The significance of this phenomenon has not been fully developed, however; a poorly organized, amateur-led army that consisted of many dozens of highly cohesive regiments was like a dinosaur, a killing machine with powerful muscles and a tiny brain. It was capable of inflicting and enduring great violence, but the lack of a highly developed central nervous system limited it to administering straight-ahead blows and prevented it from coordinating its sinews to strike at its opponents' vulnerable flanks. At the same time, the absence of a powerful brain made such an organization almost impossible to kill, since its parts could survive and function independently. When Napoleon left the field at Waterloo, the French army disintegrated in panic; in contrast, Civil War battles were full of instances where units fought successfully after the "brain" of the army departed, the stand of Thomas's corps at Chickamauga after Rosecrans's departure being the best-known example.

Since individual regiments possessed such strong internal cohesion, they usually remained intact as organizations, even after suffering casualties that would have shattered contemporary European military units. Losses of 37 percent made the Charge of the Light Brigade at Balaclava in 1854 seem disastrous, but there were at least sixty Union regiments that suffered casualties of more than 50 percent in a single engagement, many of which continued to fight. After a battle, whether won or lost, the survival of most of their regiments as functioning units made it relatively easy for Civil War armies to reassemble themselves, much more so than if they had disintegrated into mobs of panic-stricken individuals. The decentralization of loyalty and the concentration of unit identification at the regimental level made these armies so elastic that they could not be broken, yet it also made them into awkward weapons that their leaders could not wield with decisive effect.

The history of the Army of the Ohio reflects this combination of resilience and clumsiness. From its organization in 1861 to its moment of decision at Perryville in October 1862, the Army of the Ohio was characterized by regimental cohesion that was extraordinarily strong and by a "brain" (defined as its entire command and control system, not just the ability of its commanding officer) that was unusually dim. The army's regiments displayed great bravery and, in small engagements like Rowlett's Station or Mill Springs, showed considerable tactical finesse. At the army's major battles, Shiloh and Perryville, the leaders of its higher echelons of command were unable to perform their assigned functions, but the army nonetheless survived because its individual regiments maintained their organizational integrity. In each case, it was not technology or generalship but the regiment-based culture of the army, developed in the processes of recruitment, organization, and training, that determined how well or poorly the Army of the Ohio fought. Whether the same statement can be applied to other Civil War armies (as I believe it can) is a question that invites the participation of other scholars, to confirm or reject this thesis, in either case advancing the study not just of the Civil War, but of the nature of human conflict.

CHAPTER ONE

Genesis of an Army,
May to November 1861

In the late summer of 1862 seventy-five thousand men known collectively as the Army of the Ohio marched two hundred dry, dusty miles across Tennessee and Kentucky, hurrying north in a desperate effort to prevent Braxton Bragg's rebel forces from capturing the strategically vital Union base of operations at Louisville. The soldiers of the Army of the Ohio won the race against Bragg, and though they arrived in Louisville hungry, dirty, and exhausted from the chase, it took only a few days of rest and full rations to revive their spirits. After trading in their tatters for new uniforms, they looked and felt their martial best when they set out again on the first day of October, determined to find and defeat Bragg's army and to reclaim Kentucky for the Union.

The procession of the Army of the Ohio as it left Louisville that autumn day impressed everyone who saw it. More than a quarter of a century later, an otherwise plain-speaking veteran named George Herr was moved to un-characteristic Victorian excess when he recalled the scene: "Proud stepping men, proud prancing horses, blaring trumpets, flashing sabres, burnished guns, gleaming bayonets blazing in the day, with plumes and spurs and banners dancing in the sunbeams and spangling the air, presented a fine picture of the pomp, panoply and circumstance of war." To another participant, Lieutenant John Bross of the 88th Illinois, the first few days of the march that followed "seemed more like a parade than anything else." The army at night presented an equally stirring spectacle, especially for new soldiers like Major James Connolly of the 123rd Illinois, embarking on his first campaign: "As far as the

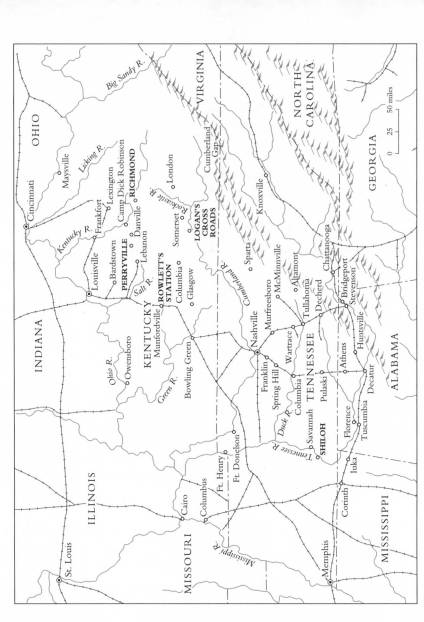

Theater of Operations of the Army of the Ohio, 1861–1862

eye can reach, the camp fires of our army can be seen, and the hum of thousands of voices, mingled with the strains of martial music, comes up to our camp."[1]

A scant eighteen months earlier, this mighty army did not exist. When Confederate troops opened fire on Fort Sumter on April 12, 1861, the officer who would lead the Army of the Ohio so splendidly out of Louisville, Major General Don Carlos Buell, held the rank of major as a career bureaucrat in the adjutant general's office. Many of the men who would command the corps, divisions, and brigades of the Army of the Ohio were also junior officers, serving out dead-end careers in the tiny Regular Army's remote frontier posts. Major Connolly, Lieutenant Bross, and the rest of the future army's field officers were politicians, lawyers, or schoolteachers in Fort Wayne or Grand Rapids or Columbus or any one of the hundreds of other small towns scattered across the Midwest. George Herr and his fellow rank-and-file soldiers labored in the fields, forests, and villages of Ohio, Illinois, Indiana, Michigan, Wisconsin, and Minnesota.

When Buell, Connolly, Bross, Herr, and thousands of others came together to form the Army of the Ohio, they created an organization that would display in battle a dogged persistence in the face of disaster as well as a frustrating inability to seize tactical opportunities that might lead to victory. These characteristics were not rare among Civil War armies, but the Army of the Ohio possessed each of them to a remarkable degree. It was in the first months of its existence that the army developed these deep-rooted strengths and weaknesses, which would emerge time and again on the battlefields of Kentucky and Tennessee.

"To Lose Kentucky Is Nearly the Same as to Lose the Whole Game"

The process that led to the formation of the Army of the Ohio began on April 15, 1861, two days after Major Robert Anderson hauled down the U.S. flag at Fort Sumter, when President Abraham Lincoln called upon the loyal states to provide 75,000 volunteers to put down what he described as "combinations too powerful to be suppressed by the ordinary course of judicial proceedings."[2] The call was an acknowledgment that the seven states that had declared themselves an independent Confederacy were beyond the reach not only of the Federal government's judges and marshals, but also of its standing military force, the 16,000-strong Regular Army. The men who answered Lincoln's call were not mustered into the Regular Army, which was destined to play a secondary role in the coming war; rather, they were organized into volunteer regiments by their respective states, which then offered the regiments to the Federal government for wartime service. These regiments, and the hundreds that would follow them, were the building blocks that Union generals would form into larger and larger units: brigades, divisions, corps, and, ultimately, field armies.

Recognizing that 75,000 soldiers would not nearly be enough to subdue the Confederacy (which was quickly joined by four more states when war broke out), Lincoln asked Congress to authorize 400,000 volunteers to serve for three years. The enthusiastic legislators responded by upping the ante to 500,000 men, even as a few dozen of the first volunteer regiments were streaming into Washington to form an improvised field army.[3] The men of the new Army of the Potomac optimistically set out to seize the Confederate capital at Richmond but came tumbling back to Washington in disarray after their encounter with an equally raw Confederate force at Bull Run on July 21. The success of the Confederacy in putting thousands of soldiers into the field and turning back the first Northern offensive made it clear that the government would have to raise not one but several field armies to fight a full-scale war stretching along a thousand-mile front from the Atlantic to the Great Plains.

Remarkably, no individual in the Regular Army or the War Department seemed to be responsible for the organization and deployment of these volunteer armies. Other than General in Chief Winfield Scott's "Anaconda Plan," a rather vague proposal for the slow strangulation of the South by blockade and the capture of the Mississippi Valley, the only strategic concept to emerge from Washington in the war's first months was embodied in the slogan "On to Richmond," an idea that led directly to the debacle at Bull Run. In the absence of any explicit strategic plan, the task of allocating the military resources of the Union as they became available largely fell to Secretary of War Simon Cameron, a notoriously corrupt career politician who haphazardly directed incoming volunteer regiments to report to whatever points seemed to be in the most imminent danger of Confederate attack. This procedure brought many of the new regiments directly to Washington, but in response to various presidential directives and the frantic requests of midwestern governors, Cameron sent other units to vulnerable locations like St. Louis, Missouri, and Cairo, Illinois.[4] At these strategically important places, agglomerations of regiments began to coalesce into larger organizations. The Union field armies that developed along the Potomac, Mississippi, and Ohio Rivers thus were not conscious strategic creations. Instead, they evolved as byproducts of the War Department's ad hoc responses to specific Southern military threats.

One such threat was to Kentucky, a border slave state that seemed on the verge of secession in the summer of 1861. The loss of Kentucky would have done enormous economic and strategic harm to the Union. Its population of 1,156,000 people included nearly a quarter of a million military-age white males, more than 40,000 of whom eventually served the Union; had the state joined the Confederacy, many of those soldiers might well have fought for the South instead.[5] In Confederate hands, Kentucky would have shielded from invasion the vital industrial city of Nashville, as well as the food-producing heartland of Tennessee, and would have provided a base for Southern invasions of Illinois, Indiana, and Ohio. Transportation would have been dramatically affected, too, since Confederate Kentucky would have secured the vulnerable Virginia & Tennessee Rail Road through the Appalachians, one of the few east-west lines of communication within the South, while denying the North use of the Ohio River and its tributaries, the Tennessee and Cumberland Rivers, either as invasion routes or for commerce. It was "a matter of absolute necessity, not only for the Northern border States but for all the Northwestern States," Wisconsin governor Alexander Randall wrote to the president on May 6, that the Union retain control of the Ohio River. Lincoln, a native Kentuckian who had piloted flatboats on the river in his youth, understood this clearly. To his friend Orville Browning he explained the importance of the stakes: "I think to lose Kentucky is nearly the same as to lose the whole game."[6]

Although Lincoln recognized the Union's vital interest in Kentucky, he did not at once direct Cameron or Scott to begin building a field army there. In part, this was because the administration's attention was absorbed by military events closer to Washington. Lincoln's cabinet was dominated by Easterners like Cameron of Pennsylvania and Secretary of State William Seward of New York who focused on the war in Virginia. When the regiments camped near Washington marched away for the "On to Richmond" campaign, their fate held everyone in the capital in suspense for days. Major General George B. McClellan, who took command of the Army of the Potomac after Bull Run, proposed that the government ignore the West altogether and concentrate its military resources in Virginia, creating an enormous army of three hundred thousand that could sweep away everything before it. Lincoln saw the impracticality of that scheme, but even he was sometimes distracted from the larger strategic picture by local military threats. "As to Kentucky, you do not estimate that state as more important than I do," Lincoln wrote to the worried governor of Indiana, Oliver P. Morton, "but I am compelled to watch all points. While I write this I am, if not in range, at least in hearing of cannon-shot, from an army of enemies more than a hundred thousand strong."[7]

However important he regarded Kentucky, Lincoln's military options were severely limited by the state's delicate political situation. In April, Governor Beriah Magoffin had contemptuously rejected the president's call for volunteers, claiming that Kentucky would "furnish no troops for the wicked purpose of subduing her sister Southern States."[8] The request for volunteers to suppress the rebellion had acted as the catalyst that triggered the secession of Virginia, Arkansas, Tennessee, and North Carolina, and Governor Magoffin was eager for Kentucky to follow their example. State legislators, reflecting the deep political divisions among their constituents, resisted Magoffin's attempts to lead Kentucky out of the Union but resolved instead to adopt a position of "strict neutrality." In such circumstances, Lincoln recognized, the open recruitment or deployment of a field army in Kentucky might upset the political balance in the nominally neutral Bluegrass state and drive it into secession.

Lincoln thus took care to act as quietly as possible in beginning to assemble the force that would become the Army of the Ohio. On May 7 he sent Brigadier General Robert Anderson, the recent hero of Fort Sumter and a native of Kentucky, to establish a headquarters on the northern bank of the Ohio at Cincinnati that would serve as a rallying point and recruitment center for loyal men from south of the river. He also sent thousands of muskets in the care of U.S. Navy lieutenant William Nelson, whose secret mission was to help organize and arm the Unionist paramilitary Home Guard as a counter to the secessionist Kentucky State Guard militia. On May 28 General Anderson's command was formally designated the Department of Kentucky, consisting of the portion of Kentucky within one hundred miles of the Ohio River.[9] Although he now had open military jurisdiction over a part of his home state, Anderson still did not receive any troops from Washington with which to begin conducting operations. He maintained his headquarters in Cincinnati and continued to recruit men in Kentucky and Tennessee primarily through clandestine agents.[10]

Most of the recruiting of Union soldiers in Anderson's territory was conducted by Kentucky citizens. After Governor Magoffin rejected the April 1861 call for volunteers, under which the state was to have furnished four regiments of infantry, Kentuckians James V. Guthrie and W. E. Woodruff obtained Federal commissions to recruit two of the four requested regiments. Early in May they established Camp Clay near Cincinnati, just across the Ohio River from their home state, where they organized what would become the 1st and 2nd Kentucky regiments. In June state senator Lovell H. Rousseau went to Washington to obtain authority to recruit two more Kentucky regiments, which he organized largely from existing Home Guard companies. As

Guthrie and Woodruff had done, Rousseau bowed to political considerations and quartered his men outside the state, establishing Camp Joe Holt across the Ohio River in Indiana. On July 1 the War Department ordered Lieutenant Nelson to organize three more Kentucky regiments, along with seven composed of Tennessee Unionists, and promised to forward another ten thousand muskets and six artillery pieces. Nelson complied and began to recruit an additional cavalry regiment for good measure.[11]

The rapid pace of Union recruiting, and the simultaneous mobilization of the secessionist State Guard, so weakened Kentucky's supposed neutrality that Nelson drew no rebuke from Anderson when he ordered his newly formed units to assemble openly on August 6 at Camp Dick Robinson, between Lexington and Danville. When Governor Magoffin complained of the presence of Union troops in his state, Lincoln replied disingenuously that he could do nothing about it. Although, according to presidential secretary John Nicolay, some of the first Kentucky regiments "in reality . . . were principally from Ohio and Indiana," Lincoln told Magoffin that he considered Nelson's men an indigenous force, one that "consists exclusively of Kentuckians, having their camp in the immediate vicinity of their own homes," and thus could not be removed.[12]

The establishment of Camp Dick Robinson, and similar camps of pro-Confederate troops, signaled the approaching end of Kentucky's vain effort to avoid the horrors of civil war. Recognizing that the state would soon be a battleground, the War Department on August 16 renamed Anderson's command the Department of the Cumberland and expanded it to include all of Kentucky and Tennessee. Anderson pressed the government for the reinforcements that he felt he would need to keep the Confederates from moving north and crossing the Ohio River once they abandoned the fiction of Kentucky's neutrality. To Secretary of the Treasury Salmon P. Chase he wrote plaintively, "We need everything." In particular, he requested the services of one of his friends from the Regular Army, Brigadier General Don Carlos Buell: "I must have him."[13]

On September 3, 1861, Confederate troops seized Columbus, Kentucky, overlooking the Mississippi River.[14] With this action, any remaining political restrictions on recruiting or maneuvering troops in the state disappeared. On the same day General in Chief Scott asked Governor Morton of Indiana to send five regiments "to such points on the Ohio as General Anderson may be supposed to approve." Anderson moved his headquarters from Cincinnati to Louisville, and Governor Morton warned Secretary of War Cameron, "The war in Kentucky has commenced." Cameron, however, was slow to respond to the danger. On September 5 he directed Morton to send to Cairo, Illinois, "all regiments organized and ready for movement," including, presumably, those that Scott had wanted him to send to Anderson. "I am very uneasy about Kentucky," Morton replied, "but I suppose the Government is not, as orders to send troops to the border are countermanded." Cameron continued to worry primarily about the military situation in Virginia, requesting the governor of Illinois to send "three or four full regiments infantry" to McClellan's Army of the Potomac and shortly afterward calling all Indiana, Michigan, and Wisconsin regiments to Washington.[15]

Cameron's neglect left Anderson with little means of resisting whatever aggressive moves the Confederates might choose to make. Surveying the scattered camps of ill-trained recruits that made up his "army," Anderson complained that "Kentucky has no armed men whose services I can command." Brigadier General Ormsby MacKnight Mitchel, who led the military department north of Anderson's, wrote to his family that "General Anderson is calling for troops with the energy of despair." When forces under Confederate general Simon Bolivar Buckner occupied Bowling Green, Kentucky, on September 18, Mitchel expected the rest of the state to fall and prepared to defend his department along the line of the Ohio River. Rumors that secessionists had already seized towns along the Kentucky-Indiana border led Lincoln personally to order Major General John Charles Frémont, in command of the next department to the west, to send a gunboat up the river from Cairo to investigate. "Perhaps you had better order those in charge of the Ohio River to guard it vigilantly at all points," Lincoln advised Frémont. Anderson, the man in charge of the Ohio River, in turn begged Lincoln to provide "all the troops from the North you can raise" and sought additional assistance from militia units, the Home Guard, and the governors of nearby states.[16]

While waiting for reinforcements, Anderson ordered his second-in-command, Brigadier General William Tecumseh Sherman, to do something to slow the progress of Buckner's invasion. The only forces available to Sherman, other than a scattering of untrained Home Guard militia units, were the men William Nelson and Lovell Rousseau had assembled at Camp Dick Robinson and Camp Joe Holt. These "half-drilled volunteers," reporter Henry Villard noted, were "very far from being ready to take the field." Comparing them to the unfortunate Union soldiers whom he had observed retreating from Bull Run in July, Villard judged Anderson's men "not half as efficient." Sherman gathered a scratch force consisting primarily of Rousseau's volunteer regiments and the Louisville Home Guard and headed south. To his relief, Sherman found that Buckner's army, which was little better organized than his own, had stopped and entrenched itself only a short distance north of Bowling Green. Sherman left most of his force at Muldraugh's Hill, some thirty miles south of Louisville, to monitor Buckner's actions and await reinforcements.[17]

Over the next month, three developments solidified Anderson's command and transformed it into an organization that could reasonably call itself an army. First, it continued to grow. Although Secretary of War Cameron was still directing most new Union regiments to Virginia or Missouri, a steady flow of reinforcements reached Kentucky to swell the ranks of the Department of the Cumberland. The first Union regiment to arrive from outside the state was the 49th Ohio, on September 21, followed shortly by more than a dozen additional regiments from Indiana and Ohio.[18] On September 24 the War Department reported sending eighteen thousand muskets to Anderson and asked the governors of Indiana and Ohio to send him artillery. The next day Cameron authorized the recruitment of another brigade in Kentucky.[19] After a disastrous train wreck killed or injured 129 men of the 19th Illinois, passing through the Department of the Cumberland en route from Missouri to Washington, the regiment was ordered to disregard its previous instructions and report to General Anderson instead.[20] At Camp Dick Robinson, where Brigadier General George H. Thomas had taken command on September 15, three regiments from north of the Ohio reinforced the six from Kentucky and Tennessee raised by Nelson, who was now busy at Maysville, Kentucky starting a new camp of recruitment and instruction.[21] By the middle of October, Anderson's force of some thirty regiments (mostly infantry, with a few cavalry units) and five artillery batteries was large enough to acquire the informal title of "Army of the Cumberland."[22]

The second development was a change in leadership. On October 8 Anderson resigned his command, for reasons of health, and was succeeded by William T. Sherman.[23] Anderson had been appointed as much for his public relations value as his military skill, and in that capacity he served well, doing nothing to alienate his fellow Kentuckians from the Union cause. Although he had also done his best to build up Northern military strength in Kentucky, he lacked the passion that his successor brought to the task. Sherman made no secret of his belief that the number of men available to him was far from adequate to defend Kentucky, much less to begin to conquer the South. He was "simply appalled" by the task that had fallen to him, which he had not sought; indeed, he claimed that he had been "forced into command of this department against my will." Sherman took to pacing up and down the corridors of the Galt House hotel in Louisville for hours at a time, according to Henry Villard, "to such an extent that . . . it was soon whispered about that he was suffering from mental depression." When Secretary of War Cameron visited Louisville on October 16 and heard Sherman's estimate that it would take two hundred thousand men to suppress the rebellion in the western theater alone, "it startled the Secretary and excited doubts as to the state of the General's mind." This was followed shortly by the publication of rumors that Sherman had gone insane.[24]

Although his meeting with Cameron on October 16 cost Sherman his reputation, at least temporarily, it went far toward strengthening his army. Up to that point in the war, as Sherman later wrote, the North had committed most of its resources to the armies of McClellan in Washington and Frémont in St. Louis, with "nobody seeming to think of the intervening link covered by Kentucky." Whatever Cameron thought of Sherman's mental stability, he was apparently persuaded by Sherman's argument that the Army of the Cumberland was not nearly strong enough for its mission. The secretary of war afterward reported to President Lincoln that things were "in a much worse condition than I expected to find them" and that a "large number of troops [are] needed here immediately." Even before his return to Washington, Cameron began to rush men and arms to Sherman's department. The 2nd Minnesota regiment, which had reached Pittsburgh on its way to Washington, D.C., was ordered to turn around and report to the West. Volunteers from Wisconsin and two companies of newly raised Regulars were sent to Sherman, as well as a brigade from Pennsylvania, the first and only unit from east of the Appalachians ever assigned to the department. In Sherman's brief tenure as commander in Kentucky, he succeeded in convincing the War Department for the first time to give adequate attention to the area.[25]

The third key to the establishment of the force that would become the Army of the Ohio was provided by President Lincoln, in the form of a strategic vision that guaranteed a continuous supply of men and material to the region in which the army would operate. Even before Sherman persuaded Cameron to take a closer look at Kentucky as an important theater of war, Lincoln had already prepared a "Memorandum for a Plan of Campaign," in which he sketched his thoughts for operations against the Confederates in Kentucky to begin "on, or about the 5th of October." The plan revealed Lincoln's concern for and detailed knowledge of the situation in his native state: "We have a force of 5000 or 6000, under General Thomas, at Camp Dick Robinson. . . . We have possession of the Railroad from Louisville to Nashville, Tenn, so far as Muldrough's Hill. . . . At the Hill we have a force of 8000 under General Sherman." Lincoln proposed that the troops at Louisville and Cincinnati concentrate with Thomas's men for a joint attack on Cumberland Gap, timed to coincide with the landing of an amphibious expedition at Port Royal, South Carolina, in November.[26]

Nothing came of the Cumberland Gap plan in 1861, but more significant than Lincoln's operational plan was his long-term scheme for the allocation of military resources. All new regiments raised in the western states, he wrote, should be sent to Frémont, while those raised east of the mountains would be earmarked for McClellan. "All from Indiana and Michigan, not now elsewhere, [will] be sent to Anderson at Louisville. All from Ohio [not needed in western Virginia, will] be sent to Mitchell [*sic*] at Cincinnati, for Anderson." Although Lincoln's program was not put into effect exactly as written, for the rest of the war the army occupying the "intervening link" of Kentucky would receive resources on a scale to match those of the armies to the east and the west.

Sherman did not stay in Kentucky to see what he had accomplished. In early November he was replaced by Major General Don Carlos Buell. Sherman's old Department of the Cumberland disappeared with him; Buell's command was designated the Department of the Ohio and expanded to include Ohio, Michigan, Indiana, Tennessee, and Kentucky east of the Cumberland River. The forces he led within that vast region would be called the Army of the Ohio.[27]

"I Had Determined to Enlist in a Company of Volunteers"

If asked to identify the Army of the Ohio in November 1861, General Buell in his headquarters in Louisville or President Lincoln in Washington would have had little difficulty in taking a map, drawing a satisfying circle around the Union regiments in Kentucky, and calling the enclosed units the Army of the Ohio. To the men on the ground, however, no such circle was visible. For them, the field army to which they belonged was a meaningless abstraction. Most of them had enlisted in the spring and summer of 1861, before the army had come into existence. Since that time, everything in their military experience had encouraged them to develop strong bonds of loyalty to their companies and their regiments, to the exclusion of any other institutional affiliation. The devotion that soldiers felt for their regiments, contrasted with their relative indifference toward other regiments and toward the army as a whole, would have long-lasting effects, both positive and negative, on the performance of the Army of the Ohio.

For most of the men who found themselves in the Army of the Ohio in 1861, military service began with an encounter with a recruiting agent. Recruiters were generally state, not Federal, agents since the government in Washington lacked the bureaucratic machinery to induct hundreds of thousands of civilian volunteers. Rather than organize its own units, the War

Department requisitioned the states for ready-made regiments, each consisting of ten companies of approximately one hundred men apiece.[28] The state governments were no better prepared to create instant armies, so they in turn delegated to private individuals the authority to recruit and organize companies. Although the details of recruiting varied somewhat among the states, in most cases recruiting agents expected to receive officers' commissions after they had enlisted enough men to form the companies they wished to lead.

Indiana, for example, issued one commission per company to be raised, "permanent commissions in the organization being conditional upon success in enlisting recruits." George Herr of the 59th Illinois observed that in his state those "who aspired to official positions recruited companies on their own account, and recruited them as fully and rapidly as possible for the purpose of securing their commissions as soon as possible." In Kentucky, colonels were appointed by the state or Federal government to raise regiments, and they in turn authorized civilians to recruit companies. The experience of a young Tennessean named Marcus Woodcock was typical; when he decided to fight for the Union, he enlisted not in the U.S. Army, but in a specific company led by a man he knew: "I had determined to enlist in a company of volunteers that Captain Hinson was recruiting for the service of the State of Kentucky."[29]

In Ohio, the state that was to furnish more men for the Army of the Ohio than any other, contingent commissions were offered to prospective company commanders who recruited volunteers and shipped them, at government expense, to designated camps. A recruiter who brought a full unit of 83 to 101 men into camp then had to submit a roll showing each volunteer's preference for the captain, first lieutenant, and second lieutenant of the company. If the recruiter was named on the roll by a majority of his men and his character endorsed by the regiment's commander, he then received a temporary appointment as captain, which became permanent when the regiment was completely organized and mustered into service.[30]

The companies raised under this system tended to consist of men from the same village, town, or neighborhood, officered by men of local prominence. Indiana adjutant general W. H. H. Terrell observed that the typical company was raised within the borders of a single county, so "the men generally know each other and are acquainted with their officers, either personally or by reputation."[31] Judson W. Bishop, who eventually became the colonel of the 2nd Minnesota, noted that in his regiment the "men and officers of each company were mutual acquaintances and friends, while they were strangers to those of other companies." Novelist Albion W. Tourgée, who served as a lieutenant in the 105th Ohio, similarly observed that in his unit all ranks shared a common background and that the officers were the "product of the same conditions as the enlisted men—field, staff, and line were the neighbors and kinsmen of the rank and file." In the 38th Indiana, a veteran recalled, the "company commanders were all men of influence in the communities in which they resided." When Ohio volunteer Joseph Sims wrote home from Camp Dennison in September 1861 that "We have a heap of go[o]d friend here thare is prety near all of Marsailles here now and upper sandusky is here now," he was not exaggerating. The webs of relationships that held civil communities together were in many cases transferred whole into the army, uniting the new companies even before they began their service.[32]

Under these circumstances, it is not surprising that soldiers soon regarded their companies as families, a metaphor commonly employed by veterans of the Army of the Ohio. Lieutenant Tourgée used the word to characterize the ten companies of his regiment, noting that "Each family has its own place and its own specific quality and character." Colonel Bishop observed that the regiment was a more important tactical unit, but "the company was the family of more intimate and brotherly relations among the men and more immediate and personal care and command by the officers."[33]

Since their commissions depended on the number of men they secured, recruiters competed to make life in their company "families" seem as attractive as possible. In addition to offering prospective soldiers the opportunity to serve with friends and neighbors, many would-be officers assured their men that they would retain much of the autonomy to which they were accustomed as freeborn American citizens by having the right to choose which regiment their company would join and (most important) the right to elect their officers. These promises were powerful recruitment tools; Adjutant General Terrell noted that among Hoosier volunteers, "the larger portion of them always selected the new regiments of their own districts."[34]

An unintended effect of such promises, however, was to encourage the new soldiers to think of themselves as members of their companies first and of the army second. When young men enlisted on the basis of guarantees made by authority figures whom they knew and trusted, they perceived that they were entering quasi-contractual relationships with those particular individuals. Unlike the professional soldiers of the peacetime Regular Army, who in essence signed away their lives for years at a time in exchange for food, clothing, and shelter, the volunteers of 1861 saw themselves as making a much more limited bargain: they would temporarily give up certain elements of their civilian freedom in return for the perquisites attached to membership in a specific company, as promised by its recruiter.[35]

This perception led men to cling fiercely to the companies in which they had enlisted. In December 1861 mutiny broke out in the 37th Indiana after the

The company was the soldier's military family. Company H, 44th Indiana (top), and an unidentified company of the 21st Michigan (bottom) pose for group portraits. *Top*: Courtesy of The Lincoln Museum, Fort Wayne, Indiana (TLM #3306); *bottom*: Massachusetts Commandery, Military Order of the Loyal Legion and USAMHI.

colonel (a former Regular Army officer) tried to break up the regiment's nonregulation eleventh company and distribute its personnel among the other ten. Rather than serve with strangers, the men of the eleventh company spent ten days under arrest; they were eventually sent home by Governor Morton, who thus implicitly confirmed the soldiers' belief that they were obligated to serve only in the company of their original choosing. Company loyalty also outweighed state patriotism for a group of volunteers from Dowagiac, Michigan, who responded to news that their state had already filled its quota of regiments by crossing the state border and enlisting as Company E of the 42nd Illinois, preferring to join a "foreign" regiment rather than to disband. Most of the 9th Missouri and 13th Missouri were likewise made up of companies that had migrated from Illinois and Ohio, respectively.[36]

Many volunteers reacted badly when they learned that their recruiters' pledges would not be fulfilled. A company recruited from Vevay, Indiana, on being told that its term of enlistment would be a year instead of three months as originally promised, simply turned around and headed home. When the officer who enlisted him was promoted out of his company, an Ohio soldier named Patrick McKernan took his case directly to the secretary of war. "I told him if he was going to *abandon* his men that I would *like* to be allowed my choice of a company in the regiment," he wrote to Cameron, presumably without effect. The self-styled Chicago Company of Sappers and Miners, consisting of men who had enlisted with the expectation that they would serve as military engineers, were greatly dissatisfied to find themselves mustered in as part of an infantry unit. It was "not that they had any objection to the regiment," according to one of their new comrades, "but they wished to enter the area of service for which they were recruited."[37]

A petition from a similarly aggrieved group of Kentucky volunteers, addressed to General Buell in February 1862, reflected the signers' contractual concept of their enlistment. The fourteen petitioners had the previous October joined "an artillery company then being organized by Capt. Rufus Sommerly . . . having a decided preference for that branch of the service & enlisted with a perfect understanding that we should be required to serve as artillery men & nothing else." When Colonel Stephen G. Burbridge, later to gain notoriety for his ruthless suppression of guerrilla activity in Kentucky, detailed the men to fill out the ranks of some infantry companies, they objected to the assignment as being "contrary to our inclinations & against our most earnest remonstrance." They refused to be sworn in as infantry and insisted that since their company was being disbanded, they "ought to have the privilege of choosing whatever branch of the service was most suitable to our several tastes & inclinations." Keenly aware of the rights and privileges that they imagined attached to their enlistments, the petitioners added what must have seemed to them an unassailable negotiating point: if they did not get their way, it would be "impossible for us under present circumstances to discharge our duties with that amount of cheerfulness which should animate every true soldier of the union." Although Buell's response was not recorded, it is unlikely that he was moved by the threat of insufficiently cheerful service, as he did not share the volunteers' view that he was obligated to fulfill, or even take notice of, the promises made by recruiters.[38]

Despite the views of professional soldiers like Buell, volunteers did manage to exercise some of the rights promised to them, in particular the right to elect their company officers. The policy of allowing company elections was widespread through the first year of the war, not only for state volunteers but also for those companies raised directly by the Federal government in areas where the state government was in rebellion, such as eastern Tennessee. By War Department orders, these companies were allowed to choose "field and company officers of their own selection," while Congress provided that any replacements for the original complement of company officers were to be chosen by company election.[39] In states that issued contingent commissions to recruiters, officers frequently pledged to resign their temporary commissions and conduct elections as soon as their companies were full.[40] Ohio journalist Whitelaw Reid, who opposed the practice as encouraging "electioneering, bribery, drunkenness, and lax discipline," noted that even without elections, democracy prevailed in the ranks: "[I]t was well known [in Ohio units] that if the men took care to represent a certain officer as unpopular he would not be reappointed." Few of the diaries and unit histories written by members of the Army of the Ohio fail to mention the election of company officers as part of the early days of service.[41]

As Reid pointed out, elections had obvious drawbacks. Candidates found it difficult to curry favor with their constituents and impose military discipline on them at the same time. Elections reduced the stability of leadership, since until its ranks were full, a company's balance of power could change daily as new batches of recruits arrived, each ready to vote for its own slate of officers. When John William Tuttle brought a dozen recruits with him to the camp of Captain Henry Taylor's company at Monticello, Kentucky, for example, he immediately found himself elected first lieutenant. The worst feature of officer elections, however, was that there was no apparent positive correlation between electability and effective military leadership. To many soldiers, the opposite seemed true. In the 3rd Kentucky, the newly elected Lieutenant Tuttle observed that schoolteachers made the best officers (Tuttle had taught school at one time), followed by preachers and lawyers; but "without exception, the politicians were the very poorest sticks in the service." Choosing officers by ballot meant that "unfortunately . . . a large percentage of the officers of our volunteer army were politicians." Colonel William B. Hazen of the 41st Ohio, a Regular Army soldier who had taught tactics at West Point, concurred that among volunteer officers "as a rule, fitness was found to vary inversely with rank."[42]

Regardless of its effects, the enlisted men of the Army of the Ohio placed a high value on their promised "right" to choose their own officers. Speaking through their governor, Ohio troops expressed "much dissatisfaction" with an 1861 War Department order that required that a third of each company's officers be men promoted from the ranks; although the order was designed to democratize the officer corps, the Ohioans had already chosen their leaders and refused to serve under any others. Members of the artillery company of the 11th Michigan balked at taking the oath of service to the Federal government in November 1861 because they had not been allowed to elect their first lieutenant, who had been appointed by the regiment's colonel instead. Applying the democratic principle a step further, a sergeant in the 9th Michigan tried to have a particularly overbearing officer recalled by circulating a petition against him, until a comrade who had served in the French army explained to him that such insubordination violated military law. The colonel of the regiment, recognizing that his men were essentially civilians in uniform who were unaware that they had given up their constitutional right to petition, wisely declined to punish anyone involved.[43]

The practice of electing officers was not entirely detrimental to the efficiency of the Army of the Ohio. The enlisted men often tried their best to choose the most qualified candidates. Jacob D. Cox, who helped organize the first Ohio regiments and eventually rose to become a major general, wrote that "The young volunteers felt so deeply their own ignorance that they were ready to yield to any pretense of superior knowledge." A Mexican War record, no matter how remote or insignificant, thus became "a sure passport to confidence." "Our commander had served in the Mexican War, and we youngsters looked with admiring and envious eyes on the gold leaf of the brevet rank which he had then won," recalled an enlistee of the newly formed 18th U.S. regiment. Sometimes the voters made good choices, as when Company A of the 59th Illinois elected S. P. Post as their second lieutenant, despite the company commander's promise of preferential treatment to those who voted otherwise. Post went on to become colonel of the regiment and eventually a brigade commander. The enlisted men of the 64th Ohio took quick advantage of the arrival of a former Regular Army soldier in their camp: "Thinking him a much more efficient commander," one of them recorded, "the boys called for an election and had him appointed Captain."[44]

The damage wrought by electing incompetent officers often proved temporary, as unfit men tended to weed themselves out. A member of Company G, 9th Michigan, recalled: "Quite a number of our first officers resigned during the first few months—some because of their self-conscious inefficiency; others because they found soldiering a more serious business than they had expected." In Colonel Hazen's tightly run 41st Ohio, bad officers "soon made their unfitness evident in many ways; and when there was no more hope, they either voluntarily resigned or were informed in a kind way that they were not likely to be useful, and quietly went home."[45]

After 1861 company elections became much less common, but the principle of company autonomy endured. The War Department continued to mandate that officer vacancies in a given company be filled by promotion from within the unit, rather than by appointment of an outsider. Though the practice of electing company officers eroded, the right to be officered by men from the same community persisted throughout the war. Reviewing the process of officer selection in an 1869 publication, Adjutant General Terrell concluded that "The true rule of promotion . . . is that each company and regimental organization is by right entitled to have all vacancies filled from its own members."[46] The identity of the company as the soldier's military "family" thus remained unchallenged by the introduction of strangers at its head.

Small unit cohesion generally contributes to the military effectiveness of an army, but the close-knit solidarity of the companies of the Army of the Ohio proved too much of a good thing when company identity became so intense that it led to conflict with outsiders. This occurred most often within the army's handful of ethnic units and standing militia companies. The latter, which had originated many years earlier as ready defense forces to resist the British or suppress the Indians, had by 1861 evolved into social institutions that offered recreation and status for wealthy young men. When the war began, many militia companies enlisted immediately and were sent to Virginia, but at least a few such units ended up in the Army of the Ohio, including the Old Infantry company of Lexington, Kentucky (which joined the 21st Kentucky), the Coldwater Light Artillery (Battery A, 1st Michigan Artillery), and the Guthrie Grays, who became the nucleus of the 6th Ohio.[47]

The Army of the Ohio might have consisted entirely of fully organized militia companies had the states of the Ohio Valley enforced the long-standing laws making annual service in the militia a universal obligation for white males, but by 1861 these state militia organizations had decayed from decades of neglect. No enrollment of the Indiana militia had been made since 1832. Where militia service survived, it was typically in the form of an annual "training" day that provided an excuse for the participants to wear elaborate uniforms, make speeches, and get drunk. An observer described the Kentucky militia as a comic-opera farce consisting of "hosts of be-feathered and epauletted officers, who were worthless, inefficient, and incompetent." Recruitment of the 10th Ohio regiment was set back by the discovery that two of its militia companies, the Montgomery Guards and the Sarsfield Guards, consisted of the same personnel, each of whom had two uniforms to wear depending on which company was on parade. The Illinois militia, in which Abraham Lincoln had served in the Black Hawk War of 1832, was in no better shape. In 1852 Lincoln made a campaign speech in which he described Springfield's last militia muster: "Among the rules and regulations, no man is to wear more than five pounds of cod-fish for epaulets, or more than thirty yards of bologna sausages for a sash; and no two men are to dress alike, and if any two should dress alike the one that dresses most alike is to be fined." The situation was little improved ten years later, when the adjutant general of Illinois reported that "there were no available, efficient, armed and organized militia companies in the State," except a few independent companies of "active and enterprising young men, whose occasional meetings for drill were held more for exercise and amusement than from any sense of duty."[48]

In practice, only those with considerable discretionary income and free time could afford to indulge in the exercise and amusement of belonging to an active militia company. A captain of one such unit, the Chicago Highland Guards (organized in 1855), bragged of the group's "honorable position" in the city and the fact that members had to "pay well for the privilege" of joining. Guardsmen contributed to the rent of the company's armory, engaged in hours of drill, and paid for their own elaborate uniforms, complete with kilts. The company was mustered into the 19th Illinois and became part of the Army of the Ohio, where fellow soldiers like Lieutenant Henry A. Buck of the 51st Illinois regarded them as "a wild, high-strung set of young Chicago bloods" who were "splendidly drilled and will fight like tigers, but . . . have some peculiarities" such as the "original and queer" habit of painting girls' names on their rifles. Brigadier General Joshua Bates, trying to organize the war effort in Ohio in 1861, encountered the Guthrie Grays, a militia company that included "many of the most promising young men" of Cincinnati. The Grays considered themselves too good to be commanded by ordinary officers and "held aloof from [other units], refusing to recognize any superior authority except the governor."[49]

If the fancy titles, colorful uniforms, and social pretensions of the exclusive

The "Guthrie Grays" militia, here parading through Cincinnati in 1861, served in the Army of the Ohio as the 6th Ohio Volunteer Infantry. From *Harper's Weekly*, June 8, 1861; photograph courtesy of The Lincoln Museum, Fort Wayne, Indiana (TLM #4530).

militia companies distanced them to some degree from the rest of the Army of the Ohio, the isolation of the army's ethnic units was even more visible, in part because there were more of them. The Turnverein, a paramilitary organization that was the political and social heart of many German American communities, proved a ready source of volunteer companies when the war began. The 9th Ohio was composed almost entirely of German-speaking volunteers formed into companies like the Lafayette Militia and the Jaegers, both organized by Cincinnati's German American community before the war. After helping to train the 9th Ohio, Adjutant Augustus Willich left to take command of the 32nd Indiana, another regiment consisting largely of German immigrants. In addition to as many as ten predominantly German units, the Army of the Ohio eventually included regiments of Irish immigrants from Illinois, Indiana, and Ohio, as well as the 15th Wisconsin Scandinavian regiment, which consisted of Norwegians, Swedes, and Danes in companies with names that included Odin's Rifles, St. Olaf's Rifles, and the Norway Bear Hunters.[50]

Native soldiers frequently commented, usually negatively, on what they perceived as the distinctive characteristics of immigrant volunteers. In April 1862 Lieutenant Tuttle of the 3rd Kentucky encountered a German American soldier from a different regiment that also claimed the name "3rd Kentucky." Tuttle's account reveals both the difficulty of mutual comprehension as well as the condescension and ridicule to which "foreign" soldiers were often subject: "[W]e were accosted by a burly Teuton with 'Vot ish dis rechemendt poys?' On being answered that it was the Third Kentucky he flew into a passion all over and yelled out 'Pogus! Pogus! Oh! you shoost pe tam mit yeselfs.' . . . Our man pushed him backward and raised his gun to strike him when others rushed up on both sides and it was [with] the greatest difficulty that a general melee was prevented." A Kentucky volunteer recommended that the soldiers camped at Louisville in December 1861 be segregated by nationality: "There seems to be a little kind of party feeling between the German and American soldiers[;] they can't understand one another[.] They seem to be suspishus of each other." Another wrote to a friend expressing his unit's resentment at being ordered to give their new muskets to the 32nd Indiana, "the duch you recollect."[51]

Some American-born soldiers admired the foreign military style of the immigrants. Captain Wilberforce Nevin of the 79th Pennsylvania found "German" soldiers fascinating, if still alien. To him, they appeared "a strange body of men" who drank an "ocean of beer" and performed unusual drills: "Their marching is like a dance. Their orders are given in German, and their execution is as smooth and beautiful as a Waltz." Not all German American regiments were so graceful, however. The men of the 24th Illinois were notorious for their drunkenness, poor discipline, and sloppy drill, which provoked General Sherman during his brief tenure in command of the Army of the Ohio to write to their colonel, "The troubles in your Regt. have long been a source of annoyance."[52]

In July 1861 the War Department attempted to prevent ethnic tensions from escalating throughout the Union field armies by the heavy-handed measure of prohibiting the enlistment of volunteers who could not speak English. Angry political response to this order forced the department to backtrack, first claiming that it meant only to restrict non-English speakers from joining "American" regiments, then withdrawing the order altogether on August 8. Both the order and the immediate reaction suggest the depth of feeling between native and immigrant soldiers in the Army of the Ohio and elsewhere. Thirty-five years after the war, the historian of the 9th Ohio remained bitter that, as he saw it, "Americans disdain immigrants and disparage whatever they do, as soon as every possible advantage has been taken of the same immigrants."[53]

If the company was the soldier's military family, the regiment became his hometown. As companies of volunteers reported to their respective state rendezvous camps, they were combined into regiments consisting of ten companies and a headquarters. There they began to transfer their primary organizational loyalty from company to regiment. "[T]he regiments, especially in our State," wrote Judson Bishop of the 2nd Minnesota, "had been recruited by companies, each company from some particular town or county; many of them had local names, and some had company flags. . . . Each company had a character of its own, too: there was the German Company G, and Scandinavian Company E with four Ole Olsons on its roll, the 'meek and lowly' F, made up mostly of lumbermen and raftsmen." The companies possessed an esprit de corps that was "not objectionable when subordinated to that of the regiment, as it was later," but was initially so strong that "it was not for the best discipline of the troops." Over the weeks or months that elapsed between a regiment's organization and its assignment to the Army of the Ohio (or whichever field army the War Department designated), "gradually the company became less and the regiment more conspicuously the unit of organization, and the regiment, as it became thus a more compact and homogenous body of troops, was better governed and more effectively handled."[54] The infantry regiment became the basic unit of command, maneuver, and administration for all Civil War armies and, for most soldiers, the source of their military identity.

Other than specifying the number of units required from each state, the Federal government in 1861 played almost no role in organizing volunteer regiments. Each state appointed its own regimental officers and in varying degrees trained, armed, and equipped its regiments before sending them off to fight. Of the nine states that provided the bulk of the regiments that made up the Army of the Ohio (Ohio, Michigan, Kentucky, eastern Tennessee, Indiana, Illinois, Missouri, Wisconsin, and Minnesota), no two followed the same procedure. Only Indiana imposed a rational system on the organization of its regiments from the start of the war; it set up eleven assembly camps, one in each of its eleven congressional districts, and assigned each new regiment to a specific camp where it could be organized from companies recruited in the same district.[55]

In contrast, many regiments raised in other states were organized by ambitious individuals who sought to become regimental commanders by finding ten unattached volunteer companies willing to serve under their leadership. The promises made by these would-be colonels echoed on a larger scale the offers of company recruiters, including the all-important right to elect officers. Where necessary, several military entrepreneurs might do some large-scale horse trading to put together a regiment, a process described by George Herr of the 59th Illinois: "[R]egiments were formed by the connivance of those in command of independent companies who came together, and upon a basis of swapping favors, parceled out the regimental officers, brought their several commands together[,] often from distant parts of the State, sometimes from other States, [until] a coalition was accomplished, and—Regiment Volunteer Infantry was formed." These regiments, Herr observed, "did not pretend to represent any special section of the State" and in some cases did not even represent a single state. Herr's own regiment was created when "gentlemen who aspired to official positions 'pooled their issues,' crossed ten Illinois companies over the Mississippi to St. Louis, and caused them to be mustered into the service as the Ninth Missouri Volunteer Infantry," later renamed the 59th Illinois.[56]

The turbulent political situation in Kentucky left even more power in the hands of entrepreneurial regimental recruiters. These men, variously appointed by President Lincoln, the War Department, or Generals Anderson, Nelson, or Sherman, were authorized to organize and command their own regiments, on the condition that they find ten companies of volunteers.[57] Even more than in Illinois, this encouraged politics and negotiation. "Kentucky is a most remarkable state in one particular," Colonel William W. Duffield observed in June 1862. "Everything runs into politics. Every Kentuckian no matter whether he accepts a commission in the present war or attends a horse race does so with the view of political advancement and for no other purpose." Judge Thomas Bramlette's experience showed how the system worked. After Bramlette received a commission from William Nelson to raise the 3rd Kentucky, he resigned his judgeship and delegated his recruiting authority to various agents, schoolmaster John W. Tuttle among them, who brought their contingents to Camp Dick Robinson in August 1861. Tuttle noted that the camp was filled with "parts of companies raised for Bramlette's regiment, two or three for Wolford's regiment, four or five for Fry's regiment, two or three companies of Home Guards, and more East Tennessee refugees." After a month of wheeling and dealing, Bramlette managed to get ten companies pledged to his regiment and even turned down requests from several more that wanted to join. He suffered a minor setback, just before the 3rd Kentucky was formally mustered in, when one of his companies defected to join a rival regiment, but within two years the newly minted colonel turned his military career to political advantage, winning the election for governor of Kentucky in 1863.[58]

Other states organized their regiments one at a time, assigning every newly enlisted company to the same regiment until it was full, then starting another. This worked well enough in states with relatively few volunteers. In Minnesota, five companies enrolled within a week of Lincoln's July 1861 call for troops, but the harvest season slowed recruitment and the additional five companies needed to complete the 2nd Minnesota were not found until October.[59] All ten of the regiments sent to the Army of the Ohio from Minnesota, Wisconsin, and Michigan in 1861 were organized in serial fashion, made up of companies from all parts of their respective states. The government of Ohio initially attempted to assign companies to regiments in the order of their arrival, but the flood of volunteers in April and May 1861 overwhelmed the state's adjutant general, who lost track of the number and seniority of the companies pouring into Columbus. For weeks, every Ohio company claimed the right to be named Company A of a new regiment, until the legislature finally worked out compromise regimental assignments based on political expediency rather than any rational organizing principle. Only the German companies of the 9th Ohio avoided this process, since they had privately organized themselves into a regiment that presented itself whole to the state government.[60]

Regimental officers, like their counterparts at the company level, were commissioned by the governors of their respective states pursuant to a May 1861 War Department order. This ensured that regimental officers would at least share a common state background with their troops and contributed to the early development of regimental spirit. The criteria for selecting such officers, however, often were unrelated to military efficiency. Since every regiment required a colonel, lieutenant colonel, and major, plus a headquarters staff that included an adjutant and a quartermaster (both lieutenants), a surgeon and a hospital steward, three staff sergeants, and twenty-six musicians, politicians tended to view the organization of a new regiment as a patronage bonanza.[61] Abraham Lincoln's friend, Judge David Davis, complained to the secretary of war that Governor Yates of Illinois was choosing officers with a view to building political support for a try at the Senate. "[T]he way regiments have been officered in the war has been lamentable," Davis wrote, "[and] all owing to this insane ambition of Yates." As a further detriment, the power to appoint officers encouraged governors to organize all recruits into new regiments, instead of sending them to reinforce existing units, to increase patronage opportunities.[62]

In practice, not all of the Army of the Ohio's regimental commanders owed their appointments to their respective state governors. Through the summer of 1861, while Robert Anderson was seeking reinforcements for his department with increasing desperation, Secretary of War Cameron was routinely refusing to accept new units from states that had already met their regimental quotas. Some of the disappointed governors gained a Pyrrhic victory by going over Cameron's head to Lincoln, who not only accepted the offered regiments but chose their colonels himself. Other regiments had their leaders selected by Cameron, who regularly authorized his political favorites to recruit new regiments, even while turning down units already organized by the state governments. The governor of Ohio responded with incredulity to one such appointment: "Is it possible you have authorized W. G. Sherwin to organize a regiment of artillery? If so, for God's sake withdraw the authority. Such commission will make a farce of the public service." After protests from the governors of Illinois, Indiana, Michigan, and Ohio to cease appointing colonels and accepting independent regiments, the War Department in September 1861 placed all new regiments under state control.[63]

The volunteers themselves also insisted on their perceived right to have a say in the selection of their regimental leaders. Some did so by choosing to enlist in companies belonging to one of the independent regiments authorized by Cameron, rather than serving under their governors' appointees. When this avenue was closed in September 1861, an Ohio recruiter warned Lincoln that the state would lose the services of several thousand men "who will not have anything to do with Governor Dennison. They will disband before they come under his administration." In other cases, soldiers sought to exercise their will by trying to elect their regimental officers. At the beginning of the war many states allowed volunteers to choose their field officers by vote, the War Department's requirement that such officers be appointed notwithstanding.[64]

The familiar civilian ritual of voting for their leaders gave soldiers an increased sense of community within their regiments, just as it had done earlier at the company level. The disadvantages of officer elections, however, grew exponentially with unit size. A bad company officer was a burden on his men and an inconvenience to his colonel, but an incompetent regimental commander could have a significant effect on the outcome of a battle. Even where good officers were chosen, the process of electing them could lower a regiment's morale by creating rival factions within the unit. Where company elections often served to build unit cohesion by affirming the status of recognized community leaders, regimental elections were more likely to be contested, since the presence of companies from different parts of a state, each favoring a local leader, made it more difficult to reach consensus.

There were many instances of divisive intraregimental politics in the Army of the Ohio. In the 36th Illinois, which was transferred to the army in 1862,

Sergeant Day Elmore wrote home of complex intrigues involving the lieutenant colonel, who was scheming with the major and two captains (who happened to be his brother and brother-in-law) to have the colonel of the regiment removed so that all the plotters could be promoted. William Nelson reported to army headquarters that a similar ploy was afoot in a regiment under his command in January 1862: "The 34th Indiana is a regiment of politicians gotten up for bunkum and personal gratification. An intrigue has been gotten up and urged ahead to overthrow the Colonel." Regimental politics divided the 74th Ohio when Colonel Granville Moody, the "Fighting Parson," saw his appointment of an unpopular chaplain overturned by a vote that the regimental historian described as "politicized"; one lieutenant who supported Moody even felt obliged to print up a card denying that he had sold his vote to the colonel. Writing after the war, Major General Jacob Cox maintained that although voting was the best way to choose company officers, "election of field officers, however, ought not to have been allowed. Companies were necessarily regimented together of which each could have little personal knowledge of the officers of the others; intrigue and demagogy soon came into play."[65]

Another practice that ultimately strengthened the identity of the regiment as a community, but sometimes at a price in efficiency, was that of internal promotion. The principle of unit autonomy that entitled companies to fill officer vacancies from within their own ranks was often applied to regiments as well. If a major left an Indiana regiment, for example, he would be replaced by that regiment's senior captain, even if there were captains with more seniority in other Indiana regiments. Regimental affiliation took priority over superior professional qualifications as well, as Colonel William Hazen recognized when he was promoted to command a brigade. In recommending his successor as colonel of the 41st Ohio, Hazen wrote: "Were it not for the principle of the thing I would have recommended Capt. Gilbert of the regular army, but I think the Regt. entitled to the promotion so long as it has worthy officers." So strong was the concept of regimental autonomy that some officers believed that they had no direct authority over men from other regiments, any more than a father would have over another parent's children. As late as mid-1862, one of Buell's generals found it necessary to issue an order to his division to correct the "idea [which] prevails to some extent that the authority of an officer is confined to the Regt. to which he belongs."[66]

Regimental names were still another point of pride and source of identity. Each regiment bore a unique designation that in most cases remained unchanged throughout the unit's existence. The Civil War was fought by thousands of units named "Company A," dozens of "First Brigades," a handful of

Each regiment carried its own flags, which were often presented to the troops with great ceremony by civilians from the soldiers' home communities. From *Harper's Weekly*, October 5, 1861; photograph courtesy of The Lincoln Museum, Fort Wayne, Indiana (TLM #4531).

"Second Divisions," and a few "III Corps" on each side, but there was only one "50th Ohio Volunteer Infantry Regiment." Soldiers were jealous of the individuality of these titles, which they proudly displayed on their regimental flags. When the Kentucky legislature adopted the units organized in Ohio in the summer of 1861 as the 1st and 2nd Kentucky, it caused a furor among the units previously known as the 1st through 5th Kentucky regiments, which were renamed the 3rd through the 7th Kentucky. Colonel Thomas Bramlette of the original 1st Kentucky, displaying the political skill that would later help him attain the governor's chair, made no complaint about his regiment's new "3rd Kentucky" name (though he considered it "no favor to us"), but he did find a "constant source of annoyance" in the "persistent obstinacy with which the Louisville Legion (5th Ky.) and the Regt. commanded by Colonel T. Garrard (7th Ky.) cling to '3rd Ky.' despite the orders from Head Quarters and the action of both state & federal authorities in changing the numbering. . . . The Louisville Legion refuse to be called 5th; seek quarrels with 3rd Ky. on account of title to (3rd)." Only after many months, and much misdirected mail, did the men of the Louisville Legion grudgingly acknowledge their new title.[67]

Once a regiment was fully organized and officered, it was a matter of days or weeks until it was sworn into Federal service and sent to Louisville (or Washington, or Cairo) to become part of a field army. There, the members of a regiment entered the war together, served together, reenlisted together, and (for the lucky ones who survived) were discharged together. Transfers from one regiment to another were rare, and even officers promoted to field command or staff duty retained their original regimental affiliations.[68] If a regiment lost most of its men to battle or disease, it might be broken up and the survivors reassigned, but more often the regiment would try to avoid such a demoralizing fate by detailing officers to return home to find recruits to bring the unit back up to strength.[69]

The regiment was the largest permanent subunit in the Army of the Ohio. Officers higher in the chain of command regarded regiments as integral units, not to be broken up even for temporary service, except under extraordinary circumstances. Lieutenant Tourgée described the companies of his 105th Ohio regiment as having "a certain organic relation to each other, and to the whole" so that even when temporarily detached "they are still part of the organization, are carried on its rolls, and return to it at the expiration of their 'detached service.'" The regiment was thus a "permanent community composed of ten families." The Army of the Ohio would go through numerous reorganizations, several changes of command, and half a dozen different names in the course of the war, but through everything its regiments remained the army's indivisible "unit[s] of force."[70]

By November 1861 the men of the Army of the Ohio were united to the other members of their companies by ties of kinship, locality, and in some cases ethnicity and social class. Through shared experiences, they were growing increasingly tightly bound to their regiments, developing the almost mystical loyalties that would in future decades inspire the veterans to memorialize those regiments by commissioning battlefield monuments and publishing regimental histories.[71] The localized recruitment and organization of companies and regiments worked to build cohesion within those units but did nothing to integrate them with other regiments into a larger whole. In the following months it would be up to the commander of the Army of the Ohio to try to bring together these independent communities of highly motivated military amateurs and forge them into a real army.

CHAPTER TWO

From Civilians into Soldiers, November 1861 to January 1862

On November 9, 1861, Brigadier General Don Carlos Buell replaced Sherman as the commander of all Union military forces in the Ohio River Valley.[1] Based on his long record of service, Buell was as qualified as any officer in the army to receive the appointment to command the newly formed Department of the Ohio. He was a West Pointer, having graduated thirty-second out of fifty-two in the class of 1841 (which included nineteen other Civil War generals-to-be), and a longtime veteran of the Regular Army. He had been wounded in action in the Mexican War, where he received two brevet promotions. For thirteen years he had served in various staff positions in the adjutant general's department. In December 1860 he was sent by President James Buchanan's secretary of war, John Floyd, to carry orders to Major Robert Anderson at Fort Sumter, where a member of the beleaguered garrison, Major Abner Doubleday, noted that Buell "did not appear to sympathize much with us" and disapproved of Anderson's defensive preparations because they might "irritate the people" of Charleston.[2] When Fort Sumter came under attack in April 1861, Buell was under orders to report to San Francisco to serve as adjutant of the Department of the Pacific. He reached California in May, but after his close friend George McClellan took command of the Army of the Potomac, Buell was made a brigadier general of volunteers and summoned to Washington. Once there, he quickly advanced to command of a division, a post he held until November, when McClellan took over from the aged and corpulent Winfield Scott as general in chief and tapped Buell to lead the Army of the Ohio.[3]

On receiving his assignment Buell instantly set out for Kentucky, to the exasperation of his aides, who were left behind to follow on the next train. He carried with him a letter setting forth what McClellan expected the Army of the Ohio to do: hold Kentucky in the Union, defeat the main rebel army in the West (which was led by Albert Sidney Johnston, then widely considered the South's greatest soldier), and march into eastern Tennessee to rescue from Confederate oppression the many Union sympathizers living there. The mission was daunting, but Buell was confident that he could accomplish it, in part because he believed that Johnston could not amass more than 25,000 troops to face him. From Kentucky, Buell wrote to McClellan that "Sherman still insists that I require 200,000 men," but added lightly, "I am quite content to try with a good many less."[4]

"Pretty Much Every Thing Necessary to Make an Army . . . Had to Be Done"

Buell's confidence soon faded. He spent his first days in command reviewing troops and assessing the condition of the army, which had swelled to fifty thousand men, with more reinforcements arriving continuously.[5] The Army of the Ohio that Sherman had left to him on closer inspection turned out to be a loose collection of regiments rather than a well-coordinated military force. "Instead of being an organizer," remarked an observer, W. F. G. Shanks, "Sherman was a disorganizer. His attempt to organize the army in Kentucky in 1861 was a most egregious failure. He gave it up in despair to General Buell, who, on assuming command, found it a mob without head or foot, or appropriate parts."[6] Regimental camps were scattered throughout the state, some established as ad hoc responses to Confederate maneuvers, others, as William Nelson complained in October, set up by officers "establishing their men in camps at places useless and inconvenient . . . [because] each man wants a camp at or near his own farm."[7]

There were no fixed levels of command between the dozens of individual regiments and the department headquarters. Worse, there were not nearly enough trained officers to command the army. Only "four or five General and perhaps as many staff officers embraced the whole military experience in the Department," Buell wrote in 1863, while the soldiers themselves "were but little instructed, some of them not at all." Inadequate state resources had left the troops poorly armed, so that "arms of two or three different calibers could frequently be found in the same regiment, and many of these were of foreign make and unfit for service." Field transportation was in an equally unsatisfactory condition. In short, Buell wrote, "pretty much every thing necessary to make an army of soldiers had to be done." To move quickly against the enemy was out of the question: "The first thing to be done was to organize, arm, equip and mobilize this heterogeneous mass; and this was both a difficult and tedious work."[8]

Buell was not alone in his opinion of the state of the army. Major John Buford, later to gain fame commanding a cavalry division at Gettysburg, visited the army in December in his role as assistant inspector general and wrote a scathing report of the condition of its regiments and batteries. A few examples convey the tone of the whole:

> Capt. W. R. Terrill's Comp. H, 5th Arty, inspected Dec. 9 1861 at Louisville. . . . *Discipline*, good compared with that of the Vol. Batteries, but nothing to be proud of. *Military Appearance*, bad . . . *Equipments*, new, not properly filled, not cared for. *Books*, not properly kept nor posted. . . . *Company fund*, none, has been neglected. . . . *Guard Duty*, too loose.
>
> Capt. Edgerton's Comp. E, Ohio V. Art. inspected December 9th, 1861 at Louisville[.] *Discipline*, some little *Mil. App.*, bad. . . . *Drill*, The batt. has been organized since August last, does not drill as well as it should do—drills four hours daily, but is careless & inattentive. *Messes*, filthy & receive no attention. *Comp[any] & Off[icer]s*, intelligent, but indolent & ignorant of their duties. *N[on].C[ommissioned]. Off[icers]s* of not much force. . . .
>
> Col. Jesse Bayle's Regt of Ky. Cav, inspected Dec. 28th, 1861 at the Fair grounds near Louisville. *Discipline*, none. The men do not stay in camp, are noisy, and are under no restraint. *Mil. App.*, very bad. Long hair, slouched hats—dirty clothing & filthy camp.
>
> Colonel Steele's 43rd Regt. Ind. Vols. *Discipline*, very poor. *Arms*, all in bad order, dirty and rusty. . . . *Company Officers* careless & ignorant. Capt. Gancy is near sixty years of age; has no soldierly qualities; was a preacher before he entered the service; has no dignity and is wholly out of place as an officer . . .
>
> Col. Hawkins' (Ky. Vols.) men are under no restraint; much like a herd of wild animals; the officers do not check them; this is owing in all probability to the fact that the proper election of officers has not yet taken place.

Buford was equally frank in his assessment of other units, but he also recognized the potential of the men to become good soldiers. He graded the 9th

Pennsylvania Cavalry "not much" for discipline but added that "the men seem well disposed & orderly." He described some Kentucky units as "under more control [than Hawkins's regiment]" and predicted that they "will, in time, make good troops." Once formally mustered into Federal service, even Hawkins's "wild animals" would, he expected, show "great improvement."[9]

Buell began the work of organizing the Department of the Ohio by grouping its many regiments into larger, more easily managed units. In selecting the men to command these brigades and divisions, he was careful to make appointments that would be favorably received by the people of Kentucky, whose political loyalty was one of his primary goals. As a career military bureaucrat, Buell also took into account the effects his choices would have on organizational politics within the army, although his concept of army politics omitted one vital constituency: the rank-and-file volunteers, who thus far had more or less organized themselves and had yet to serve under any military authority not of their own choosing. Buell's professional background left him insensitive to the wishes of enlisted men, whose rights (in the Regular Army) were extremely limited. Finally, military efficiency also played a role in his choice of subordinates, but apparently only after external and internal political considerations were satisfied.

The politically oriented command structure that Buell created left much to be desired in military terms. Theory called for a force the size of the Army of the Ohio to be divided into brigades, each of two to four infantry or cavalry regiments and a battery of artillery. Following innovations introduced in Napoleon's army over half a century earlier, two or more brigades plus an artillery reserve of several batteries formed a division, led by a major general assisted by a number of staff officers. Two or more such divisions constituted a corps, which was a miniature army of infantry, artillery, cavalry, and engineering troops, supported by medical, logistical, and other administrative services and commanded by a senior major general with a sizable staff. An army corps could operate independently and was supposed to be capable of withstanding the enemy's entire force long enough for additional corps to come to its assistance.

Rather than establishing such a modern command structure, Buell on November 30 organized his entire army into sixteen brigades, after the fashion of the mid-eighteenth century, when the brigade was the largest tactical unit in use and the typical army marched and fought as a whole, under the sole direction of its commander. Buell numbered his brigades consecutively, from one to sixteen, with additional brigades receiving further numbers as they joined the army. This differed from the organization of the Army of the Potomac and most other Union field armies, which numbered their brigades from one to three within their divisions, so that a brigade could only be identified with reference to its division and corps. The famous "Iron Brigade," for example, entered the Gettysburg campaign as the First Brigade, First Division, I Corps, of the Army of the Potomac. Although Buell combined his brigades into five divisions early in December 1861, the brigades retained their unique numbers, implying that each was a subunit of the army itself and directly subordinate to the army commander. This structure gave Buell an unwieldy sixteen maneuver units under his personal control.[10]

Buell's twenty years of service in the Regular Army may have predisposed him to see his army as a collection of numerous small units reporting directly to a central headquarters. Not since the American Revolution had the nation fielded an army large enough to require any permanent tactical units of brigade size or larger. When the United States went to war with Mexico, the army organized its regiments into temporary brigades and divisions, but as soon as the war ended these formations were disbanded and their components scattered across the frontier in company-size packets. The concept of large formations was so unfamiliar to generals on both sides at the start of the Civil War that when the War Department published new tables of organization in April 1861, it made no provision for any unit larger than a division, and at Bull Run, the victorious Confederate forces were divided into brigades directly subordinate to their two army commanders, Joseph E. Johnston and P. G. T. Beauregard.[11]

Buell's unstated motive for retaining a degree of direct authority over his brigades may have been to reduce the opportunity for state politicians to interfere in army affairs. Governor William Dennison of Ohio, Buell complained to McClellan on November 22, "evidently looks upon all Ohio troops as his army," and Governor Morton "from the beginning tried to retain a *quasi* authority over Indiana troops after they . . . had joined my army." Buell was vexed by colonels who reported to state officials instead of to army headquarters and by governors who "send their staff officers to look after the interests of their troops, exchange their arms without my knowledge, and keep up a communication in other matters which they have no business with."[12]

To counter this, Buell made sure that each of his brigades consisted of regiments from two or more states. Governors might continue to try to influence the activities of the individual volunteer regiments that they sent to Kentucky, but the army's multistate brigades were clearly responsible to Buell alone. Buell later claimed that he "made a rule . . . not to group the regiments by states, but to represent as many States as possible in each brigade," but in fact he only intermixed regiments from different states enough to make the resulting brigades governor-proof. About half of the brigades had units from only two states, and in no brigade were as many as four states represented. A week after he announced the composition of the army's brigades, Buell informed McClellan that although he "suffer[ed] yet from the officiousness of Governors," he was curtailing their acts of interference as he learned of them and "after a while will be able to correct them entirely."[13]

Buell believed that the creation of mixed-state brigades "was attended with the happiest results in the discipline and tone of the army," but he overlooked the friction that resulted within those brigades. Whereas the bond of common state citizenship contributed to the esprit de corps of companies and regiments, state rivalries made it difficult for brigades to develop similar cohesion. Members of the 10th Indiana expressed "great dissatisfaction" when they were brigaded "with a Parcel of Green Kentuckians" and wished for "a Hoosier General" to lead the brigade. Benjamin Bordner of the 11th Michigan complained, in turn, that the "hoosers" in his brigade seemed to receive preferential treatment over Michigan troops. Unlike companies and regiments (or Confederate brigades, in which most if not all of the regiments came from a single state), the brigades of the Army of the Ohio were not extensions of specific civilian communities, nor did they quickly begin to develop institutional identities of their own.[14]

Because units of brigade size or larger lacked organic ties of locality, ethnicity, or even common statehood, their cohesion and efficiency depended primarily on the quality of their leadership. Unfortunately for the Army of the Ohio, there were not enough trained, experienced officers to go around. Buell theoretically required at least five major generals, one for each division, but he had none. Indeed, Buell himself was only a brigadier general. His army was also short of brigadiers, so that one of Buell's first acts on receiving command was to ask McClellan as general in chief for "six or eight" more, "even though they should be no better than marked poles." But McClellan had none to spare, leaving the divisions of the Army of the Ohio to be led by brigadier generals instead of major generals; seven of the army's brigades were initially commanded by colonels instead of brigadiers. Throughout his tenure in command, Buell frequently expressed his belief that the army did not have enough qualified officers.[15]

The men whom Buell selected for brigade command possessed limited military experience. Of the first fourteen, only Thomas J. Wood (Fifth Brigade) and Richard W. Johnson (Sixth Brigade) were active Regular Army officers. Both were brigadier generals who had served on the frontier, and Wood had won a brevet in Mexico. Three others had graduated from West Point but were not in the army when the war began. These were Colonel Joshua W. Sill (Ninth Brigade), third in the class of 1853, who served as a West

Point instructor and ordnance officer until his resignation in January 1861; Colonel Jacob Ammen (Tenth Brigade), at fifty-three the oldest brigade commander, who had been out of the service for twenty-four years; and Colonel Milo Hascall (Fifteenth Brigade), who had resigned a year after his graduation in 1852.[16]

Several other brigade leaders had related experience. Samuel Carter (Twelfth Brigade) was an Annapolis graduate and navy lieutenant from Tennessee who had been detailed to his home state to rally support for the Union. Buell confirmed Carter's de facto leadership of the East Tennessee regiments in the Army of the Ohio by giving him command of their brigade, even though he had no official rank outside the navy; for some months after his appointment he was referred to as "Acting Brigadier General" in official papers. Brigadier General Albin Schoepf (First Brigade) had been a captain in the Austrian army until the 1848 revolution in Hungary, and Colonel John Basil Turchin (Eighth Brigade) was a former colonel of the Russian Imperial Guard who had served on the staff of the future Czar Alexander II during the Crimean War. Brigadier Generals Lovell Rousseau (Fourth Brigade) and James Negley (Seventh Brigade) and Colonel Mahlon D. Manson (Second Brigade) all had volunteered during the Mexican War, Negley as a private.[17]

The remaining three brigade leaders had no military background whatsoever. Colonel Robert L. McCook (Third Brigade) was a lawyer who entered the war when the German Americans of the 9th Ohio chose him as their colonel in spite of his inexperience, hoping that his extensive political connections would help the regiment overcome whatever bureaucratic inertia and nativist prejudice might otherwise prevent it from being accepted for service. Colonel Charles Cruft (Thirteenth Brigade), like General in Chief McClellan, had been the president of a railroad before the war. Brigadier General Jeremiah Boyle (Eleventh Brigade) was a Kentucky lawyer who, on receiving his first appointment from General Sherman in early November 1861, wrote frankly in reply, "I confess my want of military knowledge."[18]

The average age of Buell's original brigade leaders in 1861 was thirty-eight. McCook, Rousseau, Hascall, Boyle, and Cruft had been trained as lawyers. Rousseau and Manson, a druggist, were also state legislators. When the war began Ammen and Sill were teaching college mathematics, Schoepf was a government clerk, Turchin an engineer with the Illinois Central, and Negley a prominent horticulturalist.

The five divisions that Buell created on December 2, 1861, were led by an equally colorful lot with only slightly more impressive credentials. Brigadier General George H. Thomas, commander of the First Division, was the most qualified for high command. He had graduated twelfth in West Point's class of

1841 and been made a brevet major in Mexico. From 1855 to 1861 he had served in the 2nd U.S. Cavalry regiment under Colonel Albert Sidney Johnston and Lieutenant Colonel Robert E. Lee.[19] As commander of Camp Dick Robinson, Thomas had combined Nelson's Kentucky volunteers with two regiments of refugees from Tennessee into a provisional brigade, thus forming the first military organization within the Department of the Ohio larger than a regiment. As early as September 1861, he had begun preparing his forces to march to the relief of the Unionists of eastern Tennessee; he had bombarded Anderson, Sherman, and Buell in turn with requests for the additional men and supplies such a campaign would require. The four brigades that made up Thomas's First Division in December 1861 were posted along a line in south-central Kentucky from Lebanon to London, with Schoepf's First Brigade holding an advanced position at Somerset near the Cumberland River. Both Thomas's temperament and the location of his troops made his division the logical force to lead any movement into eastern Tennessee.[20]

The Second Division, the largest in the army, consisted of the troops concentrated at Camp Nevin on the road from Louisville to Bowling Green. Its commander, Brigadier General Alexander McDowell McCook, was one of Ohio's "fighting McCooks," along with his brother Robert and twelve other brothers and cousins who served the Union, four as generals. It had taken McCook five years to graduate from West Point (which he accomplished in 1852), but he learned enough on active service with an infantry regiment to return to the academy as an instructor in tactics, a post he held at the outbreak of the war. He led the 1st Ohio at Bull Run (where his brother Charles was mortally wounded) and became a brigadier general of volunteers in September 1861. He was described by one of his soldiers as "a good fighting man, but coarse, without dignity" and "much set up with his elevation" from captain in the Regular Army to general of volunteers, which made him "overbearing to his officers. . . . We have however confidence in him in battle." Another observer, Lieutenant Colonel John Beatty of the 3rd Ohio, was less charitable: "McCook is a chuckle-head." Sherman called him "a juvenile." When McCook took command of Camp Nevin in early October, he followed Thomas's example by organizing his regiments into provisional brigades. His division faced the Confederate force at Bowling Green until the end of January 1862 without engaging in any active operations beyond a few skirmishes.[21]

Not far from McCook's camp, Buell formed a Third Division under Brigadier General Ormsby MacKnight Mitchel. "Old Stars" Mitchel had graduated from West Point at the age of nineteen, but he was better known as the astronomer who had helped establish the Cincinnati Observatory and the Naval Observatory in Washington, D.C., than as a military officer.[22] Through

Some of the leaders of the Army of the Ohio. *Left to right, top*: Robert Anderson, Don Carlos Buell, George Thomas; *bottom*: Alexander McCook, O. M. Mitchel, William Nelson. From *Harper's Weekly*, January 12, 1861 (Anderson), December 14, 1861 (Nelson), May 3, 1862 (McCook), November 22, 1862 (Thomas), and *Frank Leslie's Illustrated Newspaper*, October 11, 1862 (Buell), November 1, 1862 (Mitchel); photograph courtesy of The Lincoln Museum, Fort Wayne, Indiana (TLM #4532).

the autumn of 1861 Mitchel had been responsible for the defense of Cincinnati and later for the original Department of the Ohio, which included only Ohio and a small piece of Kentucky, within fifteen miles of Cincinnati. He played an important role in keeping regiments and supplies flowing south to the Union base at Camp Dick Robinson, taking control of the Kentucky Central Railroad for the purpose, but he resented the assignment and told Governor Dennison of Ohio that it did "not suit me to become a drill-master of troops to be turned over to the command of other men." He was particularly eager to lead an invasion of East Tennessee and at the end of October submitted his resignation in frustration at not receiving a field command. After visiting with Lincoln and Cameron in Washington, Mitchel withdrew his resignation and was given the Army of the Ohio's Third Division. This division consisted mostly of regiments recently transferred into the Department of the Ohio from western Virginia, where they had campaigned successfully against local Confederate forces and paved the way for Union loyalists to create the state of West Virginia.[23]

Mitchel's prideful refusal to accept what he considered a secondary post might have alerted Buell that Mitchel lacked the temperament of the ideal subordinate officer. Mitchel's personality flaws, however, were minor compared to those of the commander of the Fourth Division, William Nelson. Nelson weighed three hundred pounds, stood six feet four inches tall, and had the face of a cherub, from which poured a steady stream of oaths and insults. Lacking any gift for self-censorship, Nelson made life miserable for everyone around him with his loud, abrasive manner. In October Sherman wrote to Thomas that "Nelson has got into difficulty with the militia." A month later, when O. M. Mitchel tried to issue some orders to troops under Nelson's command, Nelson initiated another quarrel with his blunt and tactless response. "Nelson has been in camp a day," Buell wrote to McClellan, "and . . . has already got into difficulty with Mitchel; . . . [Nelson] . . . has behaved very absurdly." Although his friends, like Sixth Brigade commander Richard Johnson, insisted that "within that rough exterior which he affected was a heart as warm and generous as ever pulsated in the bosom of man," even Johnson had to admit that "his manner appeared brusque, not to say rude" and brought him into conflict, sooner or later, with most of his colleagues.[24]

Although Nelson was widely disliked by his fellow officers, Buell considered him "an officer of remarkable merit" who could get things done. The former navy lieutenant had been instrumental in arming and organizing Kentucky Unionists in the summer of 1861, applying what reporter Henry Villard described as his "tireless, infectious energy, and . . . remarkable personality." "Nelson had the Reputation of being the Most rigid Disciplinarian of all Buell's generals," according to a private soldier who served under him, but he was not initially unpopular among enlisted men, perhaps because they were less offended by his outspoken style than were his fellow officers. One day in the fall of 1861 Nelson was crossing a river on a flat-bottomed rope ferry when his weight began to tip the craft. "—— you. You are trying to drown me," he yelled at the soldier pulling the rope, but when the private replied, "—— —— you. Get over and help trim the boat," Nelson got over. He was a successful recruiter and ran Camp Dick Robinson effectively until replaced by Thomas in September. He then organized a force at Maysville, which fought in several engagements in eastern Kentucky and became the nucleus of the Fourth Division. Of the army's high officers, Nelson was unquestionably both the most dynamic and the most disruptive.[25]

Buell established the Fifth Division at Owensboro, on the Ohio River west of Louisville, to guard the army's right flank. It was led by Brigadier General Thomas L. Crittenden, who had served as an aide to General Zachary Taylor and later commanded a regiment in the Mexican War. Crittenden belonged to one of the leading political families of Kentucky. His father, Senator John J. Crittenden, had proposed the compromise that bore his name as a last futile attempt to avert the war that would sunder his family as well as his country. Crittenden's brother George became a general in A. S. Johnston's Confederate army; his cousin, Thomas T. Crittenden, became a Union general.

The shortage of experienced military professionals available to Buell in 1861 left him no alternative to appointing a number of marginally qualified leaders for the Army of the Ohio's divisions and brigades. But the shortage of good generals, which plagued all Civil War armies, was exacerbated in the case of the Army of the Ohio by political considerations that further reduced the pool of eligible leaders. To counter Confederate propaganda that portrayed Federal troops in Kentucky as abolitionist hordes carrying out a war of aggression, the Lincoln administration made it a point to assign generals to the region who had local connections and were tolerant of slavery. The first commander with jurisdiction over Kentucky, Robert Anderson, was a native of the state and a slaveholder. His successor, Sherman, was from neighboring Ohio and had lived in Louisiana before the war. Buell was an Ohio native who had been raised in Indiana, married a Georgian, and at one time owned eight slaves. He was appointed to replace Sherman over the head of Major General David Hunter, who outranked Buell but was known for holding strong antislavery views. Buell, in contrast, clearly sympathized with the instructions he received from McClellan "to carefully regard the local institutions of the region in which you command," a euphemism for saying that Buell was to do nothing to interfere with slavery in Kentucky.[26]

Buell applied the same political criteria in choosing his subordinates, at the expense of the army's military effectiveness. Four of the Army of the Ohio's sixteen brigades were led by natives of Kentucky, and division commanders Mitchel, Crittenden, and Nelson all had Kentucky roots. Alexander McCook of the Second Division was from Ohio, as were three brigade commanders. George Thomas was a Virginian. Of the remaining brigade commanders appointed by Buell in 1861, two were from other states that had seceded, one was from Indiana, and two others had been born and raised in Europe; no New Englanders need apply.

The practice of sending "none but Southern and Western officers" to lead the Army of the Ohio was "a stroke of good policy," according to Kentuckian Richard Johnson of the Sixth Brigade, but however much it appeased local civilians, the policy was not particularly popular with the army's rank and file.

Johnson, in spite of his credentials as an active Regular Army officer, at first "did not have the full confidence of the troops because he was a native of Ky.," according to one veteran. In general, the leadership of the Army of the Ohio in 1861 did not meet the approval of those to whom it mattered most, the soldiers themselves. "We have, all of us," wrote Captain R. Delavan Mussey, "large confidence in Genl Buell though the brood of Brig Genls under him in Kentucky do not inspire much respect or confidence."[27]

"Severe and Constant Drill"

The companies and regiments that had gathered to form the Army of the Ohio in the fall of 1861 were filled with eager, highly motivated young men. Few of these recruits yet understood what soldiering meant, but they were willing to undergo the most onerous hardships and face the most extreme danger rather than disgrace themselves before the friends and family with whom they served. Sherman gauged them accurately: "These regiments are composed of good material," he wrote to the War Department shortly before he was replaced by Buell, "but devoid of company officers of experience." If properly armed and equipped and thoroughly trained by efficient officers, the Army of the Ohio had the potential to develop into a formidable fighting force.[28]

Don Carlos Buell seemed the right general for the task. He was a professional soldier who understood the importance of rigorous training, and as a longtime army administrator he was well prepared to tackle the problem of securing arms, uniforms, and equipment for his men. He did not, however, understand the nature of the volunteer army that he led. To Buell, the troops' outward lack of military appearance, their insistence on voting for their officers, and their general rambunctiousness were signs of a lack of military discipline that could only be cured through extensive drill and painstaking attention to the details of correct military behavior. W. F. G. Shanks, who had found Sherman so disorganized, discerned the opposite fault in Buell. He was "too much of a regular, so that when he came to command a great volunteer force he looked for and strove in vain to attain the perfectness in appointment, organization, drill, and all that routine duty to which he had been accustomed in the old army." Buell failed to look beyond the disorderly appearance of the volunteer regiments, as Sherman had done, to recognize that they were ready to fight and needed only to be shown how.[29]

The training of the Army of the Ohio consisted almost exclusively of close order drill, performed by individual regiments. Little training took place at higher organizational levels. Brigade and division officers rarely practiced maneuvering their units, nor did the men in the ranks gain much experience in operating as part of anything larger than their own regiments. By emphasizing the perfection of small-unit drill, Buell improved the efficiency of individual regiments, but he did nothing to encourage soldiers to see themselves as members of any larger entity. Brigades, divisions, and the army as a whole remained mere organizational abstractions. When Buell took over the Army of the Ohio in November 1861, it was little more than a multitude of local, almost tribal, groups of volunteer soldiers; he drilled those tribes into disciplined regiments, but he did not weld them together into a single powerful army.

In the winter of 1861–62 the soldier's typical day began with roll call and breakfast, followed by several hours of drill. In the greenest units, men practiced basic individual skills, like marching and performing the "manual of arms." More experienced outfits spent their mornings drilling by companies and learning to form lines and columns, although every company seemed to have its "awkward squad" that needed extra practice in the fundamentals. After lunch, the colonel assembled the companies for several more hours of what was called "battalion" drill but included the entire regiment.[30] The day concluded with the regiment marshaled for dress parade, where the men stood uncomfortably at attention while the band marched up and down in front of the line, the officers read orders aloud, and visiting dignitaries or curious bystanders got a good look at the men as they shivered in the December twilight. "It is a cold pill to stand so long, some cold days," Leroy Mayfield of the 22nd Indiana wrote to his brother. Most regiments thus spent from four to eight hours each day in various forms of drill, in many cases seven days a week.[31]

The purpose of drill was to prepare men to fight. Even the most ardent volunteer was of no use on the battlefield if he could not use his weapon and maintain his proper station relative to the other members of his company while advancing, retreating, or changing formations, all in immediate response to the commands of his officers. New troops, wrote Colonel Benjamin Scribner of the 38th Indiana, lack "that cohesion which long association and discipline give." Judson Bishop of the 2nd Minnesota summarized the goals of regimental training: "At the crucial hour the regiment must be *present* in full strength and must have its cartridge boxes full—it must be *coherent*, not to be broken up and scattered by something or anything that may happen to it—and it must be *manageable* under all circumstances. Wanting any of these qualities, it is simply a crowd of men of which nothing can be predicted with certainty except confusion and defeat." Close order drill, repeated endlessly, not only taught the actual physical movements required in battle, but also did it so thoroughly that the soldier could be expected to obey his officers' commands automatically, even under fire when every instinct of self-preservation told him to seek safety instead.[32]

Drill was hard. The physical aspect was difficult, but what the volunteers resented most was that it required their complete and unthinking submission to authority. This habit, George Herr of the 59th Illinois noted, "comes slowly and with a sense of irritation to citizen soldiers." In a report to Buell's headquarters regarding charges against Captain Samuel E. Erwin of the 6th Ohio, William Nelson described Erwin as "a strict and faithful officer, by general admission the best in the regiment" and added matter-of-factly that "Capt. Erwin has enforced a strict discipline in his command and is consequently hated by every mean man under his authority." Resentment of discipline was not limited to "mean" men, but was typical of most recruits. "For the independent American citizen," a volunteer surgeon later commented, "the habit of obedience to orders, whether the reason for them is apparent or not, is a difficult acquisition." The acquisition was made easier, for some, by the regard that they held for the officers they had elected. Albion Tourgée noted that "the use of discipline is only to establish confidence between the enlisted man and his officer," and that where such confidence already existed, "it requires very little drill to make the recruit a soldier; [but] if it has to be created, the habit of obedience must take the place of personal confidence."[33]

Most of the regiments of the Army of the Ohio soon acquired the discipline necessary for efficient operations. Not all did; the 24th Illinois was notorious for its bad behavior, and an officer of the dissension-riddled 74th Ohio admitted in his hometown newspaper that his regiment was "not a perfect model of discipline and drill," despite the efforts of its Prussian-born lieutenant colonel, who "would not allow the men even to spit [while] on dress parade." James Cole of the 49th Ohio complained in October 1861 that "Our Co. is getting poorer instead of better in drilling," but by January 1862 Oscar Chamberlain of the same regiment could write to his parents that their unit "has got the name of being about as well drilled as the Regulars, they [the Regulars] say so themselves." Lieutenant Connelly of the 31st Indiana similarly recorded that his men were "more like regulars than volunteers" due to their "severe and constant drill."[34]

One reason why the regiments to which Chamberlain and Connelly belonged seemed as well drilled as the Regulars they saw was that the Army of the Ohio initially contained only four Regular Army infantry regiments (the 15th, 16th, 18th, and 19th U.S.), all of which were new units raised as part of the expansion of the Regular Army authorized by Lincoln in May 1861.

Although the field officers of these regiments were professional soldiers, the company officers and enlisted men were recent civilians who joined the Regulars because their state regiments were full, or to avoid the politics of local units, and not in most cases out of any desire to make the army a career. "These [Regular] regiments were enlisted from the same material and were infused with the same spirit as the State regiments, and were, in fact, 'volunteers,' like all the rest," according to Captain Lewis Hosea of the 16th U.S. Infantry.[35]

Even if the Army of the Ohio's Regular Army regiments were not truly professional, the fact that the army's volunteers took pride in behaving like them was a sign that the citizen-soldiers were beginning to adopt (at least temporarily) the military virtues of discipline and automatic obedience. In the war's second year, Captain John Pierson of the 10th Michigan would look back and comment on the "great diferance between men that are well drilled and Raw recruits." "I think our Regiment can do more to day with half of our origenal number," the captain wrote home in September 1862, "than we could when we came into the field."[36]

The regiments of the Army of the Ohio practiced close order drill not only to instill discipline and teamwork (for which purposes modern armies still drill their recruits), but also because the formations and maneuvers that regiments learned on the parade ground were the same ones that they could expect to use in battle. The most common formation, used for dress parade as well as in combat, was the "line of battle," two ranks deep, with Company A (commanded by the regiment's senior captain) occupying the position of honor on the right end of the line. This formation allowed every soldier to fire his musket at the same time, generating the regiment's maximum firepower, but it had limited mobility and was easily disordered. To move quickly as a body, a regiment could form into a column of companies (one company wide and twenty ranks deep), a column of divisions (two companies wide, ten ranks deep), or, for road marches, a column of route with four men abreast and as many as two hundred ranks. Much time was spent on the drill ground learning to deploy rapidly from column into line and back again.[37]

Keeping the companies of a regiment in their established positions relative to one another while changing formation required all manner of complex evolutions. A regiment in line formation could not form a column of route to the left simply by having each man pivot ninety degrees to his left, for example, because doing so would put Company A at the rear of the column instead of in its customary position at the head. Some colonels nonetheless began to rely on this simple procedure, known as marching "by the flank," in place of the more complicated regulation maneuvers, until Buell issued an order early in 1862 prohibiting the practice. When the poorly drilled 9th Indiana joined Brigadier General William Hazen's brigade in March 1862, Hazen had to remind its colonel "that marching of regiments by flank, unless to pass defiles, is prohibited."[38]

A few regiments supplemented their training in close order drill with open order (skirmish) drill or an occasional session of target shooting. Soldiers in a skirmish line were positioned singly or in small groups spaced several yards apart, usually deployed some distance in advance of the main body of the regiment. Since they operated outside the immediate control of their colonel, skirmishers had to learn to respond to bugle calls or drumbeats instead of shouted commands. In January 1862 Nelson ordered the regiments of his Fourth Division to engage in daily skirmish drill and specified that "Particular attention will be paid to the instruction of the Officers in the bugle calls." In most regiments, however, open order drill was little practiced until the fall of 1862, after the experience of a year of fighting had made clear the importance of skirmishers.[39]

Target shooting was another combat skill rarely practiced in the Army of the Ohio. This was partly a matter of safety, as the combination of loaded weapons and inexperienced soldiers was certain to result in accidents. In October 1861 the colonel of the 31st Ohio issued an order at Camp Dick Robinson that began: "Having waited patiently for someone to shoot himself, or be shot, after first having forbidden the practice of carrying or handling loaded pistols of any description in this camp, it now having come to pass that the waited for event has transpired. . . ."[40] Weapons training was generally limited to learning how to "load in nine times," a series of nine ritualized movements by which all the men of a regiment loaded, aimed, and fired their muskets in unison. The emphasis in loading "by the numbers" was on speed, not individual accuracy. The same applied to artillery training, which also focused on rate of fire, although a member of the 5th Wisconsin Artillery wrote that his battery took the opportunity to practice target shooting at ice floes in Lake Michigan before it was sent to the Army of the Ohio. Because live fire practice was so rare, when the soldiers of the 3rd Minnesota engaged in it at Murfreesboro, Tennessee, in May 1862, the rest of the Union camp assumed that they were under fire from the enemy.[41]

Whether a regiment engaged in target practice, or skirmish drill, or any drill at all was a decision made by each unit's commander.[42] Although Buell attempted to set up "camps of instruction," the Army of the Ohio had no centralized training system. The inspector general of the Regular Army, who was traditionally responsible for instruction of the troops, could not spare any officers from his department to help train the Army of the Ohio, nor was there even a standard textbook of military tactics used throughout the army. The result was that the level of competence each regiment attained depended entirely on the character and military experience of its officers.[43]

Unfortunately for the army, few of its officers knew anything about drill in 1861. The bewilderment expressed by a brand new officer of the 59th Illinois, ordered to do nothing more complex than march his squad down a hill, was typical: "Up to this time in my life I had been a civilian. I had never attempted to form a company or give a military command." John Buford's inspection of the 43rd Indiana noted that, at drill, "The men are in advance of their officers." Lieutenant Tuttle recorded how a volunteer captain in the 3rd Kentucky, challenged by Colonel Bramlette to demonstrate the proper way to maneuver a company around some brush heaps, "turned to his men and gave the command, 'Charge 'em boys! Charge 'em!' . . . [The men] obeyed his command by rushing forward, leaping and scrambling over the brush heaps in the most ludicrous manner." But Bramlette, according to Tuttle, was little better as a drillmaster, frequently getting his men "into an apparently hopeless tangle" and then relying on his adjutant, a Mexican War veteran, to straighten matters out.[44]

Many officers worked hard to repair their ignorance by attending schools conducted by the few Regular Army veterans in the Army of the Ohio and by studying whatever military texts they could get their hands on. The most frequently used tactical manuals were those written by the first Union general in chief, Winfield Scott, and by Regular Army captain William Hardee, who joined the Confederacy and became a general. Scott's and Hardee's texts were similar but not identical; Mexican War veteran Benjamin Scribner complained that "the change in tactics from Scott to Hardee made it necessary to learn them all over again."[45]

Although most regiments were drilled according to Scott or Hardee, there were many exceptions. John Buford's inspection of the 5th Ohio Cavalry revealed that the unit had its own form of drill: "The comp. make a pretty fair show at drill—but use no prescribed tactics. The officers make commands of their own—more suitable for 4th of July occasions than for service . . . Col. Kennett drills the reg't. by a system of tactics made from day to day by himself, which is a nondescript mixture. I saw him drill the reg't. for upwards of an hour without hearing a single command given as laid down in the book."[46] A few regiments learned the exotic and fashionable Zouave drill, a set of fast-paced maneuvers inspired by the performances of French North African colonial troops, while the German-born officers of the 32nd Indiana and 9th Ohio taught their men tactics based on those of the Prussian army, complete with commands given in German. Even among regiments that used the same drill,

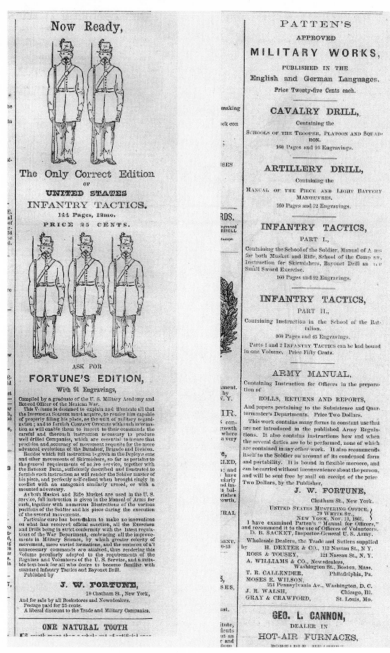

With no standard manual of tactics in use throughout the Army of the Ohio, publishers competed to convince volunteer officers to purchase various editions. From *Frank Leslie's Illustrated Newspaper*, July 20 and November 23, 1861; photograph courtesy of The Lincoln Museum, Fort Wayne, Indiana (TLM #4533).

some varied the system by deviating from the Regular Army practice of ordering companies (from left to right): B G K E H C I D F A. The 3rd Kentucky, for example, kept Companies A and B at their respective posts but deployed the rest in reverse alphabetical order: B K I H G F E D C A. By the end of 1861, a division commander in the Army of the Ohio could have been confident that all of his dozen or so regiments were reasonably adept at some form of drill, but he could have no expectation that any two of them would necessarily know the same drill.[47]

Along with inconsistent regimental training, another potential source of battlefield confusion for generals trying to coordinate their subordinate units was the absence of a standard uniform. Since the Federal government could not at first afford to clothe the hundreds of thousands who volunteered in 1861, many regiments joined the Army of the Ohio wearing outfits provided by their states or localities. Most of these approximated the Federal regulation uniform of dark blue coat and sky blue pants, but variations were common. Minnesota dressed its men in trousers of dark blue. An Indiana soldier described the overcoats issued by his state as "curiosities. They are light blue, having a long tail reaching below the knees, with a cape on shoulder, and . . . seem to have been made as much for frightening the enemy as for service to the soldier."[48]

One of the purposes of uniform military dress is to break down the individuality of the wearer, but the variety of military fashions worn by Buell's troops in 1861 had the opposite effect of reinforcing the identities of individual regiments. This was particularly true of the elaborate costumes of the militia companies, such as the "beautiful Zouave uniforms consisting of a blue Zouave jacket trimmed with yellow braid and bell buttons, red pants and red fatigue caps" worn by some companies of the 19th Illinois. Other companies of the same regiment managed to defeat the other major function of military uniform, identification of friend and foe, by wearing "pretty well made grey suit[s]." Numerous other Union regiments, in the Army of the Ohio and elsewhere, went to war clad in gray uniforms in 1861, until the War Department in September wrote to the various governors asking that "no troops hereafter furnished by your State . . . be uniformed in gray, that being the color generally worn by the enemy." As the soldiers' original clothing wore out and was replaced by Federal issue, the Army of the Ohio gradually took on a more uniform appearance, but some regiments continued to distinguish themselves with individual touches, like the white gloves purchased by members of the 3rd Minnesota for parade and guard duty.[49]

The problem of coordinating regiments that were drilled, equipped, and dressed individually might have been addressed by a program of brigade- and division-level training exercises, but these were rare in 1861. When the 18th Ohio began to practice brigade maneuvers in January 1862, Sergeant Sylvanus Bartlett thought it "the hardest drill we ever had." The 9th Michigan did not take part in its first brigade drill until May 2, 1862, and never participated in another. Colonel Benjamin Scribner later noted that brigade maneuvers were introduced to his unit in January 1863.[50] On the few occasions when such drills were held during the first winter of the war, they sometimes resembled parades more than realistic training exercises. George Landrum of the 2nd Ohio wrote home describing his unit's first brigade drill in January 1862: "There were in one field four Regts. of Infantry, a Battery of Artillery, and a Squadron of Cavalry. They were maneuvered in field movements; the Infantry was formed in squares, the cavalry charged down on us and for the first time I saw something that looked like fighting. The artillery blazed away, and we had a regular sham battle. It was a beautiful sight. We begin to think we can whip twice our weight in Rebels."[51] The use of largely obsolete tactics, like regimental squares, combined with the overconfident reaction of Landrum and his fellow soldiers suggest that this particular drill was of limited use in preparing the troops for war. A participant in a similar drill in Lebanon, Missouri, noted that his unit seemed to be put through such events "for the double purpose of exercising those [troops] and amusing the Lebanonites."[52] The lack of any meaningful training at the brigade and division levels in 1861 or early 1862 meant that the commanders of those units would have to go into battle with little experience in coordinating their regiments. They would have to learn on the job and pay for their mistakes with the lives of their men.

"One of the Handsomest Things of the Season"

Although the army's emphasis on regimental drill as the primary form of training did nothing to develop coordination among regiments, it did allow individual units to reach high standards of efficiency. In a series of skirmishes in late 1861, single regiments of the Army of the Ohio displayed the effects of their training by defeating small Confederate forces. Elements of Nelson's Fourth Division conducted successful operations in eastern Kentucky, and Albin Schoepf's First Brigade won a small battle at Rockcastle Hills on October 21. The most dramatic of these minor engagements took place on December 17, when the 32nd Indiana demonstrated what a well-trained regiment could do, even in its first combat, by repelling the attack of a Texas cavalry regiment at Rowlett's Station on the Green River.

The 32nd Indiana was assigned to Richard Johnson's Sixth Brigade, which was stationed north of Bowling Green. Buell had no plans for active operations in the area and was certain that Johnston's troops at Bowling Green would remain equally quiet. "I should almost as soon expect to see the Army of the Potomac marching up the road," he wrote confidently to McClellan on November 22. Confederate activities seemed to confirm Buell's view of the situation. On December 6 a squadron of cavalry led by John Hunt Morgan slipped past Union outposts and burned the Bacon Creek bridge of the Louisville & Nashville Railroad, between Bowling Green and Louisville; eleven days later an entire brigade, reinforced with cavalry, set out to tear up the same railroad as far north as Green River. Johnston's attacks on the main line of communication between his position and Buell's suggested that he was more concerned with preventing Yankees from marching south, using the railroad as a supply line, than he was with launching an offensive of his own.[53]

Although Buell was also content to remain in place, Morgan's raid on the railroad compelled him to "put aside the inertion which I was anxious to pursue for the present."[54] To keep open the possibility of an eventual move toward Bowling Green, he sent the Second Division to repair the bridge at Bacon Creek. One brigade of the division, the Sixth, continued on to Munfordville near Green River, which it occupied on December 12. From there a single regiment, the 32nd Indiana, was sent ahead still farther to secure the ruins of the Green River railroad bridge. Rebel troops had partially burned the bridge and destroyed one of its four massive masonry piers, but enough of the structure remained to allow engineers to quickly rebuild it to carry rail traffic.

To prevent further damage to the bridge, two companies of the 32nd Indiana crossed the river and set up a picket line guarding the site's southern approaches, while the rest of the regiment built a temporary crossing. When this was completed on December 15, four additional companies crossed the river to support the picket line, leaving the remaining four companies in reserve just north of the river. They would not wait in reserve long; on December 17 a substantial force of Confederate infantry and cavalry set out from the Bowling Green area on a mission to destroy the railroad as far north as Green River. At noon, Southern horsemen encountered the pickets of the 32nd Indiana and opened fire. The skirmish, officially recorded as "Action at Rowlett's Station," began.[55]

The 32nd Indiana was as well prepared for its baptism of fire as any regiment in the army. Mustered in on August 24, 1861, the unit consisted of companies recruited from the German American Turnverein throughout the Hoosier state. It was led by the popular and competent Augustus Willich, a Prussian army veteran who had begun his service to the Union in the 9th Ohio.

Willich nearly won the election for the colonelcy of the 9th, then accepted the post of regimental adjutant (under the mistaken assumption that it would make him second-in-command, as in the Prussian army, rather than a mere clerk) before rising to the rank of major. As the regiment's drillmaster and de facto commander, he came to the attention of Governor Morton, who was finding it difficult to appoint a colonel for the 32nd Indiana from among his state's competing factions of German voters without giving offense to those whose candidate was not chosen. Under these circumstances, Willich of Ohio was the ideal compromise candidate, since he belonged to none of the rival groups but possessed the military qualifications and Teutonic heritage to appeal to them all. With the help of another Prussian veteran, Lieutenant Colonel Henry von Trebra, Willich "molded the new unit in the German way, using the German method of drill and the German system of command," just as he had done with the 9th Ohio.[56]

On the morning of December 17 Willich was away at division headquarters, having left the regiment under the command of von Trebra. When von Trebra heard firing break out around noon, he stationed himself with the four reserve companies at the temporary bridge. From the steep banks of the Green River he could see across a mile of treeless land sloping gently away to the south, then rising in a heavily timbered ridge. The railroad and turnpike to Bowling Green ran due south across this plain. The 32nd Indiana's picket line was deployed along the far side of the distant ridge, facing a valley of cultivated fields. Company C formed the left half of the picket line; the incoming fire seemed to be concentrated on Company B on the right. In response, the two picket companies advanced, one on either side of the turnpike, toward the source of the gunfire.[57]

The men shooting at the 32nd Indiana were part of Confederate Brigadier General Thomas C. Hindman's force of 1,100 Arkansas infantry, four artillery pieces, and 250 men of the 8th Texas Cavalry, better known as Terry's Texas Rangers. The Texans embodied the stereotype of Southern superiority in riding and shooting; even Northern newspapers recognized them as "among the very gamest of the invaders." When the Indiana troops began to move forward, Hindman ordered the Rangers to fall back, hoping to lure the Yankees across the valley and up the hill on the far side, behind which Confederate artillery waited in ambush. But the impetuous Rangers spoiled the plan when they were unable to resist turning and attacking Company C as it crossed the valley to the east of the turnpike. Confederate infantry attacked Company B at the same time, and the Union line fell back under pressure.[58]

On hearing the sound of the pickets' battle, officers of the other companies of the 32nd Indiana ordered their men to prepare for action. Willich had left instructions for his company commanders in the event of an engagement, but in their excitement the men north of the river simply rushed across the bridge to the southern bank, where they formed a close column of companies, a formation that Willich described as "our usual position at alarm." Had they been attacked while in such a compact formation, the men of the 32nd would have been almost helpless to respond, but Lieutenant Colonel von Trebra quickly dispersed the regiment by sending individual companies to assist the picket line. Companies K, G, and F went to support Company B on the right, while Companies A and I marched to the aid of Company C on the left, leaving Major William Schnackenberg and the three remaining companies to follow as the reserve. The advancing companies joined the picket line in the timber on the ridge a mile from the river, where they were again attacked by Terry's Rangers. The rebel cavalry, with "infernal yelling," this time advanced to within twenty yards before falling back. When the center and left companies of the 32nd started to follow the retreating Rangers, the Confederates charged again "in larger numbers," some of them riding right through the regiment's position and circling around to attack from the rear.[59]

The cavalry was able to penetrate the Union line because some, if not all, of the companies of the 32nd Indiana were deployed in thin skirmish lines rather than two-rank shoulder-to-shoulder lines of battle. Skirmish lines were more flexible and could cover a broader area with fewer men, but they lacked the concentrated firepower and bristling hedges of bayonets that allowed infantry battle lines to repel cavalry charges. Contemporary military theory recommended that infantry attacked by cavalry in open terrain should "form square," nullifying the superior mobility of the cavalry by adopting a hollow square formation that had no vulnerable flanks or rear, but skirmish lines were too scattered to "form square" quickly by company or regiment. The skirmishers' only recourse against cavalry was to "rally by fours," forming miniature squares of four soldiers apiece. This is what the skirmishers of the left wing of the 32nd Indiana did, presumably leaving gaps that allowed the Texans to pass through their lines. Only the timely arrival of Company H from the reserve, which "advanced with a hurrah" and drove back the cavalry, prevented the rebels from exploiting their success and routing the left half of the regiment.[60]

A similar contest took place on the right of the Union position, where three companies advanced in skirmish formation followed by a reserve company in column. When the cavalry attacked, the reserve company formed a hollow square behind which the skirmishers retreated. The company square drove off the charging Rangers three times and killed their leader, Colonel B. F. Terry. About this time Willich arrived on the battlefield, immediately ordering the

At Rowlett's Station, the 32nd Indiana used several tactical formations, including the company square shown here, to defeat a Confederate cavalry attack. From *Harper's Weekly*, February 11, 1862; photograph courtesy of The Lincoln Museum, Fort Wayne, Indiana (TLM #4534).

bugle signal "fall back slowly" sounded for the entire regiment. The Confederates, who were demoralized by Terry's death and the sight of other Union regiments of the Sixth Brigade crossing the Green River to support the 32nd Indiana, withdrew from the field at the same time, ending the action.[61]

Both sides made extravagant claims of casualties inflicted. Out of 20 officers and 398 enlisted men participating in the fight, the 32nd Indiana lost 1 officer and 10 enlisted men killed, 22 men wounded, and 5 men missing, rather fewer than the Confederate estimate of 75 Yankees killed, an unknown but presumably greater number of wounded, and 7 prisoners. The rebel force, according to Willich, was "at least seven times as strong as our own" and suffered at least 40 fatalities, but the report of the Confederate commander Hindman showed only 4 men killed in action, one of them Colonel Terry, and 2 officers and 8 enlisted men missing. Both sides claimed a victory.[62]

Although the balance sheet of human lives slightly favored the Confederates, it was the Union soldiers who clearly won the skirmish. The 32nd

Indiana fulfilled its mission by preventing the rebels from further damaging the Green River bridge (even though that had not been their goal) and killed a colorful member of the Southern chivalry in the process. To a Northern public starved for good news, this looked like success. The fight at Rowlett's Station occurred during an otherwise unbroken string of Union defeats, from Bull Run in July and Wilson's Creek in August to the fiasco at Ball's Bluff in October. In these circumstances, the *New York Times* hardly exaggerated in calling it "The most brilliant National victory yet achieved."[63]

At the front, the battle had what Colonel Benjamin Scribner described as "quite a moral effect on both armies," not simply because the Northern soldiers had won, but because the outcome contradicted two prewar stereotypes. Terry's Texas Rangers were skilled riders, crack shots, and hardy outdoorsmen, the very embodiment of the boastful rebel who could lick ten Yankees. "[W]ith much ostentation and arrogance," Scribner noted, the Rangers assumed an air of superiority over all other soldiers, including their fellow Confederates. But when the shooting started, they were turned back by a regiment made up of immigrants, who were in Southern eyes (and many Northern ones) the lowest form of Yankee life. In contrast to early and repeated Confederate successes in Virginia, which gave Lee's army a psychological dominance over the Army of the Potomac that lasted until 1864, Rowlett's Station revealed that the self-proclaimed best rebel troops in Kentucky could be "Whipped by the Dutch!," as their own comrades taunted them. Further, the performance of Willich's men at Rowlett's Station seemed to inoculate the Army of the Ohio against the xenophobic practice of blaming its setbacks on foreign-born soldiers, a habit that infected the Army of the Potomac after the German American XI Corps was routed at Chancellorsville and Gettysburg in 1863. Instead, Buell's entire army shared the pride he expressed when he wrote to McClellan, "The little affair in front of Munfordville was really one of the handsomest things of the season."[64]

The tactical lessons of the skirmish at Rowlett's Station were less clear than its psychological ones. The Prussian drillmasters of the 32nd Indiana had steeped their men in classical European maneuvers, so that in their first fight they were able to fight in skirmish order or line of battle, to advance and fall back in good order in the face of the enemy, to rally by fours and form company squares, and to maneuver in response to bugle signals. But the months ahead would reveal that many of these maneuvers were no longer useful on the typical Civil War battlefield. Rowlett's Station, as one veteran observed, was "notable as one of the few fights of the war between infantry skirmishers in the open and cavalry." The mounted attack of the Texas Rangers was an anomalous event; few other units of the Army of the Ohio ever faced a traditional cavalry charge on an open field. The level, unobstructed plains necessary for a charge by a line of horsemen riding boot to boot were rare on the heavily wooded battlefields of the western theater. Where the terrain was sufficiently open to permit cavalry to attempt a charge, defending infantry could employ the full capabilities of their long-ranged rifled muskets to break up the attack by firepower, long before the saber-wielding horsemen could get close enough to do any damage. Although some units continued to practice maneuvers like the company square and rallying by fours, these tactics were in fact obsolete.[65]

The skirmish at Rowlett's Station was deceptive in another way. The ease with which the competent and experienced officers of the 32nd Indiana handled their regiment in battle gave no indication of the confusion and difficulty of communication that would be characteristic of larger engagements involving dozens of regiments, brigades, and divisions. Lieutenant Colonel von Trebra was able to command portions of the 32nd Indiana by his voice alone, and Colonel Willich communicated with all ten companies at once by bugle signals, but these methods would not suffice to control larger units. The absence of information that paralyzed McCook's division, several miles to the rear of the fighting, was a clearer portent; soldiers there could hear firing from the battlefield, but as one veteran recalled, "From its irregularity it was considered uncertain whether an engagement was progressing, or the firing was merely a practice at target." Although the Sixth Brigade and the rest of the Second Division were camped not far from the battlefield, their leaders did not respond in time to assist the 32nd Indiana. Such breakdowns in communication would continue to plague the Army of the Ohio on other battlefields, with consequences much more severe than those at Rowlett's Station.[66]

CHAPTER THREE

The First Campaign
Logan's Cross Roads, January 1862

Don Carlos Buell reluctantly ordered the inexperienced Army of the Ohio to undertake its first offensive military operation in January 1862. Under political pressure to act aggressively to save Unionist civilians in eastern Tennessee, he authorized Thomas's First Division to make a token advance against a small Confederate force camped north of the Cumberland River near Mill Springs, Kentucky. In a sharp battle at Logan's Cross Roads on January 19, Thomas's regiments maintained their cohesion under fire and used effective small-unit tactics, as the 32nd Indiana had done at Rowlett's Station. The battle ended with the Confederates on the run and their leader, Brigadier General Felix K. Zollicoffer, dead on the field. Thomas's victory exposed the eastern flank of the Confederate defensive line along the Kentucky-Tennessee border and led to the retreat of all Southern forces from Kentucky. Few Civil War battles had results so disproportionate to the numbers involved.[1]

Although the Logan's Cross Roads campaign demonstrated that the Army of the Ohio was capable of achieving decisive tactical results, at least in small engagements where its officers could exercise direct control over their troops, it also revealed the limits of Buell's ability to reconcile the political and military objectives of the Army of the Ohio. Buell understood that war and politics were interrelated, as he had shown in November 1861 when he willingly allowed political considerations to overshadow military qualifications in his selection of subordinate commanders. But when politicians in Washington, as well as elements within the Army of the Ohio, began to pressure him to send the army to eastern Tennessee, Buell underestimated the strength of their influence. Initially he clung to his professional view that Nashville was the army's proper strategic goal, and that in any case the Army of the Ohio was not yet ready for any kind of offensive activity. When he finally tried to quiet his critics by allowing Thomas's division to advance, he did so against his better judgment and made it no secret that he considered any diversion of his army's strength into eastern Tennessee a waste of resources. Though the unexpected victory at Logan's Cross Roads cast some brief reflected luster on Buell's reputation, the fact remained that he contributed little to what would turn out to be the only unambiguously successful campaign conducted by the Army of the Ohio under his leadership.

"The Necessity of Sending Something into East Tennessee"

Although Buell did not believe that the Army of the Ohio was ready to take the offensive at the beginning of 1862, the rank-and-file troops were anxious to get on with the war. By their mere presence, they had already helped to stabilize the political situation in Kentucky and to confine Confederate military forces to the southern portion of the state. They were armed and equipped at least as well as their opponents, and they considered themselves well trained. The few skirmishes they had fought had only heightened the enthusiasm with which they had entered the service. "Before I enlisted," wrote Amos Abbott, who had been a student at the University of Michigan when the war began, "I anticipated and made up my mind to meet all, aye, if necessary, much more, than I have yet seen."[2] He and most of his comrades had not yet seen very much, and they were eager to fight.

The soldiers were impatient to march against the enemy in part because they perceived that it would be safer than spending the rest of the winter in their camps. "While marching we never have any sick; when we stop the men sicken and fall like leaves," reported Colonel Bramlette of his 3rd (né 1st) Kentucky in December 1861. Regiments that served in the Army of the Ohio lost an average of 12 percent of their manpower to disease over the course of the war, a mortality rate higher than that of any of the army's battles. James Coulter's recollections of conditions in the camp of the 37th Indiana at the end of 1861 were typical: "typhoid fever, mumps Small pox and other diseases broke out in camp and Men were dying every day." Epidemics of all these diseases ran through the army's camps during the war's first winter. Measles was another killer, especially among young soldiers who had grown up in sparsely populated rural areas and failed to develop immunities. After sixty-one men had died of the disease at Camp Dick Robinson, the frustrated Colonel Bramlette "upon one occasion severely reprimanded the men of his regiment for not having had the measles while they were children."[3]

Medical treatment was often worse than useless. Jesse B. Connelly of the 31st Indiana described how the regimental doctor treated an outbreak of mumps in his unit by using the same swab to apply "caustic" to the inside of every patient's throat, unknowingly ensuring transmission of the disease. "I was taken sick . . .," George W. Squier of the 44th Indiana reported to his wife, "[and] Our regimental surgeon (which the boys call 'Instent Death') looked at me and said 'Typhoid fever.'" Fortunately for Squier, his comrades' gallows humor proved an exaggeration, as he survived his illness. Another typhoid survivor, Charles Wesley Heath of the 6th Indiana, was lucky enough to have a doctor who recognized that "if he goes to the hospital, he will die" and left him in the care of his friends in camp. Heath's prescription was a good one, as hospitalization offered few comforts but meant certain proximity to patients suffering from all manner of infectious diseases. When Marcus Woodcock of the 9th Kentucky was hospitalized for measles in November 1861, he and his fellow sufferers were placed two in a bed. "The stench was horrible from the fact that the beds were simply a continuation of the straw pile[d] around the room," Woodcock wrote, and in the absence of spittoons the patients made it a habit to spit against the wall, which "was not washed more than twice in a week." Woodcock recovered only after his father came and took him away, confirming the observation of Colonel William Hazen that the only really effective treatment for a sick soldier was to send him home before he got any worse.[4]

Soldiers were most vulnerable to disease immediately after enlisting, when they were suddenly exposed to new microbes carried by hundreds or thousands of other volunteers gathered at a state rendezvous camp. Once a regiment had been in service for several months, it was considered "seasoned." The weakest soldiers were no longer in the ranks, having died or gone home to recover, while the survivors developed immunities. "Men who live through this campaign," wrote Lieutenant George W. Landrum from the camp of the 2nd Ohio in early 1862, "will not die under hardships; they will be proof against anything but the bullets and shells of the enemy." For those undergoing the process, bullets and shells often seemed preferable to the random danger of waiting for camp diseases to run their course. The seasoning of the Army of the Ohio in the winter of 1861–62, though it was necessary and inevitable, increased the impatience of the men to leave their camps and get at the rebels. Colonel Bramlette spoke for the army when he wrote to his division commander in December 1861, "We would rather die in battle than on a bed of fever."[5]

Of all the troops in the Army of the Ohio, none were more anxious to move than Samuel Carter's brigade of Tennessee refugees. They had enlisted with the expectation of quickly liberating their home state at the head of a victorious Union army. As the months passed, new recruits from eastern Tennessee brought word of increasing hardships for the families left behind under Confederate rule, while the Army of the Ohio remained fast in its camps. Carter repeatedly urged Thomas to march to East Tennessee: "[T]he condition of affairs there is sad beyond description, and if the loyal people who love and cling to the Government are not soon relieved they will be lost." The plight of the region received national attention in December 1861, when the government of Tennessee, with approval of the Confederate secretary of war, executed several Union partisans who had responded to the rumored arrival of Thomas and his division by burning bridges to hamper the Confederate response.[6]

Meanwhile, the frustration of Carter's Tennesseans nearly boiled over into mutiny. On November 20 or 21, Thomas ordered the "East Tennessee Brigade," as Carter described his command, to march two dozen miles north, away from the Tennessee border. On receiving the order, which was intended to consolidate the subunits of the First Division, Carter assured Thomas that although his men had "a great dread of the Blue-grass country, and are most desirous of driving the rebels from East Tennessee in the quickest possible time," they would willingly comply with his instructions. In the event, however, many of Carter's troops balked at the command to march farther from their homes. Some deserted rather than obey, and Carter confessed to Tennessee congressman Horace Maynard that he was "intensely mortified at the hesitancy of some of our Tennesseeans to move on." To avoid further problems, Carter asked Maynard to see if he could arrange matters so that his men, who "would sooner perish in battle than turn their backs towards the Tennessee line again," not be ordered back to central Kentucky in the future.[7]

Maynard was more than eager to comply with Carter's wishes. Since October, he and fellow Tennessee loyalist Senator Andrew Johnson had been trying to get the Army of the Ohio to drive the Confederates from their home state. They had intrigued with Simon Cameron to replace Thomas with O. M. Mitchel as commander of Camp Dick Robinson in the hope that Mitchel would be more responsive to their will. Thomas, who ironically was a strong proponent of a campaign into eastern Tennessee, foiled the maneuver by threatening to resign.[8] Even though Thomas repeatedly pressed Buell for permission to advance over the next two months, this was not enough for Maynard, who darkly warned Thomas on December 8 that only "shameful wrong somewhere" could account for the army's prolonged inactivity. With Carter's Tennesseans suffering from their exposure to "Nelson and the measles and . . . nakedness and hunger and poverty and home-sickness," Maynard hinted that Thomas should take it upon himself to act without waiting for instructions from Buell. "I cannot," Maynard concluded, "approve your determination simply to 'obey orders.' "[9]

In addition to trying to suborn the generals of Buell's army, Maynard and Johnson worked on Buell himself. Samuel Carter was too good a soldier to violate military procedure by writing directly to Buell (going over the head of Thomas, his immediate superior), but his letter of November 21 to Maynard had the same result. In it, Carter begged Maynard "to get those in power to give us . . . permission to make at least an effort to save our people"; Maynard showed the letter to President Lincoln, who referred it to McClellan.[10] On December 7 Johnson and Maynard wrote to Buell that they had met with McClellan and Lincoln, who "concur fully with us" in their "anxious solicitude" for an East Tennessee expedition.[11] This was true, as McClellan was already bombarding Buell with increasingly urgent reminders of the need to "sacrifice mere military advantage" for the political goal of liberating eastern Tennessee quickly. On December 3 McClellan (with Lincoln's approval) had sent Buell the letter that Carter had written to Maynard. "Let me again urge the necessity of sending something into East Tennessee," McClellan wrote two days later. "Johnson, Maynard, &c., are again becoming frantic," he warned Buell on December 29, "and have President Lincoln's sympathy excited."[12] McClellan then fell ill with typhoid fever, and Lincoln himself took over the job of trying to prod Buell into action via the telegraph, asking him on January 4, 1862, "Have arms gone forward for East Tennessee? Please tell me the progress and condition of the movement in that direction. Answer."[13]

Buell resisted the pressure. As early as November 22 he began hinting to McClellan that he favored an attack on the center of the Confederate line, with Nashville as the objective, rather than a march into eastern Tennessee. A drive on Nashville would follow existing railroad lines, Buell argued, whereas a twelve-thousand-man expedition into the barren hill country would require a massive wagon train just to carry its own supplies, much less to bring the ten thousand muskets that the administration wanted to send to Union sympathizers in East Tennessee. Buell contended that without more wagons and more quartermaster officers to organize the army's supplies, the Army of the Ohio was not ready for an offensive campaign anywhere.[14]

By Regular Army standards, Buell had reason for thinking the army insufficiently prepared for war. He reported in late December that only fifty thousand of his seventy thousand men could be considered an "efficient force"; the rest were completely untrained, poorly organized, or simply absent (with or without leave). The Kentucky regiments were in particularly bad shape. Buell found "some forty or more Kentucky regiments or fractions of regiments scattered over the State in recruiting districts" that "had to be collected from remote quarters and . . . consolidated and organized." Until this was done, he claimed, "The Kentucky regiments . . . can be but little used."[15]

Through the winter, Buell focused on organizing, equipping, and training his command, while waiting for his friend and fellow professional McClellan to come around to his way of thinking. McClellan was still insisting that the Army of the Ohio make "a primary object of what I think ought to be secondary," Buell wrote to his wife in December, "However he will not disagree I think" with the plan to move toward Nashville once the army was ready. Accordingly, Buell refused to move, except when he felt it necessary to do something to placate those who demanded action. A sympathetic observer, Robert M. Kelly of the 4th Kentucky, later wrote that the reason Buell's "brigades and regiments were allowed to remain in apparently objectless dispersion" was because "he desired to do nothing to put the enemy on the alert." Buell confirmed this in a letter to McClellan: "Thus far," he claimed proudly in late November, "I have studiously avoided any movements which to the enemy would have the appearance of activity or method."[16]

McClellan did not share Buell's enthusiasm for his masterly show of inactivity and proposed in mid-December to reduce Buell's authority by transferring responsibility for the Sandy River region in eastern Kentucky to an adjacent military department headed by Brigadier General William Rosecrans. Buell forestalled this by immediately dispatching a force under Colonel James A. Garfield to secure the area. Likewise, Buell moved to counteract the mounting pressure of the East Tennessee lobby on December 29 by finally granting permission to Thomas to march south, but only as far as the Cumberland River, where he was to push back the Confederates who had established a position on the northern bank. The possibility that Thomas might actually "succeed in destroying Zollicoffer's force entirely" Buell dismissed as "too much to calculate upon."[17]

Meanwhile, he continued to temporize with his superiors. Writing to McClellan on the same day that he unleashed Thomas, Buell confessed: "It startles me to think how much time has elapsed since my arrival and to find myself still in Louisville." On January 5, 1862, he admitted to Lincoln that his heart had never been in the East Tennessee plan at all and that "my judgment from the first has been decidedly against it." His preparations were motivated "more by my sympathy for the people of East Tennessee and the anxiety with which you and the General-in-Chief have desired it than by my opinion of its wisdom."[18]

With this Buell had overplayed his hand. The letter drew a sharp rebuke from Lincoln, who wrote back that "Your dispatch . . . disappoints and distresses me" and that he could not even show it to Johnson or Maynard. Lincoln did show it to McClellan, who was equally critical of Buell's strategic ideas and sarcastically observed that "interesting as Nashville may be to the Louisville interests . . . its possession is of very secondary importance in comparison with" eastern Tennessee. On January 13 he further warned Buell, "You have no idea of the pressure brought to bear here upon the Government for a forward movement. It is so strong that it seems absolutely necessary to make the advance on Eastern Tennessee at once." McClellan also sent four hundred wagons and instructions to buy or seize as many more as necessary to get the Army of the Ohio moving immediately.[19]

Within hours of receiving McClellan's January 13 telegram, Buell replied that he was sending Thomas to fight Zollicoffer, referring to the movement he had initiated two weeks earlier. In the same message, Buell continued to maintain that his resources were inadequate. Acknowledging that reinforcements had swelled the Army of the Ohio to 90,000 men, he could not resist pointing out that "a large proportion of this is unfit for active operations." He would need eight divisions, totaling 120,000 men, before he could spare three divisions for eastern Tennessee. But even as he made his case to McClellan again, Buell could see that he had pressed it as far it could safely go. After sending his reply, he prepared a message for Thomas, telling him to expect reinforcements and encouraging him to be aggressive: "[I]f you see an opportunity, lose not a day." The advance of Thomas's division, which Buell had authorized only as a sop to his critics, suddenly represented his best hope of proving to Washington that he deserved to retain command of the Army of the Ohio.[20]

"The Continual 'Zip,' 'Zip,' of the Bullets"

The forces of Thomas and Zollicoffer had encountered one another in battle before. When Zollicoffer's troops first entered Kentucky in October 1861, Thomas immediately sought to stop them by dispatching an ad hoc brigade commanded by Albin Schoepf. Schoepf's men fought a successful skirmish with the Confederates at Rockcastle Hills on October 21. As Zollicoffer retreated to the Cumberland Gap, Schoepf's troops and Carter's eager Tennesseans pursued him as far as London, Kentucky.[21] Thomas then repositioned his brigades at London, Columbia, and Somerset, forming a line across southeastern Kentucky, with reserves at Lebanon. In early December Zollicoffer again marched north from Tennessee, this time occupying Mill Springs, a position of considerable strategic importance that protected the right flank of the Confederate army at Bowling Green and blocked the path of any Union expedition to East Tennessee. Zollicoffer's men also built a fortified position north of the Cumberland River at Beech Grove, less than twenty miles from Schoepf's brigade at Somerset. Schoepf feared that he would be outnumbered by the advancing Confederates and called for Carter's brigade to join him. Thomas persuaded Buell that Zollicoffer constituted a threat that had to be eliminated, and on December 29 he obtained Buell's permission to use the rest of his division to march to Schoepf's aid and force the rebels back across the Cumberland.

It took two weeks for Thomas and the bulk of his division to reach the vicinity of Schoepf's brigade at Somerset. Heavy rains slowed the division's progress to less than five miles on some days. "This was our first, and perhaps our hardest march. It rained almost incessantly, and roads, cut up by the heavy trains in advance of us, were well-nigh impassable," recalled one veteran. On January 17 Thomas encamped at Logan's Cross Roads, still about eight miles short of Somerset and only ten miles north of the Confederates at Beech Grove. He had with him a force consisting of four regiments, two each from the Second and Third Brigades, and two batteries of artillery. The remaining two regiments of the Second Brigade and more artillery were strung out eight miles behind, closing up as quickly as possible. From the east, three regiments of Carter's East Tennessee brigade and another battery of guns were also converging on Thomas's camp, less than a day's march away.[22]

Unknown to Thomas, the Confederate position at Beech Grove was empty. Orders had been issued earlier in the month replacing Zollicoffer with Major General George B. Crittenden (brother of the commander of the Fifth Division of the Army of the Ohio). When Crittenden, a trained soldier, reached Zollicoffer's camp on January 7, he immediately saw that his predecessor had erred in dividing his force between Mill Springs and Beech Grove, with the swollen Cumberland River between. Learning that Thomas's division was advancing, Crittenden decided that it was too late to try to withdraw the Beech Grove contingent. He instead planned to unite his four thousand men north of the river, then make an overnight march followed by a surprise attack at dawn on the Union camp at Logan's Cross Roads. Crittenden's two brigades, one commanded by Zollicoffer, departed at midnight on January 18 but were slowed by heavy rains and did not arrive at their objective until after daylight on the nineteenth, tired and discouraged by the wet weather.[23]

The first unit in the path of Crittenden's attack was the Second Brigade, commanded by its senior colonel, Mahlon D. Manson of the 10th Indiana.

Manson was a politician and druggist who had led a volunteer company during the Mexican War and commanded a three-months' regiment in McClellan's West Virginia campaign in the summer of 1861. Like most volunteer officers, he was still learning his new job. On the night of January 15, he experimented with the unorthodox procedure of deploying a two-gun section of Battery C, 1st Ohio Light Artillery, as part of the picket line that guarded his camp from surprise attacks. Apparently the experiment was not successful enough to merit repeating, and on the morning of January 19, 1862, Manson's brigade was guarded by a more traditional picket line consisting solely of infantry.[24]

The men who made up the brigade's picket line that morning belonged to two companies of the 10th Indiana. Company I was deployed about a mile south of the regiment's camp, with Company K another three hundred yards beyond. Even if the sunrise had not been obscured by early morning rain and mist, the pickets would not have been able to see far in any direction because of the nature of the ground, described by Judson Bishop (then a captain in the 2nd Minnesota) as "undulating and mostly covered with thick woods and brush, with some small open fields inclosed by the usual rail fence of the country." To complicate matters, somewhere to the west and south of the Indiana companies were several hundred dismounted Kentucky cavalry belonging to Colonel Frank Wolford's battalion who were also deployed as pickets, apparently on authority of division headquarters.[25] Wolford's unit, which had already earned a reputation within the army for drunkenness and incompetence, was not part of Manson's brigade or subject to his command.[26]

The fighting began at daylight when advancing Confederates encountered the 10th Indiana's two outpost companies. "[W]e gave them a hearty welcome as they came up in sight," Corporal Harrison Derrick of Company K enthusiastically wrote to a friend shortly after the battle, "and we gave them some of the enfield slugs which made them weak in the knees." At about the same time, Wolford's cavalry also came under fire from the leading Confederate units. Wolford and the commanders of the two infantry companies sent messengers to carry word of the attack to various higher officers, including Lieutenant Colonel William Kise as acting commander of the 10th Indiana, Colonel Manson of the Second Brigade, and Brigadier General Thomas.[27]

Although hastily scrawled notes or brief spoken messages transmitted by courier represented slow and inefficient means of communication, they were among the few sources of information available to Kise, Manson, and Thomas that morning, or to anyone more than a hundred yards away from the firing line on any Civil War battlefield. Experienced soldiers could glean some idea of the progress of the fighting by listening to the sounds of gunfire, but these could be deceptive. At Logan's Cross Roads, the initial Confederate attack was clearly audible near the camp of the 2nd Minnesota, over a mile away, where Captain Bishop heard "a musket shot, another, and then five or six more in quick succession [ring] out with startling distinctness over on the Mill Springs road, a mile or more to our left and front." But closer to the scene, some of the 10th Indiana could not hear the firing of their own picket companies. "The first we New of the Fight," according to Wesley Elmore, "we wase prepareing to Eat Breakfast when a messenger Came in from the scene of action and the Camp was Soon alarmed by the long Roll and we were Shortly arrayed in line of Battle with our guns and Cartridge Boxes on." Closer still, the deafening noise of the fighting blotted out most other attempts to communicate. When Captain Samuel Shortle ordered Company K of the 10th Indiana to fall back, Corporal Derrick noticed that his words failed to reach at least one soldier, George Shortle, who fought on alone for some time before realizing his predicament and running to rejoin the Union skirmish line.[28]

When the first messenger from the two picket companies reached the camp of the 10th Indiana, at about 6:30 A.M., Kise immediately responded by sending the next ranking officer, Major Miller, with an additional company to reinforce the pickets. In spite of this aid, the pickets soon fell back to a position about one-half mile from the regiment's camp. Shortly after Miller's departure, Colonel Manson ordered Kise to lead the rest of the regiment forward. The seven remaining companies marched in column south on the Old Road toward the sound of the fighting, passing the intersection of the Old Road and the Mill Springs road, until they were within seventy-five yards of the Union front line. "The continual 'zip,' 'zip,' of the bullets," wrote regimental historian James Shaw of Company D, "soon settled the fact that the Tenth was engaged in a battle." Kise then deployed five companies in the woods to the right, west of the road. He sent the other two companies to the left, "into an open Field Contrary to our wishes," as Wesley Elmore recalled in a letter home.[29]

From his position with the right wing companies, Kise reported that he could see "a regiment of rebels . . . advancing in line of battle and their treasonable colors . . . flaunting in the breeze." He could not, however, see the enemy advancing on the two leftmost companies and thus ordered those companies to hold their fire. After enduring a hail of incoming musket balls without replying for "some time," Elmore and his comrades on the left flank "thought it was time for us to do Some Execution" and opened fire in spite of Kise's orders. For the next hour, the men of the 10th Indiana engaged in a fierce firefight with a constantly increasing rebel force that threatened to overlap both of the regiment's flanks.[30]

While Kise and his men struggled to hold their ground, Manson headed for

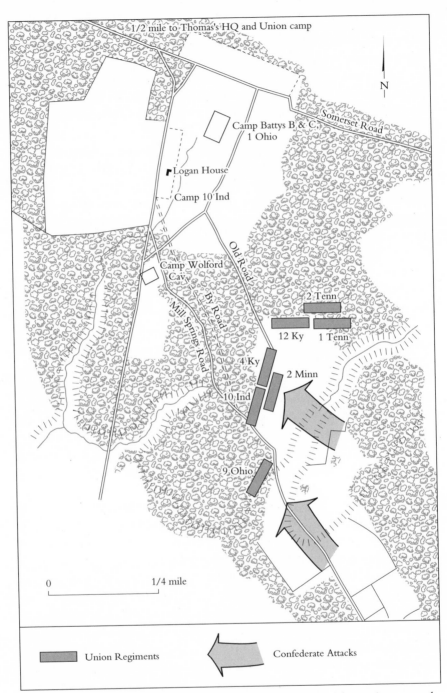

Battle of Logan's Cross Roads, January 19, 1862. Based on *Atlas to Accompany the Official Records*, plate VI, no. 3.

the rear to find the other units of his brigade and to report to Thomas. These were tasks a staff officer might normally perform, but Manson apparently had no one available. Manson first found the camp of the 4th Kentucky, where he awakened Colonel Speed S. Fry shortly after 6:30 A.M. Manson's orders, according to Fry, were to "proceed at once towards the scene of action" and "go and take a position in the woods." In his after-action report to Manson, Fry left little doubt that he considered Manson's directions inadequate, stating that "I had no information as to the strength or position of the enemy, and had to be governed entirely by my own judgment as to what was best to be done."[31]

From Fry's camp Manson hastened to Thomas's headquarters. Passing through the camp of the Third Brigade shortly before 7:00 A.M., he alerted its commander, Colonel Robert L. McCook, "that the enemy had driven in his pickets and were approaching in force." McCook immediately formed up his two available regiments, the 9th Ohio and the 2nd Minnesota, and detached Company K of the 9th Ohio to act as skirmishers in the woods on his right to protect the brigade's flank. Manson, meanwhile, finally encountered Thomas and stood before him "hatless, with disheveled hair, unwashed face, and incomplete toilet." Before Manson could explain what he had been doing and why he was so far behind the firing line during a battle, Thomas interrupted him by shouting, "Damn you sir, go back to your command and fight it."[32]

In the absence of their brigade commander, Manson's men were having a difficult time. Ammunition was running low in the picket companies of the 10th Indiana, which had fallen back and joined the main line of the regiment. Kise perceived that Confederates were extending past his position at both ends and threatening to envelope his regiment's flanks. He first sent Company F to shore up the right, then decided to pull back the entire right half of the regiment. Harrison Derrick and the men of Company K heard Kise give an order "to retreat for reinforcements which we done in order," but others became confused. Samuel McIlvaine of Company D thought that the entire regiment had been ordered to retreat, "but from some misunderstanding of the command, or other reason, only the right wing at first fell back and that only partially and in Indian style, loading and firing from behind trees as we went." Wesley Elmore's company was also ordered to fall back from its exposed position in an open field to the relative safety of some woods, where the company rallied. Adding to the general confusion, Wolford's Kentucky cavalrymen, who had been fighting dismounted in the woods not far from the 10th Indiana, joined the swelling retreat.[33]

Just as the right wing of the 10th Indiana was giving way, Colonel Fry and his 4th Kentucky infantry arrived. They formed a line of battle to the left of the Hoosiers, on some high ground in the field to the east of the Old Road, in front of and parallel to a fence bordering the field. From 250 yards away to the southeast, behind another fence that enclosed the opposite side of the field, a Confederate unit poured fire into the Kentuckians. Believing that his men were outnumbered and that the Confederates had the advantage of superior cover, Fry directed his men to fall back and take shelter behind the fence to their rear. As the regiment occupied this new position, Fry received a report from his lieutenant colonel that rebels were moving into the woods on his right, filling the position recently vacated by the 10th Indiana.[34]

Fry went to inspect the situation in person. Morning fog, combined with the smoke of thousands of black powder muskets, made it hard to see anything in the dense woods; a drummer boy in the 2nd Minnesota recalled that "smoke hung so close to the ground on account of the rain that it was impossible to see each other at times."[35] Riding into a road beyond his regiment's right flank, Fry suddenly came upon a mounted officer in a pale overcoat. "We must not kill our own men," he warned Fry, apparently concerned that the poor visibility and the inexperience of the troops were leading to casualties from friendly fire. A moment later the officer pointed to some men in the woods and added, "those are our men and let us not kill them." The conversation ended abruptly when one of the officer's aides rode out of the woods, deliberately aimed his pistol at Fry, fired it, and dashed away. Realizing at last that he had ridden among the enemy, Fry fired back at the officer who had spoken to him, General Felix Zollicoffer, and killed him.[36]

After shooting the Confederate commander, Fry looked again at the troops that Zollicoffer had pointed out. Discovering that they too were rebels, he "gave orders to our men to fire upon them which they did hitting several of them and putting the others to flight."[37] The timely arrival of the 4th Kentucky and the death of General Zollicoffer checked the momentum of the Confederate attack and allowed the Northern units time to rally. Some of Wolford's cavalry and a good portion of the 10th Indiana returned to the front and resumed fighting alongside Fry's men.

The rally of the 10th Indiana demonstrated the depth of the regimental cohesion that prevailed throughout the Army of the Ohio. After Kise ordered the right wing to fall back, the regiment had become separated into two bodies. While the men of the left half of the regiment held their ground and continued fighting under the direction of their officers, the formation of the right wing dissolved, its soldiers fighting from behind trees and seeking cover independently. In the confusion and low visibility, these men had the opportunity to go to the rear without risk of being seen. Instead of fleeing, however, most of them retreated only as far as their regimental camp half a mile away and there reformed their ranks. On his way to the front, Thomas found them "formed in front of their encampment, apparently awaiting orders." He sent them forward again to support the endangered left flank of the 4th Kentucky, where they resumed their part in the battle.[38]

The history of the 10th Indiana reveals the source of its members' collective willingness to resume fighting. They had been recruited entirely from the state's Eighth Congressional District, with each company raised within a single county in the district. Many of the men had thus known one another before they enlisted in September 1861, and at least 20 percent of the original 979 who signed up were related to other members of the regiment. Over their first four months of service, the men camped, marched, and drilled as a regiment. The 10th Indiana was their home; had any of them taken advantage of the chance to run from the battlefield, they would have had no place else to go, either in the army or out of it. Word of such behavior would get back to Indiana with the return of the veterans after the war, if not sooner, guaranteeing that anyone who forsook the regiment, even under duress, would forfeit the chance to live at home with his reputation intact.[39]

Despite the momentary repulse of their attack that followed Zollicoffer's death, the Confederates continued to threaten the right flank of Fry's 4th Kentucky. Unable to find Manson, Fry assumed the responsibility of sending for another regiment to strengthen his position. While awaiting these reinforcements, he ordered two companies from the left of the regiment's line to move to the right flank. This maneuver changed the usual position of the regiment's companies relative to one another, but Fry "considered the transfer of those companies more judicious than a change of position of the whole regiment" because it allowed the other companies to keep up their fire, which he "held important to preserve unbroken." The unorthodox formation that resulted compromised the ability of the 4th Kentucky to maneuver quickly, but this was of no immediate concern to Fry, whose only purpose at that moment was to hold on until help arrived.[40]

Fry and the other regimental commanders of the Second Brigade had to make such decisions without the benefit of meaningful leadership from their immediate superiors. Not only did Colonel Manson fail to coordinate the tactics of his own regiments, he actively intervened to disrupt the maneuvers of Samuel Carter's Twelfth Brigade as well. While returning from Thomas's headquarters, Manson happened upon one of Carter's regiments, the 1st Tennessee, and ordered Colonel R. R. Byrd to divert the unit from its course toward the left end of the Union line and to march instead to the support of the 10th Indiana. Manson had no authority to give orders to a regiment that did not belong to his brigade, but Colonel Byrd did not dispute the matter. As he was obeying Manson's instructions, however, he received an order from his own brigade commander to march his regiment back to the Somerset road behind the Union left wing. Manson then reported to Thomas that he had found Carter's Tennesseans moving in the wrong direction, away from the threatened portion of the Union line, prompting Thomas to order Carter to attack the enemy's right with all three of his available regiments. The 1st Tennessee thus resumed marching toward the left flank, in the same direction it had been going when Manson initially interrupted its progress.[41]

In addition to sending Carter's brigade forward, Thomas also directed Manson to bring up Robert McCook's troops to protect the Union right flank. Having been alerted earlier by Manson, McCook had already brought his two available regiments forward, each of them leaving behind one of its ten companies to guard its camp. McCook's men were waiting in the fields around the Logan farmhouse when Manson next saw their commander and told him that the enemy was "on the top of the next hill beyond the woods." Guided by these vague instructions, McCook advanced his regiments in a line of battle facing south, with the 9th Ohio to the west of the Mill Springs road and the 2nd Minnesota to the east.[42]

The Minnesotans were the first to find the enemy. When they began to move faster than the other half of their brigade line, Thomas personally ordered them to halt long enough for the 9th Ohio to catch up. He then directed them to take over the position being held by the men of the 10th Indiana and 4th Kentucky, who were running out of ammunition and desperate for reinforcements. To accomplish this, McCook ordered the 2nd Minnesota's Colonel Horatio P. Van Cleve to "move by the flank" past the 4th Kentucky and 10th Indiana, "then deploy to the left of the road"; in other words, to march in a column around the Kentucky and Indiana troops and then change from column to line formation in front of them. This was the prescribed method for a fresh unit to take the place of one that was exhausted by combat.[43]

Colonel Van Cleve, however, either did not receive or chose to ignore McCook's order. Instead of marching beyond the 10th Indiana and 4th Kentucky, he deployed his regiment into a line of battle behind them. William Bircher, the drummer boy of the 2nd Minnesota, described the maneuver: "We marched by the right flank, up the main road, then made a left oblique movement, then regimental front, and double-quick time until we met the 10th Indiana." This left the Minnesotans with no way to reach the front other than to march directly through the ranks of the 10th Indiana, with the risk that the two units would become intermixed. Such a "passage of lines" under fire threatened to infect the reinforcing troops with the disorganization and con-fusion of those already in combat, sapping their momentum and tempting them to seek safety by joining the ranks of the stationary unit.[44]

In this case, Van Cleve's fresh troops successfully passed through the Indiana regiment, whose lines had broken down into clumps of soldiers scattered throughout the woods, waiting for ammunition.[45] The Minnesota men then advanced to the fence where the 4th Kentucky had been fighting. Here the fortuitous results of Van Cleve's decision became apparent: "Suddenly the Second's lines came against a rail fence with an open field in front, and a line of the enemy's troops was dimly seen through the mist some twenty or thirty rods distant in the field. The firing commenced immediately, and in a few minutes the enemy's line just mentioned had disappeared. It was, in fact, his second line, the first being literally under the guns and noses of the Second Regiment, only the fence intervening."[46] Unknown to Van Cleve, the 4th Kentucky had been forced back from the Old Road fence, which was now held by the Confederate 20th Tennessee regiment. For the next thirty minutes Northerners and Southerners engaged in a vicious fight, sometimes hand-to-hand, for possession of the fence. As dire as the situation was, it would have been far worse for the 2nd Minnesota had Colonel Van Cleve tried to follow his orders to advance past the position, marching by the flank. His men would have walked helplessly into an ambush, strung out along the road four abreast when they encountered the enemy, with the great majority of them unable to return fire because of the friendly troops ahead.

While the 2nd Minnesota fought to hold the fence, an equally vicious struggle was taking place west of the Mill Springs road. There the men of the 9th Ohio, who had been advancing in line of battle next to the 2nd Min-nesota, emerged from heavy woods to encounter a Confederate regiment on the opposite side of a small farm, only two fenced-in cornfields separating the adversaries. "With loud hurrahs," the regiment's adjutant reported, "our boys . . . advanced upon the enemy, extending themselves all over the first of said two corn fields, and taking stand along and below the fence." In the course of the advance Colonel McCook was wounded, leaving Major Kam-merling of the 9th Ohio the ranking officer on that part of the battlefield. The rebels were now only sixty yards distant across the second cornfield, producing a deadly fire from the shelter of the farm's fence, log house, stable, and corn crib, as well as from the wooded ground to their rear. Four companies of the 9th Ohio wheeled to their left to outflank the western end of the Confederate line and capture the log house, but the enemy stood firm. All else failing, the wounded McCook decided to resort to a bayonet charge, first ordering his men to unload their weapons so that they would not be tempted to stop and fire. Kammerling echoed McCook's command to the ranks, adding, "If it gets too hot for you, shut your eyes, my boys—Forward!"[47]

This proved to be the decisive moment of the battle. The 9th Ohio's bayonet charge, McCook reported, "broke the enemy's flank, and the whole line gave way in great confusion, and the whole turned into a perfect rout." At almost the same time Carter's brigade came up on the left of the 2nd Minnesota and helped to drive back the Confederates in that part of the battlefield. The 10th Indiana also advanced, further precipitating what Lieutenant Colonel Kise also described as "a perfect rout" of the Confederates.[48]

The collapse of Confederate resistance brought the battle to a sudden close. "[T]he fireing seased at 12 noon," Thomas Small of the 10th Indiana entered in his diary, exulting that "we gave them a good whiping and sent them back to the River." Lieutenant Lewis Johnson of the same regiment agreed: "Secesh was now completely played out, and they all struck for their den." The Federal troops, especially the soldiers of Manson's brigade, were short of ammunition and could not pursue the rebels until they had reformed their lines and refilled their cartridge boxes. This done, Thomas's division took up the chase, which lasted the rest of the day and ended with the Confederates in their fortifications on the northern bank of the Cumberland River. Thomas had several artillery batteries brought up to shell the entrenchments until dark, after which the Confederates slipped across the river, leaving their empty camp to be occupied by Thomas's men the next morning.[49]

"I Don't Believe I Ever Spent Happier Hours"

Two weeks after the battle, Corporal Harrison Derrick of the 10th Indiana tried to capture on paper the emotional impact of his experience. "Molly it is a serious sight to see the dead and hear the groans of the dying and the prayers of the wounded," he wrote to a friend. Thirty-nine Union soldiers were killed at Logan's Cross Roads, and 207 were wounded; Confederate losses were 125 killed, 309 wounded, and 99 missing. This toll was modest by later standards, but certainly severe enough to constitute a "serious sight." "It makes the hardest heart melt and tears roll down their cheeks," Derrick added, "but still I don't believe [sic] I ever spent happier hours than when the battle was raging."[50]

In its effects on military and civilian morale, this battle was the action at Rowlett's Station writ large. Few participants may have experienced the joy of battle to the degree that Harrison Derrick did, but most of the Union soldiers who took part felt great pride in the outcome. Reflecting on the battle a few years later, one veteran wrote, "I dont see how we ever whiped so many as they was thare but we don it very Nicely." At Logan's Cross Roads, as at Rowlett's Station, a small Union detachment had repelled the assaults of a substantially larger Confederate force and compelled it to retreat. In each case, the outcome was due primarily to the tactical proficiency of the regiments of the Army of the Ohio, aided by the fortuitous fall of a Southern leader. The result of each battle was to build confidence within the army and boost morale at home.[51]

The army had considerable reason to feel satisfied with its performance at Logan's Cross Roads. Its individual regiments for the most part managed to function as coherent organizations through the confusion of battle. The volunteers of the 10th Indiana rallied themselves and kept fighting even after miscommunication caused the regiment to divide itself in half, one wing retreating while the other stood fast. The *soldaten* of the 9th Ohio displayed the fruits of their Prussian drill lessons by executing a number of maneuvers, including a disciplined bayonet charge with unloaded guns that led directly to victory. During the pursuit that followed, the companies of the 9th Ohio at one point emulated Willich's 32nd Indiana at Rowlett's Station by forming square to resist an imminent rebel cavalry charge.[52] The attack never materialized, nor would the square likely have been necessary, but the maneuver demonstrated the regiment's wide tactical vocabulary.

The Army of the Ohio did commit some tactical errors at Logan's Cross Roads, but these were relatively minor and did not affect the battle's outcome. The separation of the wings of the 10th Indiana was the most serious incident of regimental disintegration, but it proved temporary. Company K of the 9th Ohio, detached to guard the regiment's flank early in the battle, lost its way in the woods and was unable to rejoin the main body of the unit, but again the men did not flee; instead, they attached themselves to the first friendly regiment they found and fought the battle as temporary members of the 2nd Minnesota.[53] The commander of that unit, Colonel Van Cleve, took a considerable risk when he had his men pass through, rather than around, the ranks of the 4th Kentucky and 10th Indiana, but again the motivation to stay with their comrades kept the Minnesota troops moving forward as a body instead of avoiding combat by mingling with the stationary Kentucky and Indiana units. Finally, Colonel Fry of the 4th Kentucky risked throwing his regiment into confusion when he transferred companies from one flank to another, but the Kentuckians' success in holding their position justified the tactical expedient.

The Union victory at Logan's Cross Roads reflected the tactical skill of the Army of the Ohio, but like Rowlett's Station, it was too small an engagement to reveal the inadequacies of the army's command and control arrangements.

HARPER'S WEEKLY.

JOURNAL OF CIVILIZATION.

VOL. VL—No. 267.] NEW YORK, SATURDAY, FEBRUARY 8, 1862. [SINGLE COPIES SIX CENTS. $2 50 PER YEAR IN ADVANCE.

The alarmed Picket-guard.

Harper's Weekly portrayed the pickets of the 10th Indiana at Logan's Cross Roads on its February 8, 1862, cover. Like the action at Rowlett's Station, the Battle of Logan's Cross Roads made a great impression on Northern readers starved for good news. Photograph courtesy of The Lincoln Museum, Fort Wayne, Indiana (TLM #4535).

In both battles, a single officer was able to control the entire Federal force. Thomas, once he reached the battlefield, was able to discern much of what was happening through personal observation. He met and gave orders to his brigade commanders in person. At times he even went down through the next layer of command, taking direct tactical control of individual regiments. Only five Union regiments were seriously engaged, so Thomas in effect commanded a large infantry brigade rather than a whole division.

Because the battle was a straight infantry fight, it offered no test of the army's ability to employ combined arms tactics. The sole Union cavalry regiment engaged, Wolford's 1st Kentucky, used its horses only as transportation and did its fighting dismounted (anticipating the mounted infantry tactics that would eventually be adopted by the cavalry of both sides), but it played only a small part in the battle. The army's powerful artillery, which would assume a much greater role in the larger battles to follow, was rendered ineffective by the heavily wooded terrain and limited visibility. A member of Battery B, 1st Ohio Light Artillery, described how he and his comrades could not find a suitable firing position for their cannon and so became spectators standing "like so many wooden men" while bullets flew overhead so rapidly that "the twigs from the trees fell like a shower of hail."[54]

Had all the units of the First Division been present at Logan's Cross Roads, Thomas would have had to rely much more heavily on his subordinate commanders. To the extent that his brigade leaders were tested in the battle, they showed personal bravery but little professional skill. Neither Manson of the Second Brigade nor McCook of the Third was especially successful in coordinating the actions of his regiments. There was little horizontal communication between leaders of regiments within each brigade. Vertical communication, between regiments and their brigade headquarters, was not much better. There were not enough staff officers or aides-de-camp available to allow the brigade commanders to send messages as needed. When Manson decided to act as his own messenger and to report personally to Thomas, he had to leave his units to fight unsupervised. Both Manson and Thomas gave a number of orders in person that might have been more efficiently delivered by others, and Manson spent much of the battle acting as Thomas's aide-de-camp, carrying messages instead of leading his troops.

The inexperience of Manson and McCook, both civilian volunteers, was evident. Manson's attempt to commandeer the 1st Tennessee from Carter's brigade without notifying either Carter or Thomas was an egregious example of his lack of professionalism, as was his decision to leave the front and report to Thomas at the beginning of the battle. McCook, in contrast, became too involved in the tactical management of his old regiment, the 9th Ohio, making decisions regarding the deployment of individual companies. Although his presence on the firing line no doubt inspired his troops, it prevented him from exercising command over his brigade as a whole and exposed him to the enemy fire that eventually left him wounded, further limiting his ability to lead the brigade.[55]

"I never in all my military career saw a harder fight," wrote Lieutenant Colonel Kise, a Mexican War veteran, in his after-action report.[56] In the months ahead, the Army of the Ohio would engage in much larger battles that would make the personal scale of Logan's Cross Roads seem almost quaint. None of these would be decided by the fall of one enemy officer, nor would a single competent Union general be able to rectify all the mistakes of his subordinates.[57] In the larger contests to come, the problems of command and control above the regimental level that first emerged at Logan's Cross Roads would prove endemic in the Army of the Ohio, to the point of nearly paralyzing its battlefield operations. Never again would the army under Buell fight a battle that ended with the enemy in full retreat.

CHAPTER FOUR

The Army in Action

The Shiloh Campaign, January to April 1862

In the weeks that followed the battle at Logan's Cross Roads, Don Carlos Buell resumed sparring by telegraph with other Union military leaders over the proper strategic employment of the Army of the Ohio, while his troops loitered in their camps, perfecting their regimental drill and enduring the cold rain and snow of a Kentucky winter. When the aggressive Brigadier General Ulysses S. Grant captured Forts Henry and Donelson in February, Buell took advantage of the situation to occupy Nashville, abandoned by the retreating Confederates. On March 11, 1862, Lincoln appointed Major General Henry Wager Halleck to command all Union forces in the western theater, including Buell's Army of the Ohio, Grant's Army of the Tennessee, and Brigadier General John Pope's Army of the Mississippi. Prodded by Halleck, Buell's army lurched forward from Nashville while Grant pushed far to the south along the Tennessee River to Pittsburg Landing. Halleck planned for the two armies to unite there, but poor communication between Grant and Buell, coupled with Buell's dilatory leadership, slowed the pace of the Army of the Ohio to a crawl. The head of Buell's column was still a day's march from Pittsburg Landing at dawn on April 6, 1862, when a massive Confederate attack surprised Grant's force. By the next morning, three of the Army of the Ohio's six divisions were on the Shiloh battlefield, helping to stem the Confederate tide and stage a successful counterattack.

Buell may have hoped that the First Division's expedition to Mill Springs would demonstrate his concern for East Tennessee without foreclosing any of his strategic options, but George Thomas's stunning victory at Logan's Cross Roads instead raised what Buell described as the "natural expectation that our success . . . would be followed rapidly by other successful operations against the enemy." To meet this expectation, Buell sent Carter's brigade toward the Cumberland Gap to "encourage the loyal inhabitants" of East Tennessee. At the same time, however, he warned that Carter's small force "alone cannot be expected to penetrate" into Tennessee. To conduct such an invasion, Buell claimed that he would need to increase the Army of the Ohio to 120,000 men and double its artillery just to support a modest advance by only three divisions, totaling perhaps 45,000 men. Even a limited pursuit of the rebels by the rest of Thomas's First Division would be impossible, Buell asserted, for all the usual reasons: bad weather, bad roads, and lack of wagons. Perhaps it was embarrassment at repeating these shopworn excuses for the immobility of his command that caused Buell to address his report of January 27, 1862, to Adjutant General Lorenzo Thomas, "for the information of the General-in-Chief," rather than writing directly to his friend George McClellan, as he had done many times before.[1]

"All my plans are delayed for the want of transportation," Buell complained to his wife in mid-January. It was not the lack of wagons that was the greatest obstacle to an East Tennessee campaign, however, but the fact that Buell's heart remained set on capturing Nashville. The correct Union strategy, he believed, was for his army not to march east into the desolate and inhospitable mountains, but to drive south against the Confederate main body at Bowling Green. Meanwhile, Union troops to the west (belonging to Halleck's Department of the Mississippi) could advance along the Mississippi, Cumberland, and Tennessee Rivers, supported by gunboats and supplied by steamers. Halleck's advance would force the rebels either to disperse their forces to counter the multiple threats or to evacuate Bowling Green and its fortifications without a fight. The virtue of such simultaneous offensives was not lost on President Lincoln, who had suggested something similar to Halleck in December 1861: "When [Buell] moves on Bowling Green, what hinders it from being re-enforced from Columbus? A simultaneous movement by you on Columbus might prevent it."[2]

Halleck agreed in principle that his forces should cooperate with those of Buell, but the two generals shared a number of traits that made it difficult for them to translate any kind of plan into meaningful action. Halleck, who in the

Regular Army had acquired the nickname "Old Brains" for his familiarity with military theory, rivaled Buell as a perfectionist in regard to the preparation of his forces. Like Buell, Halleck tended to overestimate the enemy's resources; neither general realized that the total Confederate strength in Kentucky and Tennessee was substantially less than that of either one of their two armies alone.[3] Finally, each envisioned himself as the leader of the main Union effort in the West, and each held stubbornly to what he conceived to be correct strategy.

Halleck discounted Nashville as a strategic goal and wanted the Army of the Ohio to play the secondary role of supporting Halleck's forces in the upcoming campaign. For Buell, this was no more palatable than Washington's insistence that he go into the wilderness of East Tennessee. Rather than pursue either of these options, he kept his divisions dispersed, thus "concealing my design as long as possible," as he explained to McClellan. Through the end of January 1862, Buell avoided committing his army, keeping his design concealed not only from enemies in the South, but from rival strategists in the North as well.[4]

While their commander stalled for time, the men of the Army of the Ohio suffered through the winter of 1861–62 in their camps, waiting for something to happen. These were tedious weeks, dominated by bad weather and repetitious drilling. "It rains, then snows a little, then freezes a little, then thaws a good deal, and finally everything on the surface of the ground seems liquid earth," wrote O. M. Mitchel, commanding the Third Division. The Second Division's historian recalled it as "a time of deep mud, incessant toil and weary exhaustion." An Ohio surgeon found camp life so monotonous that it was "almost impossible to tell one day from another," while his fellow officers passed the time in vigorous arguments over how many weeks they had spent in camp. Some soldiers, like the boys of Company C of the 17th Ohio, found enough energy to entertain themselves by playing "round town ball" in their spare time, but most days the weather kept the men confined to their tents, where they endured what C. C. Briant of the 6th Indiana described as "long, dreary winter evenings" with "nothing to read, nothing to do." Long association at such close quarters led to frayed tempers. "I am sometimes washing my face plain to be seen," Alford Sampson of Kentucky complained in a letter to his mother, "[and] Some one will ask me what I am doing. This I call foolery."[5]

News of the victory at Logan's Cross Roads was a welcome tonic for the rest of the army, but it only increased the troops' desire to take an active part in the war. J. Ross Ingerson wrote to a comrade in the 49th Ohio who was away on sick leave that "old Jollycoffer . . . has been whipped and what is better has

An image of bored soldiers dominates this collection of scenes from the Army of the Ohio's Second Division, sketched by a newspaper artist in January 1862. From *Harper's Weekly*, February 1, 1862; photograph courtesy of The Lincoln Museum, Fort Wayne, Indiana (TLM #4536).

been *killed*[,] is not this glorious news," but then added, "I for one do not wish to criticize the movements of our great men but to tell the truth I am getting considerably discouraged."[6]

Although the soldiers were frustrated at their leaders' apparent lack of activity, the weeks of delay in fact brought new strength to the army. By the middle of January enough new regiments had entered the Department of the Ohio to enable Buell to organize a Sixth Division, which he placed under the command of Brigadier General T. J. Wood, formerly a brigade commander in McCook's division. The army gained in quality as well as quantity, as the Federal government began to supply adequate amounts of arms, clothing, and equipment, in uniform pattern, to replace the miscellany that the troops had brought with them from their respective states.

The most welcome piece of new equipment was the Sibley tent, a conical structure thirteen feet high and eighteen feet in diameter, which the men found "incomparably superior to the other kinds in common use." "No one improvement in these respects," wrote one veteran, "was received with more gratification by the soldiers of the division than the entire substitution of

Sibley for the bell and wedge tents." General Nelson observed that William Hazen's 41st Ohio was "the best reg't under my command, and the best commanded, but it is being decimated by disease. . . . I have come to the conclusion that the source of the diseases lies in their tents," which were small and overcrowded. "The remedy in my opinion is *Sibley tents!*" Nelson's analysis of the way disease was transmitted (involving "exudation from the skin") was faulty, but his conclusion was correct. After three to five Sibley tents were issued to each company in the army, overcrowding and sickness decreased dramatically.[7]

New muskets were an even more important acquisition. The most modern shoulder arm available in any numbers to the soldiers of either side in 1862 was the muzzle-loading rifled musket with percussion cap ignition. The two most common models of this weapon were the Springfield .58 and the British-made Enfield .577, both of which had an effective range of approximately five hundred yards and a rate of fire of two or three rounds per minute. The Springfield and Enfield rifled muskets were similar in most respects, and soldiers in the Army of the Ohio were happy enough to get either. Those who expressed a view seemed to prefer the former; Frederick Marion wrote to his sister in May 1862, "Our regiment [the 31st Ohio] has got new guns[;] we have got the splendid Springfield rifle they are the prettiest gun I ever saw they are inprovement [*sic*] to the Enfield rifle," and James Jones of the 57th Indiana described his new Springfield as the "splendidest gun I ever saw."[8]

Regiments that could not obtain either of these had to settle for smooth-bore muskets, which had a similar rate of fire but were not effective beyond two hundred yards at most and inaccurate at any range. Smoothbore weapons had the marginal advantage of being able to fire "buck & ball," a cartridge containing a musket ball and a small load of buckshot that in theory combined the best features of both kinds of ammunition. In reality, as Ulysses S. Grant wrote, "At the distance of a few hundred yards a man might fire [buck and ball] at you all day without your finding it out." Most smoothbores used percussion caps, although some unreliable flintlock weapons were in service.[9]

When the war began, there were far from enough rifled muskets available to supply every regiment of the Army of the Ohio. Many companies went to war carrying the scourings of Federal and state arsenals. The weapons originally issued to Indiana troops, for example, were "of an inferior character," wrote Governor Morton, "being old muskets rifled out, and in very many instances the bayonets have to be driven on with a hammer, and many others are so loose that they can be shaken off." In addition to these obsolete weapons, other regiments carried muskets of varying patterns imported from Europe. The regiments of the Fourth Division, according to a report dated January 12,

1862, were armed with Enfields, smoothbores, smoothbores that had been rifled (but still fired caliber .69 bullets), Belgian rifles, Greenwood rifles, and Prussian muskets; even after exchanging arms within their brigades, some regiments still carried more than one type of weapon. The proliferation of small arms models made it hard for quartermasters to supply each unit with the right ammunition and complicated the problem of tactical command for brigade leaders who had to take into account the different capabilities of the muskets carried by each of their regiments.[10]

The artillery of the army faced similar difficulties. An inspection of nine batteries in December 1861 revealed four varieties of smoothbore cannon (6-pounders, mountain howitzers, 12-pounder howitzers, and 12-pounder Napoleons), as well as two kinds of rifled guns (6-pounder James rifles and 10-pounder Parrotts), with at least two different types of ordnance in each battery. Increases in domestic manufacturing and foreign importation made rifled muskets more widely available, so that by the spring of 1862 most of the Army of the Ohio's infantry were equipped with Springfield or Enfield muskets of uniform caliber, but the diversity of artillery types persisted at least into 1863.[11]

"The Way Open to Nashville"

The strategic inertia that gripped the Union forces in Kentucky at the beginning of 1862 finally ended on January 30. Recognizing that Buell was unlikely to agree to any plan but his own, Halleck decided that the Army of the Ohio's cooperation was "at present not essential" and ordered Grant to capture Fort Henry on the Tennessee River and Fort Donelson on the Cumberland River. Buell responded with petulance to the news by warning Halleck to expect to encounter ten thousand Confederate reinforcements in his path, transferred from Bowling Green. To Halleck's request for a diversionary attack to fix the Bowling Green garrison in place, Buell answered: "My position does not admit of diversion. My moves must be real ones." The limit of his cooperation was an offer to lend Halleck the assistance of a single brigade, "if you find that you absolutely require it."[12]

The real move that Buell proposed in response to Halleck's plan was a deliberate, massive advance of the entire Army of the Ohio toward Bowling Green. "Progress will be slow for me," Buell informed Halleck, noting that he would need twelve days to cover the forty miles to his objective. In Washington, McClellan was disappointed that Buell had found yet another reason to delay the effort to liberate East Tennessee, but he did not overrule the attack on Bowling Green. Halleck, who was even less happy with Buell's plan, argued against it on the grounds that the Tennessee and Cumberland Rivers were the proper strategic route into the heart of the Confederate position in Tennessee.[13]

It was not lost on Buell that he had earlier made the same point in support of his pet idea of taking Nashville, which would give the Union control of the Cumberland River. Seeing an opportunity to revive the Nashville plan, Buell began to vacillate. On February 6, he wrote to McClellan that Halleck's advance was "right in its strategical bearing" and that he was thinking of using most of the Army of the Ohio to reinforce Grant and approach Nashville from the west. Such a move, Buell claimed, would have to be made "in the face of 50,000 if not 60,000 men" at Bowling Green. After Grant took Fort Henry on February 6, Buell reconsidered: "I cannot, on reflection, think a change of my line would be advisable." The next day he remained uncertain: "I am concentrating and preparing, but will not decide definitely yet."[14]

Buell struggled to keep his options open as long as possible. On February 10 he finally began the army's long-awaited advance, sending O. M. Mitchel's Third Division toward Bowling Green. At the same time Buell ordered the rest of the army to be prepared for either of two possibilities: to follow Mitchel and attack the rebels head-on at Bowling Green or to head north to Louisville, board steamboats, and sail down the Ohio and up the Cumberland to reinforce Grant, who had moved rapidly overland to attack Fort Donelson.

Mitchel, later described by a subordinate as "determined to make all understand that he was the greatest of living soldiers," exulted at the opportunity to put his division at the head of the army's advance. "I am at last in the position to which my rank entitles me," he wrote to a friend on February 12. Leaving camp on February 10, Mitchel's troops by the twelfth had passed south through the Second Division at Munfordville. Mitchel was aware that the Confederates were pulling troops out of Bowling Green to reinforce Fort Donelson, and he hoped to arrive before they could evacuate the town completely and destroy the Barren River railroad bridge. He hurried his men along, at one point impressing civilian horses and wagons to carry their knapsacks, but when they reached Bowling Green on February 14, they found its fortifications empty, the bridge destroyed, and only the last of the rebel garrison visible in the distance, marching away to join the rest of A. S. Johnston's army.[15]

News of the evacuation of Bowling Green caused Buell once again to reverse his course. He had already dispatched Nelson's division to assist Grant's army, and was planning to send more troops, when he learned that the rebels before him were retreating. The next day, February 15, he wrote to McClellan that "leaving the way open to Nashville makes it proper for me to resume my

Wagons belonging to Mitchel's Third Division advance through a camp of Sibley tents at Bowling Green in February 1862. From *Frank Leslie's Illustrated Newspaper*, March 15, 1862; photograph courtesy of The Lincoln Museum, Fort Wayne, Indiana (TLM #4537).

original plan." Halleck continued to assert that Buell should join Grant on the Cumberland River, bluntly telling McClellan: "General Buell telegraphs that he purposes to move from Bowling Green on Nashville. This is bad strategy." Halleck repeated his objection directly to Buell, writing, "To move from Bowling Green on Nashville is not good strategy." But Buell ignored him and ordered the rest of the Army of the Ohio (except Nelson's division, already en route for Fort Donelson via the Cumberland River) to head for Nashville.[16]

The march to Nashville revealed how much the Army of the Ohio had to learn about conducting a large-scale campaign. Slogging through rain, sleet, snow, and foot-deep mud, the soldiers found that their accustomed standard of living required far too many wagons for the kind of roads available. Most regiments started the march with one wagon per company, plus three more for the headquarters and staff, to carry their baggage and other equipment, including the large Sibley tents that had added so much to their comfort in camp. These tents proved impractical to transport, Jacob van Zwaluwenburg of the 16th U.S. noted in his diary, "as the wagons carrying them could not keep up with the troops on the march." The army accordingly began to shed itself of the Sibley tents and other impedimenta. R. M. Kelly of the 4th Kentucky recorded that in mid-January his comrades held "the general opinion . . . that it would be impossible to move" with fewer than two wagons for each company but soon discovered that half that number was adequate. The men of the 2nd Minnesota, who had embarked on the Logan's Cross Roads campaign with thirteen baggage wagons "loaded to their roofs," left their overcoats and dress coats behind when setting out for Nashville and by the end of 1862 had reduced their regimental train from twelve wagons to six.[17]

Inexperience slowed the army in other ways. Tramping through atrocious weather, the men and horses of Battery A, 1st Ohio Light Artillery, covered only six miles on February 14. The next morning the troops found their guns and limbers frozen into the earth, as they had not yet learned the trick of ending each day's march by running the wheels up onto fence rails laid over the liquid mud. In the infantry, some officers were slow to enforce the discipline necessary to conduct grueling road marches, afraid to risk the popularity that had gotten them elected in the first place. Others were simply unaware of the limits of their men. Edgar Kellogg of the 16th U.S. observed: "Theory alone, a mere knowledge of what text books teach will not qualify an officer to conduct a march of infantry. He can learn the art only by experience." Many veterans later recalled being worn out unnecessarily on their first marches because their officers had yet to discover that under most circumstances a moderate pace, with regular rest breaks, produced the best results.[18]

Traffic control was another element of the art of marching that the men began to learn on the road to Nashville. Spread out in a column of route, a Civil War army was transformed from a compact fighting force into a thin, vulnerable animal that could be broken at almost any point. In battle formation, a single infantry brigade might occupy five hundred yards of ground from flank to flank, whereas the same unit, stretched out along a road in marching order, measured nearly a mile. To minimize their units' vulnerability on the march, officers tried to keep their men from straggling and to reduce the intervals between regiments by endlessly repeating the order to "Close up!" Keeping each regiment close to the one in front of it, however, meant that when the head of the column stopped for any reason, the units behind it had to stop almost immediately to avoid a chain reaction collision. When the lead unit resumed marching, some time inevitably passed before the next regiment could get under way, after which it would have to double-time to close up with the troops ahead. This process would be repeated, and the time lag multiplied, for each succeeding regiment. Men at the end of a long marching column thus faced hours of idleness followed by desperate forced marches, often ending after dark, to catch up with the rest of the army.

Although close intervals made for inefficient marching, there were few alternatives. Captain S. S. Canfield of the 21st Ohio thought that he had found one when, during one of his company's first long marches, he tried to avoid the stop-and-go phenomenon by keeping his company marching at a steady pace regardless of its distance to the unit ahead, figuring that his men would reach their assigned position sooner or later and would be in better shape when they got there. As Captain Canfield proudly led his easy-marching company past the Fourth Division commander, however, General Nelson was unimpressed and made only a single comment to the captain: "Close up!"[19]

Regimental pride helped inspire men not to fall out of the ranks during difficult marches, but that same pride occasionally created its own traffic problems. One of the most effective means of avoiding the accordionlike motion of long columns was to divide the army into several shorter columns marching on parallel roads. This worked until the columns converged at a crossroad, where two colonels jealous of their respective regiments' prerogatives might each refuse to yield the right-of-way, bringing whole divisions to a standstill while the issue of precedence was resolved. Alternatively, if the officers of one regiment recognized that another unit was marching to the same destination, they might push their men hard to get there first, as much to win bragging rights as to secure the best campsites. In January 1862 the men of the 10th Indiana engaged in such a race to be the first to reach camp at the end of a day's march. "[T]he 14th Ohio tried to run in before our regt," James A. Price proudly noted in his diary, "and got defeated in it after getting some six or eight of their men knocked down and their Lieut. Colonel run off a bridge and injured some." Events like this, or the epic twenty-three-mile contest between the 17th and 31st Ohio on February 25, 1862, reinforced regimental spirit at the cost of the army's unity and wore out men and animals for no good strategic reason.[20]

"There Is No Need of Haste; Come On by Easy Marches"

Despite the confusion attending its first major strategic movement, most of the Army of the Ohio reached Nashville by the beginning of March 1862. There was no fighting to be done there, because Johnston had gambled on defending the city by concentrating his forces against Grant. The unconditional surrender of fifteen thousand Confederates at Fort Donelson on February 16 left Johnston's strategy in ruins and Nashville untenable. Soldiers from Mitchel's Third Division reached Edgefield, on the north bank of the Cumberland River opposite Nashville, on February 23. Since the retreating Confederates had destroyed all the bridges, no Union troops were able to cross the river, but Nashville's mayor nonetheless offered Mitchel and Buell the city's formal surrender on February 24. Nelson's division arrived by steamboat from Fort Donelson that evening and occupied Nashville the next morning.[21]

"There has been another success without a battle," Buell triumphantly informed his wife on February 27. "You can see I am in Nashville." It took another week to finish ferrying the rest of the army across the Cumberland, a process Buell described as "difficult and tedious." "You can hardly realize this," he wrote, "until you have seen thousands of men and horses, with their wagons and artillery carriages crowded into narrow avenues, waiting or searching for their opportunity to get to the boat that is to take them over a river that is running like a torrent." In the same letter home, Buell noted that his horse, a "vicious" beast, had thrown him from the saddle, leaving him stunned, bruised, and "a good deal cut" about the face. This was not the first time that his horse had thrown and injured Buell, nor would it be the last.[22]

In Nashville the army began to prepare for its next campaign in various ways. The men of the 2nd Minnesota spent "all our spare time drilling and learning the manual of arms." Colonel William Hazen, promoted to command of the Nineteenth Brigade, kept his troops "very busily engaged with drills and in preparation for moving forward." He had to work particularly hard at straightening out the 9th Indiana, which had just been assigned to his brigade after service in West Virginia and had there become "fixed in many vicious habits." On March 12, the anniversary of the birth of Andrew Jackson, William Nelson exercised the Fourth Division with a twelve-mile hike to Jackson's home, the Hermitage. After paying their respects at the grave of the late president, Nelson's men returned to Nashville the same day, "well pleased with the trip, though weary, for they had marched not less than twenty-three miles."[23]

While Nelson indulged his political loyalties by visiting the Hermitage, other officers found plenty of opportunity to play politics without leaving Nashville. When Colonel Thomas Bramlette found that he was the senior colonel in the brigade to which his 3rd Kentucky regiment had just been transferred, he objected to serving under a junior officer and tried to secure command of the brigade for himself. Buell instead transferred the 3rd Kentucky to still another brigade, one commanded by a brigadier general who decisively outranked Bramlette. Major Thomas Jefferson Jordan of the 9th Pennsylvania Cavalry thought that politics were behind the decision to divide his regiment into battalions and assign it to unglamorous patrol missions. Jordan complained to fellow Pennsylvanian Simon Cameron (who had recently lost his position as secretary of war) that the rough-and-ready Westerners who led the army were prejudiced against his well-disciplined men and had determined that there should be "no glory here for Pennsylvania troops."[24]

Personal jealousies also affected the deployment of the army's lone regiment of engineers, the 1st Michigan Mechanics & Engineers. Detachments of this valuable unit were assigned to assist the various divisions in building bridges, repairing roads, and other construction tasks, but in the Second Division they came into conflict with a "pioneer corps" that Colonel August Willich had organized for the same purpose. The division's commander, Alexander Mc-Cook, settled the issue by disbanding Willich's pioneers, a move that would soon prove costly.[25]

The routine of drilling, conducting foraging expeditions, and manning the picket lines around the city was periodically shattered by Confederate raids. On March 7 a company of rebels in captured Union uniforms attacked the picket line of the 30th Indiana, and two days later a mixed force of three hundred Confederate infantry and cavalry surprised the outposts of the 1st Wisconsin, who at first thought they were friendly troops returning from a scouting expedition.[26] These raids, which were of no military significance, nevertheless kept the men of the Army of the Ohio on edge. When Nelson and his mounted bodyguard returned to Nashville from a reconnaissance to the south, they were fired on by nervous Union pickets who mistook them for enemy cavalry.[27]

In March 1862 many people in the North and South alike still conceived of the war as a contest to be resolved solely in open battle between organized bodies of soldiers drawn up in formal array. In that context, the sudden violence inflicted by John Hunt Morgan, Nathan Bedford Forrest, and other Confederate raiders seemed (to its victims at least) little short of murder. William Sumner Dodge of the Second Division revealed the mixture of fear and frustration these attacks caused when he described one such incident as "merely a dash upon an exposed part of the line, to gratify a lust for butchery," rather than a "legitimate" act of war. Actions that killed men without other-wise affecting the course of the war, Dodge protested, "are contrary alike to the plainest precepts of humanity and the recognized code of modern war-fare—expressly interdicted in this struggle in general orders by the com-manders of each side. . . . No where do such acts constitute war."[28]

Some Confederate raids had even more far-reaching psychological effects. On March 8 Morgan and a mere two dozen followers managed to wreck a train of Union supply wagons outside of Nashville. (In the process they cap-tured a Captain Braden, whose father-in-law Brigadier General Ebenezer Dumont had just been assigned responsibility for the security of the city; Morgan's men took Braden's horse and let him return to Nashville on a mule, which prompted Dumont to remark, "Well, Braden, I am glad to see you, but I think you have made a damn bad swap.") A week later Morgan launched another successful raid in which he destroyed a railroad engine and a large quantity of rolling stock. The ease with which Morgan's cavalry rode through the army's rear areas must have made clear to Buell that once he left the security of the Cumberland River and began to rely entirely on rail lines and wagon roads for supplies, his army would become extraordinarily vulnerable to the depredations of Confederate cavalry.[29]

Meanwhile, Buell and Halleck continued to haggle over details of strategy. In broad terms, they agreed that the next Union objective should be to sever the Memphis & Charleston Railroad, one of the South's main east-west arteries. Buell wanted to do this by marching due south from Nashville toward Huntsville, Alabama, but Halleck wanted Buell's army to sail from Nashville down the Cumberland to the Ohio River, then south up the Tennessee River to join Grant, whose army was already under way along the river's eastern bank. The route Halleck proposed was extremely roundabout but made sense in an era when water transportation was as much as thirty times more efficient than overland travel.[30] On March 11, 1862, Halleck won what appeared to be a decisive victory over Buell in the form of Presidential War Order No. 3, which abolished the Department of the Ohio and put all Union forces in the West (including the armies of Buell and Grant) under Halleck's command. Buell had to accept Halleck's strategy of combining forces but successfully argued that he could do so best by marching directly from Nashville to unite with Grant and his army at Savannah, on the Tennessee River.[31]

Before starting out, Buell arranged to protect the territory his army had already won. He consolidated the scattered forces that had been left behind in eastern Kentucky into a new Seventh Division, commanded by Brigadier General George W. Morgan, and sent it to seize the Cumberland Gap and advance as far as practicable into East Tennessee. Buell detailed a brigade to garrison Murfreesboro, left another in Nashville, and deployed additional troops to hold other key points in middle Tennessee, in part to placate the state's new military governor, Andrew Johnson, who continually harassed Buell, Halleck, and Secretary of War Edwin Stanton to assign more men to protect Tennessee. Finally, Buell continued to pursue his original objective by sending the egocentric commander O. M. Mitchel and his Third Division to cut the Memphis & Charleston Railroad at Huntsville. Collectively, these detachments meant that about half of the Army of the Ohio's 73,000 men were committed to various secondary missions, leaving only 37,000 to join Grant.[32]

The army's cavalry left Nashville for Savannah on March 15, followed by McCook's Second Division on the sixteenth. Over the course of the next week the divisions of Nelson, Crittenden, and Wood broke camp and moved out, with at least one day elapsing between the departures of each. Thomas's First Division was last in the column and did not leave Nashville until April 1. Buell remained in the city until March 25, watching his troops file out day by

High water in the Duck River delayed the Army of the Ohio for two weeks in March 1862, while troops built a pontoon bridge and repaired the permanent crossing (background). Before they finished, the river had fallen far enough to be forded (foreground). From *Harper's Weekly*, May 3, 1862; photograph courtesy of The Lincoln Museum, Fort Wayne, Indiana (TLM #4538).

day and becoming so worried about the possibility of a Confederate counterattack that he directed Wood's Sixth Division to halt when it got to Columbia, about forty miles southwest of Nashville and less than halfway to Savannah. This left only four divisions moving to Grant's support.[33]

During the two weeks it took to get the main body of the Army of the Ohio back on the road, the head of the column progressed no more than forty miles from Nashville, then halted at the Duck River and Rutherford's Creek, where Union cavalry arrived just too late to prevent rebel troops from burning the bridges. Though the Duck River was swollen with spring rain and melted snow, it was not so broad or deep to offer much of an obstacle to an experienced army. "At a later period of the war," according to a history written by one of Thomas's staff officers, "the high water in Duck river would have hardly caused a halt." In 1863 the Army of the Ohio would demonstrate its engineering ability by improvising a crossing of the much larger Tennessee River in less than twenty-four hours.[34]

In March 1862, however, Buell did not trust his inexperienced volunteers to exercise their initiative in constructing makeshift crossings. He wanted the

old permanent bridge rebuilt properly and put the Second Division to the task. McCook sorely missed Colonel Willich's recently disbanded pioneer unit, as it took considerable time to organize a detachment of men with engineering skills and to find adequate tools. The process was so slow that a temporary pontoon bridge was also put under construction, to be used until the permanent structure was completed. As it turned out, it took just as long to build the pontoon bridge as to complete the repair of the original structure. Both bridges were ready for traffic on March 29, 1862, two weeks after the first Union troops reached the river and one day after the level of the water had dropped enough to allow the impetuous Nelson to order his troops to ford the river without using any bridges at all.[35]

Buell insisted on carefully rebuilding the Duck River bridge, rather than immediately forging ahead over an improvised crossing, in part because neither Grant nor Halleck had indicated to him that there was any need to hurry. Communications among Buell, Grant, and Halleck were so slow that as of March 30, 1862, Halleck had yet to receive any of the dozen messages that Buell had sent him since March 14. Over the same two weeks Buell received

Halleck's messages within a day or two of their dispatch, but Halleck's instructions were based on outdated information and of little help to Buell. None of Halleck's communications included the important information that Grant had crossed his army to the western bank of the Tennessee River at Pittsburg Landing; Buell continued to believe that Grant was still safely camped at Savannah, with the broad Tennessee River between his army and the nearest Confederates. When Grant finally established contact with Nelson's division, in the vanguard of Buell's army, the message he sent did nothing to shake Buell's complacency: "There is no need of haste; come on by easy marches."[36]

"Instantly Each Man Grasps His Gun"

William Nelson was the only one of the Army of the Ohio's generals, Buell included, who showed any sense of urgency in keeping his men moving toward the junction with Grant's forces at Savannah. At the Duck River, Nelson exhorted one of his brigade commanders, "d—n you, get over, for we must have the advance and get the glory." When Nelson's division successfully forded the river, correspondent Henry Villard reported, the exploit "was looked upon as an uncalled-for piece of bravado by his fellow-commanders and the rank and file." Although a Second Division soldier later wrote, "I remember some of our officers saying Nelson was a tyrant" for driving his men on, those who actually made the crossing were generally pleased to have gotten the jump on the rest of the army and not too discomfited by having to wade through the icy water. "We pulled off our clothes and put them and our cartridge boxes on the point of our bayonets and waded in," wrote Maurice Williams of the 36th Indiana. "The water was about waist deep and very swift and most awful cold and still it was only sport for us."[37]

Buell's other divisions followed at a more leisurely pace, in part because the men were still learning how to conduct a military river crossing. August Willich, who had been appointed to direct the construction of the pontoon bridge, had to teach the volunteer cavalry how to ford the river by fours; he also had to instruct the infantry to use route step (rather than marching in cadence) on the bridge in order not to set up vibrations that could destroy it. Willich's expert advice provided little reassurance to soldiers like the 6th Indiana's C. C. Briant, who remembered the experience of crossing the rapidly flowing river on a fragile, swaying pontoon bridge as more terrifying than going into battle.[38]

While the other division commanders eased their men along, Nelson pushed his troops ahead through the mud and bad weather that limited the rest of the army's progress to less than a dozen miles each day. Rain fell continuously, and at night soldiers tried to warm themselves by standing around blazing fires made from dry fence rails. "[W]e would very near freeze on one side and cook on the other," drummer boy Bircher of the 2nd Minnesota recalled. Exhausted men grew drowsy standing in front of the fires, and some unlucky ones were burned when they fell asleep on their feet and pitched over into the flames. In spite of such hardships, Nelson's division made it to Savannah by the mid-afternoon of April 5. Buell, who had hurried forward after his belated departure from Nashville, arrived there the same night.[39]

At 5:20 A.M. on April 6, according to a staff officer who carefully noted the time, the rattle of heavy volleys of musketry reached Nelson's camp. The sounds of battle, carried on the still morning air across the Tennessee countryside, were soon audible to units of the Army of the Ohio as far as thirty miles away.[40] The troops were electrified by the prospect of action. "Instantly each man grasps his gun more firmly. . . . The speed is doubled; the mud is not in the way any more," recalled C. C. Briant, describing the moment his regiment heard the guns of Shiloh. "From early morning on the march, we . . . heard the booming of cannon off to the southwest as we hurried in that direction," wrote a captain of the 16th U.S.; the eager men of his regiment promised onlookers that "we would [show] them how to play ball" when they reached the battle. In one of his classic accounts of the war, "What I Saw of Shiloh," Ambrose Bierce (then serving in the ranks of the 9th Indiana) described the impact of "the long, deep sighing of iron lungs" on Nelson's men that morning: "the division, as if it had received the sharp word of command, sprang to its feet. . . . I have since seen similar effects produced by earthquakes."[41]

Buell quickly sent orders to the nearest divisions, those of Crittenden and McCook, to hurry to Savannah, where they could board steamboats to take them the few miles upriver that would bring them to Grant's camp at Pittsburg Landing, where the battle was developing. At Nelson's headquarters, messages from Grant arrived throughout the morning describing a massive Confederate attack and requesting assistance. Communications problems continued to hamper the Army of the Ohio. Buell received Grant's messages but failed to inform Grant that he was with Nelson's division; thus Grant did not know of Buell's presence until the two generals met later that day at Pittsburg Landing. The aide carrying Buell's orders for the Fifth Division did not find General Crittenden until he was just about to send his troops directly to Pittsburg Landing on foot, rather than by steamboat via Savannah, which would have delayed his arrival at the battlefield by many hours.[42]

Buell and Nelson waited impatiently for boats from Grant's army to take the Fourth Division upstream. When none came, they tried to find someone who could guide the division along the river's eastern bank to a point where it could be ferried across. Shortly after 1:00 P.M. the division finally started marching south, over a route so waterlogged that artillery and wagons had to be left behind. Nelson's infantry struggled along a narrow path that meandered through five miles of swamps, reaching a point opposite Pittsburg Landing at around 5:00 P.M. For the rest of the night and into the next day, while rain fell without cease, steamboats busily ferried Nelson's men across or shuttled up and down the river to Savannah to fetch the troops of McCook and Crittenden. By the morning of April 7, most of the three divisions had reached the landing and gone ashore.[43]

The scene that met the soldiers as they arrived at Pittsburg Landing was appalling. The landing and the bluff above were covered with the routed remnants of Grant's army. As each reinforcement-laden steamboat landed, Ambrose Bierce recorded, "this abominable mob had to be kept off her with bayonets." Henry Villard, who accompanied Nelson's men, found himself "amid an immense, panic-stricken, uncontrollable mob" consisting of "between seven and ten thousand men, of all arms and of all ranks, from field officers downward, all apparently entirely bereft of soldierly spirit, with no sense of obedience left, and animated by the sole impulse of personal safety." Grant himself estimated the number of refugees at the landing as only "four or five thousand," but he admitted that they were "panic-stricken" to the point that "most of [them] would have been shot where they lay, without resistance, before they would have taken muskets and marched to the front to protect themselves."[44]

From these stragglers, the men of the Army of the Ohio learned what had happened. Five of Grant's six divisions had been surprised by an overwhelming Confederate attack at dawn on April 6 and in a long day of brutal fighting had been driven back to the river's edge. The survivors warned Buell's newcomers that the same fate, or worse, awaited them at the front. " 'You will see.' 'You will come back, or be killed.' 'It's murder,' " were among the comments that greeted Nelson's men. "As we pushed our way in the dim light of dawn through the crowd of demoralized fugitives cowering under the bank," Captain Lewis Hosea wrote, "we were treated to about all the dismal prognostications the human mind is capable of." Grant's men, Bierce confirmed, "expressed their unholy delight in the certainty of our destruction."[45]

Frank Jones, a brigade staff officer in Crittenden's division, recalled that the arriving units of the Army of the Ohio found it all they could do to maintain their organization while "threading our way up the bank [through] the disorganized mass of soldiers driven from the line of battle." Crittenden was so "disgusted" that he asked Buell for permission to drive the stragglers away at bayonet point, later explaining that "I did not wish my troops to come in contact with them." Nelson, typically, went further and "asked permission to open fire on the knaves," whom he found "insensible to shame or sarcasm" or even to his well-developed stock of profanities. When permission was denied, one of his aides wrote, Nelson arrayed his mounted staff officers in a tight formation and shouted, " 'Gentlemen! Draw your sabres and trample these — — sons of — into the mud! Charge!!' and away we went slashing through the crowd, which crawled over each other like maggots on a dead horse."[46]

The fear and confusion of the refugees on the banks of the Tennessee are well attested. Yet the regiments of the Army of the Ohio, landing in the midst of hordes of frightened stragglers, appeared immune to the contagion of panic. The contempt expressed by officers like Nelson and Crittenden was shared by their rank and file, who marched confidently through the demoralized mob and on toward the enemy. This was not because they were any braver than the men of the Army of the Tennessee, who, after all, had grown up in the same midwestern townships and villages, joined the army for much the same reasons, and undergone the same kind of training (or lack thereof). Nor did Buell's troops have any legitimate reason to consider Grant's men to be inferior soldiers merely because they had retreated in the face of a devastating surprise attack that would surely have routed any Civil War army.

The primary reason that Buell's regiments were unfazed by the specter of defeat on the night of April 6, 1862, was their insularity. The average soldier in the Army of the Ohio refused to be panicked by events, or stories and rumors of events, that took place outside of his self-contained regimental world. Blinkered by loyalty to the friends and neighbors who made up his company and his regiment, he simply regarded the experiences of outsiders (like Grant's people) as irrelevant. As they marched up the slope from Pittsburg Landing to the high ground where the Confederates waited, Buell's men heard warnings of " 'Oh, you'll catch it when you get over the hill there!' 'Oh, boys, I pity you!' 'You'll never come back again, comrades—mark that!,' " but they kept going, replying only, "Fall in here; this is a good regiment; it's not going to run, neither!" "They told us we would be torn to pieces," B. Frank Dysart of the 34th Illinois wrote to his brother afterward, "but we cared not what they said."[47]

"We Could See Nothing but the Flash of Our Own Muskets"

The next morning Buell ordered his army to advance and recapture the ground that the rebels had seized the day before. Grant gave his troops similar orders, but the two generals developed no plan for cooperation beyond an agreement that the Army of the Ohio would attack on the left and the Army of the Tennessee on the right. Buell later denied the existence of even this rudimentary understanding between himself and Grant, claiming that when he ordered his men forward, he "did not expect much assistance from General Grant's troops." Buell had so little information about the terrain and the enemy that his order to advance, as simple as it was, exhausted his ability to direct the fighting. In his own words, his "entire ignorance of the various roads and of the character of the country at the time rendered it impossible to anticipate the probable dispositions of the enemy." Buell tried to learn more by visiting sections of the battlefield on the night of April 6, but the thick woods limited what he could see. When the battle resumed the next morning, he confessed, "It was my misfortune to know nothing about the topography in front."[48]

Despite his lack of information, Buell was able to infuse his generals with confidence for the fight. Colonel William Hazen, who eventually rose to the rank of major general, later wrote of Buell's demeanor on the night of April 6 that "nothing in the war impressed me more." But inspiration was the limit of the contribution that Buell could make to the upcoming day's battle. The ground on which it would be fought was heavily forested, cut by numerous ravines, and choked with dense undergrowth that made it impossible for him to see what was happening and restricted the kinds of tactical orders that he and his division commanders could give. Further, the field was hemmed in by the Tennessee River to the east, Lick Creek to the south, Owl Creek to the west, and Snake Creek to the north. With tens of thousands of soldiers jammed into such a compressed area, Buell and his generals would have had little scope for maneuver even if it had been as flat and clear as a barracks square. As it was, the battle inevitably degenerated into a series of frontal attacks and counterattacks.[49]

Since their tactical options were so limited, the three Army of the Ohio division commanders present were reduced to exercising leadership by displaying their physical courage and exhorting their men to go forward in a series of aggressive head-on assaults against the Confederate line. At this, Nelson excelled. During the night of April 6, he ordered Union gunboats in the Tennessee River to shell the Confederate camps every thirty minutes, just to disturb the enemy's sleep. His three brigades went forward on April 7 before 5:00 A.M., on the left of the army, with the river protecting his division's left flank. They advanced steadily at first, interrupted only by a brief halt to wait for Crittenden's division on the right to catch up. Once they engaged the enemy, Nelson's men spent the rest of the day alternately attacking the Confederates and repelling their counterattacks, sometimes falling back for short distances before resuming the advance, with Nelson himself always somewhere in the middle of the fighting. "Old Nelson is a gay fellow he was cool as a cucumber during the whole fight," wrote a soldier in the 6th Ohio.[50]

Alexander McCook's Second Division held the right end of Buell's line. McCook handled his division adequately, advancing when he could and shuttling his reserves back and forth to repel counterattacks against both flanks. At times, however, he could not resist the temptation to give orders directly to individual regiments instead of operating through their brigade commanders, a practice that inevitably resulted in confusion.[51]

Thomas Crittenden was the least effective of the Union divisional leaders. The erratic pace of his Fifth Division caused vulnerable gaps to develop between it and the two other divisions, delaying Nelson's men and forcing McCook to commit reserve units to protect his left flank. Later in the day, when one of his brigades temporarily moved out of contact with a neighboring division while successfully charging a thicket held by the rebels, Crittenden overcompensated for his earlier errors by ordering the brigade to restore flank contact at the cost of abandoning its objective and falling back to its previous line. The rebels reoccupied the thicket, and when the Fifth Division resumed its advance, the brigade had to charge the position a second time, suffering further casualties in the process. By the end of the battle, Crittenden had allowed his command to become so scattered as to draw Buell's attention. He did, however, match Nelson and McCook in his willingness to lead by example, as his aide-de-camp Louis Buford discovered to his dismay. Accompanying Crittenden into battle, Buford found, meant that "instead of having the safest position I had the most dangerous."[52]

Moving down through the chain of command, the Army of the Ohio's brigade leaders occupied positions that were just as dangerous and close to the action (if not more so), but with no greater ability to exercise tactical control over the battle than belonged to Buell or the division commanders. Colonel William Sooy Smith found it difficult to position the regiments of his Fourteenth Brigade on the night of April 6, according to his adjutant, because he "had but little knowledge of the exact location of the enemy or the point to which Grant's army had been driven back." Brigadier General Lovell H. Rousseau, commanding the Fourth Brigade, was ignorant of the enemy's position in the dense woods to his front, but before sending his troops forward he "made a ringing speech" that drew three cheers and "cheered us up amazingly," reported one of his men; "I tell you we w'ld have faced anything after that," another wrote home enthusiastically after the battle.[53]

Other brigadiers found the terrain so inhospitable that they were not even able to provide their troops with inspiring speeches. William Hazen tried to lead his inexperienced soldiers into battle, but as he went forward with them he became lost in the woods, leaving his Nineteenth Brigade leaderless for much of the battle and convincing at least one of his regimental commanders that he had run away. Even less useful to his men was Colonel Sanders D. Bruce of the Twenty-second Brigade, described by Lieutenant Horace Fisher of Nelson's staff as a "real Kentucky-Colonel type [who] kept a barrel of whisky on tap." Bruce, who was among the many officers with whom Nelson had quarreled, was ignored by the Fourth Division commander throughout the battle in favor of his ranking subordinate, who served as the de facto brigade commander. In his postbattle report Nelson praised his other brigade leaders (even the missing Hazen) but was pointedly silent as to Colonel Bruce.[54]

The limitations that terrain imposed on division and brigade commanders made Shiloh a "soldier's battle." Generals had little to do but go forward with their men. The battle's outcome thus devolved upon the individual enlisted man and his decision to stay with his regiment or run away. As long as enough men in his regiment chose to stand and fight, he would stay too, unaware and unconcerned that his brigade, division, and army commanders were confused, out of touch, and blinded by the unfamiliar terrain. His regiment would carry on, and after the battle, win or lose, its survivors would rally together and prepare for the next campaign. But should the regiment begin to disintegrate, all was lost. If enough regiments lost their cohesion, then all higher forms of organization would disappear as well, and the Army of the Ohio would degenerate into a helpless mob.

For most of Buell's men, Shiloh was their first battle and they were anxious to "see the elephant." Colonel Jacob Ammen contrasted the eager anticipation of some of his troops, who had yet to experience combat, with the reserved behavior of the veterans of the 24th Ohio, who "had seen the elephant several times, and did not care about seeing him again unless necessary."[55] As the soldiers neared the field, eagerness turned to apprehension. Captain Lewis Hosea described the Fourth Brigade's approach to the battlefield: "Each hour the roar of the battle grew more distinct; our pace was quickened; the ranks were closed up; the usual chaffing and jokes of the march ceased; and every one was seriously and earnestly animated by one overwhelming desire—to reach the battlefield before it might be too late."[56]

Fear of missing the fighting was mixed with fear of its consequences. A soldier of the 15th Ohio noted that the wounded men coming back from the front "were without exception in good spirits and told us to go in," but the dead and badly wounded on the ground "looked heavy to us new soldiers."

The volunteers of the 29th Indiana lost much of their enthusiasm for the fight when they marched by a pile of amputated limbs outside a field hospital. When the men of the first regiment of the Army of the Ohio to reach the battlefield, the 36th Indiana, formed a line of battle at the top of the bluff above Pittsburg Landing on the evening of the sixth, they were horrified to see one of General Grant's aides struck by a cannonball that decapitated him and ricocheted into the ranks of Company G, where it tore off the legs of an unfortunate soldier. "These death scenes caused the men in the line near thereto to curve by a step or two back," one of the Hoosiers recalled, before the colonel's order straightened them out "as though the Regiment had been on drill or dress parade."[57]

Eager as they were to "see the elephant," the men soon found that they (like their officers) were prevented by the dense vegetation and undulating terrain from seeing much of anything. Even the enemy was invisible until almost in contact. H. W. Engelbracht recalled how his company of the 2nd Kentucky was held in reserve in an open field, under fire but unable to see who was doing the shooting. When the regiment finally advanced, Engelbracht wrote, the situation worsened: "The battle field was covered with woods and in places there was extensive underbrush. When we approached one of these thickly wooded sections, we realized that the enemy was before us. A bullet killed our captain. We prepared to fire, when suddenly we were met by a terrific rifle fire, from the unseen enemy, a fire so rapid that I cannot understand today that our whole company, which was exposed to the full force of the fire, was not completely wiped out." Colonel Benjamin C. Grider of the 9th Kentucky reported that his unit similarly advanced to within ten paces of an enemy position hidden in a hollow covered with a "very thick growth of timber and underbrush." Jacob van Zwaluwenburg wrote of the increasing tension that gripped his regiment, the 16th U.S., as it marched toward the sound of enemy fire without seeing anything. A line of advancing rebels finally came into view, only to disappear again into a creek bottom. "There were moments of intense nerve strain[;] we were not allowed to fire until the order was given, we knew they were slowly but surely coming right on us."[58]

The stress of waiting to meet the unseen enemy was so great that actual combat was welcomed by some soldiers. Edwin Payne recalled the order for his 34th Illinois to advance as "a relief from that always 'knee weakening' occupation of supporting a firing line without knowing whether the order to 'engage' will come in a minute or an hour." But for others, the moment of truth was even worse than anticipated. Lieutenant Ambrose Bierce found himself in a 9th Indiana skirmish line, with orders to cross a small open field and flush out any rebels among the trees on the opposite side. The Union soldiers advanced to within thirty or forty yards of the woods. "Then—I can't describe it—the forest seemed all at once to flame up and disappear with a crash like that of a great wave upon the beach—a crash that expired in hot hissings, and the sickening 'spat' of lead against flesh." Bierce had expected to find no more than a few enemy skirmishers: "What we had found was a line of battle, coolly holding its fire till it could count our teeth."[59]

Since the soldiers could see so little of the enemy, those not in the battle line tried to piece together what might be happening from the sounds of the fighting, at least until their regiments opened fire and the immediate roar of battle drowned out everything else. Captain Hosea of the 16th U.S. described the experience of waiting for an enemy attack to materialize: "The battle began on our left, and the noise of musketry, deepening from the skirmish fire into the roll of the line of battle, crept nearer and nearer." The next sign of imminent combat for Hosea's men was the arrival of Union skirmishers, carrying their wounded and seeking the safety of the main battle line. Following closely behind them "we saw battleflags amid the leafage of the trees, and beneath, the surging line of butternut and grey, which halted at about fifty yards and commenced firing." After waiting for the last Union skirmishers to enter their lines, Hosea's regiment returned the fire. Soon "the stifling fog of powder-smoke" filled the forest so that "we could see nothing but the flash of our own muskets." Again sound became Hosea's primary source of information, when after an hour of firing "the angry buzz of whistling bullets became less and less violent, and we knew by a sort of instinct that the opposing lines were wavering and melting away. Thus the first attack was repulsed."[60]

The battle flags mentioned in Hosea's account were among the few visual landmarks available during the battle. Most Federal regiments carried two, a national flag (the "Stars and Stripes") and a regimental flag, which was usually a variation of the unit's state flag with the name of the regiment prominently added. These banners, which were large and colorful enough to be visible even through the smoke of battle, served the practical purposes of identifying the regiment and indicating the center of its line.[61] As long as a regiment's companies maintained the same relative positions that they had rehearsed on the drill ground, men could use the flags to orient themselves within their regimental formations. When officers' commands were drowned out by the din of fighting, soldiers knew that they should advance when their flags advanced, fall back when the flags retreated, and hold their ground as long as the color-bearers held theirs. "As the christian finds comfort and feels security and protection in an hour of danger 'clinging to the cross,'" wrote Spillard F. Horrall of the 42nd Indiana, "so the soldier by 'clinging to the flag' gets courage." The phrase "rally 'round the flag" reflected tactical reality as well as patriotic sentiment, and the loss of a flag in battle was a calamity that often signaled the end of the regiment as a coherent body of men.[62]

A regiment's flags were its most prized possessions, not only for their tactical importance but also because they were tangible links between the regiment and the civilian community from which it was raised. Most regiments received their flags before they left home. The flags were usually professionally made and purchased for the regiment by funds raised from local citizens, although in some communities women made the flags by hand. The presentation of a regiment's colors was an important civic ceremony marked by speeches that emphasized the mutual obligations between the regiment and its place of origin. The symbolic value of these flags was increased by recording on them the names of the regiment's battles, a practice sanctioned by the War Department in February 1862.[63] Flags were so important that soldiers competed for the honor of belonging to the regimental color guard, eight men who carried or marched next to the flags in combat, in spite of the fact that the flags' visibility ensured a high volume of enemy fire; the 41st Ohio lost four color-bearers at Shiloh, the 34th Illinois all but one. The flag was to the regiment what the church spire was to the town: physical landmark, symbol of community, and source of inspiration.[64]

The behavior of field and company officers was another vital source of regimental cohesion at Shiloh. Officers led by example, encouraging their men by demonstrating their willingness to risk wounds and death. " 'Lie down, there!' a captain would shout and then get up himself to see that the order was obeyed. 'Captain, take cover, sir!' the lieutenant-colonel would shriek, pacing up and down in the most exposed position that he could find," was how Ambrose Bierce depicted the self-conscious bravery of the 9th Indiana's officers. Such conspicuous displays of valor sometimes backfired when the inevitable (and highly visible) casualties that followed depressed the morale of entire regiments. While the enlisted men of their brigade obeyed an order to lie down to avoid enemy fire, Captain Hosea and Lieutenant P. T. Keyes of the 16th U.S. stood arm-in-arm watching the battle, "the traditional *esprit* of the service not permitting officers to hug the earth as we came to do later," Hosea wrote. Both men were almost immediately knocked to the ground by the impact of a bullet that struck Keyes in the arm, wounding him mortally. The Second Division's historian recorded that when the commanders of the 34th Illinois and 30th Indiana were hit in quick succession, "The intelligence of the disaster sped like a flash along the lines, and despair seemed to settle upon them." After Shiloh, officers in the Army of the Ohio would moderate their displays of bravery.[65]

Although the terrain and tactical circumstances at Shiloh did not permit

A contemporary illustration of the 1st Ohio advancing across a clearing at Shiloh highlights the short range of the fighting, the closeness of the surrounding woods, and the prominence of regimental flags. From *Frank Leslie's Illustrated Newspaper*, May 17, 1862; photograph courtesy of The Lincoln Museum, Fort Wayne, Indiana (TLM #4539).

much fancy maneuvering, some regiments performed notable feats of arms. Lovell Rousseau reported that his Fourth Brigade regiments fought until they had used up their ammunition, then executed a passage of lines with the Fifth Brigade "without the least confusion or even excitement," bringing fresh troops to the front without disrupting either unit.[66] At another point in the battle the 49th Ohio swung back like a gate, changing its front ninety degrees to meet a threat to its left flank, and then returned to its original position. Later it repeated the process to defeat a second flank attack.[67] Colonel August Willich's 32nd Indiana used traditional European tactics with success, as it had at Rowlett's Station the previous December, this time executing a bayonet charge in a tightly packed column formation.[68]

But even units as skilled as the 32nd Indiana could fall victim to tactical inexperience. Captain Hosea saw "Willich's regiment of Germans. . . . [formed] in a compact mass, closed by companies in the center, and with flags flying and drums beating," ready to advance again. Before they could move forward, however, they came under fire from Union troops behind them, because of what Willich described as "bad management in our squeezed-up position." Under the impact of the unexpected fire from the rear, the 32nd Indiana fell back in disorder. "When to our dismay Col. Willich's regiment of dutch that fought so bravely at Green River came pell mell thorugh our lines in full retreat," wrote Captain A. P. Dysart, the men of the 34th Illinois also began to fall back, so that Dysart "thought for a few moments that our regiment was disgraced." After trying four times without success to rally his company, Dysart decided "not to leave the field living and be disgraced by retreat"; enough of his comrades eventually joined him that the regiment was able to hold its ground and later resume its advance. Meanwhile, Willich took the extraordinary measure of halting his men and drilling them in the manual of arms, under fire, until they had regained their composure. So remarkable was the behavior of the 32nd Indiana that it attracted the attention of two of Grant's division commanders, who mentioned it in their after-action reports.[69]

The 32nd Indiana was not the only unit in the Army of the Ohio to experience "friendly fire." A particularly macabre example took place in the 16th U.S. After the regiment divided its line in two in order to pass around both sides of an obstacle, the two halves moved too far as they came back together, making the regiment four ranks deep instead of two in the center where the wings overlapped. The men were then ordered to lie down and fire. Accustomed to firing from two ranks, a soldier in the front rank stood up just as a man in one of the rear ranks discharged his musket and was killed by a ball that blew off his head.[70]

"The Ardor Was Completely Cooled"

Victory at Shiloh was not decided in a single climactic moment, like the repulse of Pickett's Charge at Gettysburg or the arrival of A. P. Hill's Light Division at Antietam. Its outcome was instead the sum of the results of hundreds of smaller combats, separated from one another by tangled ravines, thick woods, and heavy clouds of smoke. Some of these engagements, like the ambush of Ambrose Bierce's skirmish line, were Union reverses. Others, such as the first bayonet charge of the 32nd Indiana, were victories. When night fell on April 7, it became apparent that the balance sheet of these engagements favored the North. The Army of the Ohio had advanced more than it had retreated, and most of its men had stayed with their regiments. Through their perseverance, they and the Army of the Tennessee had recaptured all the ground that had been lost on April 6 and had driven the Confederates from the field, although at such cost (241 men killed, 1,807 wounded, and 55 captured or missing, out of approximately 20,000 Army of the Ohio soldiers engaged) that no thought could be given to pursuing the enemy.[71]

The Battle of Shiloh had a profound effect on the soldiers of the Army of the Ohio. Most of them had looked forward to the experience, and there were some who found it as exhilarating as they had imagined. For Alex Varian of the 1st Ohio, nothing could compare to the "awful grandeur of a raging battle" and the "splendid" behavior of officers under fire. As for himself, he proudly wrote of his skill with "The Widow," as he called his musket: "She spoke to the Rebels 31 times during the day—I think to some purpose." Thomas Prickett of the 9th Indiana was undismayed, even after being wounded by a skull fragment from another soldier who had been hit by a cannonball. When his regiment charged, Prickett wrote shortly afterward, "[I] never felt so good in my life, I thought we were just going to play smash with them generally." He admitted that when the tide of battle turned momentarily, "I did some tall running as well as the rest," but he returned to join in a "grand charge of [the] whole division." C. C. Briant of the 6th Indiana relished the sight of General Rousseau proclaiming "The rebels are flying! The victory is ours!" followed by "one universal handshaking" among the troops: "Oh, was'nt that a glorious meeting!"[72] The army's sense of superiority over the rebels, born at Rowlett's Station and nurtured at Logan's Cross Roads, was strengthened by the thrill of victory at Shiloh, where the Army of the Ohio (in its own eyes, at least) had saved Grant's forces from defeat and disgrace.[73]

Even more than pride, however, the primary emotion of the battle's survivors was an earnest wish not to repeat the experience. Shiloh gave them their fill of combat. "Mother I have all ways want to see one battle field and now I have seen it and I never want to see a nother one," Torah Sampson wrote, after describing how his brother Alford had been killed in the fight. In a similar mood, Michael Truxhall declared to his uncle, "I am perfectly satisfied with war now, and I don't care how soon it is over. There is no fun in having the bullets whizzing around a fellow's head for a whole day." After the men of the 6th Indiana enjoyed a fleeting moment of celebration, C. C. Briant later wrote, they acknowledged that war "meant neither fun nor pastime." Levi H. Sipes recalled that in the 29th Indiana, "the Ardor was Completely Cooled" after Shiloh. Before the battle, B. Frank Dysart "longed" to fight and "was willing to run the risk but I never dreamt that we would ever get in a fight like this." Afterward, he commented, "I don't care how soon we go home now I have been in a fight that is what I wanted." The same applied to Dysart's regiment, the 34th Illinois, which arrived at Shiloh "spoiling for a fight . . . but now being as they were pretty well smoked they will be able to go a long time again" before wanting to enter another. The battle did not shake the army's faith in its leaders or its cause, but it disabused the men of the idea that there was fun to be had in combat.[74]

In the days following the battle, two more divisions of the Army of the Ohio arrived at Pittsburg Landing. These soldiers, who saw the carnage without having participated in the battle, were even more chastened than those who had fought. Lieutenant Tuttle described how the men of the 3rd Kentucky encountered "the most shocking and sickening sight of the day or any other day during the war. It was two or three wagon loads of amputated hands, arms feet and legs thrown in a heap. We had *expected* to find dead and mangled bodies on the field and our minds were prepared for the spectacle but we were not prepared to come in sudden contact with that naked and ghastly mass of human flesh."[75] Another latecomer, 2nd Minnesota drummer boy William Bircher, was struck by the way that "the warm sun caused a stench that was almost unbearable." There were dead men and animals who had been hurt in every imaginable way, including some who had been burned to death by fires that had crept through the woods on the first day of the battle. It took days to recover the wounded and to find and dispose of all the bodies on the field, during which looters rifled the pockets of the dead, or almost dead.[76]

Although the Battle of Shiloh was a victory, it was far from decisive. The Confederates' losses were very high, but their morale remained firm and their army intact, ready to fight again after a few weeks' recuperation. Rather than demonstrating to the South the futility of its cause, it showed the North the magnitude of the struggle to come. "Up to the battle of Shiloh," Grant stated, "I, as well as thousands of other citizens, believed that the rebellion against the Government would collapse suddenly and soon. . . . [Afterward] I gave up all idea of saving the Union except by complete conquest."[77]

The success of the Army of the Ohio at Shiloh indicated that man for man and regiment for regiment, it could stand the most severe punishment and give out the same in return. But the army's inability to destroy its opponents also showed the limits of what it could accomplish without more effective leadership. At the army level, Buell failed to bring half of his divisions to the battle at all, and he had so little knowledge of the ground and the condition of the enemy that all he could do with the forces at hand was to send them straight ahead into an unknown tactical situation. His division commanders, who could not see more than a fraction of their men at a time because of the terrain, were reduced to acting as junior officers, leading charges, and maneuvering individual regiments. Brigade and regimental officers became even more involved in the thick of the fighting; some provided inspiring personal leadership, but many were wounded (or got lost) before they could influence the battle. The Army of the Ohio fought the Battle of Shiloh as a large collection of individual regiments rather than a single well-coordinated, centrally directed military organization; as such, it proved to be a blunt instrument that could maim but could not kill.

CHAPTER FIVE

Promise Unfulfilled
The Corinth and Chattanooga Campaigns,
May to July 1862

For the first six months of its existence the Army of the Ohio experienced an unbroken trajectory of progress, culminating in the victory at Shiloh. Extensive drill transformed its regiments from masses of enthusiastic but ignorant recruits into confident and relatively capable military units. Successes at Rowlett's Station, Logan's Cross Roads, and especially Shiloh left the men convinced that there were no better troops in the country, North or South. Their confidence in themselves was reflected in the boast of the 19th Illinois's Henry Haynie, who wrote that he belonged to "the best drilled regiment in the [Army of the Ohio], which is to say, the best in all the Northern armies."[1] Buell's men had every reason to expect that, given the right leadership, they would soon finish what they had started and put an end to the war in the West.

Instead, the spring and summer of 1862 proved to be a time of frustration and disappointment. In April the army was merged with two other Union armies into a huge conglomeration commanded by Henry Halleck. In June, after a slow and tedious campaign to capture Corinth, Mississippi, Halleck restored Buell's status as commander of an independent field army but gave him the manifestly impractical assignment of capturing and repairing the Memphis & Charleston Railroad as far east as Chattanooga, Tennessee. The entire two hundred–mile stretch of railroad lay within easy reach of rebel raiders, and Buell lacked the resources to defend the railroad and conduct an offensive campaign against Chattanooga at the same time.

Buell remained aloof from his volunteer soldiers during this difficult period, paying little attention to their morale, even when political struggles over the nature and purpose of the war threatened to divide the army. In July and August poor staff work combined with a series of devastating enemy raids left the army chronically short of supplies and raised doubts about the competence of its leadership. When Buell refused to let his troops forage from Southern civilians to alleviate their hunger, some of them began to question his concern for their well-being. As a result, the army that fought as a collection of regiments at Shiloh failed to coalesce during the summer of 1862. Although the average soldier's regimental loyalty remained as strong as ever, by the end of the summer of 1862 he no longer took any particular pride (if indeed he ever had) in serving in Don Carlos Buell's Army of the Ohio.

"Most of Our Time . . . Was Employed by Building Corduroy Roads"

"Don't you think this month will settle the fate of the Rebellion?" George Landrum of the Third Division asked his brother-in-law in April 1862. The strategic picture looked promising for the Union. In the East, McClellan had outflanked the rebels by transporting the Army of the Potomac onto the Virginia Peninsula, where he was besieging Yorktown. On the Mississippi, Major General John Pope had opened the great river as far south as Memphis by capturing the enemy stronghold at Island No. 10, on the same day that the Confederates began their retreat from Shiloh. By the end of the month Halleck had concentrated the armies of Buell, Pope, and Grant at Pittsburg Landing and was ready to push south into the heart of the Confederacy.[2]

After Shiloh, Buell's men had begun to compare themselves favorably to both of the armies that had retreated during the battle, Grant's Army of the Tennessee and the Confederate Army of Mississippi.[3] As early as April 9, Buell asserted in a private letter that his men had "saved the army of General Grant which otherwise was doomed to destruction." Along with many of his soldiers, Buell imagined the story of Shiloh to be that of the rescue of Grant's helpless, unprepared, defeated army by the timely arrival of his own well-trained, brave, efficient forces. This narrative, had it taken hold in the public memory, could have become the institutional legend around which the Army of the Ohio forged a strong collective identity. Buell, however, naively imagined that he need do nothing to bring this about. Of the battle, he wrote home, "I shall not speak boastfully to anyone, unless it is to you, my wife, of the part the 'Kentucky Army' has acted in it." Determined to "let the world draw its own conclusions as to what kudos my troops are entitled to," Buell was hurt and surprised when Grant's superior public relations skills persuaded the public to accept a very different version of what had happened at Shiloh. "[T]he troops whom we rescued have so far forestalled public opinion by false ungrateful and boastful reports of their exploits and by silence in regard to the services of the Army of the Ohio, that it seems our presence in the battle is hardly recognized," he complained to his wife in early May. To Buell's lifelong chagrin, most Americans came to perceive Shiloh as Grant's victory, not his. In later years, long after it might have helped the Army of the Ohio, Buell undertook to change this perception by writing a series of letters and articles promoting his version of the battle, but with little success.[4]

Whatever nascent pride Buell's troops had in belonging to the one army that did not retreat at Shiloh was dashed on April 28, 1862, when the Army of the Ohio was amalgamated with the forces of Grant and Pope into a single, massive Army of the West, led by Halleck, in which Buell's divisions were designated the "Center" corps. If the old Army of the Ohio had always placed a distant third in the hearts of its soldiers, behind their regiments and companies, the new army had no claim on their loyalty at all. Halleck lacked any hint of charisma to draw the volunteers' affection or to overcome the rivalry between Grant and Buell (and their armies) born at Shiloh.[5]

The new army numbered more than a hundred thousand men. A few of its members were impressed by the idea of a force so big that those stationed on one flank might have no knowledge of what was happening on the other. "Our army extends several miles in length," Lieutenant Henry Buck of the 51st Illinois bragged to his sister. "What would you think of there being a fight on our extreme right . . . ," he added wonderingly, "and we, hearing of it for the first time through the Chicago papers? Such a case has happened." More typically, however, soldiers responded to the apparent demise of the Army of the Ohio by making their regiments the sole object of their institutional loyalty, encouraged by the continuing routine of endless drills that made the regiment the focus of their daily activity. "[T]here is nothing in this country," one officer complained in May 1862, "either to eat, to wear, to read, or anything else but to drill." A few officers tried to introduce brigade-level drills, but for the most part regiments continued to drill independent of one another.[6]

On May 2, 1862, Halleck's ponderous army began a painfully slow advance. The swampy, trackless, heavily wooded terrain of southwestern Tennessee proved a more formidable obstacle to Halleck than the Confederates, who were still reeling from the loss of ten thousand men (including their leader, Albert Sidney Johnston) at Shiloh. Halleck's objective was the railroad junc-

Two versions of Shiloh. *Top*: Grant's disintegrating army is about to be saved by the Army of the Ohio, the vanguard of which is just visible on the far shore of the Tennessee River. *Bottom*: Grant (mounted, center) leads the decisive charge of the battle in person, defeating the enemy without need of assistance. To Buell's chagrin, the public largely accepted the latter interpretation of events. From *Frank Leslie's Illustrated Newspaper*, May 3, 1862 (top), and *Harper's Weekly*, April 26, 1862 (bottom); photograph courtesy of The Lincoln Museum, Fort Wayne, Indiana (TLM #4540).

tion at Corinth, but there were neither railroads nor rivers leading there from Pittsburg Landing, forcing the Union army to rely on inefficient horse-drawn wagons to haul its supplies. Since the roads were inadequate for the number of wagons the army needed, the men had to construct new ones. "Most of our time in April was employed by building corduroy roads over swamps and bayous," wrote James Shaw of the 10th Indiana. This was a labor-intensive process that involved the felling of enormous numbers of trees, which were hewn into logs ten feet in length and laid across the roadway. With luck, a dozen logs would extend the road by as many feet, but where the mud or water was especially deep, many layers of logs might be needed to raise the surface of the road sufficiently. "[W]oe to the man or beast that was unfortunate enough to step or fall off of the roads," Shaw added. "Some of the mules that fell off of the corduroys were never found."[7]

The army's progress was further slowed by Halleck's requirement that the men build fortifications every night. Halleck, already cautious by nature, wanted no chance of a repetition of the surprise attack that had almost brought disaster at Shiloh. As the country's leading scholar of military theory, Halleck was one of the first generals to appreciate the full value of fortifications in the Civil War. His belief in their importance was confirmed by the rank and file of both sides later in the conflict, when they adopted the practice of digging in for protection whenever combat appeared likely, whether ordered to do so or not. In May 1862, however, Halleck's theoretical understanding was misapplied to a situation where the Confederate threat was minimal. The constant labor of building temporary fortifications seemed a meaningless waste of energy, especially after the campaign came to an anticlimactic end on May 30 with the discovery that the Confederates had secretly abandoned the fortifications of Corinth the night before.[8]

To the east, meanwhile, O. M. Mitchel's Third Division continued to conduct its independent campaign to break the Memphis & Charleston Railroad at Huntsville, with mixed results. Since March, when Buell detached Mitchel's eight thousand men from the Army of the Ohio, the astronomer-general had gained control of northern Alabama up to the Tennessee River and captured intact a substantial section of the rail line.[9] This disrupted transportation between the eastern and western sections of the Confederacy and gave the Union a supply route from the head of navigation on the Tennessee River (at Florence, Alabama) to the approaches to Chattanooga. Mitchel was not shy about claiming credit for his achievements, at some length, in dispatches that he sent over Buell's head directly to Secretary of War Stanton.[10]

Mitchel's successes were counterbalanced by his unreliability. He indulged in schemes like an attempt to steal a Confederate locomotive (which resulted in seven of his men and a civilian being executed as spies), and he was heavily involved in the sale of contraband cotton. His frequent communications to Washington alternated between grandiose victory announcements, which Buell characterized as "marred by exaggeration and false coloring, and inconsistency and self-seeking," and dire predictions of disaster if his shrill demands for reinforcements were not met at once.[11] In late May, Mitchel rashly ordered his troops to burn the railroad bridges across the Tennessee at Decatur and Bridgeport to protect his division from a threatened counterattack that never took place; the destruction of the bridges had no effect on the Confederate war effort but impeded Union operations in the area for months.[12] Mitchel's private correspondence with the secretary of war, his boastful dispatches, and his attempts to wriggle from under Buell's authority and operate his division as a separate entity all supported Buell's description of him as "ambitious in an ostentatious way" and unsuited for independent command.[13]

"It Would Have Taken 50,000 Men to Keep That Railroad in Running Order"

Following the capture of Corinth, Halleck broke up his command into its original components, restoring the forces of Grant, Buell, and Pope to the status of separate field armies.[14] The revived Army of the Ohio included the divisions of Thomas, McCook, Nelson, Crittenden, and Wood, plus Mitchel's division in northern Alabama and G. W. Morgan's in eastern Kentucky. The army's mission, Halleck decided, was to capture Chattanooga, about two hundred miles to the east. Chattanooga was not only a critical railroad hub, linking Virginia and northern Georgia to points west, but it also guarded the southern gateway into the Tennessee mountains, where Unionist spirit still thrived. Once again, Buell found himself responsible for fulfilling the government's cherished goal of relieving the Union sympathizers of East Tennessee.

From its start on June 11, the campaign against Chattanooga was plagued by logistical problems that lowered the army's morale. Halleck directed Buell to draw his supplies from Memphis (which had fallen on June 6) via the Memphis & Charleston Railroad.[15] But since the road from Memphis to Chattanooga ran parallel to the line dividing Union and Confederate territory, it was a simple matter for Southern horsemen to sally forth and tear up the tracks behind the army at almost any point they chose. Further, there was little rolling stock available and no easy way to add more, as the line did not connect to any Northern railroads. Buell issued the appropriate orders to have work done to put the line into operation, but he considered the project impractical. As far back as April he had remarked that the railroad "would hardly be a proper line of communication for us against Chattanooga." Events would prove him right; Alexander McCook later testified that "it would have taken 50,000 men to keep that railroad in running order," more than the total strength of Buell's four divisions at Corinth. Within weeks, Buell reported to Halleck that in spite of his efforts the railroad was "useless as a channel of supplies for this army."[16]

Without a working railroad, the men had to carry their own supplies. The first stage in the campaign was the fifty-mile haul from Corinth to the Tennessee River bridges at Tuscumbia, Alabama. The land was dry and barren, and the heat oppressive. "You load a man down," wrote C. C. Briant of the 6th Indiana, "with a sixty-pound knapsack, his gun and forty rounds of ammunition, a haversack full of hard tack and sow belly, and a three-pint canteen full of water, then start him along this narrow roadway, with the mercury up to a hundred, and dust so thick you could taste it, and you have done the next thing to killing this man outright."[17] The troops experienced some relief on reaching the Tennessee River, but Buell found his hope of receiving supplies by steamboat frustrated by dry weather that had lowered the water level and reduced the river's navigability. Only by kidnaping local river pilots and forcing them to guide boats through the shoals (damaging three steamers in the process) were Union supply officers able to bring up ten days' rations for the army.[18]

At Tuscumbia, where the soldiers marveled at the town's natural spring, the divisions of McCook, Nelson, and Crittenden crossed the river by ferry, a slow process that took until June 26 to complete. Thomas's division remained behind to guard the particularly exposed stretch of the Memphis & Charleston Railroad between Iuka and Decatur, which lay south of the Tennessee, while Wood's division was detached to hold the crossing at Decatur. As the Second, Fourth, and Fifth Divisions resumed their march toward Chattanooga, scarcity of food became a problem. Beyond Muscle Shoals, a few miles east of Tuscumbia, the river was no longer navigable at all. Although Buell detailed thousands of men to defend and repair the railroad (and to improvise pontoon bridges and ferries to replace the railroad bridges destroyed by Mitchel's troops in May), few trains arrived from Memphis. There were not enough locomotives or cars available, and Confederate raiders continued to wreck many of the trestles and bridges along the line faster than Thomas's men could repair them. Most discouraging of all, Buell discovered that Mitchel had failed to stockpile supplies for the army at Athens, Alabama, as he had been ordered to do long ago.[19]

Attempts to supply the Army of the Ohio by rail from Memphis in the summer of 1862 were handicapped by the destruction of the railroad bridge over the Tennessee River at Decatur, Alabama, which had been burned by Union troops in May. From *Harper's Weekly*, August 16, 1862; photograph courtesy of The Lincoln Museum, Fort Wayne, Indiana (TLM #4541).

By June 30 even Halleck could see that it no longer made sense to try to supply the army from Memphis, so he authorized Buell to open a new supply route from Nashville.[20] Buell promptly assigned Nelson's Fourth Division to repair the Central Alabama Rail Road from Nashville to Decatur, leaving only two divisions to continue the advance on Chattanooga. Six weeks earlier, such a force could likely have taken the city without a fight, but now it boasted a substantial garrison, more than strong enough to resist an attack by a division or two. Buell ordered McCook and Crittenden to stop at Bridgeport, some thirty miles west of Chattanooga. By the first week of July, the Army of the Ohio had ground to a complete halt.

Some of Buell's men blamed him for the slow pace of the campaign. Staff officer Ephraim Otis thought that the army could have seized Chattanooga had it not conducted such a "leisurely march" that seemed "like holiday soldiering," with each day's hike ending by 10:00 A.M. But Buell, with considerable justification, pointed to Halleck's order that the army trace its supply line to Memphis as the real cause for delay. Halleck, in turn, accused Buell of detaching too many troops for defense and not putting enough men to work on the railroad.[21] The debate was pointless, even more so than most bickering among Civil War generals, because of what had happened on June 7. On that day, while Buell was still in Corinth, a small force operating under O. M. Mitchel's auspices approached Chattanooga from across the Tennessee River and threw in a few artillery shells, alerting Confederate authorities to the possibility of attack. The city was reinforced at once, eliminating any chance for Buell to seize it without fighting a battle, whether he arrived sooner or later.[22]

Buell's forty-five thousand men outnumbered the Chattanooga garrison, but they were scattered far and wide across northern Alabama and central Tennessee. Relieved from the need to guard the railroad to the west, Buell called for Thomas and Wood to bring their divisions up, but at the same time he was forced to spread many of Nelson's regiments along his two new lines of supply from Nashville, both the main route to Stevenson (via Murfreesboro, Wartrace, Tullahoma, and Decherd) and an auxiliary route to Decatur (via Franklin, Spring Hill, Columbia, Pulaski, and Athens). As he had done in Kentucky, Buell offered the rationale that he was dispersing his troops "to conceal the object . . . of my campaign," but this time there was little mystery about the destination of the Army of the Ohio. The only question was how long it would take Buell to secure his communications and build up a sufficient surplus of provisions to allow him to resume the offensive. Until he did, the advance on Chattanooga was stalled indefinitely.[23]

"Oh! For an Active, Earnest Leader!"

In his attempts to put the Army of the Ohio on a firm logistical footing, Buell consistently rejected the option of allowing his men to live off the land. It was doubtful that the hardscrabble farms of the Cumberland foothills could have supplied all the needs of the Army of the Ohio, but Buell refused even to consider the possibility, for political as well as military reasons. He felt strongly that foraging from civilians was corrosive to discipline and if unchecked would undermine the tone of the army. Further, he believed that the best way to pacify the residents of the South was to be as solicitous of their rights as possible, thus encouraging them to rediscover their loyalty to the government that protected them.[24] In spite of this policy, many civilians within the Army of the Ohio's lines continued to display open hostility, while others engaged in armed resistance, including sabotage and assassination. As the summer wore on, Buell's "soft war" policy of strict regard for civilian property rights became increasingly unpopular with his soldiers.

The sack of Athens, Alabama, on May 2, 1862, like the massacre at My Lai in the Vietnam War, became the single representative incident around which support for and opposition to official policy crystallized. Athens, a town about ten miles south of the Tennessee border, was occupied late in April by the Eighth Brigade of Mitchel's division. The commander of the brigade, Colonel John Basil Turchin, was a veteran of the Czar's armies who had a reputation for disregarding the property rights of secessionist civilians.[25] After a rebel cavalry attack temporarily drove the Eighth Brigade out of Athens, some of Turchin's men apparently claimed that local civilians had joined in the fighting and fired at the retreating bluecoats. Turchin responded by ordering his brigade back into the town and announcing, "I shust shuts mine eyes for two hours." The men took advantage of the license to do thousands of dollars worth of damage, and to commit several assaults or rapes against enslaved women.[26]

Mitchel, Turchin's immediate superior, rebuked him but refused to make restitution to the victims or punish any of the accused, contemptuously rejecting a stack of affidavits from the citizens of Athens listing their losses on the grounds that they failed to name the guilty individuals; he could not, he said, "arraign" an entire brigade. Buell took stronger action, ordering the court-martial of Turchin and several others, relieving Turchin of his command, and breaking up the Eighth Brigade by reassigning its regiments to other units. In response, all of the officers of the 19th and 24th Illinois resigned, as did Colonel Turchin.[27] Although Turchin was convicted, he returned to the army a few months later in triumph bearing a presidential pardon and a brigadier general's star, thanks to an outpouring of political influence on his behalf and in spite of Buell's protest to Stanton that Turchin was "entirely unfit" for promotion.[28]

Mitchel's career, in contrast, failed to recover from the incident. Up to that time, he had been popular with his troops, in part because he had few qualms about allowing them to make themselves comfortable at the expense of secessionist civilians. "Gen. Mitchell is the man, in him we have confidence," one wrote in his diary in May 1862. It was not his harsh attitude toward the victims of Turchin's act, but his refusal to stand by Turchin in its aftermath that turned his men against him. Mitchel's lust for glory and pettiness toward fellow officers was hard to hide and led some soldiers to suspect that he had persuaded Buell to break up the Eighth Brigade because he was jealous of Turchin's achievements.[29] Turchin himself thought that Mitchel owed his military reputation to the Eighth Brigade and told him so: "Yes, Gen., [my brigade] placed dot star on your shoulder too, Got dam; my Brigate do dat too." By the end of June one officer went so far as to claim that Mitchel's soldiers had come to "look upon him as a lunatic." Having alienated his commander, his officers, and his soldiers, Mitchel asked his patron Stanton for another assignment, then denied to Buell that he had made any such request. In July he was sent to the coast of South Carolina as commander of the Department of the South, where he died of yellow fever within a few months.[30]

By the end of the summer of 1862, the official response to the sack of Athens had polarized the Army of the Ohio into "hard war" and "soft war" factions. Buell's punishment of the Eighth Brigade and Colonel Turchin gave many soldiers the impression that he cared more for the people of the South than for his own troops and "embittered them against the commander of the army," according to Colonel Marcus Mundy of the 23rd Kentucky. James Shaw of the 10th Indiana agreed that Buell's policy "prejudiced the men against him." John Beatty, colonel of the 3rd Ohio, disapproved of Turchin's behavior but resented what he called the "dancing-master policy" of Buell even more: "[Buell says to] the bushwhacker: '. . . Now do, my good fellows, stop, I beg of you. . . . [I]n the meantime we propose to protect your property and guard your negroes.'" "General Buell with kid-glove policy uses all his influence to dismiss the energetic General Turchin," wrote Joseph Johnston, a frustrated member of the 19th Illinois. The great contrast in popularity between Turchin, an extrovert who was not above playing leapfrog with his men, and the "cold, smooth-toned, silent" General Buell personalized and intensified the conflict over policy.[31]

The treatment of escaped slaves became an increasingly controversial aspect of Buell's "soft war" policy. Initially, when the Army of the Ohio was fighting to keep the slaveholding state of Kentucky in the Union, opposition to slavery was incompatible with the army's mission. In September 1861 Robert Anderson had warned Lincoln that on hearing of an emancipation decree issued by General Frémont in Missouri, "a whole company of our Volunteers threw down their arms and disbanded." Speaking at the 10th Indiana's flag presentation ceremony in Louisville in December 1861, Colonel Mahlon D. Manson assured his Kentucky audience that "We wage no Abolition crusade" and that his men would "scorn the imputation" of abolitionism. Many other generals, notably Lovell Rousseau, made no secret of their antiabolitionist opinions, and Alexander McCook proudly stated in December 1862 that "I have been abused by the Abolition press North and I hope I shall continue to be."[32]

Such views were not limited to the army's leaders. Daniel Finn, a musician with the 10th Ohio, noted in his diary that after taking advantage of the services of an escaped slave, he and his comrades had "sent our *niggar* home to his master, with a letter stating we were no abolitionists." The Emancipation Proclamation "was not received with good grace by the common soldier" of the 42nd Indiana, according to a member of the regiment, and fifteen officers resigned from the 38th Indiana in 1862–63 because they objected to the policy of enlisting African American soldiers. The exclusively midwestern origin of the Army of the Ohio, unleavened by the presence of regiments or generals from abolitionist New England, was reflected in the widespread racism and antiabolitionism of its members.[33]

According to Rousseau, the former slave owner Buell "desired to have as little to do with the slaves as might be," but with the army's advance into Confederate territory in 1862, the ever-growing numbers of self-emancipated African Americans who flocked to the camps of the Army of the Ohio forced him to make decisions exposing his belief that slaves were a species of property like any other. Buell "desired that loyal men should have their negroes" and on occasion personally ordered the return of slaves to their owners. His lack of sympathy for the refugees from slavery following his army emerged most clearly in a brutal order issued on June 21 to Alexander McCook, whose division was being ferried across the Tennessee River at Tuscumbia. McCook was instructed to prevent any fugitive slaves from crossing the river with his command, thus leaving hundreds, perhaps thousands, of escaped slaves stranded on the southern bank, at the mercy of local authorities.[34]

Over time, more and more soldiers in the Army of the Ohio began to oppose the institution of slavery. Some were shocked by their first exposure to its realities. Colonel Beatty of the 3rd Ohio recalled being taken aback by the sight of a "Negroes Bought and Sold" sign he saw south of Louisville in November 1861. A few may have been troubled by the army's abandonment of the refugees at Tuscumbia. A larger number, like the officers of the 42nd Indiana who considered resigning over the Emancipation Proclamation but reconsidered and accepted it as a war measure, came to see abolition as a way of bringing the war home to the South.[35]

As antislavery sentiment spread, William Sumner Dodge of the Second Division recorded, "the growing radicalism of the army found [Buell's] administration faulty." In March 1862, the same month that Congress prohibited army officers from returning fugitive slaves, Buell issued orders that all such fugitives be returned to their owners or expelled from the army's camps. When loyal Kentucky slaveholders tried to enter regimental camps to retrieve their runaway "property," however, they found themselves increasingly likely to be thwarted by enlisted men and officers who refused to cooperate, even under direct orders. Angry soldiers of the 21st Wisconsin and 24th Illinois went so far as to threaten the otherwise popular Lovell Rousseau with a beating when he tried to punish some of them for driving off a slave catcher. As late as August 1862, Brigadier General T. J. Wood made it a practice "without particularly inquiring into the question of the owner's loyalty, to allow citizens to reclaim fugitive negroes in our lines" in order to "convince the people it was not our design to interfere with the slaves of the country," but when the wife of a known rebel officer insisted on the return of a slave to her Tennessee plantation, even Wood felt compelled to ask Buell if the policy ought to be changed. Buell agreed that such slaves should not be returned, but he specified that fugitives who could not be put to work for the government had to be expelled from the army's lines, which in most cases doomed them to be recaptured.[36]

"I wish we had fewer pro-slavery Gen[eral]s," Lieutenant George Landrum wrote home in July 1862. The Army of the Ohio certainly waged no abolition crusade, but by the end of the summer of 1862 it was no longer in sympathy with Buell's policy toward slavery. In his diary, Major James Connolly of the 123rd Illinois expressed the army's emerging view: "Oh! for an active earnest leader from the free states! One who sees nothing sacred in negro slavery."[37]

Buell's insistence on maintaining a "soft war" policy, regardless of the growing opposition of his troops, was symptomatic of his leadership style, which in turn played a significant role in the army's failure to coalesce in 1862. As the army increasingly disagreed with its commander over the right way to fight the war, Buell continued to give orders rather than explanations. He thought that his men ought to do as they were told simply because they were soldiers. He never took seriously the volunteers' belief that their opinions on politics, strategy, or anything else deserved any consideration from him. Grant, who had a better understanding of the psychology of the volunteer soldier, wrote that Buell "was a strict disciplinarian, and perhaps did not distinguish sufficiently between the volunteer who 'enlisted for the war' and the soldier who serves in time of peace. One system embraced men who risked life for a principle, and often men of social standing, competence, or wealth, and independence of character. The other includes as a rule, only men who could not do as well in any other occupation."[38]

If Buell recognized a distinction between volunteers and Regulars, it was only to consider the former inferior soldiers. A quarter of a century after he commanded the Army of the Ohio, he looked back with nostalgia on his Mexican War experience in a letter to fellow West Pointer William F. Smith. The war with Mexico, Buell wrote, "was substantially fought by educated soldiers. Even the volunteers were largely moulded and inspired by West Point men—Davis, Clay, Sidney Johnston, Marshall, and a host of others." Whatever success came to the volunteer forces in Mexico was owed to the support of the

Regular artillery and "the influence of an army command and staff that were wholly and thoroughly *Regular*." In Buell's affectionate memory, volunteers could never measure up to Regulars, not even such Regulars as Jefferson Davis and Albert Sidney Johnston, who later turned against the flag for which Buell fought.[39]

Placed in command of a volunteer army, Buell had little idea how to motivate his troops. When they performed poorly, he berated them publicly and appealed to their "professional pride" to do better. When he tried to praise them, he focused on their discipline and appearance, not their service to the Union cause or the glory of the Army of the Ohio.[40] Henry Halleck, hardly the most inspirational leader of the war, wrote a farewell to the armies of the West on his appointment as general in chief in July 1862, ending with: "Soldiers! you have accomplished much toward crushing out this wicked rebellion, and if you continue to exhibit the same vigilance, courage, and perseverance it is believed that, under the providence of God, you will soon bring the war to a close and be able to return in peace to your families and homes."[41] Compare the closing passage of Buell's last message to his army, later the same year: "The general reflects with pride that the army under his command has for the most part been free from petty jealousies and intrigues; that it has neither indulged in vain boasting nor tarnished its high character by bickerings and low criminations. . . . He will pray that it may be the instrument of speedily restoring the Union to its integrity, and there is no individual in its ranks in whose honor and welfare he will not feel a special interest."[42] Buell's reference to himself in the third person, the laundry list of sins that the army "for the most part" managed to avoid, the double negative in the last phrase, and the generally lukewarm tone of the message are indicative of the emotional distance that separated Buell from his soldiers.

Don Carlos Buell was, in the memorable characterization of T. Harry Williams, "a McClellan without charm or glamor." Buell rivaled McClellan as a successful administrator, but was too absorbed in details to provide the kind of grand, symbolic leadership necessary to unite a large volunteer army. "I have frequently felt that had he visited his camps more, reviewed his troops more, and shown himself more to his soldiers," Alexander McCook testified in December 1862, "a different state of feeling would have existed." Instead, Buell neglected to consult with his subordinates, spent no time chatting with enlisted men, and gave no grand speeches. He did not engage in Napoleonic posturing or turn his army into a cult of personality, as McClellan did with the Army of the Potomac, nor did he draw attention to himself by modestly affecting the appearance of a "simple soldier," as did Grant. He was even reluctant to have his picture taken, unlike Lincoln, whose willingness to pose for photographers made him at once more accessible and more popular. If Buell had cared more deeply about his image in the eyes of his men, or had done more to create a mystique and enhance the sense of identity of the Army of the Ohio, he would have provided his men with an icon to which they could have given their love and loyalty beyond the confines of their regiments. His failure to do so was not critical only as long as he commanded the army's respect for his professional competence. When a series of setbacks brought his ability into question in the summer of 1862, Buell found no reserve of good-will among his men.[43]

"I Need More Good Staff Officers"

Buell's administrative ability was tested to its limit by the problem of keeping the army supplied during the Chattanooga campaign. Like all Civil War generals, he had to rely on a network of staff officers to secure and distribute the food, fodder, equipment, arms, medical stores, and other commodities needed to maintain his command as an efficient fighting organization. In theory, there should have been an adjutant general, quartermaster, ordnance officer, engineer, inspector, medical officer, and provost marshal at Buell's headquarters, and a similar staff at the headquarters of each brigade and division, to perform these vital administrative tasks. In fact, the Army of the Ohio (like most of the other improvised field armies of the war) was critically hampered by a shortage of professionally trained staff officers.

From its inception, the Army of the Ohio needed more staff officers at every level. "[E]very moment of my time is occupied until one or two o'clock at night," Buell wrote on assuming command of the army in November 1861, in part because he had to do so much of his own staff work, including answering requests for furloughs from individual volunteers who felt themselves entitled to meet with the commanding general on demand. O. M. Mitchel had no staff at all when he took command of the Third Division in 1861, his son recorded, which meant that "every captain of a company, hospital steward, or wagon-master, felt at liberty to address the general direct for any required article, be it a hundred rounds of ammunition or a bottle of medicine." As late as June 1862, Mitchel was still complaining to Halleck that "I have not a single brigade quartermaster in my entire division." George Thomas's division was short of staff officers in September 1861, but when he asked Robert Anderson for more, he was told: "I regret that you have not been able to get staff officers. I am in the same condition." Buell received much the same answer when in November 1861 he wrote to McClellan: "I am greatly in need of general and staff officers. My own staff force is entirely insufficient." On December 8 Buell repeated his plea: "We are greatly in want of staff officers and brigadiers."[44]

McClellan, however, did not have enough staff officers for his own army, much less any to spare for the Army of the Ohio. In 1861 there were few enough professional staff officers in the Regular Army, and on the outbreak of war most of them (including Buell himself) sought and received more glamorous appointments as commanders of combat units. Those who stayed in staff positions tended to remain near Washington, where they were "absorbed by the Army of the Potomac," as Halleck informed Buell in June 1862. Of necessity, many staff roles had to be filled by volunteer officers, but few of them relished such duty, since it took them away from their military "families." "I do not like the idea of leaving my company and mess," wrote Lieutenant George Landrum when he was detailed to the Third Division's newly formed signal corps.[45]

Those volunteers who accepted staff appointments were not always the best qualified, an example being the ingenuous patriot who wrote to the secretary of state in April 1861: "Not being sufficiently acquainted with military details to take a Captaincy or Lieutenancy, I have been advised to seek a staff appointment." Even the most efficient volunteers had to go through a period of trial and error as they learned the mysteries of army staff work. Sergeant Samuel McIlvaine of the 10th Indiana described in his diary how he spent nine days preparing his regiment's payroll, only to be told that he had been given the wrong forms and had to start again.[46]

To compound the problem, although the War Department could not possibly find enough specialists to meet the staff needs of every Union field army, it issued a general order in February 1862 reminding commanders that although they could detail subordinates to temporary staff duty, they were not authorized to make permanent staff appointments, which were the prerogative of the chief executive. The assistant adjutants general, assistant quartermasters, commissaries of subsistence, surgeons, and paymasters for each division and brigade all had to be formally appointed by Abraham Lincoln, which made the busy commander in chief's desk into a bottleneck through which staff appointments passed too slowly to suit General Buell. "I need more good staff officers in every department" was an unending refrain in Buell's correspondence with Washington.[47]

Where staff resources were available, Buell and his division commanders did not always take full advantage of them. This was particularly evident in the mishandling of the signal corps of the Army of the Ohio. The innovative idea of a unit dedicated to communications, using the wigwag flag system, colored rockets, and field telegraph stations, was introduced to the army early in 1862.

Buell had each division organize a signals unit, which entailed the usual difficulties of finding qualified volunteers to leave their regiments. In the First Division, the men detailed to the signals unit continued to march with their own regiments, rather than travel with the division headquarters. In the Second Division, four lieutenants and eight soldiers from each brigade were assigned to signals duty in January 1862, but the detachment had limited success, as even the scientifically inclined astronomer-general O. M. Mitchel "don't [sic] understand the signals, and so won't use them," according to one of his officers. In May 1862 Buell temporarily disbanded the army's signal corps, needlessly forfeiting a potentially valuable capability.[48] Once the army was out of the forests of northern Mississippi, the divisional signals units were re-established, on one occasion using improvised flags made from petticoats, but communications continued to be a problem for the army.[49]

The shortage of competent staff officers directly interfered with operations. In June and July 1862 the Army of the Ohio needed a minimum of fifty tons of food daily just for sustenance. To meet the army's current needs and to build up a reserve to support an attack on Chattanooga, Buell's staff tried to secure from two hundred to three hundred tons of food each day, plus forage for the army's thousands of horses and mules.[50] Since this was far more than the vulnerable Memphis & Charleston Railroad could supply, Buell ordered his staff to accumulate a substantial amount of food and forage at Athens, Alabama, by June 22, so that the campaign against Chattanooga could continue without delay. Buell's order went unexecuted. "We expected 150,000 rations of forage at Athens and found none," Buell's chief of staff Colonel James B. Fry telegraphed angrily to his subordinate in Nashville, "Why is this?"[51] Part of the problem, Fry learned, was that some staff officers were neglecting their duties by failing to relay messages to their proper destinations and by working only during normal business hours. "This method of doing duty will not answer," Fry warned one quartermaster, but results did not improve. The price for such neglect was paid by the men in the ranks, like those in the 6th Indiana who marched across northern Alabama singing "Aaway down South in the land of cotton / They give us half rations and they're half rotten."[52]

"They Rushed Down upon Us Like a Wild Tornado"

Rebel cavalry roamed seemingly at will through Tennessee and Kentucky in July 1862, disrupting the already strained logistics of the Army of the Ohio. On July 4 John Hunt Morgan and a thousand mounted raiders set out from Knoxville, headed for Kentucky via the Cumberland Gap. Over the next twenty-four days Morgan's men rode a thousand miles, tearing up railroads and tele-graph lines, capturing or destroying military stores, blowing up bridges, and otherwise wreaking havoc. "They are having a stampede in Kentucky," Lin-coln advised Halleck, his new general in chief. "Please look to it."[53]

Bureaucratic confusion hobbled Union efforts to stop Morgan. In May, the War Department had appointed Brigadier General J. T. Boyle to command all Union troops in Kentucky except those already belonging to the Army of the Ohio. On June 8 Kentucky and Tennessee were made part of the Department of the Mississippi, then under Halleck. When Morgan roared through the Bluegrass state, responsibility for its defense was divided between Buell and Boyle, who were unable to coordinate their forces. Boyle, who later admitted that in July 1862 he was not even certain in whose district his command lay, did little more than issue urgent calls to Buell, Halleck, and Stanton for reinforcements. The apparent helplessness of these leaders in the face of Mor-gan's tiny force did nothing to shake the conviction of the average soldier in Buell's army that no military organization beyond his regiment was worthy of his trust.[54]

While Morgan was traveling through Kentucky, Confederate cavalry wiz-ard Nathan Bedford Forrest was preparing to undertake an even more de-structive raid. Forrest's objective was the Union camp at Murfreesboro, Ten-nessee, on the railroad between Nashville and the main body of the Army of the Ohio near Chattanooga. Murfreesboro was a critical link in the army's supply line and the site of a large concentration of stores that Buell was amassing in preparation for a renewed advance. The garrison of Murfreesboro consisted of about eight hundred men of the Twenty-third Brigade, including nine companies of the 3rd Minnesota, six companies of the 9th Michigan, four guns of Hewitt's Kentucky artillery, and two cavalry companies from Pennsyl-vania. The senior officer of the Twenty-third Brigade was Colonel William W. Duffield of the 9th Michigan, who was absent on leave at the beginning of July, leaving command of the post in the hands of Colonel Henry C. Lester of the 3rd Minnesota.[55]

Although Murfreesboro was of obvious strategic importance, it received little attention from army headquarters. Back in April, Colonel Duffield had been informed that his brigade was independent of any division, but that he should report to O. M. Mitchel for instructions. At the same time Colonel Lester had received instructions from Brigadier General Ebenezer Dumont, the commander of Union forces in Nashville, to report to him directly rather than through Duffield, Lester's brigade commander. Duffield's difficulties were compounded when his requests for additional cavalry were refused, and various bits and pieces of the Twenty-third Brigade were assigned to duty elsewhere. By July, units of the Twenty-third Brigade not at Murfreesboro included the 8th Kentucky, which had been sent to Nashville in answer to Governor Andrew Johnson's repeated requests for more men, and the 23rd Kentucky, which had been detached since May.[56]

The men of the garrison were fiercely loyal to their individual regiments but cared little for the other units with which they were brigaded. Lester had quarreled with the acting commander of the 9th Michigan, Lieutenant Colonel John G. Parkhurst, over the locations of the Minnesota and Michigan regiments' camps, and the ill will had spread to the men of the two units, creating what Colonel Duffield later described as "a great lack of discipline and a bitter feeling of jealousy between the different regiments, manifesting itself in the personal encounters of the men when they met upon the street." Colonel Lester moved the 3rd Minnesota's camp two miles away from the Michigan troops, well out of supporting distance in the event of an attack. Parkhurst was eager for Duffield to return, anticipating that Duffield would favor the 9th Michigan over the Minnesotans and arouse the jealousy of Colonel Lester.[57]

Colonel Duffield returned to Murfreesboro on July 11. With him came Brigadier General Thomas T. Crittenden, a cousin of the Fifth Division's commander, who had orders to assume command of the post. Duffield and Crittenden were surprised to find that Colonel Lester had scattered the garrison and done nothing to prepare for the defense of the vital supply depot, an omission that even the author of Minnesota's official history of the war admitted was "somewhat remarkable." To reduce the vulnerability of the position, Crittenden and Duffield agreed that the entire garrison should be consolidated into one camp, but they took no further action on the day of their arrival, relying on Lester's assurance that there were no enemy troops nearby.[58]

At 4:00 A.M. the next day, Forrest's horsemen swept into the town. The first troops they encountered were the two companies of Pennsylvania cavalry, still asleep in their tents. While the Confederates overran the cavalry camp, the men of the 9th Michigan nearby struggled to grab their weapons and form a defensive line. One of them, John C. Love, "caught the sound of cavelry [sic] as they rushed down upon us like a wild tornado[;] I sprung from my bed and began to shriek for the men to turn out." Among the first casualties was Colonel Duffield, who suffered wounds in the right testicle and left thigh, which he described as "very painful and bleeding profusely." Lieutenant Colonel Parkhurst tried to form the regiment in a square, but the men knew how to make a square only if they were already formed in a line or column, and there was no time for that. Many of them were still dressed in their underwear as they rushed about trying find their places in the regimental formation.

Before they could do so, the enemy cavalry were upon them, forcing most of the Michiganders to fight as individuals. Hiding behind trees and fences, they fired at Forrest's troopers as the opportunity offered. After about fifteen minutes, the Confederates galloped off as quickly as they had arrived, leaving the survivors of the 9th Michigan to gather their wounded and stake out a defensive position in the fenced yard of a nearby log house.[59]

While some of Forrest's raiders were battling the main body of the 9th Michigan, others were confronting Company B of the same regiment, which was serving as provost guard in the center of Murfreesboro. The men of Company B, cut off from their comrades by the sudden onslaught, occupied the town's brick courthouse. Protected by the walls of their improvised fortress, they held their position until the building caught fire, when they were forced to surrender. By mid-morning Forrest had undisputed control of Murfreesboro. He put his men to burning all that they could not carry away of the supplies that Buell had so painstakingly collected.[60]

In the camp of the 3rd Minnesota, Colonel Lester and his men could hear the sounds of fighting only a mile away. The regiment quickly fell in, advanced toward the town, and then halted, supported by Hewitt's battery. Here the regiment remained, while parties of Confederate cavalry slipped behind the line of infantry and burned their camp. Messengers arrived from Parkhurst begging Lester to advance to the relief of the remnant of the 9th Michigan, still holding out at the log house. The Minnesota soldiers were eager to fight, but Lester refused to order them forward. At 1:00 P.M. Parkhurst and his troops finally surrendered, having lost twelve killed and at least fifty wounded, including Colonel Duffield, who had fainted from pain and loss of blood. Forrest then invited Lester to meet him in the middle of the town, under a flag of truce, where Forrest paraded his force in Lester's view and produced an officer of the 9th Michigan to convince him that the rest of the garrison had surrendered.[61]

Lester returned to his regiment and put the question of surrender to a vote of his company leaders. When they urged him to fight, he called for another vote. This time they gave in to their commander's apparent wish to surrender, much against the will of the rank and file.[62] A Michigan soldier relayed to his wife an account of the scene, as described to him a few days afterward: "The men did not want to surrender & said they would rather die on the spot. . . . brave men were seen to shed tears & were unwilling to yield & others, broke their guns by striking them against trees & rocks. They charge their Col[onel] with cowardice."[63] The surrender of the 3rd Minnesota made Lester a pariah. Before leaving Murfreesboro, the Confederates paroled the enlisted men they had captured and sent them north to be held at Camp Chase, Ohio, until they could be exchanged for a like number of Southern prisoners. On their way to captivity, a 9th Michigan veteran wrote, "the Minnesota boys spent a good share of their time in cursing Col. Lester for his cowardice." Forrest's men, who carried off the officers they had captured, shared the same view of Lester and treated him with a disdain that they did not show their other prisoners. Fifty years later, in a history of Buell's 1862 campaigns, veteran Henry Stone still could not bring himself even to write Lester's name, referring to him only as the "pusillanimous colonel" who had surrendered the 3rd Minnesota at Murfreesboro.[64]

The fiasco at Murfreesboro showed the high price of Buell's failure to unite the army's regiments into effective brigades and divisions. He tried to defend against further raids by stationing garrisons at every vulnerable point along his lengthy supply lines, which led to what Colonel John Beatty described as an "insane effort to garrison the whole country." Morgan nevertheless continued to inflict humiliating defeats on Union detachments—at Gallatin, Tennessee, on August 12, Clarksville on August 18, and Hartsville on August 21. At Gallatin Morgan's men destroyed a vital railroad tunnel, and at Hartsville they added General Richard Johnson to the hundreds of other Union troops they had captured. Buell's garrison commanders sent out regiments of infantry in pursuit of the raiders, in the vain hope that the mounted troops of Morgan and Forrest would hold still long enough to be trapped by foot soldiers.[65]

The success of these raids offered further proof of the bankruptcy of Buell's attempt to pacify the population of Tennessee and northern Alabama by zealously guarding their property rights. In spite of the solicitous treatment they received, many civilians supplied the rebel raiders with the food, water, and information they needed to travel light and stay ahead of their pursuers. Other civilians even engaged in guerrilla warfare in the Union army's rear areas. Such behavior occasionally tried the soldiers' patience with Buell's "soft war" policies beyond its breaking point, notably on August 6, when guerrillas attacked a party of cavalry escorting Brigadier General Robert McCook, who was ill and confined to an ambulance. The guerrillas lured the escort away and murdered the helpless general. The soldiers of the 9th Ohio, McCook's original regiment, responded to the atrocity in kind, hanging civilians and burning houses for miles around.[66]

Buell expressed regret for McCook's death but did not publicly condemn the guerrillas or reconsider his policy toward civilians. He used much harsher language to criticize his own troops after the debacle at Murfreesboro, when he vented his frustration by indiscriminately lashing out at the entire garrison. "Take it in all its features," Buell wrote of the surrender in General Orders No. 32 on July 21, "few more disgraceful examples of neglect of duty and lack

The death of General Robert McCook at the hands of Confederate guerrillas in August 1862 received national attention. Buell alienated many of his soldiers by refusing to undertake reprisals. From *Frank Leslie's Illustrated Newspaper*, August 30, 1862; photograph courtesy of The Lincoln Museum, Fort Wayne, Indiana (TLM #4542).

of good conduct can be found in the history of wars." When the major commanding the 9th Michigan's four companies that had not been at Murfreesboro submitted a requisition for supplies, Buell allegedly responded that "The Mich 9th has lost enough property belonging to U.S. and could wait a while."[67]

Buell's anger was understandable, for the loss of the supply depot crippled his plan for resuming the advance on Chattanooga. As one of his staff officers later noted, the fall of Murfreesboro would prove to be "a fatal blow" not only to the campaign, but to the general's career as well.[68]

CHAPTER SIX

The Invasion of Kentucky, August to September 1862

The Murfreesboro disaster, in Buell's opinion, set back his already lengthy preparations for the Chattanooga campaign by a full two weeks. In the aftermath of the raid, the men of the Army of the Ohio doggedly went back to work, collecting supplies, securing their lines of communications, and attending to the "thousand other details" that their commander considered "infinitely important to our existence, and absolutely necessary for the first step in advance."[1] Some observers, like journalist Henry Villard, thought that Buell required "a greater degree of readiness" than necessary and that even without the raid, the Army of the Ohio would never meet Buell's exacting standards.[2]

Ready or not, Buell found himself forced into action on August 14, when an enemy corps led by Major General Edmund Kirby Smith left its base in Knoxville and headed north, seizing the strategic initiative. Kirby Smith's troops marched around the isolated Union garrison at Cumberland Gap and entered central Kentucky, threatening Frankfort and Cincinnati. While Buell pondered his response, an even more immediate danger arose. On August 28 the main Confederate army in the West, led by General Braxton Bragg, crossed the Tennessee River near Chattanooga and launched a counteroffensive that threatened to trap and destroy the Army of the Ohio.

Over the course of the next month, Bragg's troops marched around the Army of the Ohio, through middle Tennessee, and deep into Kentucky toward Louisville. Buell could not afford to risk the loss of Louisville with its vital railroad bridges over the Ohio River, and he drove his men relentlessly northward in pursuit of Bragg. Buell's soldiers reached the city first, by a slim margin. Although the long retreat from the Tennessee to the Ohio River sapped their strength and destroyed their faith in their leader's strategic ability and willingness to fight, they retained their confidence in themselves and their regiments. After taking a few days to rest and to assimilate several dozen newly recruited regiments fresh from the North, the Army of the Ohio resumed its march, this time to seek a battlefield showdown with the forces of Bragg and Kirby Smith.

"As Good a Regament as Their Is in Servise"

In April 1862, when the end of the war had seemed imminent, the War Department had optimistically stopped accepting volunteers. Three months later, with the Army of the Ohio stalled in front of Chattanooga and the Army of the Potomac equally immobile before Richmond, it was clear that the restoration of the Union would take more time and blood than anyone had previously imagined. In July Lincoln issued a call for another three hundred thousand men to fill the depleted ranks of his armies. Many of these reinforcements were sent to the Army of the Ohio, which by August 1 could muster no more than sixty-four thousand men, including G. W. Morgan's Seventh Division at Cumberland Gap and the troops scattered across Tennessee and Alabama, to protect the army's lines of communication.[3]

Some of those who answered Lincoln's call enlisted in existing regiments, which periodically sent officers home to find replacements from the same communities that had supplied their initial personnel.[4] But most of the July volunteers chose to sign up with their friends as charter members of new, locally raised companies. These companies, in turn, were assigned to serve in the new regiments that their states continued to create. It suited Northern politicians to organize fresh regiments instead of reinforcing old ones because new units required new officers whose appointments could be dispensed as patronage, but the result of this practice was that the Army of the Ohio (and other Union armies) received most of its reinforcements in the form of whole regiments, each of which was as completely innocent of military knowledge and experience as the rest of the army had been a year ago.

These new regiments were as geographically homogeneous as the army's original units, if not more so. Volunteers were harder to come by than they had been in the feverish weeks that followed the attack on Fort Sumter, as Albion Tourgée found when raising a company for the 105th Ohio, since "the men who cared for military glory or adventure" and the "excitable or impressible" boys had long since enlisted. To make recruiting easier, the states of Michigan, Illinois, Wisconsin, and Ohio in 1862 all adopted Indiana's practice of assigning a specific recruiting district to each new regiment. This stimulated local pride, reduced competition among recruiters, and gave each regiment a distinct character based not only on state pride, but also on identity with a specific county or township. Finding volunteers was still slow work for recruiters like Lieutenant Tourgée, who spent weeks "traveling from town to town, holding personal interviews by day and public meetings usually at night" to fill out his company.[5]

If perhaps less "excitable or impressible" than earlier volunteers, the men who became part of the Army of the Ohio in the summer and fall of 1862 brought the same loyalty to their companies that distinguished their predecessors. James G. Theaker was among a small group of volunteers from Belmont County, Ohio, who arrived at Camp Dennison to discover that they might not be allowed to serve as a company. "When we arrived here we found that Col. [Daniel] McCook's reg. was about full, nine full companies and two fractions (ours one of them)," Theaker wrote to his brother. "He (the Colonel) said he would give us that night to consolidate with other cos. If we did not, *he would* for us the next day, when we would perhaps be divided up and lose our officers. This, you may know, caused no little excitement. All very much dissatisfied, uncomfortable, and unhappy. . . . We resolved to stick together and to Capt. Clark." To the relief of the Belmont men, the colonel of another regiment offered to give them a few days to fill their ranks, after which he would fill the ranks himself (if they had not succeeded) in exchange for the right to choose one of the company's officers. They accepted his proposition and thus became part of the 50th Ohio.[6]

As the "boys of '62" began to experience army life, they expressed the hopes, fears, and reactions typical of new soldiers. In the privacy of his diary John Wesley Marshall of the 97th Ohio faced the future bravely, proclaiming "let the hardships be what they may I will never regret volunteering to defend and perpetuate these noble institutions." He and his comrades spent their first week in Kentucky digging trenches and sleeping in wet clothes, hardships that Marshall naively considered "as hard as any regiment was ever called on to pass through in the start." In September a new member of the Chicago Board of Trade Battery complained about receiving nothing to eat but "Hard Bread, Bacon, Sugar & Coffee[,] Rice & Beans," a full menu that would have been very welcome to the army's veterans, then living on half rations at the far end of a supply line that stretched to the banks of the Tennessee. Concerns more serious than food were on the minds of recruits like John Daniel Shank, of the 125th Illinois, who wrote bleakly to his parents and sister, "I will right again meby. I don't now how soon I may be killed." Others doubtless harbored similar fears but tried to suppress them beneath the pride they took in their units. "I think we have as good a regament as their is in servise," Thomas Frazee boasted to his parents on behalf of the 73rd Illinois.[7]

The new volunteers proved just as reluctant to give up their civil rights and yield to military discipline as those who enlisted earlier had been. In a letter he wrote sixty years later, Silas Stevens of the Chicago Board of Trade Battery still resented his wartime commander. "A West-point officer and a strict disciplinarian may make good machine soldiers," Stevens claimed, "but to us free born citizens of a free republic, we could not present him the affections that men give toward a real commander, or a mighty leader." As in 1861, many volunteers felt entitled to choose their own officers. The men of the 18th Indiana Light Artillery elected Eli Lilly their captain on August 7, then eight weeks later signed a petition to Governor Morton to have him removed because his harsh discipline denied the men their "writes" as citizens. But Morton ignored the petition, and, as Wilbur F. Hinman of the 65th Ohio observed, the officer elections held in the fall of 1862 often were no more than charades to soothe the pride of the citizen-soldiers and were not considered binding by the state and Federal authorities that issued officers' commissions. James Theaker recognized this when he wrote home to announce that he had been elected a first lieutenant, adding that "The Colonel intended to make me 1st Lieut. anyhow."[8]

Although enlisted men (in old units as well as new) could no longer count on being able to choose their officers with the ballot, some of them expressed their awareness of the more fundamental power of the bullet, a power that all combat soldiers hold over their officers. In September 1862 a disaffected member of the 86th Illinois wrote that his brigade commander Daniel Mc-Cook was "held in utter contempt by all who know him, so much so that the boys say that if ever they get into battle he is the first man who will fall by their own lead." Threats of this kind were almost unimaginable in 1861, but by the war's second summer such murders had already taken place. When Captain Lewis Hosea wrote of the seemingly heroic death of Lieutenant P. T. Keyes, who had fallen at his side on the second day at Shiloh, he was perhaps unaware of the likelihood that Keyes had been killed by one of his own men. The day before the battle Keyes had abused and struck some soldiers for marching too slowly, provoking a straggler to yell, "I'll shoot you the first chance I get." After the battle another man in Keyes's regiment wrote privately, "Whether Jim shot him or the enemy [did] we never knew but the co[mpany] were glad to be rid of him."[9]

It would take time for the volunteers of 1862 to complete the same tedious and inefficient self-education in drill, discipline, and camp life that had turned their predecessors into soldiers. With veterans in the ranks to share the lessons learned in a year of campaigning and "seeing the elephant," the process might have gone much faster. John Pierson of the 10th Michigan explained to his wife that "it would Strengthen the Army very much to fill up the old Regiments[,] as the new recruits mixed in with Drilled Soldiers would Stand fire much better." Buell felt the same way, writing that "a vast waste of time, and material, and efficiency was caused by this plan of throwing large numbers of raw troops suddenly into service in distinct bodies." But there is no evidence that he ever considered trying to remedy this by breaking up his regiments and reforming them as mixed units of new and old companies. Even as an army commander, Buell was powerless to violate the sanctity of the regiment.[10]

"The Result Was What Might Have Been Expected"

Few of the regiments recruited in July had left their home states by August 16, the day that Kirby Smith's force entered Kentucky. Since the main body of the Army of the Ohio was almost two hundred miles to the south, unable to interfere with the invaders' progress, responsibility for stopping Kirby Smith fell on J. T. Boyle, commander of all Union troops in the state except those already subordinate to Buell. To reinforce Boyle, an inexperienced officer whose propensity to panic had been amply demonstrated during Morgan's recent cavalry raid, Buell hastily called on dozens of the new, untrained regiments to leave their camps in Indiana and Ohio and hurry to Louisville or Cincinnati.[11]

Rather than rely on Boyle, Buell on August 17 dispatched William Nelson to take over the defense of Kentucky. Despite Nelson's prickly reputation, Buell considered him "always solicitous about the well-being of his troops" and expressed "great confidence in his energy and ability" to organize and discipline the inexperienced men of his new command. Nelson, however, was as arrogant and difficult to work with as ever. He had no regard for Boyle, of whom he had written to Buell on July 19, "Boyle telegraphs me to death. I think he has lost his senses." Before leaving the Fourth Division to take up his new assignment, Nelson antagonized the paroled Union prisoners from the Murfreesboro garrison by ordering them to disregard their paroles and participate in his division's operations. When they rightly refused, he berated them for the surrender of the post "as if it had been their fault" and allegedly ordered one of them shot for speaking in defense of his regiment.[12]

Nelson's mission was hampered by tangled lines of military authority. Officially, Kentucky had been part of Halleck's Department of the Mississippi until July 16, when Halleck left for Washington to become general in chief. On that day the District of the Ohio, including Kentucky and Tennessee east of the Tennessee River, was removed from the Department of the Mississippi so that Buell (the district commander) could continue to report directly to Halleck. Although central Kentucky lay within Buell's district, Boyle was independently responsible for most Union forces in the state. Nelson's appointment seemed to supersede Boyle entirely, which upset Boyle so much that Buell had to coax him out of resigning. To complicate matters further, on August 19 the War Department created a new Department of the Ohio, which included Kentucky east of the Tennessee River, under Major General Horatio G. Wright. Halleck explained to Buell that the new department "does not affect Tennessee or your army . . . but includes all troops now in Kentucky," adding, "You, however, will continue the general direction of affairs in that State until General Wright arrives."[13]

This was news to Nelson, who reached Louisville on August 23. There he was surprised to meet Wright, "who arrived in this city one hour before, and is announced to command the new Department of the Ohio." Nelson immediately asked Halleck if he should return to Buell's army in Tennessee. On August 24 Wright formally replaced Boyle as commander of Union forces in Kentucky but then gave Boyle control of the troops in Louisville. The same day Nelson relieved Major General Lew Wallace, who had assumed temporary command of the raw regiments gathering at Lexington, in the path of Kirby Smith's invading army. With Halleck, Wright, Buell, Boyle, Wallace, and Nelson all at one time or another issuing operational orders relating to the defense of Kentucky, confusion was inevitable. Halleck, for example, ordered Wright to make the relief of Morgan's division at Cumberland Gap his priority, contrary to Buell's orders to Nelson that protecting Louisville was the most important objective.[14]

Nelson immediately set to work organizing his raw troops into a new Army of Kentucky. To assist him, he brought along Mahlon D. Manson, who had been promoted to brigadier general; in Kentucky, Nelson was assigned two more brigadier generals, James S. Jackson and Charles Cruft. Manson and Cruft had served under Nelson before, not always to his satisfaction. From the newly arrived regiments Nelson created three brigades, each with four infantry regiments and an artillery battery, for his three brigadiers.[15] On August 27 Nelson reported to General Wright on the condition of two of the brigades, stationed at Richmond just north of Kirby Smith's forces: "I find that there is no discipline among these troops. Straggling, marauding, plundering is the rule; good conduct the exception. I find this town literally overrun. I have ordered everybody to their camps, and shall enforce the strictest discipline."[16]

Nelson then returned to Lexington. For the time being, the situation seemed under control. Edmund Kirby Smith, Nelson asserted, was "a much smaller potato than I took him for." Kirby Smith's forces had fallen back across the Rockcastle River, apparently content to hold their position and await the starvation and surrender of the Union garrison trapped far to their rear at Cumberland Gap. Nelson issued orders to his brigades to concentrate at Danville, twenty-five miles west of Richmond. From Danville, Nelson could in theory march his troops west to aid Buell or south to break through Kirby Smith's lines and relieve the Union force at Cumberland Gap, while other regiments that were just arriving from the North guarded Cincinnati and Louisville.

In reality, the ability of Nelson's raw regiments to accomplish any kind of mission was highly questionable. Many of the units raised in July had received only minimal training and others none. The 50th Ohio drilled a total of ten days before leaving camp to defend Cincinnati, the 105th Ohio left its home state to join Nelson's force after no more than three hours of drill, and the 121st Ohio "had not been drilled an hour" when it went to war in mid-September. Battery F, 1st Michigan Light Artillery, had been in service for nine months when it was assigned to Nelson's Army of Kentucky, but its members had no experience operating their guns, which were not issued to them until the last week of August. The Michiganders were ready to do "the service that we enlisted to perform but the Government or rather these Red Tape Officials were too indolent and lazy to perform their part of the compact."[17]

From Bowling Green, veteran soldier James W. Bingham expressed his contempt for the ignorance of the new units in a letter to his mother: "You ought—no you ought *not* to see what miserable officers we are now getting to command our new levies—They have whole regiments here in which there was not one officer who knew how to get a battalion properly in line of battle." The new regiments learned their trade slowly, Brigadier General Cruft reported, "owing to the almost entire ignorance of the officers." Still, with sufficient training these officers and men doubtless would have become as competent as any who had entered the Army of the Ohio a year earlier. It was their misfortune that their first test of battle would occur before they could begin to prepare for it.[18]

At 2:30 A.M. on August 30, Nelson was startled to receive a dispatch from Manson at Richmond stating that the Confederates had reached his position in force and that he expected a battle. Nelson immediately sent couriers to

Manson ordering him to fall back and join the rest of the army at Danville, but it was too late. On the twenty-ninth, when Manson had learned from his pickets that the Confederates were advancing toward him, he had moved his brigade several miles forward to meet them and had already engaged in some preliminary skirmishing. Early on the thirtieth, Kirby Smith's veterans attacked Manson's recruits. Unable to retreat safely, Manson instead called for the support of the other Union brigade at Richmond, commanded by Cruft. The regiments of Manson and Cruft, a member of Buell's staff wrote, "were all perfectly raw, recently mustered into service, only just brigaded, and had never been under fire. . . . The result was what might have been expected."[19]

The untrained Union volunteers fought bravely at first. Soon, however, confusion set in as casualties mounted and units tried to perform maneuvers under fire that they had scarcely practiced on the parade ground. When Manson withdrew the 69th Indiana from his left flank to strengthen another portion of the line, he confused the regiment by failing to allow it to recall the three companies of skirmishers that it had sent to the front. After Cruft's men tried to charge a battery and were driven back, the entire Union line wavered and then retreated in disarray. Twice Manson was able to rally enough of the fleeing troops to make a stand, but each time the pursuing Confederates quickly routed them. Hurrying from Lexington, Nelson arrived on the battlefield in time to try to stop the flight of his army. With his imposing physical presence and colorful vocabulary, he immediately began to stem the tide of panic and to organize a new line of defense, but his efforts were cut short by a musket ball that wounded him in the foot. Without Nelson, the Union position collapsed for the final time.[20]

Federal casualties were listed as 206 killed, 844 wounded, and 5,303 captured or missing (out of fewer than 7,000 engaged), while total Confederate losses were only 451.[21] No other Civil War battle of comparable size had such one-sided results, which were universally ascribed to the inexperience of the Northern soldiers. Mahlon Manson, who was captured in the final stages of the battle, called his men "undisciplined" and "inexperienced" and reported, "Some of the regiments never had had a battalion drill and knew not what a line of battle was." Charles Cruft described his brigade as "but a mere collection of citizens, hastily assembled, armed, and thrown together without the least knowledge of military rules or discipline." Back in Louisville, Boyle observed that "The new troops will not stand before drilled rebels" and warned the president with characteristic alarm, "We must have help of drilled troops unless you intend to turn us over to the devil and his imps."[22]

For those Union soldiers who survived it, the Battle of Richmond served as an initiation into the regiment-oriented culture of the Army of the Ohio. It so vividly demonstrated the value of regimental drill that even John Patton, a veteran of just six weeks whose regiment helped to cover the retreat from Richmond to Lexington, could judge that the routed troops "had not been sufficiently drilled to be handled readily or shifted on the battlefield." Manson's rashness and Nelson's antagonistic personality taught the new men the futility of looking for competent leadership anywhere outside of their own regiments. Veteran soldiers, an aide to General Rousseau later observed, could often camp for a month "without knowing or caring what regiment was encamped next to them." After Richmond, the horizons of the new regiments would be just as limited.[23]

"The Most Terrible March That Soldiers Ever Did Make"

Long before Kirby Smith's divisions began their invasion of Kentucky, the Army of the Ohio had lost whatever momentum it had generated in its advance from Corinth. After the Murfreesboro raid on July 13, the soldiers returned to their routine of trying to build bridges, lay railroad track, and dig tunnels faster than enemy cavalry raiders could destroy them. Their commander, meanwhile, was increasingly distracted by rumors that Braxton Bragg was gathering an enormous army near Chattanooga. By early August Buell was convinced that the Confederates had "a superior force assembled in east Tennessee . . . and there could be no doubt that our position in middle Tennessee was about to be assailed." Buell's defensive mentality was communicated to Washington, where the ever-cautious Halleck grew so worried that on August 8 he offered Buell the use of two divisions from Grant's army at Corinth if required for the safety of the Army of the Ohio. Buell accepted the offer within a week and relocated his main supply depot from Stevenson, Alabama, to a more easily defended position thirty miles to the rear, at Decherd, Tennessee. By August 19, when Buell ordered the divisions of McCook and Crittenden to fall back in response to a false report that rebel troops had crossed the Tennessee River, he was much less concerned with finding and destroying the enemy than with extricating his own forces.[24]

In Buell's eyes, the strategic situation was deteriorating rapidly. Through the end of August, he remained unsure of the location or destination of Bragg's army, which he estimated to number sixty thousand men (double its actual strength). On August 23, certain that Bragg was on the move in the Sequatchie Valley northwest of Chattanooga, Buell directed Thomas, McCook, and Crittenden to concentrate their divisions at Altamont in the barren Cumberland hills, overlooking the valley. The position proved untenable, as artillery and wagons could not ascend the roads, and there was no water for the troops. With the railroad from Nashville once again out of operation, cut by the continuing depredations of Confederate cavalry, the army was forced to go on half rations. Buell commanded Nelson to use his Army of Kentucky to repair and reopen the road but found his orders countermanded by Halleck and Wright, who instructed Nelson to focus instead on the relief of Cumberland Gap. With only ten days' provisions left, Buell on August 30 ordered the entire army to withdraw some forty miles to Murfreesboro, two-thirds of the way to Nashville. The campaign for Chattanooga was over, and now the Army of the Ohio was fighting for its survival.[25]

Buell's decision to fall back toward Nashville was based on his belief that the Tennessee capital was Bragg's objective. Many in the army disagreed. George Thomas, with whom Buell frequently consulted, believed that Bragg was headed for Kentucky and recommended to Buell that the army move to Sparta, sixty miles east of Murfreesboro, exposing Nashville but blocking Bragg's path to the north. When Buell overruled Thomas, Bragg took full advantage of the undefended route into central Kentucky. The Confederate army, which did not cross the Tennessee River in force until August 28, dashed through Sparta on September 3 and kept going. The defeat of Nelson's force at Richmond on August 30, coupled with Bragg's rapid movement, convinced Buell not to halt at Murfreesboro but to continue retreating all the way to Nashville. Once there, Buell belatedly realized that the city was not Bragg's target after all, and that Bragg meant to invade Kentucky, where his army might seize Louisville and cut the Army of the Ohio's lifeline across the Ohio River or join forces with Kirby Smith and take Cincinnati. Either result would be a disaster for the Union. Buell had no choice but to hurl his divisions north in a series of desperate forced marches, trying to overtake and defeat Bragg's army before it was too late.

Buell had clearly been outgeneraled by Bragg, and the bloodless defeat cost him much of his officers' confidence. At subsequent hearings on the conduct of the campaign, division commanders Thomas and Wood expressed their disagreement with Buell's decision to retreat to Murfreesboro instead of seeking out Bragg's army and engaging it. Although Alexander McCook later testified in Buell's defense that the plan to concentrate at Murfreesboro was "as perfect as it possibly could be," at the time he was overheard to mutter to one of his brigadiers, "Don Carlos won't do."[26] Brigade commanders Albin Schoepf, R. B. Mitchell, and Speed S. Fry, among others, shared that opinion. Officers of the First Division drafted a petition to the president to have Buell removed.[27]

Doubt in Buell's competence was not limited to the officers of his army.

Attract Attention	Rockets. and no.	Signification
White	One Red followed by one Plain	All quiet in front
Red	Three Red in rapid succession	The enemy are reinforced in front
Red White	Three Plain in rapid succession	Strike Camps and advance
Red White	One Plain	Send us reinforcements
Red	One Red	The enemy are advancing
White	Two Plain	The enemy are retreating
Red White	Without Rockets	Send report by Rocket Code

The fires in cases will be always used when obtainable

The Rocket Code should be used only in cases of quick notification being desired, or when the Torch cannot be used to advantage.
"Extract"
The "Code of Rocket Signals" is confided to the Commander in chief & to the officers of the Signal Corps. To none others must it be given.

Lieut. T. R. Shattuck
Chief Asst Signal Officer
Department of the Ohio —

In August 1862 signal officers of the Army of the Ohio used a code based on colored rockets in an effort to overcome the difficulty of communicating across the mountainous terrain near Chattanooga. From Buell Papers, Filson Club, Louisville.

General in Chief Halleck warned Buell that, in Washington, "So great is the dissatisfaction here at the apparent want of energy and activity in your district" that it was only due to Halleck's personal intervention that he still had his job. Halleck did Buell the favor of ignoring his touchy response, in which he asked to be relieved if his superiors had so little confidence in him, but even Halleck's patience was wearing thin, as shown by his curt reply to Buell's announcement that the army was retreating to Murfreesboro: "March where you please, provided you will find the enemy and fight him." Tennessee's military governor, Andrew Johnson, was equally disillusioned with Buell and panicked when Union troops began to retreat from Nashville. He angrily accused Buell of abandoning him, even though a substantial garrison stayed behind to protect the city. Most significant of all, the rank and file of the Army of the Ohio now lost their remaining confidence in their leader's professional ability. Buell had never been popular, but the army's successes in the spring and summer had earned him a measure of grudging respect from his troops. As he led them north, giving up much of the ground they had gained, he gave up that respect as well.[28]

The "Race to Louisville" proved to be the most tortuous march ever made by the men of the Army of the Ohio. They began to leave Nashville on September 7, several days behind Bragg's troops, and maintained a killing pace in their effort to overcome the rebels' head start. There was little fighting along the way, but the men suffered intensely from dust and thirst. The summer of 1862 had been extraordinarily dry and hot in Kentucky, and the high limestone content in the state's dirt roads produced choking clouds of dust that all but suffocated the thousands of soldiers who plodded through them. "I never saw such a place for dust," marveled Arza Bartholomew, Jr., of the 21st Michigan. "It is from one to two and four inches deep, just as light as snow and when we march it is so thick that we can't hardly see the man in front of us." "Dust so bad that we could not see the men in front of us," Captain James Biddle of the 16th U.S. confirmed in his diary. Spillard Horrall of the 42nd Indiana estimated its depth at three to six inches. Forty-nine-year-old W. R. Claspill of the 21st Illinois described Kentucky as "the dryest and dustiest country I have seen in thirty-five years travel." When Lewis Penfield of Battery B, 1st Ohio Light Artillery, filled out an application to join a veterans' organization many years later, it was the march to Louisville that he remembered most vividly: "Never can I forget those terrible hot dusty days."[29]

The heat and dust were harder to bear because there was so little water available. In July and August the ponds that were the primary source of water for local farmers normally stagnated and became undrinkable, even for livestock. In 1862 persistent drought left many of these ponds entirely dry. Those that held any water at all were eagerly sought, even if they contained dead animals left behind by Bragg's army. "It was no unusual thing to see comrades clearing the green scum from this water near where a dead mule or horse lay, and then to fill their canteens," wrote an Indiana officer. Major H. B. Freeman of the 18th U.S. recalled that after a day of enduring the "dreadful" glare of the sun on the limestone road and thirst that swelled his tongue so that he could hardly speak, his unit camped near a stagnant pool: "the men, barely waiting to stack their arms, rushed into the water, which they swallowed in great mouthfuls."[30]

Conditions grew worse still when food as well as water ran short. The army's enormous wagon train could not keep up with the infantry, and after weeks of living on half rations the soldiers now found that provisions were "played out entirely." Left with nothing else to eat, Silas Mallory of the 64th Ohio recorded how his hunger led him to catch a frog, tear it in two, and grind it up together with an ear of foraged corn to make a mush for his dinner. The men of the 42nd Indiana "started on that long and dusty march for Louisville with nothing but flour to eat—not even salt"; they improvised by opening a barrel of flour and letting each man dump in a quart of water (if he had one) and scoop out a handful of dough to bake into rock-hard "sinkers." For soldiers who became too weak on such sustenance to continue putting one foot ahead of the other, the alternative of falling out of ranks and waiting for a half-empty wagon to come by was almost as daunting, for it had already become an old joke that the wise veteran, if given a choice of transportation when going to hell, would choose an unsprung army wagon, "'Cause I'd be glad when I got thar." But there was little joking on the march to Louisville, which was remembered by all who experienced it as "the most terrible march that soldiers ever did make in this country."[31]

By September 15 the army was concentrated at Bowling Green. Buell was uncertain of Bragg's location but believed him to be near Glasgow, marching north on a parallel route, about thirty miles to the east of the Nashville–Bowling Green road. While at Bowling Green, Buell learned that the vanguard of the enemy army was laying siege to the small Union garrison at Munfordville, which lay twenty miles north of Glasgow, blocking Bragg's way to Louisville. Munfordville was within two days' hard marching from Bowling Green, but Buell hesitated to send his army to its relief. He remained unsure of the strength and position of Bragg's main body and received no useful information from the Munfordville garrison, which reported to Wright's Department of the Ohio and not to Buell.[32] While Buell was considering his next move, the force at Munfordville surrendered on September 17.[33]

Shortly after the fall of Munfordville Buell sent for Thomas's division, which had been left behind to protect Nashville. Buell then set out cautiously from Bowling Green, feeling his way toward Bragg's army. On September 20 he found it at Munfordville, occupying a strong defensive position and barring the way to Louisville. The next day Buell's men found to their surprise that the Confederates had abandoned their lines and were marching northeast toward Bardstown, inexplicably leaving open the road to Louisville, only sixty miles away.[34] Buell took advantage of the opportunity by ordering a series of forced marches beginning on September 21. Just four days later the head of the army entered the city, although many thousands fell out along the way and did not drag themselves into Louisville for another several days.

Louisville was saved, but the men of the Army of the Ohio were spent. One regimental chronicler recorded that his unit had covered 414 miles in twenty-two days of marching: "There was no regularity in our movements; sometimes we rested by day and marched by night; at others, rested at night and marched by day. We were pushed forward when we should have halted, or halted when we should have advanced; and throughout the conduct of the march exhibited shameful mismanagement, or an utter disregard of either the health or comfort of the troops." The hardships of the march prompted one soldier to write home earnestly to his parents, presumably in regard to a younger brother, "Now laying all fooling aside, I don't want him to enlist he is too young and might not stand the privations we do. . . . Dont let him enlist." John Easton of the 44th Indiana compared the "suffering and privation we had in crossing the Cumberland mountains [with] the scarcity of water and food" to the legendary "Retreat of the 10,000" chronicled by Xenophon. "We have had the damdest time of getting here that ever was," George Alverson of the 10th Wisconsin wrote to his father on September 26. "We left Alabama the 31 of Aug. And have been on a force march ever since and have just arrived at Louisville." The same day Jackson E. Webster wrote in his diary of his "almost intolerably sore" feet that carried him along a road "lined with hundreds of straglers."[35]

For many soldiers, the discomfort of the march was intensified by the belief that the trials they had undergone could have been avoided had Buell not been so reluctant to fight. "It was the desire of the army," wrote James Shaw of the 10th Indiana, "to get into an engagement if nothing more than to relieve the monotony of constant marching." The troops were critical of Buell's decision not to attack Bragg at Munfordville, especially after the paroled garrison of that post joined the march to Louisville. When the men of the 44th Indiana saw them, John Easton wrote, "Deep were the curses heaped on buell's [sic] head. I felt so mortified that I had not words to express my rage when I found that Bragg was out of the way." In an account by a veteran of the 59th Illinois

The Army of the Ohio enters Louisville. From *Harper's Weekly*, October 18, 1862; photograph courtesy of The Lincoln Museum, Fort Wayne, Indiana (TLM #4543).

published three years later, the anger at Buell was still fresh: "Why was it that General Buell did not reinforce that bravely defended garrison? . . . Had [Buell] have been seen and known along the lines at the time those brave men were passing to the rear, his hide would never have held bran."[36]

Easton exaggerated little when he claimed that his anger at Buell was shared by everyone "from the major General to the lowest private." Private Thomas Small entered in his diary on September 22, "old Buell is a coward or a Rebel[;] Shoot him let us go." Junior officers such as Captain John Tuttle (promoted from lieutenant in May 1862) heard epithets like "traitor, tyrant, fool, and coward" used freely in regard to Buell. An officer in the 16th Illinois, staying overnight in a Bowling Green tavern in mid-September while returning to his regiment from detached service, overheard in the next room a conference "mainly of colonels and generals" who were making arrangements, "in the event of its becoming necessary in their judgment, to depose General Buell from the command of the army, place him under arrest," and install Thomas in his stead. Captain R. Delavan Mussey of the 19th U.S., who had written of the army's "large confidence" in Buell in February, complained on September 30 that "the truth is that Buell has lost, by his vacillation and incompetence, nearly or quite all we have gained" and thus brought "every officer in Buell's Army to the conclusion that he is either a Traitor or an

Imbecile." The Army of the Ohio had yet to lose a battle, but its men were demoralized and discontented with Buell's leadership.[37]

"Too Good an Organizer"

Louisville in the last week of September 1862 was a scene of enormous confusion and activity. From the south came a constant flow of what Captain Lewis Hosea called "the raggedest, dirtiest, lousiest, and hungriest lot of soldiers ever on this continent." Waiting in the city to reinforce them were various newly recruited units that had been rushed to the defense of Kentucky, described by Buell as "perfectly raw, undisciplined and in a measure unarmed troops." "It was very easy to discern between the soldiers of our army and the garrison of Louisville," wrote Marcus Woodcock of the 9th Kentucky, which had entered the town with fewer than half of the six hundred men who had begun the march a month earlier, "by the dirty and ragged clothing and rusty guns of the former, and the shining uniform and polished guns of the latter." David Lathrop recalled how the 59th Illinois entered Louisville "[w]ithout shoes, ragged and dirty, . . . contrasting beautifully with the neatly uniformed recruits about the city, with their paper collars and blacked boots." "Regiments & officers being mostly green, everything is rather confused," another observer noted with considerable understatement. Many of the veterans took advantage of the confusion to desert temporarily for the purpose of visiting friends and family across the river in Indiana before voluntarily returning to the ranks.[38]

While the veterans recovered from their brutal march from Nashville, the Army of the Ohio's newest members demonstrated how green they were at every opportunity. Recruits of the 125th Illinois mistook the sound of a few pickets routinely emptying their muskets for a full-fledged battle and began to fire their own weapons wildly. Erastus Winters of the recently mustered 50th Ohio gawked at the difference between his regiment's fresh uniforms and the tatters worn by Buell's veterans. When a member of the 4th Michigan Cavalry, riding atop a train car bound for Louisville on September 25, was injured by a low bridge, hospital steward James Vernor of Detroit stitched up the victim's wounds while "5 or 6 came near fainting just watching us work at him"; they would soon see much worse.[39]

Of more immediate value than the July volunteers were the two divisions from Grant's army that had joined the Army of the Ohio at Nashville in time to experience the Race to Louisville. These divisions, one of which had seen combat at Pea Ridge under the leadership of Brigadier General Jefferson C.

Davis, totaled about ten thousand men and represented a significant accretion to Buell's numerical strength. If Buell was glad to see them, however, the sentiment was not reciprocated. George Herr of the 59th Illinois, one of Davis's regiments, later wrote: "The conduct of General Buell was a subject of bitter comment among the men who made the march from Nashville to Louisville. The men of Davis' division were particularly severe on the general. They were marched and countermarched and bobbed about as though somebody was playing a game of shuttlecock and battledoor with them, and they were unable to understand it in any manner favorable to General Buell."[40] Several officers of Herr's regiment were arrested in Louisville for taking fence rails to make fires, a rude introduction to Buell's severe strictures on the use of civilian property. Another member of the 59th Illinois recorded the rumor that "Buell wants no such ragged regiment as we are in his army. Buell says he don't want that dirty, ragged division."[41]

Whatever Buell may have thought of his troops, old and new, he immediately set to work getting them ready. Such administrative activity was what he did best, and Boyle, still in command of the post of Louisville, was impressed by what he saw: "I think the work of arming, shoeing, clothing, paying, and supplying [the troops] in every respect; combining the new with the old and organizing them into brigades and divisions and army corps; preparing them to march against the enemy; preparing the provisions and supplies of subsistence and ammunition, and actually moving them, showed what struck me as wonderful energy, industry and ability."[42]

Most of the new units in Louisville displayed similar energy in preparing for the coming campaign by drilling as often as possible. "I am rapidly becoming initiated into all the tactics of the military school," Levi Ross wrote to his father, as a result of eight hours' daily drill with the 86th Illinois.[43] John Patton and his comrades in the 98th Ohio were led by "an energetick wide awake officer [who] embraced every opportunity to make his regiment as perfect, as possible, in the various movements of the drill." Some units, however, left Louisville without having drilled much or at all. "The commanders of many regiments wer at falt in this respect," Patton wrote, in reference to units that expected to go into battle with the Army of the Ohio even though "they had never spent an hour in drill." Such units included the 123rd Illinois, which up to October 1, 1862, "never had battalion drill, and hardly an attempt at company drill, as all the officers, except the Colonel, were 'raw recruits,' " according to the Illinois adjutant general.[44]

Buell thoroughly reorganized the army. Although he did not go to the extreme of breaking up regiments to mix old and new troops by company, he took care to assign most of the raw regiments to established brigades where they would have an opportunity to learn from experienced men. This made sense to old soldiers like Morris Fitch, who recognized that "we have a great many green regts here which will not fight as well as old ones." Similarly, the 10th Indiana's James Shaw noted, "The government had wisely decided to brigade the new troops with the old vets." The cost of this policy was that it disrupted the teamwork and esprit de corps that were beginning to develop in some of the brigades that had remained intact since the formation of the army, but on balance most soldiers seemed to agree that it was a good idea for the new units to be "sandwiched in between regiments" of veterans.[45]

The addition of two new divisions brought the Army of the Ohio's total to nine, making it impractical for Buell to continue his practice of giving orders directly to each division commander. On September 29 he reorganized the army into three corps of three divisions each. To lead these new organizations, Buell looked to Alexander McCook (First Corps) and Thomas Crittenden (Second Corps), favoring the two generals who had publicly supported his decision to retreat to Murfreesboro, although neither had shown any particular military talent. For the Third Corps, Buell intended to appoint William Nelson, who had recovered from the wound he received at Richmond, but events intervened. On the same day that Buell announced the army's new organization, Nelson was confronted in the lobby of the Galt House hotel by Jefferson C. Davis, in the company of Indiana Governor Oliver Morton. Davis demanded that Nelson apologize for some past rudeness and tossed a crumpled calling card at his face. In response, Nelson contemptuously slapped Davis and walked away. Davis refused to accept the insult. From one of the small crowd that had gathered to see the altercation, he borrowed a pistol, then followed Nelson down a corridor and shot him dead.[46]

News of Nelson's death instantly reverberated through the entire army. Buell, who believed that the men who served under Nelson had been devoted to him, arranged for extra provost guards in the streets of Louisville to cope with the violence he expected between Nelson's and Davis's troops. Feelings certainly ran high among Davis's men, who overwhelmingly supported what their leader had done. R. V. Marshall of the 22nd Indiana reported: "Every man in the 22nd deeply sympathized with General Davis, and believed him fully justified in the course he pursued." Day Elmore of the 36th Illinois assured his parents that Nelson "got the wrong man" when he "undertook to use a Brig[adier] Gen[eral] as he would a private." Outside of Davis's unit, contrary to Buell's expectations, "Almost everybody says [it] served him right," as John Bross of the 88th Illinois wrote to his wife the same night. Albion Tourgée heard soldiers throughout the city cheering for Davis, and in his diary entry for September 29, 1862, Daniel Howe of the 79th Indiana

The assassination of William Nelson by Jefferson C. Davis. Buell expected Nelson's troops to react with violence on behalf of their general; instead, they shared the opinion of the rest of the army that Nelson deserved his fate. From *Harper's Weekly*, October 18, 1862; photograph courtesy of The Lincoln Museum, Fort Wayne, Indiana (TLM #4544).

noted succinctly: "Gen. Nelson shot by Jeff C. Davis at Galt House. Great rejoicing among soldiers and citizens." In time, the celebration spread to the interned Union parolees from Murfreesboro, who had endured Nelson's abuse for surrendering. "[W]hen the news came to us at Camp Chase . . . ," wrote Charles Bennett of the 9th Michigan, "instead of mourning, some of our boys cheered and swung their caps."[47]

Some in the army respected Nelson as a soldier, but even they seemed to regard his murder without surprise or real regret. Nelson was "a rough old customer, and but very little of the true gentleman about him, but he was brave, and a good general, a fighting man, for these qualities I mourn his loss . . . ," wrote Thomas Prickett, a member of Nelson's division, "but I suppose he gave Davis sufficient cause." Ephraim A. Otis, an officer who claimed that Nelson was "greatly beloved by his soldiers," admitted that his murder was "not wholly unexpected" by those who knew Nelson's temper. One of the few soldiers to express disapproval of Davis's act was Levi Ross, who thought that the "provocation was trivial, and without the shadow of justice." Ross complained that "Davis . . . will probably go scot free, unwhipped of justice, because he wears a star," but his anger toward Davis was unmixed with any expression of sorrow for Nelson. No event in the first year of the Army of the Ohio's existence evoked such an outpouring of feeling as Nelson's assassination, but far from inciting the troops to disorder, the killing was met with expressions of almost universal satisfaction. As John H. Tilford observed in his diary, "The soldiers as a general thing seem to be glad th[e] Gen. is shot, he was considered a great tyrant by his men." J. F. Culver, in a letter home written shortly after the shooting, agreed: "I have heard no one express any regret. He was disliked by the whole army." Buell's fears of violence on Nelson's behalf were another sign of how little he understood the volunteers he led.[48]

The Galt House incident deprived Buell of the services of two experienced division commanders at a single stroke, as Nelson was buried and Davis was put under arrest.[49] To replace Nelson at the head of the Third Corps, Buell made the curious choice of Captain Charles C. Gilbert. Buell knew Gilbert from the Regular Army and had employed him on his staff in July and August as inspector general of the Army of the Ohio. In mid-August Gilbert was detailed to Nelson's staff as inspector general of the Army of Kentucky. He served in that post until just after the Battle of Richmond on August 30, when he unexpectedly found himself in charge of the army after Nelson was wounded, Manson was captured, and Cruft and Jackson both declined the command. Major General Wright, the officer who appointed Gilbert to lead the Army of Kentucky, also gave him the rank of major general of volunteers, disregarding the fact that legal authority to make such a promotion resided only in the U.S. Senate. (President Lincoln commissioned Gilbert a brigadier general later in September, but the Senate never confirmed him, and he remained legally a captain throughout his tenure as commander of the Third Corps.) In Louisville, an observer commented, "Gilbert did not hide either himself or his Major General's uniform under a bushel." When Buell suddenly needed a high-ranking officer to take command of the Third Corps, he gave the position to "Major General" Gilbert because, as he later stated, "I thought his rank entitled him to it." Although Buell may not have had reason to doubt the authenticity of Gilbert's rank, he must have known that Gilbert had spent his entire career as a staff officer and had never commanded so much as a regiment in the field before his startling "promotion."[50]

On the same day that Davis killed Nelson, the army's command structure was further shaken by a message from the War Department relieving Buell and putting George Thomas in his place. For some days high-ranking officers had openly discussed the desirability of Buell's removal, and Halleck had sent Colonel Joseph C. McKibbin to Louisville to report on the state of the army.

McKibbin confirmed that there was "Much dissatisfaction with General Buell" among the officers, a party of whom openly toasted Alexander Mc-Cook as the army's future commander at the Galt House on September 27. When the long-expected order arrived, however, Thomas declined the appointment on the grounds that Buell was finally about to undertake an offensive campaign and that a change of command at that moment would be ill advised. The governors of Indiana, Illinois, Ohio, and Tennessee all wanted Buell removed, but the opposition of Thomas and several important Kentucky politicians who spoke up in favor of Buell was enough to persuade Halleck reluctantly to withdraw the order. Word of Halleck's decision to replace Buell spread quickly through Louisville, and Thomas's intervention was, a staff officer later wrote, "a source of regret in the army." Buell's already shaky hold over his troops was thus further compromised by the War Department's public indication of its lack of confidence.[51]

Possibly out of gratitude for Thomas's action, Buell named his most trusted and talented subordinate as second-in-command. Buell clearly valued Thomas's ability but made poor use of it by awarding him the military equivalent of the vice presidency. Halleck had given Grant a similar assignment as a means of getting him out of the way after the Battle of Shiloh, and Thomas was to find (as Grant had) that the position of second-in-command had no real authority. Although he may not have so intended, Buell placed his best officer where he could do the least good in the upcoming campaign.[52]

The reorganization of the army required the appointment of new division commanders to replace Thomas, McCook, Crittenden, and Nelson. If none of Buell's choices were as bizarre as the elevation of Charles Gilbert to corps command, neither were any of them especially promising. For the First Division, Buell selected Albin Schoepf, one of Thomas's longtime brigade commanders. Once while leading his brigade, Schoepf was put under arrest by Buell for allowing his men to forage and (according to Frederick Marion of the 31st Ohio, a member of the brigade) in reply "told Buell he was a traitor to his country and pulled out his revolver and was [going] to shoot him and would have don [sic] it if it was not not [sic] for the interferance of some officers." Schoepf continued to hate Buell with a passion.[53]

Buell appointed Brigadier Generals Joshua Sill and Lovell H. Rousseau to lead the Second and Third Divisions, respectively. Rousseau had led a brigade in the Second Division since the formation of the army, but when O. M. Mitchel was called to Washington in July 1862, Rousseau was given command of the Third Division. Sill, who had led a brigade in the Third Division, was named to replace Alexander McCook as the head of the Second Division. Sill and Rousseau, popular and reasonably competent officers at the brigade level, thus found themselves leading each others' divisions. The Fourth Division (formerly Nelson's) went to William Sooy Smith, who had led both the Third and Fourth Divisions on a temporary basis in the past, while Crittenden's Fifth Division was assigned to Horatio P. Van Cleve, one of his brigadiers. Of all the division commanders in the Army of the Ohio on September 30, 1862, only Thomas J. Wood of the Sixth Division could claim as much as three months' experience in his post.

Three new divisions were added to the army at Louisville: the Ninth, Tenth, and Eleventh.[54] The Ninth, led by Jefferson C. Davis, was one of the two divisions transferred from Grant's Army of the Tennessee. Davis remained under arrest for shooting Nelson, so the division was commanded by its next ranking officer, Brigadier General Robert B. Mitchell, a Kansas Free-Soil politician who had been wounded at Wilson's Creek in 1861. The Tenth Division consisted almost entirely of raw regiments that had briefly served in the ill-fated Army of Kentucky. It was led by Brigadier General James S. Jackson, a thirty-nine-year-old former congressman from Kentucky with little military experience. Two brigades of new units were combined with Brigadier General Philip Sheridan's veteran "Pea Ridge Brigade," just arrived from Grant's army, to form the Eleventh Division. The division was originally assigned to J. T. Boyle, but Sheridan went to Buell's chief of staff and "while not questioning Buell's good intentions nor his pure motives, insisted that my rights in the matter should be recognized." Sheridan, who had been relieved as chief quartermaster of the Army of the Southwest for insubordination earlier in the year, got the division.[55]

Just as Buell mixed old and new regiments in his reorganized brigades, he made an effort to join old and new divisions to form his three army corps. The experienced Second and Third Divisions supported the raw Tenth in Alex McCook's First Corps. The veteran First Division, the Ninth Division from Grant's army, and Sheridan's hybrid Eleventh Division formed the Third Corps under Gilbert. The old Third, Fourth, and Fifth Divisions made up Crittenden's Second Corps.

In the last five days of September, Don Carlos Buell accomplished a great deal. He saw that the demoralized, hungry, and tired regiments of the Army of the Ohio were rested, reequipped, and rejuvenated. He assimilated into the army a mass of untrained regiments, including the remnants of the defeated Army of Kentucky, and did all that was possible in a few days to drill them into fighting condition. When the Army of the Ohio left Louisville on October 1 to find and fight Bragg's army, George Herr of the 59th Illinois thought that the men were "newly rested, well fed and newly dressed, [and] in the very best of spirits."[56]

"And yet this army . . . ," wrote W. F. G. Shanks, who was serving on the Third Division staff, "was the weakest in organization of any great army that ever existed." The problem, Shanks noted, was that "Buell was too good an organizer." The details of preparing regiments for the campaign "absorbed too much of his mind" and distracted him from the larger task of integrating those regiments into a cohesive army. The retreat to the Ohio had cost Buell whatever personal loyalty the army and its officers ever had for him. The turmoil in the army's upper echelon at Louisville and the selection of uninspiring nonentities as corps commanders did nothing to restore the army's confidence in Buell's leadership. After a full year of training and active service, the Army of the Ohio prepared to undertake its most important campaign still as a fragmented collection of regimental communities.[57]

CHAPTER SEVEN

Crisis of Leadership
The Perryville Campaign, October 1862

On October 8, 1862, near the village of Perryville, the men of the Army of the Ohio fought with Braxton Bragg's troops to decide the fate of Kentucky. Inadequate staff resources and a series of poor decisions by Buell and his generals led to a breakdown in communications that resulted in two of the army's three corps taking little or no part in the battle, while the remaining corps came under attack from the bulk of the Confederate army. Buell's failure to employ all of his forces meant that the regiments engaged, which included many of the new units added to the army at Louisville, were forced to rely on their bravery and internal cohesion to redeem the extremely unfavorable tactical situation in which they found themselves. Enough of them were successful to save the Army of the Ohio from disaster, deny Bragg a victory, and give Buell what would prove to be his last, best opportunity to achieve a decisive, Napoleonic-style battlefield triumph.

"A Brilliant, a Gaudy Picture"

When the seventy-five thousand men of the refreshed, reequipped, and reorganized Army of the Ohio paraded out of Louisville on October 1, they presented "a brilliant, a gaudy picture [that] moved the blood, fired the passions" even of hard-bitten veterans like George Herr.[1] Still more encouraging to Herr and his comrades was the prospect of at last coming to grips with the enemy. For the first time their objective was not a fixed point on the map, like Chattanooga or Louisville, but the enemy army itself. They marched toward Bardstown, where Buell expected to find Bragg, and entered the village on October 4. There Buell learned that Bragg had retreated (probably toward Danville) and heard reports that Kirby Smith was concentrating his force at Frankfort, forty miles to the northeast. Buell sent the Second Division, of Alexander McCook's First Corps, off to Frankfort to keep Kirby Smith in check, while the rest of the army pursued Bragg's army along the road from Bardstown to Danville, via Perryville. Buell pushed his troops hard, for if the reports were accurate, then the Army of the Ohio was closer to the two Confederate forces than they were to each other. Until they united, Buell had a rare opportunity to attack and defeat each of them in detail.[2]

His chances of doing so seemed good. The troops were marching light, having left Louisville without waiting for their wagon train; the seventeen-mile-long caravan of two thousand vehicles was still toiling up the road from Nashville, bringing back supplies that had been collected for the abortive advance on Chattanooga. Since the army would have stretched for an un-wieldy ten miles if strung out along a single road, even without the supply wagons, Buell had the three corps march on parallel roads whenever possible, both to reduce the length of the column and to enlarge the area in which to find water and good camping grounds. When the army left Bardstown, Gilbert's corps took the direct road to Perryville, with McCook's corps on its left approaching Perryville via Mackville and Crittenden's corps to the right on the Lebanon-Danville road. The use of multiple columns increased the army's speed but also made coordination more difficult, as evidenced by Mc-Cook's October 5 note to Thomas in which he confessed himself "in blissful ignorance" of the movements of the rest of the army.[3]

Since January, when the army's citizen-soldiers had undertaken their first campaign with the conviction that every company needed its own baggage wagon, the number of wagons employed by each regiment had dropped from ten or more down to three, two, or even one. By October, troops ordered to move "light" were to bring no vehicles at all, except ambulances and ammuni-tion wagons; an order to march with "half baggage" allowed one wagon for each regiment, brigade, and division "to carry a few necessary articles for the officers." Officers had to do without their personal trunks, and the men in the ranks got by with nothing but the compact loads on their backs. James Shaw of the 10th Indiana described the things they carried: "At this time we were travelling light. Gun, cartridge box, canteen, haversack, blanket and oil cloth constituted the equipment on this march."[4]

In contrast, most of the recruits who joined the army at Louisville had yet to learn the secrets of the soldier's craft. Shaw described them as well: "[T]he new troops were loaded down with all kinds of trumpery. Knapsacks were a foot above their heads. Overcoats, two suits of clothes and underwear, all kinds of trinkets, bear's oil for the hair, etc., gifts from loving and well meaning friends but useless to the soldier. On the back of their knapsacks were strapped frying pans, coffee pots and stew pans, pairs of boots hanging to the knapsack, blankets and ponchos, making in weight one hundred pounds to the man, while the 'vet' carried about twenty-five pounds."[5] A month earlier William Nelson had requested fifteen wagons per regiment to move the raw troops that made up the Army of Kentucky with all their gear.[6] But the new men learned quickly. James Congleton of the 105th Illinois thought that he was "loaded like the old time Jew pack peddler" on the march from Louisville and quickly jettisoned some of his superfluous cargo. By October 4, John Wesley Marshall noted in his diary, his comrades in the 97th Ohio were discovering the "stern reality" of soldiering: "three fourths of them have already thrown away a portion of their extra clothing, to lighten their loads[,] and numbers of their overcoats and blankets." The roads behind the army soon were filled with blankets, clothing, and all manner of personal items.[7]

Even with lightened packs, the new troops still found it difficult to keep up with the rest of the army. On the first day out of Louisville, veteran William Patterson kept an eye on the men of the 101st Ohio, a new regiment recently assigned to his brigade. The Buckeyes "began throwing away blankets and clothes" early on, Patterson wrote, but by the end of the day "The 101sters were about played out." On October 6 Corporal George Morris's 81st Indiana regiment "was stretched out for miles, the men completely worn out." Major J. M. Wright, Buell's assistant adjutant general, observed that "a great many of the regiments broke down" on the march and that the "great number of stragglers from the new regiments . . . was remarked upon throughout the army." Lieutenant Colonel Francis Darr noticed "that all the old troops . . . marched in their usual close order," while the thousands of stragglers he saw consisted "entirely of the new troops."[8]

One reason that so many soldiers fell out of ranks was the drought that continued to afflict Kentucky through the summer and fall of 1862. Like the Race to Louisville, the October march was characterized by dust, excessive and unseasonable heat, and lack of water. On October 2 the men of the First Corps had so little water that their commander felt "absolutely compelled" to change the corps' line of march to find some. "I fear I am about 5 miles out of position, but it cannot be helped," McCook reported to Thomas. The little water that was available to the army was rarely good. "Much of the water we drink is mixed with the filth of the mules, hog and goose," complained Levi

Ross of the 86th Illinois, adding that the men "are very much worn down by marching, short rations and this miserable water." The thick layer of fine, powdery dust that covered the roads, and everything else, added to the difficulty of the march.[9]

In spite of the hardships, most of the soldiers remained optimistic, confident that they were finally going to whip the rebels. When John Wesley Marshall asked a secessionist civilian for a drink, she taunted him that his army would not be able to last another three days without water. "I told her," he replied, "we would send their army to a dryer and hotter place than we were in, in less than three days." Lucius Wood of the 121st Ohio wrote home on October 5 to complain about the water ("I have drank water from ponds which Northern horses wouldn't drink") but added enthusiastically, "Speaking of Genl Bragg I can tell you we are after him hot & heavy." In the midst of a grueling all-night march on October 6, the men of the 10th Indiana demonstrated that they had not lost their high spirits. They were taking a brief midnight break, many of them sleeping where they had stopped on either side of the road, when "General" Charles Gilbert came riding through with his staff and demanded that the exhausted troops form up and salute him properly. Colonel William Kise told Gilbert that after marching day and night for a week, "he would not hold dress parade at midnight for any d—d fool living"; the only salute the men offered was to jeer and apply their bayonets to the hindquarters of the horses of Gilbert and his staff, who continued down the road rather more promptly than they had come.[10]

"The Cannonading . . . Was Not Supposed to Proceed from Any Serious Engagement"

As the Army of the Ohio closed in on Bragg's troops, the frequency and intensity of contacts between the two armies increased. By October 7, skirmishing between the lead units of Gilbert's Third Corps and a Confederate rear guard under Major General Leonidas Polk was almost constant, and a full-scale collision appeared imminent. That evening, Third Corps regiments began to deploy into lines of battle about four miles west of Perryville. At seven o'clock, Buell sent out orders to concentrate the two flanking corps for what he anticipated would be a major battle the next day. To George Thomas, who was traveling with Crittenden's headquarters, Buell gave instructions to move the Second Corps several miles forward, until it was aligned with the right flank of Gilbert's line. McCook was ordered to bring his corps up on Gilbert's left.

Both movements were to begin at 3:00 A.M.; if everything went as planned, all three Union corps would be in line by 7:00 A.M., ready to attack.[11]

By seven o'clock the next morning, it was evident that nothing had gone according to plan. Buell's orders for the Second Corps crossed paths with a message from Thomas explaining that he had moved Crittenden's men two and a half miles from where they were supposed to camp in order to find some water. As a result, Buell's order did not reach Thomas until 3:00 A.M., the hour when he was supposed to put the Second Corps in motion. McCook received his orders from Buell at about the same time and did not get his two First Corps divisions on the road until 5:00 A.M. James Jackson's inexperienced Tenth Division was due to lead the corps (the divisions alternated places daily, taking turns marching through each other's dust), but with combat likely, McCook chose to put Rousseau's veteran Third Division at the head of the column. Despite McCook's precaution, Jackson's recruits managed to disrupt the corps' order of march by entering the road after only two of Rousseau's three brigades had passed, thus cutting off Colonel John C. Starkweather's Twenty-eighth Brigade, which had to wait and bring up the rear of the column.[12]

At army headquarters, the news that the two flanking corps had not reached their places in time was taken to mean that the long-awaited battle with Bragg would be deferred at least one more day. Buell's assistant adjutant general, Major Wright, recalled that word of Crittenden's arrival was "eagerly waited for. . . . but no battle was expected that day." Buell himself wrote that he "no longer anticipated a battle that day" after McCook and Crittenden had failed to move into position on time.[13]

Buell may have privately welcomed the delay, since he had been thrown from his still-vicious horse the day before and was nursing a painful cut in his thigh that kept him from leaving his headquarters. In a gesture reminiscent of Alexander the Great, who in the Gedrosian Desert publicly spilled the last helmetful of water left in his army rather than drink while his men could not, Buell refused to allow a doctor to wash his wound while water for his men was so scarce. Unlike Alexander, whose inspirational act cemented the loyalty of his troops, Buell gained no popularity from his sacrifice because he characteristically did nothing to communicate it to the army.[14]

While the men of the First and Second Corps were belatedly working their way forward, those of Gilbert's Third Corps confronted the enemy. In common with everyone else in the area, they had water foremost on their minds. One Indiana soldier saw five hundred men standing in line at a well. "[W]hat an awful time that was for water," Corporal William P. White of the 59th Illinois recalled years afterward. Another member of the same regiment wrote in his journal, "The boys had to go two miles after water, and there were three hundred men for every cupful they had." Those who went found "the most execrable water that ever moistened the tongues of men; yet, wretched as it was, it was a boon for which two armies were willing to fight."[15]

Between the lines of the Third Corps and the Confederates lay Doctor's Creek, a small, nearly dry tributary of Chaplin River. Sheridan's Eleventh Division was the closest to the creek, and at Gilbert's instruction Sheridan sent Colonel Daniel McCook's Thirty-sixth Brigade to secure its meager supply of water for the Army of the Ohio. McCook's men were so inexperienced that they did not realize that the order to pile their knapsacks meant they were about to go into combat and thought that wagons were coming to haul their packs for them that day.[16] Unaware of what awaited them, they went forward, supported by a lone regiment (the 10th Indiana) from another brigade. Their objective was Peter's Hill, which overlooked Doctor's Creek to the north and Bull Run to the east. Rebel soldiers, equally desirous of controlling the precious water of Doctor's Creek, occupied the woods on the hill's eastern slope.

The Battle of Perryville began before dawn, when the Confederates opened fire on Colonel McCook's troops. The rebels held the men of the Thirty-sixth Brigade at bay until 10:00 A.M., when Sheridan rode up to the firing line to see what was happening. He brusquely ordered the 10th Indiana to the rear, leading to a "spirited confab" with Colonel Kise, who was under orders from his own division commander not to retreat. Sheridan then sent forward two regiments of veterans who drove the Confederates eastward across Bull Run and over the hill beyond.[17]

As Sheridan's men pursued the retreating rebels, they saw to their left the head of Alexander McCook's column advancing on the Mackville Pike toward the town. The First Corps soldiers betrayed no sense of urgency as they approached the battlefield. McCook had not received any word that the enemy was directly in his front, and he failed to notice the flags that Sheridan's signalers were using to try to warn him of the presence of the Confederates. When his cavalry scouts ran into opposition, McCook simply halted his column in the road, ordered up a single infantry regiment to support the cavalry, and had two long-range cannons from Battery A, 1st Michigan Light Artillery (more commonly referred to within the army as "Loomis's battery"), placed on a hill to shell the woods on the far side of Doctor's Creek.[18] He then held a brief conference with his lead division commander, Lovell Rousseau, in the course of which he believed that he ordered Rousseau to deploy his Third Division in a defensive formation, linking up with Gilbert's corps on the right. Leaving Rousseau in temporary command, McCook then rode back to Buell's headquarters for a consultation. Rousseau, however, understood Mc-

Cook only to have indicated a provisional line of battle "to be adopted if the enemy advanced upon us." Since there was no enemy advance, the bulk of the First Corps stayed where it was, stretched out in a long, vulnerable column on the Mackville Pike.[19]

After waiting for an hour, Rousseau on his own initiative decided to advance his division to the still, muddy water of Doctor's Creek, as his men were "suffering intensely for the want of it." As they went forward they encountered more artillery fire than Rousseau expected, prompting him to halt the column again and order up Captain Simonson's 5th Indiana Battery. A noisy artillery duel began shortly after noon and continued for over an hour, with little result. "Loomis['s] battery had so few good rammer staves and sponges, that they used rails trimmed down with an axe," an ordnance officer later noted. The drought that so tormented the men posed a technical problem for Simonson's gunners, who did not have enough water to sponge out their cannon properly. (Guns needed to be sponged out after each shot, to prevent lingering sparks in the barrel from igniting the next round prematurely.) While the ineffectual artillery exchange continued, Rousseau finally deployed the two infantry brigades he had at hand. He also learned that his third brigade, which had been delayed by the march of Jackson's division, was taking a cross-country shortcut around Jackson's men and was somewhere off to the left of the Union line. There was no sign of General McCook.[20]

Back at Buell's headquarters, two and a half miles from the front, preparations were continuing for the next day's attack. McCook arrived at half past noon to report to Buell that his corps had reached its assigned position. The sounds of the First Corps artillery in action were plainly audible, but Buell was not worried: "I had somewhat expected an attack early in the morning on Gilbert's corps while it was isolated; but, as it did not take place, no formidable attack was apprehended after the arrival of the left corps." Buell instructed McCook to link his line with Gilbert's as rapidly as possible (which McCook thought he had already done) and authorized him to make a reconnaissance ahead to Chaplin River to get water for his men. It is unknown exactly how Buell phrased the orders, but apparently McCook felt pleased with the degree of latitude that Buell left him, for Buell's staff officers "all saw McCook going serenely away like a general carrying his orders with him."[21]

Those who remained at the headquarters were equally serene in their confidence that the rest of the day would pass in relative quiet. The artillery fire continued, at one point swelling into a "heavy and furious cannonading" that drew Buell out of his tent to complain about the waste of powder. Otherwise, the army commander took no notice of it, convinced that "the cannonading . . . was not supposed to proceed from any serious engagement." Certainly it was not an unusual event. "It was common enough in those days to waste artillery ammunition in an idle way," a Kentucky gunner later wrote, explaining how Buell and his staff could remain so unconcerned. Artillery fire alone was inconsequential; a real battle would be marked by thousands of distant muskets firing, making a noise like the continuous ripping of canvas. No such sound reached army headquarters that day.[22]

It was thus with complete astonishment that Buell received at 4:00 P.M. the news that McCook's corps was under attack, that it could not stand without reinforcements, that both of its flanks were giving way, and that the battle had been raging for several hours. Buell simply could not believe that a major battle could be taking place and so doubted the rest of the message. "It was so difficult to credit the latter [that a battle had been under way since noon] that I thought there must even be some mis-apprehension in regard to the former [that McCook's corps was in danger]." Unfortunately for Buell, the messenger was not in error. Rather, the command and communications system of the Army of the Ohio had failed completely and irretrievably. Don Carlos Buell had missed the Battle of Perryville.[23]

"No Military Science, but Simply Brave Men"

Following his meeting with Buell, McCook returned to his corps at a few minutes after 1:00 P.M. He found the batteries of Simonson and Loomis firing at the distant Confederates and ordered them to stop, as there were no enemy infantry visible. The two batteries were well positioned on a hill to the north of the Mackville Pike, facing east. Rousseau had placed Colonel William Lytle's Seventeenth Brigade to the right of the guns, in a line that stretched down the hill to the pike and continued a little beyond. Still farther south, the men of the 42nd Indiana (also of Lytle's brigade) were preparing dinner in the nearly dry bed of Doctor's Creek, where Rousseau had sent them to get water and then apparently forgotten about them.[24]

Rousseau had deployed Colonel Leonard Harris's Ninth Brigade to the left of the artillery position, leaving the 10th Wisconsin regiment directly behind the guns to provide support against an infantry attack. The remaining one-third of Rousseau's infantry, Starkweather's Twenty-eighth Brigade, was still well to the rear, trying to regain its place with the rest of the division after Jackson's men blocked its path. Without advising Rousseau, McCook detached two of the 33rd Ohio's companies from Harris's brigade and sent them forward in skirmish formation into the woods that led down toward Doctor's Creek. McCook also met with Jackson of the Tenth Division and Brigadier

The Battle of Perryville, seen from the position of Rousseau's division looking east. From *Harper's Weekly*, November 1, 1862; photograph courtesy of The Lincoln Museum, Fort Wayne, Indiana (TLM #4545).

General William Terrill, recently promoted from captain of artillery in the Regular Army to the command of the Thirty-third Brigade in Jackson's division. McCook directed Terrill to deploy his infantry and artillery on some high ground to the left of Harris's brigade, facing a wooded hill that bordered Doctor's Creek on the west. When his men were in position, McCook continued, Terrill was to "advance a body of skirmishers cautiously down the slope of the hill to the water." "I'll do it, and that's my water," Terrill replied.[25]

At two o'clock, the woods in front of Harris's brigade came alive with gray-clad soldiers. Well to the front of the rest of the Union line, the skirmishers of the 33rd Ohio fell under heavy attack. McCook, usurping the roles of his subordinate division, brigade, and regimental officers, sent the rest of the 33rd Ohio forward, followed by the 2nd Ohio. He then ordered Rousseau to bring up the 24th Illinois from his reserve infantry (Starkweather's brigade, which had just reached the battlefield), an order that Rousseau chose to carry out in person.[26]

While Rousseau was leading the 24th Illinois forward, more and more Confederates emerged from the woods on the far side of Doctor's Creek and swarmed across the valley toward the Union lines. Loomis withdrew his battery, which had used up most of its long-range ammunition. Rebel infantry soon appeared within four hundred yards of Simonson's sweating gunners, who frantically fired round after round of canister at the enemy. "This was our first real fight," wrote artillerist Daniel Chandler, "and we soon began to realize what a battle means. . . . often through the smoke we could see the enemy marching and forming in line to attack, and as often when we turned the guns on them they would disappear." "I cannot imagine a more terrible fight than that which took place on this spot for an hour or more, the battery firing double shotted canister as fast as the pieces could be loaded," wrote another gunner, Henry Kendall. By half past three, Simonson's battery was retreating to a safer position, leaving the 10th Wisconsin alone on that portion of the battlefield. Rousseau had posted the 94th Ohio to help the 10th Wisconsin support Simonson's guns, but an aide from McCook had brought orders sending the Ohio men elsewhere. Having left the 10th Wisconsin vulnerable and outnumbered, McCook tried to rectify the situation by directing Harris to commit his last reserve, the 38th Indiana, to assist the Wisconsin men.[27]

The Confederate attack quickly spread to the southern portion of the First Corps's line, manned by Lytle's brigade. Around three o'clock the men of the forgotten 42nd Indiana had their afternoon meal interrupted. "The first intimation we had of the immediate presence of the rebels," wrote Captain Spillard Horrall of Company G, "was a shot from their cannon" that smashed into a tree above the headquarters' mess. The next shot "knocked away a stack of guns. . . . It was then we understood we were 'in for it.' " Ordered to "break by companies to the rear," each company scrambled up out of the creek, "not . . . without great confusion," and made its own way to a hilltop where the rest of Lytle's brigade was deployed. William Stuckey of Company K saw his friend Oliver Busenham struck in the back by a bullet but could not stop: "he fell and ask[ed] me to help him but there was no place to stop and help wounded men [as] the Secesh was in all over that ground in [a] few minutes." After they reached the hilltop, the men of the 42nd Indiana moved to the rear and began to pull themselves back into a unit. Several company officers steadied their men by putting them through the manual of arms, calming them with the familiar ritual of drill even as bullets filled the air around them. Within minutes, the regiment had regained its cohesion, which it maintained for the balance of the day.[28]

The rest of the Seventeenth Brigade did not have long to wait for its part in the battle to begin. Colonel Lytle had deployed his regiments in two lines, with the 3rd Ohio and 10th Ohio in front, supported by the 15th Kentucky and 88th Indiana. To reduce casualties from Confederate artillery fire, most of

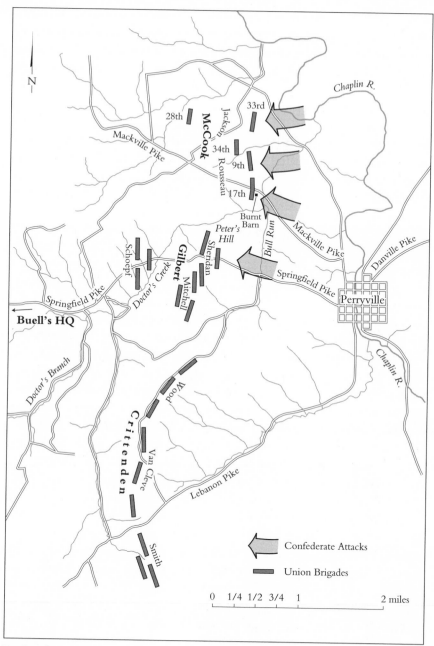

Battle of Perryville, October 8, 1862. Based on *Atlas to Accompany the Official Records*, plate XXIV, no. 2.

the men were lying down, although regimental commanders like John Beatty of the 3rd Ohio and Curran Pope of the 15th Kentucky made a point of continuing to ride on horseback along their unit's lines, exposing themselves to danger. Beatty waited until the enemy infantry were within 150 yards before he ordered his men to stand up and begin firing. The furious close-range exchange of musketry that ensued ignited a barn full of hay near the right end of the 3rd Ohio's line. The heat, Beatty wrote, forced the Ohio men back across the crest of the hill, but they "steadied themselves on the colors" and stood in support of the 15th Kentucky men who took their place in the brigade's front line.[29]

But the Kentuckians were no more successful in holding the line; they fell back after their lieutenant colonel and major were killed. As the Confederates pressed their attack, Lytle began to lose control of his brigade. Seeing that his unit's defensive position was deteriorating, he sent a staff officer to tell the individual regiments to retreat. Before the orders could be delivered, however, the regimental commanders took matters into their own hands. Pope and Beatty met and agreed that their regiments had to fall back. Without waiting for orders, Colonel George Humphrey of the 88th Indiana likewise decided to retreat to avoid being outflanked. These movements exposed the right flank of the 10th Ohio, which occupied the left half of the brigade's front line. The men of the 10th Ohio were still lying prone to avoid the artillery fire coming from over the hill to their front when they were overwhelmed by a Confederate assault from the position vacated by the rest of the brigade. Unable to change their formation to meet the unexpected onslaught from the flank, they fell back in some confusion, with Colonel Lytle among the casualties. Shortly afterward Beatty was told that the brigade commander had been killed (he was actually still alive but wounded and captured). Although four of its five component regiments continued to fight effectively, the leaderless Seventeenth Brigade temporarily ceased to exist; by the end of the day both Beatty and Humphrey had informally attached their regiments to other brigades.[30]

A few hundred yards to the north, Harris's Ninth Brigade was equally hard-pressed. Three volleys from the muskets of the 10th Wisconsin kept the approaching Southern infantry at bay just long enough for Colonel Benjamin F. Scribner's 38th Indiana to occupy the ground recently vacated by the batteries of Loomis and Simonson. Fighting side by side with Scribner's men, the Wisconsin troops kept up a continuous fire for ninety minutes. In so doing, they exhausted the forty rounds that each soldier carried, "together with all in the boxes of the dead and wounded," according to their colonel, Alfred R. Chapin. The struggle was fierce and straightforward, Colonel Chapin wrote: "the nature of the fight was such as to require no military science, but simply brave men." Courage was indeed at a premium, but tactical skill mattered as well. When Harris pulled Chapin's weary soldiers out of the line to replenish their cartridge boxes, the maneuver left a gap of two hundred yards in the Union line next to the men of the 38th Indiana, who had also used up most of their ammunition. The retreat of Lytle's brigade and the 10th Wisconsin left the Hoosiers in an untenable position, with both flanks exposed. Scribner ordered his troops to fix bayonets and stand their ground anyway, but Harris soon ordered them to retire with the rest of the Ninth Brigade, which they did in good order.[31]

The Confederate attack on the right flank of the First Corps killed or wounded hundreds of men and forced the survivors of Rousseau's division to retreat. Unlike the recruits who panicked at the Battle of Richmond, however, these veteran soldiers remained under the control of their regimental officers. Comparing their behavior to that of troops who lacked experience, Colonel Scribner observed that "when old soldiers retreat, they will keep together as if attracted to each other by a sort of moral gravitation, and will halt [when out of the enemy's range]. On the contrary, when raw troops become panic-stricken they cannot be rallied within the noise of battle."[32] Rousseau's aide-de-camp William Shanks confirmed that when retreating soldiers "are beyond the reach of the enemy's guns they generally halt, look back, and examine into matters." If they were not too scattered, they could be rallied, but "it is next to impossible to induce a demoralized man to fight with any other than his own regiment."[33]

The men of the Third Division had been driven back, but they were not scattered. Rousseau described how some of them responded when he sought to rally them: "On approaching the Fifteenth Kentucky (though broken and shattered) it rose to its feet and cheered, and as one man moved to the top of the hill, where it could see the enemy." He put Loomis's battery back into action, overriding its commander's objection that McCook had ordered him to save his ammunition for close work: "Pointing to the enemy advancing, I said it was close enough, and would be closer in a moment." Encouraged by the fire of Loomis's guns, Rousseau and Colonel Harris were able to improvise a defensive line by pulling together the remnants of Harris's and Lytle's brigades, as well as a stray regiment from another division.[34]

The veteran regiments of Rousseau's division withstood every form of battlefield stress at Perryville. The eight experienced regiments in the brigades of Harris and Lytle went into battle with fewer than five hundred men apiece, and each suffered more than a hundred casualties without disintegrating. (The average loss in these regiments was 163, whereas the two new regiments in these brigades suffered only 71 casualties combined.) The 33rd Ohio and 42nd

Indiana were at times separated into two or more groups of companies, but both regiments reunited themselves and continued to function. When troops from another regiment retreated in haste through the ranks of the 38th Indiana, the Hoosiers calmly held their ground, oblivious to the near-panic of men they did not know. The soldiers of the 80th Indiana similarly withstood a retreat through their ranks by the 2nd Ohio. Shared backgrounds, months of drill, and personal leadership by officers like Beatty and Scribner rendered the veteran regiments almost indestructible.[35]

The cohesion of Rousseau's regiments contrasted sharply with the disarray of larger organizations within the Army of the Ohio at Perryville. Once the battle began, brigade commanders Lytle and Harris were unable to control their units effectively. Their difficulties were exacerbated by their superior officers, Rousseau and McCook, who repeatedly bypassed established chains of command and gave orders to specific regiments without notifying the appropriate brigade leaders of their actions. "I now sent back for the Ninety-fourth Ohio . . . ," Harris wrote in his after-action report, "but was informed that they had been directed by Major General McCook to support a section of artillery. . . . The positions of the other regiments had all been changed." The meddling of McCook and Rousseau in the maneuvers of individual regiments and even companies resulted in confusion and intermixing of formations among the brigades of Lytle, Harris, and Colonel George Webster (of Jackson's Tenth Division), rendering the brigades impossible to command.[36]

At the division level, Rousseau and Jackson had similar problems. When the Confederate attack began, one of Jackson's two brigades was deploying to the north of Rousseau's line, but Webster's Thirty-fourth Brigade was in the rear of Rousseau's division. Jackson's division was thus separated when the battle began and never fought as a unit. Rousseau's division was likewise split, with Starkweather's brigade fighting the entire battle from a position on the left wing of the First Corps, behind Jackson's division. Rousseau spent much of the afternoon lending his inspirational presence to this brigade, during which time he was completely out of touch with events affecting the other two-thirds of his division. The disintegration of the brigades and divisions of the First Corps eliminated the possibility of large-scale tactical maneuvers. Whether the Army of the Ohio survived the onslaught would depend entirely on the ability of individual regiments to preserve their cohesion and hold whatever piece of ground they happened to occupy.[37]

While the veteran regiments of Rousseau's division were falling back in relatively good order from the Confederate assault, the raw recruits of Jackson's Tenth Division were receiving their initiation into the mysteries of combat. Like the rest of the army, they had had little food or water for the past twenty-four hours. Alden F. Brooks of the 105th Ohio recalled that "the night before we went into the battle we had no food and a dry, poor ear of corn was issued to us which we parched and pounded and ate in our coffee." On the morning of the eighth they had done their best to hurry in response to the sounds of gunfire from the vicinity of Perryville, but in McCook's words, they were "raw troops [who] understood their duties imperfectly, and consequently could not march rapidly." McCook left word for Jackson to pull his men off the Mackville Pike into a reserve position when they arrived, but there was some delay in getting the wagons of the leading brigade out of the way so the second one could move up. Webster's Thirty-fourth Brigade eventually deployed behind and to the left of Harris's brigade. To Terrill's Thirty-third Brigade, McCook gave orders to occupy a ridge farther to the north and send skirmishers ahead to Doctor's Creek.[38]

It was shortly after two o'clock when Terrill reached his unit's assigned position, on high ground separated by a narrow gully from a wooded hill that rose to the east and then fell away to the valley of Doctor's Creek. A gunner by training who had commanded a battery at Shiloh with much distinction, Terrill chose to deploy his brigade's artillery first. This consisted of a recently organized eight-gun battery, led by Terrill's friend Lieutenant Charles C. Parsons and manned by untrained infantrymen from the 105th Ohio. Parsons unlimbered his guns in a line facing to the northeast, presumably to prevent an enemy force from sweeping around the left flank of the army.[39]

Following Parsons's battery came the 123rd Illinois. These men had just come up behind the artillery when thousands of Confederate soldiers appeared in the woods on the hill to the east, advancing down through the trees toward the gully that lay between them and Terrill's ridge. Terrill saw that Parson's battery was facing the wrong way and that its right flank was exposed to the unexpected attack. To gain time for the artillery to change front, Terrill ordered the 123rd Illinois to charge. Unfortunately for the regiment, it had been marching in column by the right flank, meaning that the first company in the column was the one that normally occupied the right end of the regiment in line of battle. When the colonel ordered the men to face to the right, the brigade adjutant noted, this maneuver "unluckily threw the rear rank in front, which produced much confusion, the regiment being a new one." No longer in their accustomed places relative to one another within the unit, what little drill the inexperienced Illinois soldiers had practiced would be of no use to them that day.[40]

The men of the 123rd made it into the gully and up to the edge of the woods, where a high rail fence checked their progress. They fired a volley at the Confederates sheltered behind the trees but soon began to waver. As more and more gray-clad soldiers filled the woods, threatening to envelop their flanks, the Illinois volunteers one by one turned and ran across the gully and back up the ridge, trying to reach the temporary safety of its far side. The rebels burst from the forest, crossed the gully, and pressed up the slope behind them, but by this time Lieutenant Parsons had managed to get five or six of his eight guns wheeled around to face eastward. They swept the slope of the ridge with canister, temporarily driving the Southerners back to the woods.[41]

At about the same time that the 123rd Illinois was retreating, the equally inexperienced men of the 105th Ohio regiment came up from the south, passed behind Parson's battery, and formed a line to the left and rear of the guns. They were panting with fatigue after covering half a mile at the double-quick to reach their position and had been thrown into confusion by a runaway team of six horses pulling a caisson that had galloped through their ranks. To make matters worse, they soon found themselves in the same backward formation as the 123rd Illinois. According to Lieutenant Albion Tourgée, the regiment was ordered to halt and "face front" (or left), which put the companies in their proper relative places but facing west, away from the Confederates. The colonel then ordered the men to "about-face" and advance with the rear rank in front. For a unit that had conducted battalion drill only once before, the unfamiliar maneuver meant trouble. "The commanding officer made a mistake," wrote another member of the regiment, "and we had to face by the rear rank. It *was a hot place.*"[42]

In the confusion that ensued, the regiment's formation fell apart. Some men advanced to the crest of the ridge, while others remained below it, unable to see or fire at the enemy. Private Josiah Ayre's journal entry for the day portrayed the helplessness of undrilled men trying to fight: "By some reason or other we could not form into proper line and after going through several maneuvers in order to do so we became mixed and confused, not knowing what our officers said or anything about it. Finally we were ordered to load and fire the best we could."[43] Those of the regiment who stood in the open atop the ridge to fire saw that they were at a disadvantage against the Southerners, who were fighting from the cover of the woods less than a hundred yards away. The Confederate troops, many of whom were veterans of Shiloh, quickly seized the initiative, gave the blood-chilling rebel yell, and charged up the slope again, driving the Ohioans away in disorder.

The situation of Terrill's brigade quickly deteriorated. The makeshift crews of Parsons's battery fled, abandoning seven cannon to be captured; they had to drag with them the broken-hearted Lieutenant Parsons, who was "perfectly unmanned" by the loss of his guns. The brigade was essentially leaderless, as division commander Jackson had been killed by one of the first shots fired in the attack, and his nominal successor William Terrill was too busy trying to rally the men of the 105th Ohio and 123rd Illinois to exercise tactical leadership over his brigade, much less to take over the division. The brigade made a brief stand at a fence bordering a lane a hundred yards behind the ridge where it first deployed, but then it retreated again through a belt of woods and into a field of corn so tall that the men could no longer see one another. This especially affected the luckless 105th Ohio, which did not have its own regimental flag to serve as a beacon above the corn. (Curiously, the 105th did carry a flag at Perryville, but it was that of the 101st Indiana, which had been placed in its custody as a punishment to the latter regiment; the men of the 105th kept the Indiana colors cased throughout the battle rather than fight under a "foreign" flag.) The 105th Ohio fell into further confusion in the cornfield when some of the men heard an order from Terrill to march by the flank to a new position, while others continued to mill about in place.[44]

Meanwhile, Terrill's other two regiments encountered problems of their own. One of them, the 80th Illinois, had been misdirected by a guide on its approach to the front line and arrived too late to prevent Parsons's battery from being overrun. The other was "Garrard's detachment," a composite unit made up from three understrength Kentucky and Tennessee regiments. Both Garrard's men and the 80th Illinois were swept up in the brigade's retreat, falling back almost a mile. They eventually halted and regrouped behind the protection of Starkweather's brigade, which had fortuitously occupied a hill far to the rear of the ridge where Parsons's battery had been captured.[45]

"Our Brigade in less than an hour ceased to be a Brigade," was the observation of Captain Robert B. Taylor of Garrard's detachment. The brigade commander agreed; believing that his unit had been "wholly dissipated," Terrill gave up the role of brigadier general and reverted to his professional roots as a Regular Army artillerist. Captain Taylor saw Terrill on the hill among Starkweather's gunners with his sleeves rolled up, "whirling the rammer of a field gun around his head . . . with that peculiar grace only acquired by drill in the Artillery School." The Thirty-third Brigade had suffered 527 casualties, but as fragments of its regiments began to assemble behind Starkweather's hill, Terrill apparently regained hope of rallying them. Before he could do more than begin to reform his shattered brigade, however, he was fatally wounded by a shell fragment.[46]

While Southern troops were overwhelming Terrill's men, the Tenth Division's other brigade, commanded by Colonel George Webster, was faring little better. Webster's artillery battery, the 19th Indiana, was unlimbered on the same ridge as Parsons's guns, several hundred yards to the south. The infantry of the Thirty-fourth Brigade was supposed to be placed behind the artillery to provide support, but Webster found his regiments unwieldy, not only because of their lack of discipline but also because of their unusually large size, which averaged more than 750 men. Deployed in line of battle, the 98th Ohio could not fit into its assigned place and had to double up into a formation four ranks deep instead of two. When the Confederate attack began, Webster sent the 121st Ohio and half of the 98th Ohio to the left to help protect Parsons's battery, but the 121st lost its way, and both contingents arrived too late to help. The detachment from the 98th turned around and returned to its original position, but when the men of the 121st saw gray-clad soldiers in possession of the Union guns, many of them lost their nerve and ran from the field. "It was not cowardice," the brigade adjutant wrote, "but want of discipline and the unfortunate position to which they were assigned that caused disorder in the ranks."[47]

Elsewhere in Webster's brigade, Colonel J. R. Taylor of the 50th Ohio panicked at the outset of the action. "The first position I saw him in," wrote Captain Percival P. Oldershaw, of the Tenth Division staff, "was lying on his face, crouched behind a stump." Lieutenant Colonel Silas A. Strickland guided the regiment through the rest of the battle, while Taylor (who would resign from the army after the battle) retreated to a safer position, unable to master his fear. Colonel Taylor left his men in a difficult position, close behind the 19th Indiana battery, where for thirty minutes they lay on the ground under enemy fire, unable to reply. "[T]o say it was demoralizing would be putting it very mild indeed," one of them later wrote. When the 50th Ohio was ordered to rise and attack the enemy, fifty of its members headed for the rear instead. The last misfortune to strike Webster's brigade occurred late in the afternoon, when McCook called for assistance to stabilize the situation on the right wing of the First Corps. Colonel Webster personally led the 98th Ohio into action, helping to slow the Confederate advance against Lytle's retreating brigade, but in the process he fell from his horse with a fatal wound.[48]

The rout of the First Corps's left wing was finally checked by the veterans of Starkweather's Twenty-eighth Brigade. Bringing up the rear of the First Corps, they had covered fifteen miles in five hours to reach the battlefield. Although "their parched lips had not tasted water all that terrible day," the men in Captain Wilberforce Nevin's company of the 79th Pennsylvania marched "the last four miles as hard as we could go in a direct line for the sound of the cannon over fields, hills, woods, fences and everything." Starkweather, on his own initiative, moved his brigade cross-country to the extreme left of the Union line, in part because the road ahead was blocked by Jackson's slow-moving division, and in part because he considered the flank position "one that should be held at all hazards."[49]

The Battle of Perryville, seen from the position of Starkweather's brigade, as sketched by A. E. Mathews of the 31st Ohio. Photograph courtesy of The Lincoln Museum, Fort Wayne, Indiana (TLM #4546).

Starkweather's infantry regiments were deploying on a hill behind his two artillery batteries when refugees from the wreck of Terrill's brigade overran them, but, as happened elsewhere at Perryville, regimental boundaries proved impervious to panic. In Captain Nevin's words, "Our first sight of the field was the new levies in full rout—wounded men—officers without swords—men without guns—horses without riders pitching full at us. We just fell down on our faces, and let the cowardly herd pass over us, rose up and found our selves in their lost position."[50] Starkweather placed his one inexperienced regiment, the 21st Wisconsin, lying down in a cornfield in front of his hillside artillery position. When the unsuspecting Confederates pursued Terrill's men into the corn, the Wisconsin soldiers stood up and delivered a staggering volley. Starkweather then ordered them to charge but discovered that "no field officer was left to carry the command into execution." The 21st Wisconsin, he reported, instead "retired in some disorder and confusion." Under continuing pressure the rest of the brigade eventually retreated as well, but the men remained in sufficiently good order to serve as a rallying point for what was left of the First Corps's left wing.[51]

On the corps' right flank, Harris's improvised line and Loomis's battery, now down to its last few rounds of ammunition, appeared to be the only force left to withstand the onrushing rebels. Finally, at five o'clock, a single brigade of reinforcements came up from the Union rear. They were from Jefferson C. Davis's old division and included two regiments of "Pea Ridge men," the 59th

Illinois and 22nd Indiana. Although they were still so new to the Army of the Ohio that Rousseau did not yet know the name of their brigade commander (he was Colonel Michael Gooding), their appearance was greeted with joy. They met the enemy in a confusing twilight engagement, described by George Herr as "a disordered and terrible melee . . . almost a hand-to-hand encounter," in the course of which Colonel Gooding lost his way and was captured. Confederate general Leonidas Polk almost suffered the fate of Zollicoffer at Logan's Cross Roads when he ordered a regiment to stop firing at friendly troops, only to discover that he was among the ranks of the 22nd Indiana. Gooding's men were eventually forced back, but, like Starkweather's brigade, they halted the enemy advance long enough to sap its momentum and prevent any further Confederate gains before nightfall and the end of the battle.[52]

"No More Fit to Lead an Army . . . Than the Horses on Which They Ride"

The afternoon of October 8, 1862, was relatively quiet at the headquarters of the Army of the Ohio. The steady banging of artillery at the front continued, but Buell reported that "no sound of musketry reached my headquarters by which the sharpness of the action on the left could be known or even suspected." That the sound of infantry fire could have been inaudible a mere three miles from the battlefield challenges credulity (considering that the fighting at Shiloh was audible from as far as thirty miles away, and the Battle of Stones River in December 1862 could be heard from forty miles), but several staff offices and visitors to army headquarters confirmed that what they could hear that afternoon sounded like nothing more than an artillery skirmish. This was due to the physical phenomenon of "acoustic shadow," caused by the terrain, the wind, or both.[53] Major Wright of Buell's staff experienced its effect vividly as he rode toward the front some time after four o'clock. "Now up to this time I had heard no sound of battle; I had heard no artillery in front of me, and no heavy infantry-firing," but as Wright passed an ambulance train that was hurrying forward, he began to sense that something was happening: "I suddenly turned into a road and there before me, within a few hundred yards, the battle of Perryville burst into view, and the roar of the artillery and the continuous rattle of the musketry first broke upon my ear. It was the finest spectacle I ever saw. It was wholly unexpected, and it fixed me with astonishment."[54]

The central irony of the Battle of Perryville is not simply that Buell was unaware that his army was engaged, but that it was engaged in exactly the battle he had been trying to arrange. The entire Army of the Ohio was massed against a fraction of the Confederate force in Kentucky. All of Kirby Smith's troops and one division of Bragg's were still at Frankfort. No more than sixteen thousand Southern soldiers participated in the attack that broke the First Corps. The two other corps of Buell's army were each as large as the entire Confederate force engaged. Had they both advanced boldly once the battle was under way, they could have seized the town of Perryville, cut off the attackers from their supply depots in central Kentucky, and very possibly achieved a decisive battlefield victory on the model of Austerlitz or Waterloo. Instead, the commanders of the Second and Third Corps took almost no aggressive action, while the generals of the First Corps failed to manage their troops effectively, leaving individual regiments to resist the Confederate assault as best they could.[55]

Buell's ignorance of the very existence of the battle obviously prevented him from taking advantage of his opportunity, but the near-destruction of one-third of the army, while the other two-thirds stood idle, was the result of leadership failures throughout the organization. One problem was that many of the army's officers (with notable exceptions like Colonel Taylor of the 50th Ohio) displayed an excess of physical courage. Reckless behavior like that of Colonels Beatty and Pope, who casually rode their horses in full view of the enemy while their men took cover, demonstrated their fitness to lead and gave confidence to their troops, but only as long as they survived. Had Beatty been killed or seriously wounded, as many field officers were, his regiment's morale would have fallen, and tactical command of the 3rd Ohio would have passed into the hands of the unit's lieutenant colonel or major, who might not have been fully aware of the tactical situation and who would certainly have lacked Beatty's experience.

At higher command levels, officer casualties were still more disruptive. Since a brigade occupied more ground than a regiment, when its leader was incapacitated it took more time for staff officers to locate his successor, generally the brigade's senior regimental commander, who might be hundreds of yards away. Further, the new commander might well have no idea of the location of the other regiments in the brigade or the orders under which they were operating. If more than one officer in the same chain of command happened to fall, the already delicate succession arrangements could fail completely. This is what happened to the Tenth Division, which was effectively decapitated by the deaths of its three highest ranking officers; command of the entire division ultimately devolved onto Colonel Albert Hall, of the 105th Ohio, who was fully occupied with the disintegration of his own regiment. The display of bravery by Union officers like Lovell Rousseau, who "rode up and down the line encouraging the men" of his Third Division until an observer wondered that he was not "perforated" by enemy bullets, certainly played a role in rallying the First Corps and eventually bringing the Confederate attack to a halt. But such bravery also resulted in the loss of a division commander and three brigade leaders (out of five engaged), plus the capture of Colonel Gooding of the Thirtieth Brigade as he led his men to the relief of the First Corps, losses that made it impossible for the corps to carry out any kind of tactical plan other than trying to hold its position.[56]

Even if they were not injured, commanders who led from the front tended to become too deeply involved with their immediate surroundings and to lose sight of the larger picture of events. An axiom of military theory states that generals should give orders to units that they command directly and be aware of the locations of subunits two levels down. By this rule, McCook as the commander of the First Corps should have issued instructions to his division leaders and had a good idea of where each of their brigades was, but he should have left the direction of specific regiments to his subordinates. Instead, he treated the corps as an undifferentiated collection of regiments, to each of which he could give orders directly without bothering to inform their brigade or division commanders. He also allowed the brigades of Jackson and Rousseau to become intermixed, further confusing the chain of command for each division. Rousseau similarly indulged in overmanagement of his regiments and admitted that his personal direction of the stand of Starkweather's brigade meant that he "could not look after the interests of the Seventeenth Brigade" of Colonel Lytle until the battle was nearly over. Terrill, the artillery captain promoted to brigadier general, became so involved with the activity of Parsons's battery that he left the deployment of the rest of his Thirty-third Brigade to his staff officers.[57]

Communication to and from First Corps leaders during the battle was limited, due in part to their tendency to assume the roles of junior officers, leading charges and rallying regiments. Since Rousseau was not fully aware of what was happening to his division, for example, he could not communicate its condition to the corps commander. It was Alexander McCook, however, who was largely responsible for the worst communications breakdown of the day: the failure to inform Buell that a battle was taking place. At two-thirty, half an hour after the Confederate attack began, McCook dispatched an aide to Sheridan, whose division lay only a few hundred yards south of Rousseau's, asking him to keep an eye on the right flank of the First Corps. At three o'clock McCook sent Captain Horace Fisher bearing a more urgent message, directed "to the nearest commander of troops," asking for assistance. Shortly afterward he sent another messenger, this time to Brigadier General Albin

Schoepf, who commanded the reserve of Gilbert's Third Corps. To army headquarters, he sent no messages at all.[58] This is all the more remarkable because signal officers had managed to establish a telegraph link between the headquarters of Buell and McCook, which remained operational through the afternoon of October 8. Officers at McCook's end used the otherwise idle system to send news of the attack informally to their counterparts at Buell's headquarters, but the latter did not pass along the intelligence, as it was not their prerogative to deliver information that McCook had not chosen to send officially.[59]

Why McCook failed to communicate with Buell directly remains a mystery. Buell, who was hardly disinterested in the matter, later blamed McCook for the "grave error" of believing "that he could manage the difficulty without the aid or control of his commander." McCook might be excused from knowing of the acoustic shadow that prevented Buell from hearing the battle, but he was certainly aware from his visit to headquarters earlier in the day that Buell's injury would prevent him from easily investigating any such sounds. By neglecting to provide even the most basic information regarding the size and location of the attack until an hour after it was under way, by which time he had to admit that "the safety of my corps was compromised," McCook put the entire army at risk.[60]

As long as no orders were forthcoming from Buell, the rest of the army could do nothing but sit and wait. The nearest troops, those of Sheridan's Eleventh Division, could plainly see the attack on the First Corps. Although some commentators have argued otherwise, Sheridan had no reason to communicate what he saw to Buell, as it was not the role of a division commander to report everything that he witnessed directly to army headquarters. (If it were, army leaders would have had time to do nothing but read redundant reports; Meade at Gettysburg would have received twenty messages from his divisional generals informing him that Pickett's Charge was under way.)[61]

Around three o'clock Sheridan's division, which was firmly dug in atop Peter's Hill, was attacked by a substantial Confederate force. Colonel Dan McCook ordered his men to "to lay low and reserve the fire until the enemy was near," which the 86th Illinois's Levi Ross considered "a terrible ordeal for green troops who had been in the service scarcely one month." John Sackett and his comrades in the 36th Illinois likewise waited until the rebels were two hundred yards away, then fired until their muskets "got so hot that we could hardly hold them." Edwin Benton of the 44th Illinois wrote home of his regiment that "we did our duty amidst the unpleasant whipping of Bullets[,] solid shot and shell which came around us seeming almost to say 'where is ye? where is ye?' " The colonel of the raw 73rd Illinois misconstrued an order and began to retreat in the face of the attack, but he recovered from his mistake and put the regiment back in its place in the line, where the men did "good execution" with their old-fashioned smoothbore muskets firing buck and ball ammunition.[62]

Supported by two batteries, Sheridan's men resisted a series of attacks that lasted more than an hour. The Union artillery was particularly effective, Levi Ross wrote, "dealing out grape, Canester and death to the advancing rebels."[63] Silas Parker of the 44th Illinois described the engagement in a letter to his family: "the Rebels thinking that our Batteries was poorly supported, charged on us. [I]t was the grandest sight I have ever witnessed. On they came yelling like devils. Bayonets glisning in the sun. But a change come over their dreams . . . [when] they charged on the Flag that has made them powerful. Again we drive them, and they leave their dead on the field."[64] After the Confederates finally backed away, Sheridan did not order a pursuit, in part because the retreat of McCook's corps had exposed the left flank of his division. Further, Sheridan had already tried to advance a few hours earlier and had been ordered back by his corps commander, Gilbert, who knew that Buell did not want an engagement that day and was determined to enforce those orders to the letter, regardless of circumstances.

The refusal to allow Sheridan to exercise his initiative and move in support of the beleaguered First Corps was typical of Gilbert's style of leadership. In the few weeks since his curious appointment to command the Third Corps, his rigid enforcement of the most trivial regulations, combined with his evident inability to meet the larger responsibilities of a major general, had made him one of the most unpopular officers in the entire army. He had nearly starved Sheridan's men by his literal interpretation of the regulation limiting wagon trains to ambulances and ammunition wagons. As Sheridan put it, he "construed the order so illiberally that it was next to impossible to supply the men with food." Another general accused Gilbert of reserving the only pool of water for miles around "for his own use, his staff, and escort, while the soldiers were perishing for it. He had a guard over it and would not let them have a drink."[65]

Gilbert's response to events on October 8 revealed how badly Buell had miscast him as a corps commander. He was at army headquarters when the attack began and had a midday meal with Buell. Sometime between three and four o'clock the increase in artillery fire from Sheridan's front prompted him to return to his corps. On the way he met Captain Fisher, riding hard from McCook's headquarters with the news that the First Corps was, in Gilbert's words, "upon the point of being overpowered." "Instead of sending Captain Fisher back to General McCook with my answer to his appeal for help, I advised him to continue on and bear to General Buell the astounding news."[66] Gilbert sent no troops to McCook, but to protect the flanks of his own corps he ordered two of his divisions (led by Schoepf and R. B. Mitchell) to close in upon Sheridan's left and right, respectively. Continuing toward the front, Gilbert encountered Gooding's Thirtieth Brigade, of R. B. Mitchell's division, on the left of the Springfield pike. This unit was closer to McCook's corps than any other brigade in Gilbert's reserve, but he ordered it back to its parent division on Sheridan's right, thus moving it away from the scene of the fighting where it was most needed.

Gilbert next came upon Schoepf with one of his brigades, just as McCook's third messenger arrived with an urgent request for help. Gilbert was more concerned with the attack on Sheridan: "judging from the sound that it must soon culminate, I detained Captain Hoblitzell to await the issue." When he was finally assured that Sheridan's line was safe, he prepared to send Schoepf's First Brigade to the aid of the First Corps but changed his mind. Gilbert claimed that the First Brigade, the oldest in the army, with four of its five regiments having been in service for over a year, "did not seem to be sufficiently familiar with the tactics to make the simplest movements with promptness and intelligence." He then recalled Gooding's brigade and sent it to the right flank of the First Corps, where it arrived in time to help to stem the last Confederate attack of the day. Shortly afterward, Gilbert received an order from Buell to send two brigades from Schoepf's division to the First Corps. Exercising the discretion that he denied to his own subordinates, Gilbert chose to send only one. The result of these decisions, a Third Corps veteran later wrote, was that Gilbert's command "did no heavy fighting during this engagement . . . despite the earnest appeals and advice of his subordinates," even though the corps "enveloped the enemy's left flank, and could have crushed it like an egg shell."[67]

The Battle of Perryville could have been one of the great military turning points of the Civil War, in either direction. Had the regiments of the First Corps been forced back another half mile, all of their wagons would have been captured, and in all probability the Army of the Ohio would have had to retreat in disgrace to Louisville, leaving Bragg in control of most of Kentucky. Rather than celebrate their narrow escape from disaster, however, Buell's soldiers saw the battle as a great missed opportunity. Lyman Widney of the 34th Illinois, a regiment that was not engaged at Perryville, wrote in his diary that night: "Nothing weakens the soldier in battle more than the suspicion that his Commander is neglecting him. . . . [this feeling] was shared equally by the rank and file of the five Divisions who stood obediently in line anxious and able to decide the day but waiting for the order."[68]

Three weeks earlier, a disgruntled volunteer had sent a letter home complaining that "the majority of our officers high in rank are no more fit to lead an Army onto the battle field than the horses on which they ride. Many privates in the ranks are better qualified."[69] Perryville seemed to bear out this opinion. Buell failed to play any role in the battle, in part because of his injury and the freakish physical conditions that blocked the sound of the battle from reaching his tent, but more fundamentally because of his limited view of what was possible in war. Once the proper time for his army to launch an attack on the morning of October 8 had passed, Buell focused on nothing but his plans for the following day; it was beyond his imagination that the enemy might attack him. When it did, his troops paid the price for his failure in the preceding months to have overcome, or even addressed, the decentralization of organizational loyalty within the Army of the Ohio. McCook's refusal to make timely calls for help, and Gilbert's tardiness in responding to those calls when they finally came, reflected how little Buell had done to build a sense of community and mutual responsibility within the component units of his army. The inability of so many division and brigade leaders to maintain control of their commands on the battlefield was a product of both their indifferent qualifications and the neglect of any training beyond small-unit close order drill. The result was that at Perryville, it was every regiment for itself.

Epilogue

The Army of the Ohio lost 845 men killed, 2,851 wounded, and 515 missing at Perryville, almost all of them from the First Corps.[1] Measured as a percentage of the number of men engaged, this was an extraordinarily high casualty rate. Yet the survivors of the First Corps were not dismayed. Daniel Chandler of Simonson's battery recalled, "We knew we had been whipped but we knew too we had help and done our best to get ready to fight next day." Lucius Wood of the 121st Ohio told his sister how eager he was to fight again, partly to help redeem his regiment's reputation: "when duty calls me again into another contest I am ready to respond and give *sech.* the best there is in the shop." Among the two-thirds of the army that had not been engaged, the sentiment for an immediate renewal of the struggle was even stronger. The army, Lieutenant John Bross wrote to his father, was "chafing like a spirited horse" in its anxiety to renew the battle and defeat Bragg once and for all.[2]

Buell, however, was slow to pursue, and his failure to capitalize on what the army had accomplished cost him the last vestiges of the men's trust. Wild stories circulated about his conduct during the battle. "It is stated," an Illinois soldier wrote, "that Gen. Buell, lay on his back in his tent, reading, coolly indifferent to how the battle was going." Major Connolly of the 123rd Illinois heard by the "grape vine telegraph" that Buell had allowed the First Corps to be defeated out of personal spite—he was mad at Alex McCook for bringing on a battle against orders and so "left him to fight it out without his help." Lucius Wood was among those who repeated the story that Buell and Bragg had slept in the same tent the night before the battle, and many soldiers spread the tale that the opposing generals had colluded to ensure that the Confederates escaped, sometimes adding the detail that Buell went easy on Bragg because the opposing generals were brothers-in-law. In his history of the 10th Indiana, James Shaw discounted some of the rumors about Buell's relationship with Bragg, "but," he added, "we do know he never would fight Bragg if he could help it." The Third Division's chief surgeon, who was responsible for the care of most of the Union wounded, opined that if "30,000 troops stood to arms on our right, ready, willing and anxious to aid their comrades, only waiting for orders . . . I feel we may say that some one blundered."[3]

Over the next two weeks the men were mystified and angered by the pace of their pursuit of Bragg's army. The chorus of opposition to Buell swelled as it became apparent that he was going to allow Bragg to retreat to Tennessee without another battle. A member of the 33rd Ohio, Thaddeus Minshall, groped for words to express his contempt for his commander: "he is a great big lump fish . . . either a traitor or a failure." Eugene Lyford of the 88th Illinois called Buell "an old granny. . . . Shame forever and infamy on his name! We are all disgusted with the man." Even the chaplain of the 58th Indiana agreed that Buell's failure to pursue Bragg transformed the battle into "a useless slaughter of men without any substantial benefit." Some of the blame spilled over onto Gilbert, who was viewed as Buell's "pet." Henry Stone, who served on Buell's staff, noted that the "general feeling among McCook's friends is that Gilbert did nothing and was an indifferent spectator of the former's discomfiture." R. Delavan Mussey expressed the army's consensus: "Every officer in the army feels and knows that Bragg was in our grasp there if Genl B[uell] or Gen G[ilbert] had either of them done their duty. . . . If Gen. Buell is not removed by the President immediately the Army will go to the Devil." A number of regiment and brigade commanders went so far as to sign a petition to Lincoln requesting Buell's removal. "With one voice, so far as it has reached me," Governor Tod of Ohio complained to the secretary of war on October 30, "the army from Ohio demand the removal of General Buell."[4]

Even as Tod wrote, the army's demand had already been granted. On October 24 General in Chief Halleck issued an order to Major General William Rosecrans placing him in command of "the Department of the Cumberland and of the army of operations now under Major-General Buell." It took six days for Rosecrans to make his way from northern Mississippi, where he had defeated an attack on his forces at Corinth on October 3 and 4, to Buell's headquarters in Louisville. Buell continued to busy himself by shuffling detachments of cavalry from post to post, but he was not deaf to the rumors that his job was in jeopardy. "If, as the papers report, my successor has been appointed, it is important that I should know it," he wrote to Halleck on October 29. The answer came in the form of Rosecrans's arrival the next day, marking the moment when, as C. C. Briant of the 6th Indiana recalled, "General Buell's official head fell into Halleck's waste basket."[5]

"The whole army was electrified by the news that 'Don Carlos' was relieved . . . ," wrote artillerist Daniel Chandler, "[and] the change raised the spirits of the troops." "Great joy in camp today over the intelligence that the rebel sympathiser, Gen. Buell, has been superceded," the cynical Levi Ross entered in his diary. Colonel John Beatty was among the minority who viewed the matter with more perspective, predicting that in a year Rosecrans would "be as unpopular as Buell." Most, however, reveled in the moment, as "shout after shout . . . echoed forth" through the army's camps to celebrate the news. "The removal of Buell gives such general satisfaction," one soldier wrote on November 16, "that it is a wonder it was not accomplished sooner."[6]

Rosecrans brought a number of superficial changes to the Army of the Ohio. The mellifluous "Army of the Cumberland" name was revived for the department's troops as a whole, but the army in the field was given the more prosaic title of "XIV Army Corps," a bureaucratic label hardly calculated to inspire institutional loyalty. McCook's First Corps was designated the Right Wing of the XIV Corps, Crittenden's Second Corps became the Left Wing, and the Third Corps (commanded by George Thomas in place of the unlamented Gilbert, whose commission as a brigadier general was eventually submitted to the Senate but never confirmed) was renamed the Center.[7] Rosecrans reorganized the army's signal corps, raised morale by reestablishing daily mail service, and reduced straggling by instituting an Army Directory tent where lost soldiers and returning convalescents could go to find out where their regiments were camped.[8] There was an increase in the frequency of brigade drills.[9] In leadership style, there could have been no sharper contrast than that between the reserved, distant Buell and the jovial, talkative Rosecrans.

The army's next battle, however, showed that many of the flaws exposed at Perryville had not been repaired. At Stones River on the last day of 1862, Rosecrans planned to attack the Confederate army's right flank near the town of Murfreesboro, but Bragg struck first. An early morning assault took Alexander McCook by surprise and crushed the Right Wing of the XIV Army Corps. As at Perryville, the command structure of McCook's unit collapsed. The Confederates came close to destroying McCook's force altogether and cutting off the rest of the army from its base. But as they had done before, individual regiments fought doggedly without direction from above and purchased enough time for reinforcements to arrive and stabilize the Union line. Rosecrans was content to hold his ground, and on January 3, 1863, the enemy withdrew from the field, conceding a bloody, indecisive victory to the formation once known as the Army of the Ohio.[10]

In strategy as well as in battlefield success, Rosecrans seemed to differ little from Buell. When Halleck began pressuring Rosecrans to secure East Tennessee, noted C. C. Briant, "It is sufficient to say that the order was treated as the idea of a crank by Rosecrans, just as it had been by general Buell."[11] Like Buell, Rosecrans took a long time to get ready and preferred marching to fighting. Unlike Buell, however, his elaborate plans eventually led to significant strategic accomplishments. It took Rosecrans six months after the Battle of Stones River to launch an offensive campaign, but when he finally moved in June 1863 he completely outmaneuvered Bragg, forcing the Confederate army out of central Tennessee and capturing Chattanooga without having to fight a major battle.

His success was soured, however, when his divisions pursued the rebels too far into the dense forests of northern Georgia. At the Battle of Chickamauga in September 1863, Bragg turned and delivered an unexpected counterattack, supported by a corps from the Army of Northern Virginia led by James Longstreet. Rosecrans had little idea where his troops were, and a misunderstanding among Union generals caused an entire division to march out of the line of battle at a critical moment, creating an irreparable breach. Rosecrans fled to Chattanooga with most of the army, unaware that George Thomas's men were still on the battlefield, making a heroic stand that earned their leader the nickname "Rock of Chickamauga."

The Union army that fought at Perryville, Stones River, and Chickamauga proved amazingly resilient in the face of devastating flank attacks, but incapable of following up any of its limited battlefield successes. These traits remained constant, no matter who was in command, because they were inherent in the army's social structure. As long as its members identified themselves primarily with their regiments, the army remained a decentralized aggregation of military communities. Since other field armies, both Union and Confederate, were recruited and trained in much the same way as the Army of the Ohio, they tended to share its characteristic disjointedness and fought battle after battle in which they absorbed enormous punishment without shattering, the loser withdrawing sullenly to lick its wounds, the victor too badly damaged to pursue.

The exception to this pattern proved the rule. The Battle of Chickamauga left Rosecrans stunned "like a duck hit on the head" (in Lincoln's words), with his reputation for personal courage in ruins and his army besieged in Chattanooga. He was replaced by Thomas, who vowed that the Army of the Cumberland (as it was once again called) would hold the city or starve. Grant's

Army of the Tennessee came to the rescue, reversing the roles the two armies had played at Shiloh, aided by two corps under Joseph Hooker dispatched from the distant Virginia front. Hooker's troops, many of them German-speaking immigrants, had been the scapegoats for the Army of the Potomac's defeats at Chancellorsville and the first day at Gettysburg, but now they joined with the men of the Army of the Tennessee in looking down on Thomas's army, which Grant regarded as demoralized and ineffective after its defeat at Chickamauga. In mid-October, after Grant was promoted to command all Union troops in the West, he planned to use the Army of the Tennessee (now under William T. Sherman) and Hooker's corps to drive the Confederates from Chattanooga, not trusting the Army of the Cumberland to play a significant role in the coming battle.

On November 24, 1863, Grant ordered the Army of the Tennessee to make what he expected would be a decisive flanking maneuver against the powerful Confederate position on Missionary Ridge, while Thomas's divisions were assigned a minor diversionary attack against the front of the apparently impregnable hillside. The battle that followed vindicated the reputation of the old Army of the Ohio. Having been let down by their generals in every major battle, the enlisted men and their regimental officers took matters into their own hands. They executed their orders to seize the entrenchments at the foot of Missionary Ridge but found that they could not safely stay there under fire from above. Rather than retreat, they spontaneously went forward and began to scramble up the steep incline. To the surprise of every observer, the Cumberland men made it to the top and routed the Confederates, driving them from the battlefield in disorder at the cost of relatively few casualties. In its greatest victory, as in the indecisive stalemates and near-disasters of its first years, it was the action of individual regiments that determined the army's fate.[12]

In closing this paper I must say that the reports are badly mixed up
both as regards time and distance, and everybody seems to have littered
up his report with praise of his adjutant, or orderly, or drummer boy,
or something of that kind, to the exclusion of everything else.
—HENRY M. KENDALL, 5th Indiana Battery,
"Battle of Perryville"

Notes

ACFWHS
Allen County Fort Wayne Historical Society, Fort Wayne

AL
Roy P. Basler, ed., Marion Dolores Pratt and Lloyd A. Dunlap, asst. eds., *The Collected Works of Abraham Lincoln*

BHC
Burton Historical Collection, Detroit Public Library, Detroit

B&L
Robert U. Johnson and Clarence C. Buel, eds., *Battles and Leaders of the Civil War*

Buford, Inspection Reports
Inspection Reports of Maj. J. Buford, NA RG 393.1.880

Campaigns
Military History Society of Massachusetts, *Campaigns in Kentucky and Tennessee, including the Battle of Chickamauga, 1862–1864: Papers of the Military Historical Society of Massachusetts*, vol. 7

CHS
Chicago Historical Society, Chicago

DC Commandery, *War Papers*
Commandery of the District of Columbia, Military Order of the Loyal Legion of the United States, *War Papers*

FC
Filson Club Historical Society, Louisville

GAR records
Application records of George H. Thomas Post, No. 5, Grand Army of the Republic of Chicago Papers

IHS
Indiana Historical Society, William H. Smith Memorial Library, Indianapolis

ISHL
Illinois State Historical Library, Springfield

ISL
Indiana State Library, Indiana Division, Indianapolis

Kansas
Report of the Adjutant General of the State of Kansas, 1861–'65, vol. 1. *Kansas* citations take the following form: volume number(part number):page number(s).

LC

Library of Congress, Washington, D.C.

LL

Lilly Library, University of Indiana, Bloomington

MHC

Michigan Historical Collections, Bentley Library, University of Michigan, Ann Arbor

Minn. Comm.

Minnesota Board of Commissioners

Minnesota Commandery, *Glimpses*

Minnesota Commandery of the Military Order of the Loyal Legion of the United States, *Glimpses of the Nation's Struggle: Papers Read Before the Minnesota Commandery of the Military Order of the Loyal Legion of the United States*

Mississippi

Military History Society of Massachusetts, *The Mississippi Valley, Tennessee, Georgia, Alabama, 1861–1864: Papers of the Military Historical Society of Massachusetts*, vol. 8

NA RG

Record Group, National Archives, Washington, D.C.

Ohio Commandery, *Sketches*

Ohio Commandery of the Military Order of the Loyal Legion of the United States, *Sketches of War History, 1861–1865: Papers Read Before the Ohio Commandery of the Military Order of the Loyal Legion of the United States: 1883–1886*

OHS

Ohio Historical Society, Columbus

OR

U.S. War Department, *The War of the Rebellion: A Compilation of the Official Records of the Union and Confederate Armies. OR* citations take the following form: volume number (part number, where applicable): page number(s). Unless otherwise noted, all citations are to series 1.

SCWC

Schoff Civil War Collection, William L. Clements Library, University of Michigan, Ann Arbor

SNMP

Shiloh National Military Park, Tennessee

SRNB

Stones River National Battlefield, Murfreesboro, Tennessee

UC

University of Chicago, Chicago

USAMHI

U.S. Army Military History Institute, Carlisle Barracks, Pennsylvania

Wisconsin Commandery

Commandery of the State of Wisconsin Military Order of the Loyal Legion of the United States, *War Papers: Being Papers Read Before the Commandery of the State of Wisconsin Military Order of the Loyal Legion of the United States*

INTRODUCTION

1. John Patton Memoir, 3:60–66, LC.

2. After the Battle of Perryville, the Army of the Ohio was reorganized and renamed, first as the "XIV Army Corps" in November 1862 and later as the "Army of the Cumberland," the name by which it is most commonly remembered, in large part because of the victories it won at Missionary Ridge in 1863 and Nashville in 1864 under the leadership of Major General George H. Thomas. A second Army of the Ohio, unrelated to the first, was created in 1863 under Ambrose Burnside and later was led by John Schofield.

3. The word "army" can refer to three very different kinds of military organizations in Civil War narratives. In its broadest sense, the entire military force of the United States during the Civil War constituted a single "Union Army," composed mostly of civilian volunteers enlisted in Federal service for the single purpose of fighting the South. For operational purposes, the Union Army was divided into several smaller "field armies," which were self-contained organizations of all arms and staff departments. In most cases, a field army was associated with the particular geographic area in which it operated; all the military forces in the District of the Ohio, for example, constituted the Army of the Ohio. A third kind of "army" was the small prewar Regular Army, made up of long-service professional soldiers, which was not employed as a separate field army but main-tained its identity as a separate institution through the war; the Army of the Ohio, like most Union field armies, included a few Regular Army infantry units along with its dozens of volunteer regiments.

4. As long ago as 1866, a veteran of the western theater complained of the Virginia-centric focus of Civil War writing, noting "that there are thousands of people in the East who do not know aught of the geographical position of Western battle-fields." Shanks, *Personal Recollections*, 197. Richard McMurry's 1989 work, *Two Great Rebel Armies*, was seminal in reversing this trend.

5. Weigley (*Age of Battles*) argues persuasively that the norm of decisive battle never existed in the first place. Even if eighteenth- and nineteenth-century battles in Europe were not typically decisive, it is clear that Civil War soldiers initially expected that theirs would be.

6. The most articulate and detailed exposition of the traditional view that tactics lagged behind technology is found in McWhiney and Jamieson's *Attack and Die*, al-though the book is marred by its dubious conclusion that the aggressive tactics of Southern armies were culturally determined. Those who have challenged this view, such as British author Paddy Griffith, have found that they have poked a stick into a hornet's nest. Many Civil War buffs in the United States have passionately rejected any argument that "soft" factors like training and morale mattered more than weaponry, perhaps be-cause the traditional view that the war's tactical futility was technologically inevitable

comfortably absolves the generals they admire from responsibility for the slaughter. Albert Castel's review of Griffith's *Battle Tactics of the Civil War*, in *Civil War History* 35 (December 1989): 335–38, is an intelligent and comparatively mild example of the negative American response to Griffith's thesis. See also Griffith, McWhiney, and Jamieson, "The Rifle Revolution: Fact or Myth?," *North and South* 1 (July 1998): 16–30.

7. McPherson (*For Cause and Comrades*) contrasts Civil War soldiers with twentieth-century American soldiers (among whom open expressions of political or patriotic motivation were not fashionable) and finds that Civil War soldiers on both sides were motivated by political ideology as much as by loyalty to their units. McPherson's argument, which is a useful corrective to the idea that Civil War soldiers were ignorant of the war's political issues, is consistent with the idea that the regiment was the focus of unit loyalty, which was extremely strong.

8. Long, *The Civil War Day by Day*, 716.

CHAPTER I

1. Herr, *Nine Campaigns*, 110 ("Proud stepping men"); John A. Bross to [Mrs. John A. Bross], Camp near Lancaster, Ky., October 15, 1862 (written October 5), Bross Letters, Private Collection ("more like a parade"); Connolly, *Three Years*, 19 ("As far as the eye").

2. Abraham Lincoln, "A Proclamation," [Washington, April 15, 1861], *OR*, 3d ser., 1:67.

3. *AL* 4:431–32.

4. Typical requests for troops, with Cameron's responses, are Cameron to Gov. Yates, War Department, April 20, 1861, *OR*, 3d ser., 1:93; Gov. Morton to Cameron, Indianapolis, April 23, 1861, *OR*, 3d ser., 1:102; Gov. Yates to Cameron, Springfield, Ill., April 25, 1861, *OR*, 3d ser., 1:113.

5. U.S. Bureau of the Census, *Historical Statistics*, 1:28. Kentucky's white population was 919,000. Of the state's total population of 1,156,000, 51.3 percent were male and 51.6 percent were between the ages of 15 and 44, inclusive. Using the crude assumption that these percentages applied equally to the white and black populations, approximately 243,000 of Kentucky's inhabitants in 1860 were white males of military age.

6. Gov. Randall to Lincoln, Madison, Wis., May 6, 1861, *OR*, 3d ser., 1:167–70 ("matter of absolute necessity"); Lincoln to Orville H. Browning, "private & confidential," Washington, September 22, 1861, *AL* 4:532 ("to lose Kentucky").

7. Lincoln to Oliver P. Morton, Washington, September 29, 1861, *AL* 4:541.

8. B[eriah] Magoffin to Simon Cameron, Frankfort, Ky., April 15, 1861, *OR*, 3d ser., 1:70.

9. General Orders No. 27, Adjutant General's Office, May 28, 1861, *OR* 52(1):147; Dyer, *Compendium*, 1:255.

10. The story of the clandestine Union operations in Kentucky in the summer of 1861 and the early operations of Anderson's headquarters can be pieced together from Lincoln [to Anderson], [Washington], May 7, 1861, *OR* 52(1):140–41; Special Orders No. 3, Dept. of the Cumberland, Louisville, September 10, 1861, *OR* 4:257; Anderson to G. H.

Thomas, Louisville, September 17, 1861, *OR* 4:260; Kelly, "Secret Union Organization in Kentucky in 1861," in Ohio Commandery, *Sketches*, 3:278–91; Van Horne, *Army of the Cumberland*, 1:1–20; Nicolay, *Outbreak of Rebellion*, 130–32; Shanks, *Personal Recollections*, 207–29; Villard, *Memoirs*, 1:204–6; and Stevenson, "General Nelson, Kentucky, and Lincoln Guns," 118–21.

11. For the recruitment of the first Union regiments in Kentucky, see L. Thomas, Adjutant-General, to Nelson, Washington, July 1, 1861, *OR* 4:251–52; Nelson to Adjutant-General, Cincinnati, July 16, 1861, *OR* 4:252; Villard, *Memoirs*, 1:205–6; Van Horne, *Army of the Cumberland*, 1:12, 15–17; Dodge, *Old Second Division*, 39–44, 46–48, app. p. 7; Nicolay, *Outbreak of War*, 132; and Shanks, *Personal Recollections*, 213–18. For modern accounts, see Current, *Lincoln's Loyalists*, 29–30, and Hughes, *Camp Dick Robinson*.

12. Nicolay, *Outbreak of War*, 131 ("principally from Ohio and Indiana"); Lincoln to Magoffin, Washington, August 24, 1861, *AL* 4:497 ("exclusively of Kentuckians"). In June 1861 many of the original recruits in these regiments refused to reenlist when their terms were extended from three months to three years, at which time they were in fact replaced by Kentucky recruits. Van Horne, *Army of the Cumberland*, 1:14–15.

13. General Orders No. 57, Adjutant General's Office, Washington, August 15, 1861, *OR* 4:254; Anderson to Chase, Cincinnati, September 1, 1861, *OR* 4:255–56 ("We need everything").

14. The circumstances of the movement of Confederate troops into Kentucky are described in *OR* 4:179–95 and amplified by Woodworth, " 'The Indeterminate Quantities,' " 289–97.

15. Scott to Morton, Washington, September 3, 1861, *OR*, 3d ser., 1:479 ("such points on the Ohio"); General Orders No. 2, Dept. of the Cumberland, Cincinnati, September 7, 1861, *OR* 4:257 (moving department headquarters); Morton to Cameron, Indianapolis, September 12, 1861, *OR* 4:257 ("war in Kentucky"); Cameron to Morton, War Department, September 5, 1861, *OR*, 3d ser., 1:487 ("all regiments organized"); Morton to Col. Thomas A. Scott, Assistant Secretary of War, Indianapolis, September 7, 1861, *OR*, 3d ser., 1:490 ("uneasy about Kentucky"); Cameron to Yates, *OR*, 3d ser., 1:486–87 ("three or four full regiments"); and Cameron to Governors Morton, Blair, and Randall, War Department, September 12, 1861, *OR*, 3d ser., 1:501.

16. Anderson to Lieutenant-Colonel Oliver, Louisville, September 19, 1861, *OR* 4:263 ("no armed men"); Mitchel, *Ormsby Macknight Mitchel*, 220 ("energy of despair"); O. M. Mitchel to E. D. Townsend, Assistant Adjutant-General, [Cincinnati], September 26, 1861, *OR* 4:276; Lincoln to Frémont, Washington, September 22, 1861, *OR* 4:265 ("send a gunboat"); Anderson to Lincoln, Louisville, September 30, 1861, *OR* 4:281–82 ("all the troops").

17. Villard, *Memoirs*, 1:207–8 ("half as efficient"). For Sherman's brief campaign against Buckner, see Sherman, *Personal Memoirs*, 1:225–27; Cist, *Army of the Cumberland*, 2–3; [Fitch], *Annals*, 361–62; Van Horne, *Army of the Cumberland*, 1:28–29; Kelly, "Secret Union Organization," Ohio Commandery, *Sketches*, 3:278–80; Dodge, *Old Second Division*, 61; and Shanks, *Personal Recollections*, 225–27.

18. Dyer, *Compendium*, 3:1519. The historian of the 6th Indiana claimed the same

honor for his unit, which entered Kentucky at about the same time, although without uniforms. Briant, *Sixth Regiment Indiana*, 77. For the arrival of additional regiments, see Oliver D. Greene, Assistant Adjutant-General, to L. Thomas, Louisville, September 21, 1861, *OR* 4:264.

19. Thomas A. Scott, Assistant Secretary of War, to Morton, War Department, September 24, 1861, *OR*, 3d ser., 1:536; Thomas A. Scott, Assistant Secretary of War, to Dennison, War Department, September 24, 1861, *OR*, 3d ser., 1:537; Cameron to Jeremiah T. Boyle, War Department, September 25, 1861, *OR*, 3d ser., 1:539.

20. The 19th Illinois was one of two regiments redirected to Anderson after being ordered to Washington from Frémont's department. See Frémont to Lincoln, St. Louis, September 22, 1861, *OR* 4:266, and Dyer, *Compendium*, 1:1053.

21. Special Orders No. 3, Hdqrs. Dep't of the Cumberland, *OR* 4:257. The three arriving regiments were the 14th and 31st Ohio and the 33rd Indiana. See Hughes, *Camp Dick Robinson*, [10].

22. Enclosure to L. Thomas, Adjutant-General to Cameron, Washington, October 21, 1861, *OR* 4:315.

23. General Orders No. 6, Department of the Cumberland, Louisville, October 7, 1861, *OR* 4:296.

24. Sherman to Garrett Davis, Esq., Louisville, October 8, 1861, *OR* 4:297 ("forced into command"); Villard, *Memoirs*, 1:210–13 ("to such an extent"). See Shanks, *Personal Recollections*, 31–34, for an alternative contemporary account. Royster, *The Destructive War*, 95–99, is a thorough modern analysis of Sherman's state of mind.

25. Sherman, *Memoirs*, 1:222 ("nobody seeming to think"); Cameron to His Excellency the President of the United States, Louisville, October 16, 1861, *OR* 4:308 ("much worse condition"). For the transfer of units to Sherman's department, see Cameron to Lt. Treadwell, War Department, October 16, 1861, *OR*, 3d ser., 1:577; Thomas A. Scott to General Negley, War Department, October 17, 1861, *OR*, 3d ser., 1:578; Thomas A. Scott to Governor Randall, War Department, October 17, 1861, *OR*, 3d ser., 1:578; Thomas A. Scott to Governor Randall, War Department, October 21, 1861, *OR*, 3d ser., 1:582; Thomas A. Scott to Governor Randall, War Department, October 22, 1861, *OR*, 3d ser., 1:588; and Bircher, *Drummer*, 13–14.

26. Abraham Lincoln, "Memorandum for a Plan of Campaign," [ca. Oct. 1, 1861], *AL* 4:544–45.

27. General Orders No. 97, Headquarters of the Army, A.G.O., Washington, November 9, 1861, *OR* 4:349.

28. The company was the smallest infantry unit described in the tables of organization promulgated by the War Department. Officially an infantry company consisted of sixty-four to eighty-two privates (plus two musicians and a wagoner) under the command of a captain, two lieutenants, and thirteen noncommissioned officers, but in service this ideal was rarely met. L. Thomas, Adjutant-General's Office, Washington, April 16, 1861 (*OR*, 3d ser., 1:76), gives the "organization for the militia force called for by the President." General Orders No. 15, War Dept., Adjt. General's Office, Washington, May 4, 1861 (*OR*, 3d ser., 1:151–54), prescribes the organization of the first three-year volunteer

regiments. The organization of companies and regiments was not substantially modified thereafter.

29. Terrell, *Indiana*, 20 ("permanent commissions"); Herr, *Nine Campaigns*, 20 ("securing their commissions"); Woodcock, *Southern Boy*, 15 ("determined to enlist").

30. Examples of Ohio state documents authorizing recruitment and transportation of companies (for the 41st Ohio) are in Aquila Wiley Papers, file 2127, WRHS.

31. Terrell, *Indiana*, 110 ("men generally know"); Memoir, pp. 11–12, Coulter Papers, LL. Company muster rolls often recorded where the men were enlisted rather than where they lived, exaggerating the companies' geographic homogeneity, but those companies that did not originate entirely in a single community often consisted of no more than two or three groups of local recruits, each from a nearby area. See, e.g., Rowell, *Yankee Cavalrymen*, 22.

32. Bishop, *Story of a Regiment*, 193 ("mutual acquaintances"); Tourgée, *Story of a Thousand*, 39 ("product of the same conditions"); Perry, *Thirty-Eighth Regiment Indiana*, 16 ("men of influence"); Joseph Sims to Sarah Ann Sims, [Camp Dennison], September 17, 1861, Sims Letter, USAMHI. Mitchell (*The Vacant Chair*, p. 21 and chap. 2) elaborates on the idea that "the company—the basic military unit—functioned as an extension of the soldier's home community."

33. Tourgée, *Story of a Thousand*, 36 ("each family"); Bishop, *Story of a Regiment*, 194 ("intimate and brotherly relations").

34. Terrell, *Indiana*, 20. For descriptions of the recruitment of various Army of the Ohio regiments, see Tapp and Klotter, *Tuttle*, 22, 42; Farmer Memoir, p. 265, LL; Rowell, *Yankee Cavalrymen*, 19–23; Tourgée, *Story of a Thousand*, 20–26; Bennett and Haigh, *Thirty-Sixth Regiment Illinois*, 12–13; and Grebner, *"We Were the Ninth,"* 5–8. Union recruitment procedures in general are discussed in Wiley, *Billy Yank*, 17–24; James I. Robertson, *Soldiers Blue and Gray*, 3–18; and Lord, *They Fought for the Union*, 1–20.

35. A related argument appears in Frank and Reaves, *"Seeing the Elephant,"* 23–24, which postulates a contract between soldiers and the communities from which they came. Cf. Anderson, *A People's Army*, which argues that the effectiveness of the Massachusetts militia in the French and Indian War was influenced by the soldiers' view of their service as covenant-bound, i.e. contractual, as opposed to the professional soldier's acceptance of absolute duty.

36. For the mutiny of the 37th Indiana, see Memoir, pp. 15–16, Coulter Papers, LL. For companies serving outside their own states, see John Robertson, *Michigan in the War*, 745, and Norton GAR records, CHS.

37. Heath Diary, transcripts printed in *Vevay Reveille-Enterprise*, March 7, 1946, Heath Papers, LC; Patrick McKernan to Simon Cameron, Camp Chase, Columbus, January 17, 1862, Cameron Papers, LC; Herr, *Nine Campaigns*, 26.

38. [Fourteen petitioners] to Brig. Genl. Comd. Dept of the Ohio, Camp Calhoun, February 10, 1862, NA RG 393.1.880.

39. Cameron to [General Scott], War Department, June 27, 1861, *OR*, 3d ser., 1:299–300; General Orders No. 49, War Department, August 3, 1861, *OR*, 3d ser., 1:381.

40. See, e.g., Bremner, "Early History of Company E," CHS, citing a letter printed in the *Chicago Tribune* on January 29, 1861, stating that officers of the Chicago Highland Guards will resign to allow the election of new officers. Blackburn, *Letters*, 24.

41. Reid, *Ohio in the War*, 1:27, 55. Examples of elections for company officers in the Army of the Ohio include Beatty, *Citizen-Soldier*, 89–90; Herr, *Nine Campaigns*, 438; Gates, *Rough Side of War*, 15; Floyd, *Seventy-Fifth Regiment of Indiana*, 12–18; Tapp and Klotter, *Tuttle*, 24, 41; Diary Typescript, September 5, 1861, Connelly Papers, IHS; Mallory, "Not in a Useless Cause," pp. 6–7, WRHS; Diary Typescript, September 2, 1861, Inskeep Papers, OHS; Ross Diary, August 13, 1862, ISHL; McClurkin Memoir, p. 1, USAMHI; Hinman, *Sherman Brigade*, 44; and C. C. Andrews, "The Surrender of the Third Regiment Minnesota Volunteer Infantry," in Minnesota Commandery, *Glimpses*, 1:337. For a general discussion of officer selection, see Wiley, *Billy Yank*, 24; Lord, *They Fought for the Union*, 192–95; and James I. Robertson, *Soldiers Blue and Gray*, 13.

42. Tapp and Klotter, *Tuttle*, 41, 45–46 ("without exception"); Hazen, *Narrative*, 9 ("as a rule").

43. Gov. Dennison to Cameron, Columbus, May 29, 1861, *OR*, 3d ser., 1:154, 242–43 ("much dissatisfaction"); Benjamin F. Wells to "Dearest Mother," Bowling Green, Ky., November 2, 1861, Wells Letters, MHC; Bennett, *Ninth Michigan*, 7.

44. Jacob D. Cox, "War Preparations in the North," in *B&L* 1:92 ("sure passport"); H. B. Freeman, "Eighteenth U.S. Infantry From Camp Thomas to Murfreesboro and the Regular Brigade at Stone River," in Minnesota Commandery, *Glimpses*, 3:106–25, 109 ("admiring and envious"); Herr, *Nine Campaigns*, 438; Mallory, "Not in a Useless Cause," p. 6, WRHS ("much more efficient").

45. Bennett, *Ninth Michigan*, 7 ("self-conscious inefficiency"); Hazen, *Narrative*, 8 ("voluntarily resigned").

46. Terrell, *Indiana*, 110.

47. See Speed, Kelly, and Pirtle, *Union Regiments of Kentucky*, 488–504; John Robertson, *Michigan in the War*, 509–10; George M. Finch, "In the Beginning," in Ohio Commandery, *Sketches*, 1:223; and Bates, "Ohio's Preparations," Ohio Commandery, *Sketches*, 1:131. The 1st and 2nd Ohio were "mostly made up of well known militia organizations," including the "Rover Guards," "La Fayette Guards," "Columbus Fencibles," and a Zouave company. Reid, *Ohio in the War*, 1:27; Finch, "In the Beginning," 1:223. The 19th Illinois contained several militia companies. See Bremner, "Early History of Company E," CHS.

48. Terrell, *Indiana*, 51; Stevenson, "Kentucky Neutrality in 1861," in Ohio Commandery, *Sketches*, 2:52 ("worthless, inefficient, and incompetent"); Joshua H. Bates, "Ohio's Preparations for the War," in Ohio Commandery, *Sketches*, 1:128–31; [Lincoln] "Speech to the Springfield Scott Club," August 14, 26, 1852, *AL* 2:149–50 ("rules and regulations"); Reece, *Illinois*, 1:7 ("active and enterprising").

49. Bremner, "Early History of Company E," CHS; Henry A. Buck to "My Darling Sister," Nashville, October 4, 1862, BHC; Bates, "Ohio's Preparations," in Ohio Commandery, *Sketches*, 1:130. See also Burton, *Melting Pot Soldiers*, 43.

50. Lonn, *Foreigners in the Union Army and Navy*, though outdated, remains the stan-

dard source on the subject. For the organization of the 9th Ohio and 32nd Indiana, see Grebner, *"We Were the Ninth,"* 6–7, 26–27, and Burton, *Melting Pot Soldiers*, 80–83, 93–96. The other German regiments in the Army of the Ohio included the 2nd Missouri, 24th Illinois, and four more Ohio regiments. Burton (pp. 44–45) discusses the difficulty of determining which regiments were "ethnic." Cox ("War Preparations," in *B&L* 1:98) describes the 10th Ohio as an "Irish regiment . . . proud to call themselves the 'Bloody Tinth.' " For Scandinavian units, see Blegen, *Heg*, 23–25, and Minn. Comm., *Minnesota*, 149.

51. Tapp and Klotter, *Tuttle*, 86 ("a burly Teuton"); A. H. Sampson to "Dear Friends," Louisville, December 29, 1861, Torah W. Sampson Papers, FC ("kind of party feeling"); James M. Cole to "Old Friend Jim," Camp Wood, Ky., January 18, 1862, Cole Papers, ISHL ("duch you recollect").

52. Wilberforce Nevin to "My Dear Sister," Camp Wood, Munfordville, December 22, 1861, transcript, Nevin Letterbook, LC ("strange body of men"); W. T. Sherman to Geza Mihalotzy, Headquarters, Department of the Cumberland, October 26, 1861, Mihalotzy Papers, ISHL ("source of annoyance"). For troubles in the 24th Illinois, see Burton, *Melting Pot Soldiers*, 72–77, and "Ethnic Regiments."

53. General Orders No. 45, War Department, July 19, 1861, *OR*, 3d ser., 1:339; General Orders No. 51, War Department, August 5, 1861, *OR*, 3d ser., 1:385; General Orders No. 53, War Department, August 8, 1861, *OR*, 3d ser., 1:391; Grebner, *"We Were the Ninth,"* 184 ("Americans disdain immigrants").

54. Judson W. Bishop, "The Mill Springs Campaign: Some Observations and Experiences of a Company Officer," in Minnesota Commandery, *Glimpses*, 2:76–77.

55. For state quotas, see War Department, April 15, 1861, *OR*, 3d ser., 1:69, and Cameron to governors, May 10, 1861, *OR*, 3d ser., 1:203–4. For Indiana regiments, see Terrell, *Indiana*, 19–20. The units raised under Illinois's "Ten Regiment Act" of May 1861 were likewise recruited within single congressional districts. See Reece, *Illinois*, 1:10–12.

56. Herr, *Nine Campaigns*, 20–21. For the change of the regiment's name as a result of a petition to the secretary of war, see Herr, *Nine Campaigns*, 56–57, and Gates, *Rough Side of War*, 6. The 19th Illinois "Chicago Zouave Regiment" was another example of a coalition of independent companies.

57. Saml. Gill to L. Thomas, Adjutant-General's Office, Frankfort, Ky., January 17, 1862, *OR*, 3d ser., 1:800. Although the Kentucky legislature approved the raising of 40,000 Union soldiers in September 1861, it did not raise any regiments itself because forty-five or forty-six regimental commissions had already been granted by various Federal authorities. See, e.g., Lincoln to Gentlemen of the Kentucky delegation . . . , Executive Mansion, July 29, 1861, *OR*, 3d ser., 1:364, and Cameron to Jeremiah T. Boyle, esq., War Department, September 25, 1861, *OR*, 3d ser., 1:539–40.

58. Wm. W. Duffield to Colonel James B. Fry, Louisville, June 6, 1862, NA RG 393.1.880 ("most remarkable state"); Tapp and Klotter, *Tuttle*, 42 ("parts of companies"), 58; Hughes, *Camp Dick Robinson*, [5].

59. Minnesota originally had enough volunteers to offer a second regiment in May,

which the War Department rejected. See Cameron to Gov. Ramsey, Washington, May 14, 1861, *OR*, 3d ser., 1:201–2; Minn. Comm., *Minnesota*, 79–146; and Hicks, "Organization of the Volunteer Army," 340.

60. Reid, *Ohio in the War*, 1:29; Gov. Dennison to Cameron, Columbus, April 22, 1861, *OR*, 3d ser., 1:101–2; Aaron F. Perry, "A Chapter in Inter-State Diplomacy at the Beginning of the War—1861," in Ohio Commandery, *Sketches*, 3:333–63.

61. See General Orders No. 15, War Department, May 4, 1861, *OR*, 3d ser., 1:152–54; Cameron to Gov. Curtin and other governors, War Department, May 22, 1861, *OR*, 3d ser., 1:227–28; and General Orders No. 45, War Department, July 19, 1861, *OR*, 3d ser., 1:339.

62. David Davis to Simon Cameron, Lincoln, Ill., October 13, 1861, "Confidential," Cameron Papers, LC ("insane ambition"). The colonelcy of a new regiment was a particularly rich political prize, as nearly all of its members would be eligible voters within a few years if not immediately. In 1860 approximately 18 percent of the total U.S. population was eligible to vote, so a block of one thousand voters (the nominal size of a new regiment) equaled the political population of a town of over five thousand people. U.S. Bureau of the Census, *Historical Statistics*, 1:8, 2:1072, 1074. In 1860 there were only 229 cities and towns of such size in the entire country, and most of them had fewer than 10,000 residents (1:11).

63. Gov. Dennison to Cameron, Columbus, August 23, 1861, *OR*, 3d ser., 1:447 ("Is it possible"). Other complaints against independent regiments include Gov. Morton to Cameron, Indianapolis, June 22, 1861, *OR*, 3d ser., 1:290; Gov. Yates to Cameron, Springfield, Ill., August 14, 1861, *OR*, 3d ser., 1:409–10; Gov. Blair to Cameron, Jackson, Mich., August 19, 1861, *OR*, 3d ser., 1:428; and John Robertson, *Michigan in the War*, 313–14. See also Shannon, *Organization and Administration*, 1:261, and Meneely, *War Department*, 167–68, 210–14. Independent regiments were placed under state control by Special Orders No. 243, Adjutant-General's Office, September 10, 1861, *OR*, 3d ser., 1:495–96, and General Orders No. 78, Adjutant-General's Office, September 16, 1861, *OR*, 3d ser., 1:518–20. Independent units already raised were put under the control of their respective governors by General Orders No. 18, Adjutant General's Office, Washington, February 21, 1862, *OR*, 3d ser., 1:898; see also Shannon, *Organization and Administration*, 1:261.

64. Jno. A. Gurley to Lincoln, Cincinnati, September 16, 1861, *OR*, 3d ser., 1:519–20 ("They will disband"). For regimental elections, see Reid, *Ohio in the War*, 1:27, and Reece, *Illinois*, 1:10. The congressional act of July 1861 authorizing 500,000 volunteers called for elections to fill any regimental offices that became vacant during a unit's service, but only commissioned officers were eligible to vote. General Orders No. 49, Adjutant-General's Office, August 3, 1861, *OR*, 3d ser., 1:383.

65. Day Elmore to "Dear Father and Mother," Camp Rolla, January 5, 1862, Elmore Papers, CHS; Nelson to Captain Fry, A.A. Genl., Chief of Staff, Head Quarters 4th Division, Army of the Ohio, Camp Wickliffe, Ky., January 2, 1862, NA RG 393.2.843, p. 32 ("gotten up for bunkum"); Blackburn, *Letters*, 41; Cox, "War Preparations," in *B&L* 1:91, 93 ("intrigue and demagogy").

66. Terrell, *Indiana*, 110–11; W. B. Hazen to "My Dear Capt" [Aquila Wiley], Gar-

rettsville, Ohio, June 22, 1862, Aquila Wiley Papers, file 2127, WRHS ("principle of the thing"); General Order No. 71, Head Qurs 2nd Division, Stevenson, Ala., July 15, 1862, NA RG 393.2.6465 ("authority of an officer").

67. Tapp and Klotter, *Tuttle*, 53; Speed, Kelly, and Pirtle, *Union Regiments of Kentucky*, 320; Thomas E. Bramlette to [T. J. Wood], In the field near Corinth, Miss., May 14, 1862, NA RG 393.1.880.

68. See, e.g., George W. Landrum to Mrs. Obed J. Wilson, Camp Jefferson, Ky., January 23, 1862, Landrum Papers, WRHS.

69. See, e.g., A. Pirtle to "Dear Ma," Tyree Springs, Tenn., December 2, 1862, Pirtle Papers, FC, expressing fear that the 10th Ohio might be consolidated due to losses. General Orders No. 3, Adjutant General's Office, Washington, January 11, 1862, *OR*, 3d ser., 3:788.

70. Tourgée, *Story of a Thousand*, 36.

71. See the Bibliography for dozens of regimental histories written by (and for) veterans of the Army of the Ohio. Contrast this with the much smaller number of histories of companies (which were ten times more numerous), brigades, divisions, or corps.

CHAPTER 2

1. General Orders No. 97, Hdqrs. of the Army, A. G. O., November 9, 1861, *OR* 4:349.

2. Doubleday, *Reminiscences*, 50–51. Like many Civil War officers, Buell simultaneously held multiple ranks: in May 1861 he was a lieutenant colonel in the Regular Army as well as a brigadier general of volunteers. His brevet promotions, to captain and major, had been superseded, but the confusing practice of rewarding officers with brevet promotions (which were largely honorary) continued into the Civil War. An officer could theoretically hold real and brevet ranks in both the Regulars and the volunteer forces at the same time, for a total of four different titles.

3. Engle, *Buell*, is the only full-length biography of Buell and is quite useful for the details of his career before and after the war. In sections dealing directly with the Army of the Ohio, it uses a number of primary source quotations that first appeared in identical form in Gerald J. Prokopowicz, "All for the Regiment: Unit Cohesion and Tactical Stalemate in the Army of the Ohio, 1861–1862" (Ph.D. diss., Harvard University, 1994), from which the present book developed.

4. Diary, November 12, 1861, Rockwell Collection, LC; McClellan to Buell, Washington, November 7, 1861 (*OR* 4:342), and November 12, 1861 (*OR* 4:355–56); Buell, *Statement*, 4; Buell to McClellan, November 22, 1861, *OR* 7:444 ("Sherman still insists"). See Buell, *Statement*, 2, for his initial estimate of A. S. Johnston's strength, which was accurate, although Buell revised his estimates sharply upward once he took command of the Department of the Ohio. For Johnston's numbers, see A. S. Johnston to J. P. Benjamin, Bowling Green, Ky., December 8, 1861, *OR* 7:745–46 ("between 18,000 and 19,000" near Bowling Green); Abstract from return of Western Department . . . ,

December 12, 1861, *OR* 7:762 (approximately 53,000 total, with 19,000 at Bowling Green).

5. For the strength of the army, see Abstract from consolidated report of the Department of the Cumberland . . . , November 10, 1861, *OR* 4:349 (49,586 aggregate present and absent). For reinforcements, see E. D. Townsend to Buell, Adjutant-General's Office, November 16, 1861, *OR* 4:358, and Buell, *Statement*, 3.

6. Shanks, *Personal Recollections*, 42–43.

7. Nelson to Captain Greene, Asst. Adjutant General, Maysville, Ky., October 9, 1861, NA RG 393.1.880.

8. Buell, *Statement*, 3.

9. W. B. Switzer to Buell, Washington, February 19, 1862, enclosing extracts from Buford, Inspection Reports.

10. For the organization of the army, see Special Orders No. 16, Hdqrs. Dept. of the Ohio, Louisville, November 30, 1861, *OR* 7:460–61, and Special Orders No. 19, Hdqrs. Dept. of the Ohio, Louisville, December 2, 1861, *OR* 7:467–68. In place of numerous small units under one central command, modern armies have favored pyramid organizations based on the "rule of three": three battalions to a regiment, three regiments to a division, three divisions to a corps, etc. Sir Basil Liddell Hart was one of the few twentieth-century military theorists to argue in favor of placing numerous maneuver units directly under a single commander, because "the fewer the intermediate headquarters the more dynamic operations tend to become." Liddell Hart, *Second World War*, 1:261.

11. L. Thomas, Adjutant-General's Office, Washington, April 16, 1861, *OR*, 3d ser., 1:76.

12. Buell to McClellan, Louisville, November 22, 1861, *OR* 7:444 ("all Ohio troops"); Don Carlos Buell, "East Tennessee and the Campaign of Perryville," in *B&L* 3:42–43 ("from the beginning"); Buell to McClellan, Louisville, December 8, 1861, *OR* 7:482 ("send their staff officers").

13. Buell, *Statement*, 3–4 ("made a rule"); Buell to McClellan, Louisville, December 8, 1861, *OR* 7:482 ("officiousness of governors"). For the organization of brigades, see Special Orders No. 16, Hdqrs. Dept. of the Ohio, Louisville, November 30, 1861, *OR* 7:460–61. The Fourth Brigade was the most diverse, with one regiment each from Indiana, Kentucky, Ohio, and the Regular Army.

14. Buell, *Statement*, 4 ("the happiest results"); Wesley Elmore to "Dear Father and Mother," Camp Ben Spaulding, December 4, 1861, Elmore Papers, IHS ("Green Kentuckians"); Benjamin Bordner to "Dear Brother," Bardstown, Ky., January 10, 1862, Bordner Letters, Ness Collection, folder 64, MHC. Multistate brigades were the norm in all Union armies but were less common in the Confederacy. One reason for this, as Colonel Benjamin Scribner of the 38th Indiana noted, was that single-state brigades tended to "destroy the national spirit" in favor of state pride. Scribner, *How Soldiers Were Made*, 33.

15. Buell to McClellan, Louisville, November 22, 1861, *OR* 7:444 ("marked poles"). See Special Orders No. 16, Hdqrs. Dept. of the Ohio, Louisville, November 30, 1861, *OR* 7:460–61, for the initial assignments of brigade and division command.

16. See Warner, *Generals in Blue*, and Boatner, *Civil War Dictionary*, s.v. generals' names, for all information about generals in this chapter not otherwise referenced. Note that the Fourteenth and Sixteenth Brigades were not assigned commanders when they were formed.

17. Samuel Carter was finally commissioned a brigadier general on May 1, 1862, and later became the only American ever to hold the ranks of rear admiral and major general. Current, *Lincoln's Loyalists*, 31–32.

18. Jeremiah T. Boyle to Genl. W. T. Sherman, Lebanon, Ky., November 5, 1861, Miscellaneous Collection, FC.

19. For Thomas's prewar career, see McKinney, *Education in Violence*, and Cleaves, *Rock of Chickamauga*. Piatt and Boynton's *Thomas* is an entertaining exercise in hagiography; Donn Piatt, chief legal officer of the military commission that reviewed Buell's performance as army commander, was not shy about expressing his views of the leaders of the Army of the Ohio. Van Horne, *Life of . . . Thomas*, contains little regarding Thomas's role with the Army of the Ohio that does not appear in Van Horne's history of the Army of the Cumberland.

20. Van Horne, *Army of the Cumberland*, 1:48–54. For Thomas's eagerness to initiate an East Tennessee campaign, see, e.g., Thomas to Sherman, Headquarters Camp Dick Robinson, Ky., October 28, 1861, *OR* 4:321.

21. Hough, *Soldier in the West*, 63 ("good fighting man"); Beatty, *Citizen-Soldier*, 235 ("chuckle-head"); Shanks, *Personal Recollections*, 249 ("juvenile") (Shanks himself described McCook as "an overgrown school-boy, without dignity," 249); Dodge, *Old Second Division*, 69, 71–73, 116–18.

22. For Mitchel's career as an astronomer, see F. A. Mitchel, *Biographical Narrative*. The author, General Mitchel's son, accompanied him to war as an aide-de-camp.

23. See Mitchel, *Biographical Narrative*, 214–23; Mitchel to Olcott, Cincinnati, September 8, 1861, printed in ibid., 214 ("become a drill-master").

24. Sherman to Thomas, Louisville, October 25, 1861, *OR* 4:318 ("difficulty with the militia"); Van Horne, *Army of the Cumberland*, 1:41; Mitchel, *Biographical Narrative*, 230; Buell to McClellan, Louisville, November 27, 1861, *OR* 7:451 ("behaved very absurdly"); R. W. Johnson, "War Memories," in Minnesota Commandery, *Glimpses*, 1:14 ("rough exterior").

25. Buell, "Perryville," in *B&L* 3:43 ("remarkable merit"); Villard, *Memoirs*, 1:205 ("infectious energy"); Sipes GAR records, CHS ("Most rigid Disciplinarian"); Anonymous [Memoir of Co. C, 59th Ohio], July 14, 1906, p. 3, SNMP ("—— you").

26. Villard, *Memoirs*, 1:176–77; McClellan to Buell, Washington, November 7, 1861, *OR* 4:342 ("regard the local institutions"). Hunter complained to Cameron and Lincoln about Buell's appointment, drawing a stinging rebuke from the president. Maj. Genl. David Hunter to Cameron, "Private & Confidential," Ft. Leavenworth, Kans., December 19, 1861, Cameron Papers, LC; Lincoln to David Hunter, Executive Mansion, Washington, December 31, 1861, *AL* 5:84–85.

27. Johnson, "War Memories," in Minnesota Commandery, *Glimpses*, 1:13 ("Southern and Western"); —— Reynolds to William Bourne, Sycamore, Va., January 23, 1866, Reynolds Letter, LC ("have the full confidence"); R. Delavan Mussey to Joseph R.

Barrett, Elizabethtown, Ky., February 21, 1862, Mussey Letters, UC ("brood of Brig Genls").

28. W. T. Sherman to L. Thomas, Louisville, November 4, 1861, *OR* 4:332.

29. Shanks, *Personal Recollections*, 247 ("too much of a regular").

30. A battalion was a subdivision of a regiment, consisting of one or more companies. Technically each volunteer infantry regiment consisted of a single ten-company battalion, so for all practical purposes "battalion" and "regiment" were synonymous. Cavalry regiments, in contrast, were organized into three battalions of four companies each. Regular Army infantry regiments also had more than one battalion each.

31. Soldier writings from the Army of the Ohio are filled with references to the ubiquity of drill in 1861 and early 1862. See, e.g., Oscar Chamberlain to "Dear Parents," Muldroughs Hill, October 8, 1861, in Chamberlain and Chamberlain, *Civil War Letters*, 7; Diary Typescript, December 9, 1861, Connelly Papers, IHS; Memoir, pp. 14, 20, Coulter Papers, LL; Wm. Jasper Ralph Diary, August 23, 1861, Civil War Miscellany Collection, box 2, folder 3, photocopy and typescript, IHS; Mallory, "Not in a Useless Cause," p. 2, WRHS; Wilberforce Nevin to "My dear Father," Camp Wilkins, October 14, 1861, Nevin Letterbook, LC; Minn. Comm., *Minnesota*, 149; Diary Typescript, December 19, 1861, Inskeep Papers, OHS; Blackburn, *Letters*, 59; Tapp and Klotter, *Tuttle*, 45; Diary, January 7, 1862, Montgomery Papers, LC; Scribner, *How Soldiers Were Made*, 35; Leroy S. Mayfield to [Jos. M. Mayfield], Linn Creek Town, February 2, 1862, Mayfield Papers, LL ("a cold pill") (although the 22nd Indiana was not attached to the Army of the Ohio until September 1862, dress parade was similar in all Civil War armies).

32. Scribner, *How Soldiers Were Made*, 259 ("long association and discipline"); Bishop, *Story of a Regiment*, 197 ("At the crucial hour").

33. Herr, *Nine Campaigns*, 29 ("citizen soldiers"); Nelson to Capt. J. B. Fry, A.A.G., Chief of Staff, HdQrs 4th Division, Camp Wickliffe, Ky., January 1, 1862, NA RG 393.2.843, p. 30; J. R. Weist, "The Medical Department in the War," in Ohio Commandery, *Sketches*, 2:79 ("habit of obedience"); Tourgée, *Story of a Thousand*, 39 ("use of discipline"). Wilbur F. Hinman, a veteran of the Army of the Ohio, captured the attitude of the volunteer toward authority in his barely fictionalized novel, *Corporal Si Klegg and His "Pard,"* 60. See also Mitchell, *Civil War Soldiers*, 56–60, and McPherson, *For Causes and Comrades*, 47.

34. Blackburn, *Letters*, 57 ("not a perfect model"); Diary, October 14, 1861, Cole Papers, ISHL ("getting poorer"); Oscar Chamberlain to "Dear Parents," Camp Wood, January 11, 1861, in Chamberlain and Chamberlain, *Civil War Letters*, 11–12 ("has got the name"); Diary Typescript, December 22, 1861, Connelly Papers, IHS ("more like regulars").

35. Kellogg, "Recollections," p. 2, USAMHI; Freeman, "Eighteenth U.S. Infantry," in Minnesota Commandery, *Glimpses*, 3:107; Hosea, "Regular Brigade," in Ohio Commandery, *Sketches*, 5:328 ("the same material").

36. John Pierson to "Dear Wife," Camp 3 Miles South [of] Nashville, September 12, 1862, Pierson Papers, SCWC ("great diferance"). The volunteers' acceptance of the Regulars was not reciprocated by the professional officers of the Regular Army at first; it took until the third year of the war, according to Colonel B. F. Scribner, for "the low

estimate with which the regular army officers regarded the volunteers" to change. Scribner, *How Soldiers Were Made*, 252.

37. The details of close order drill can be found in military textbooks like Casey, *Infantry Tactics*. See Fratt, "American Civil War Tactics," for the relationship between parade ground drills and tactics used in battle.

38. Hazen, *Narrative*, 22. At least one professional officer, Colonel Benjamin Scribner of the 38th Indiana, considered Buell's order "absurd." Scribner, *How Soldiers Were Made*, 258.

39. General Orders No. 4, Fourth Division, Camp Wickliffe, Ky., January 6, 1862, Nelson Papers, CHS. Few diaries or letters of members of the Army of the Ohio mention skirmish drills until the fall of 1862. See Diary Typescript, December 28, 1861, Inskeep Papers, OHS; Diary, October 24, 1862, Cole Papers, ISHL; Diary Typescript, November 14, 1862, Howe Papers, IHS; Diary, September 30, 1862, H. C. Patton Papers, IHS; Ross Diary, November 27, 1862, ISHL; and Michael Bright to "Dear Uncle," August 10, 1862, Camp Battle Creek, in Truxhall, *"Respects,"* 79.

40. General Orders No. 15, Camp Dick Robinson, Ky., October 14, 1861, Headquarters 31 Regiment O.V. U.S.A., NA RG 393.2.843.

41. Young "Biographical Sketch," USAMHI; Minn. Comm., *Minnesota*, 150. The reverse also sometimes occurred, as when the men of McCook's division mistook the engagement at Rowlett's Station in December 1861 for target practice. See Dodge, *Old Second Division*, 104.

42. For examples of individual units engaging in target practice, see Diary, January 2, 1862, Montgomery Papers, LC; Diary Typescript, November 8, 1861, Inskeep Papers, OHS; and Davidson, *Battery A*, [6].

43. See Clary and Whitehorne, *Inspectors General*, for training in the peacetime Regular Army and the shortage of training officers in 1861.

44. Herr, *Nine Campaigns*, 445 ("Up to this time"); Buford, Inspection Reports, 43rd Indiana, December 4, 1861, NA RG 393.1.880 ("advance of their officers"); Tapp and Klotter, *Tuttle*, 48–49, 72, 112 (" 'Charge 'em boys!' ").

45. Scribner, *How Soldiers Were Made*, 15. As the war progressed, the texts of Scott and Hardee were supplanted by those of Upton and Casey. McWhiney and Jamieson (*Attack and Die*, 49–56) describe some of the inconsistencies in the various drill manuals authorized for use by the Union armies; Lord (*They Fought For the Union*, 39–52) discusses tactical manuals in detail.

46. Buford, Inspection Reports, 4th Ohio Cavalry, December 16, 1861, NA RG 393.1.880.

47. For German tactics, see Burton, *Melting Pot Soldiers*, 82–83; for ordering companies in the 3rd Kentucky, see Tapp and Klotter, *Tuttle*, 60. In February 1862 Buell received a written description of still another new system of tactics from a fellow West Pointer, Brigadier General Thomas Williams, but apparently chose not to impose it on the Army of the Ohio. See T[homas] Williams to Buell, Camp Winfield, Hatteras Inlet, N.C., February 22, 1862, Buell Papers, FC.

48. Diary Typescript, November 17, 1861, Connelly Papers, IHS. For Minnesota uniforms, see Minn. Comm., *Minnesota*, 147.

49. [Captain D. F. Bremner?], "History of the Cairo Expedition," p. 8, CHS ("beautiful Zouave uniforms"); Thomas A. Scott, Acting Secretary of War, to "several Governors and others," Washington, September 23, 1861, *OR*, 3d ser., 1:531 ("no troops hereafter"). For Union soldiers in Confederate colors, see also Payne, *Thirty-Fourth Regiment of Illinois*, 2; Diary, July 17, 1861, Johnston Papers, CHS ("pretty well made"); and Minn. Comm., *Minnesota*, 150.

50. Bartlett Diary Typescript, January 7, 1862, USAMHI; Bennett, *Ninth Michigan*, 9; Minn. Comm., *Minnesota*, 150; Diary, April 1, 1862, H. C. Patton Papers, IHS; Scribner, *How Soldiers Were Made*, 112–14.

51. George W. Landrum to Mrs. Obed J. Wilson, Camp Jefferson, Ky., January [15?], 1862, Landrum Papers, WRHS.

52. Herr, *Nine Campaigns*, 48–49 ("for the double purpose"). For other examples of sham battle as training for the Army of the Ohio, see Ewbank Diary, January 11, 1862, IHS, and Diary, April 1, 1862, H. C. Patton Papers, IHS.

53. Buell to McClellan, Louisville, November 22, 1861, *OR* 7:444 ("Army of the Potomac"); Report of Capt. John H. Morgan, Camp Burnam, December 7, 1861, *OR* 7:12–13; Report of Brig. Gen. Thomas C. Hindman, Cave City, Ky., December 19, 1861, *OR* 7:19.

54. Buell to McClellan, Louisville, December 8, 1861, *OR* 7:483 ("put aside the inertion").

55. Dodge, *Old Second Division*, 89–91; Report of Col. August Willich, Camp George Wood, [Ky.], December 18, 1861, *OR* 7:16.

56. Grebner, *"We Were the Ninth,"* 7–8, 14, 26 ("molded the new unit"). See also Burton, *Melting Pot Soldiers*, 80–81, and Cox, "War Preparations," in *B&L* 1:97.

57. Burton, *Melting Pot Soldiers*, 83; Dodge, *Old Second Division*, 95–96; Willich report, *OR* 7:16. Quotations and details of the fight, unless otherwise specified, are from the Willich report.

58. Hindman report, *OR* 7:19–20; PONTIAC, "Affairs in Kentucky (Louisville, December 19, 1861), *New York Times*, December 25, 1861, p. 3, col. 3 ("gamest of the invaders"); Duke, *Morgan's Cavalry*, 103–4.

59. Willich report, *OR* 7:16–17.

60. Cist, *Army of the Cumberland*, 24; Willich report, *OR* 7:17; Casey, *Infantry Tactics*, 207–8.

61. Willich report, *OR* 7:18; Dodge, *Old Second Division*, 93–95, 101; Hindman report, *OR* 7:20.

62. For losses, see Willich report, *OR* 7:18; Hindman report, *OR* 7:20; and Special Orders No. 46, Central Army of Kentucky, December 21, 1861, *OR* 7:20. For victory claims, see congratulatory orders of Buell, Louisville, December 17, 1861, *OR* 7:15–16, and Major General Hardee, Special Orders No. 46, Central Army of Kentucky, December 21, 1861, *OR* 7:20.

63. "Important From Kentucky," *New York Times*, December 19, 1861, p. 8, col. 2.

64. Dodge, *Old Second Division*, 104; Scribner, *How Soldiers Were Made*, 34–35 ("quite a moral effect"); Buell to McClellan, Louisville, December 23, 1861, *OR* 7:511 ("The little affair"). Michael C. C. Adams, *Our Masters the Rebels: A Speculation on Union Military*

Failure in the East, 1861–1865 (Cambridge: Harvard University Press, 1978; reprinted in 1992 as *Fighting for Defeat: Union Military Failure in The East, 1861–1865*), is the fullest exposition of the argument that Union military failure in the East was primarily psychological.

65. R. M. Kelly, "Holding Kentucky for the Union," in *B&L* 1:386 ("one of the few"). For units still practicing squares, see Blakely Diary Typescript, December 17, 1862, SRNB. By the fall of 1862, Army of the Ohio skirmish lines routinely drove off cavalry without forming a square or rallying by fours. See Diary Transcript, October 6, 1862, Culp Papers, FC; Tapp and Klotter, *Tuttle*, 123; and Diary, October 8, 1862, Montgomery Papers, LC.

66. Dodge, *Old Second Division*, 93 ("it was considered uncertain").

CHAPTER 3

1. The battle at Logan's Cross Roads is variously known as Mill Springs, Fishing Creek, Beech Grove, and Somerset. Beech Grove was the site of the camp from which the Confederates marched to attack the Union position at Logan's Cross Roads. Judson W. Bishop, who as a captain led Company A of the 2nd Minnesota in the battle, observed that "Mill Springs, by which name the campaign and the battle are known in our history, was on the south bank of the Cumberland opposite Beech Grove, and had no relation to the battle so far as I know. Neither had Fishing Creek, by which the Confederates named the affair that took place on the 19th at Logan's Cross-Roads." Bishop, "Mill Springs Campaign," in Minnesota Commandery, *Glimpses*, 2:62. Somerset was seven miles to the east of the battlefield.

2. Amos W. Abbott to "Dear Sister Julia," Muldraugh's Hill, Ky., December 16, 1861, Abbott Papers, MHC.

3. Colonel Thomas E. Bramlette to Thomas, Columbia, Ky., December 23, 1861, *OR* 7:513 ("fall like leaves"); Memoir, p. 21, Coulter Papers, LL ("typhoid fever, mumps"); Tapp and Klotter, *Tuttle*, 52–53 ("severely reprimanded the men"). Few soldiers failed to mention disease in their descriptions of the winter of 1861–62. See, e.g., Peter L. Hornbeck to Isaac Bush, Bacon Creek, Ky., January 2, 1862, Hornbeck letters, LL; Haddock, "Historical Sketch," August 18, 1880, IHS; Diary Typescript, p. [6], Connelly Papers, IHS; John [R. Steele] to M. C. Steele, Crab Orchard, Ky., December 23, 1861, Hill Papers, LL; William Stuckey to Helen Stuckey, Camp Gillet, December 20, [1861], Stuckey Papers, IHS; Speed, Kelly, and Pirtle, *Union Regiments of Kentucky*, 303–4; Beatty, *Citizen-Soldier*, 97; Briant, *Sixth Regiment Indiana*, 82–84; Diary Typescript, November 5, 9, 11, 1861, January 1, 1862, Inskeep Papers, OHS; Ephraim S. Holloway to "Dear Father," Camp Wickliffe, Ky., January 21, 1862, typescript, Holloway Papers, OHS; Freeman, "Eighteenth U.S. Infantry," in Minnesota Commandery, *Glimpses*, 3:108; and Hazen, *Narrative*, 13.

4. Diary Typescript, December 1, 1861, Connelly Papers, IHS; George W. Squier to "Dear Wife" [Ellen Squier], Calhoon, Ky., February 5, 1862, Squier Letters, TLM ("'Instent Death'"); Heath Diary, transcripts printed in *Vevay Reveille-Enterprise*, March

14, 1946, Heath Papers, LC ("he will die"); Woodcock, *Southern Boy*, 37–38 ("stench was horrible"); Hazen, *Narrative*, 14.

5. George W. Landrum to Mrs. Obed J. Wilson, January [15?] 1862, Landrum Papers, WRHS ("Men who live"); Bramlette to Thomas, Columbia, Ky., December 23, 1861, *OR* 7:513 ("rather die in battle").

6. Carter to Thomas, Camp Calvert, November 24, 1861 (*OR* 7:447) ("condition of affairs"), November 20, 1861 (*OR* 7:441), and November 25, 1861 (*OR* 7:448). For the execution of the bridge burners, see Humes, *Loyal Mountaineers of Tennessee*, 138–51. Buell had apparently attempted to stop the "ill-timed" sabotage but failed. Buell to McClellan, Louisville, December 9, 1861, *OR* 7:485.

7. Carter to Thomas, Camp Calvert, November 22, 1861, *OR* 7:445; Carter to Maynard, Camp Calvert, November 21, 1861 (*OR* 7:469) ("intensely mortified"), and November 25, 1861 (*OR* 7:470) ("would sooner perish"); Kelly, "Holding Kentucky," in *B&L* 1:383.

8. The Thomas-Mitchel affair, in which political considerations nearly deprived the Army of the Ohio of its best general, is described by authors sympathetic to Thomas in McKinney, *Education*, 114–18, and Cleaves, *Rock of Chickamauga*, 86–87. Mitchel's version is given in Mitchel, *Biographical Narrative*, 226–35.

9. Maynard to Thomas, Washington, December 8, 1861, *OR* 7:484–85.

10. Carter to Maynard, Camp Calvert, November 21, 1861, *OR* 7:469.

11. Johnson and Maynard to Buell, Washington, December 7, 1861, *OR* 7:480.

12. McClellan to Buell, Washington, November 25, 1861 (*OR* 7:447), November 27, 1861 (*OR* 7:450), November 29, 1861 (*OR* 7:457–58), December 3, 1861 (*OR* 7:468–70) ("sacrifice mere military advantage"), December 5, 1861 (*OR* 7:473–74) ("Let me again urge"), and December 29, 1861 (*OR* 7:926) ("Johnson, Maynard, &c.").

13. Lincoln to Buell, Washington, January 4, 1862, *OR* 7:530. See also Cameron to Buell, Washington, January 7, 1862, *OR* 7:535.

14. Buell to McClellan, Louisville, November 22, 1861 (*OR* 7:443–44), December 8, 1861 (*OR* 7:482–83), December 10, 1861 (*OR* 7:487–88), December 18, 1861 (*OR* 7:504), and December 29, 1861 (*OR* 7:520–21).

15. Buell to Genl. Lorenzo Thomas, Adjutant-General, Louisville, December 23, 1861, *OR* 7:511 ("efficient force"); Buell, *Statement*, 2–3 ("some forty or more"). See also Buell to McClellan, Louisville, November 22, 1861 (*OR* 7:443–44), and November 27, 1861 (*OR* 7:452). Sherman had earlier complained that the numerous incomplete regiments authorized "by the President and by General Anderson" made the Kentucky volunteers "a source of weakness instead of strength." Sherman to J. T. Boyle, Louisville, November 5, 1861, *OR* 4:336.

16. Buell to [Margaret Buell], Louisville, December 10, 1861, Buell Papers, FC ("will not disagree"); Kelly, "Holding Kentucky," in *B&L* 1:385–86 ("brigades and regiments"); Buell to McClellan, Louisville, November 27, 1861, *OR* 7:451 ("I have studiously avoided").

17. L. Thomas, Adjutant-General to Buell, Washington, December 17, 1861, *OR* 7:501; Buell to L. Thomas, Louisville, December 17, 1861 (*OR* 7:501), December 29,

1861 (*OR* 7:522); Buell to McClellan, Louisville, January 13, 1862, *OR* 7:548–49 ("succeed in destroying").

18. Buell to McClellan, Louisville, December 29, 1861, *OR* 7:520 ("It startles me"); Buell to Lincoln, Louisville, January 5, 1862, *OR* 7:530–31 ("decidedly against it").

19. Lincoln to Buell, Washington, January 6, 1862, *OR*, 7:927–28 ("disappoints and distresses"); McClellan to Buell, Washington, January 6, 1862 (*OR* 7:531) ("very secondary importance"), and January 13, 1862 (*OR* 7:547) ("You have no idea"). McClellan's shipment of wagons was a direct response to Buell's most recent complaint of insufficient transportation. See Buell to McClellan, Louisville, January 12, *OR* 7:546.

20. Buell to McClellan, Louisville, January 13, 1862, *OR* 7:548–49; Buell to Thomas, Louisville, January 13, 1862, *OR* 7:549–50.

21. Report of Brig. Gen. George H. Thomas, Camp Dick Robinson, Ky., October 22, 1861, *OR* 4:205; Thomas to W. T. Sherman, Camp Dick Robinson, October 23, 1861, *OR* 4:206; Reid, *Ohio in the War*, 2:105; Sherman to Thomas, Louisville, November 11, 1861, *OR* 4:350. It was Sherman's order to Thomas, to call off the pursuit and regroup to the north, that had caused such dismay to Carter's men.

22. Freeman, "Eighteenth U.S. Infantry," in Minnesota Commandery, *Glimpses*, 3:110 ("our hardest march"). See also Thomas to Buell, Camp near Webb's Cross-Roads, Ky., January 13, 1861, *OR* 7:550; Shaw, *Tenth Regiment Indiana*, 137–38; Report of Brig. Gen. George H. Thomas, Somerset, Ky., January 31, 1862, *OR* 7:79.

23. Report of G. B. Crittenden, Camp Fogg, Tenn., February 13, 1862, *OR* 7:105–6.

24. Report of Col. Mahlon D. Manson, Camp near Mill Springs, January 27, 1862, *OR* 7:84.

25. Report of Lieut. Col. William C. Kise, Camp opposite Mill Springs, Wayne County, Ky., January 23, 1862, *OR* 7:90; Judson Bishop, "Narrative of the Second Regiment," in Minn. Comm., *Minnesota*, 83 ("undulating and mostly covered"); Manson report, *OR* 7:84; Report of Col. Frank Wolford, Camp Brents, January 22, 1862, *OR* 7:100.

26. Wolford's men had been reported as drunk while on picket before the skirmish at Rockcastle Hills. After a brief encounter with Zollicoffer's troops near Mill Springs on December 8, Schoepf reported that "The cavalry under my command [Wolford's] behaved badly, as usual. The sooner they are disbanded the better." Captain Dillion's company of Wolford's unit panicked at the outset of that action. T. T. Garrard to Thomas, Camp Wildcat, [Ky.], October 10, 1861, *OR* 4:301; Schoepf to Thomas, Somerset, Ky., December 8, 1861, *OR* 7:9; Report of Col. Van Derveer, Camp near Somerset, Ky., December 8, 1861, *OR* 7:9.

27. Diary Transcript, January 19, 1862, Small Papers, IHS; Harrison Derrick to "Dear Friend Molly," Camp Mill Springs or Zilicofers fortifications, Wayne Co. Ky., 16 miles from Somersett on the Chamberlan River, January 30, 1862, photocopy, Derrick Letters, IHS ("weak in the knees"); Wolford report, *OR* 7:100.

28. Bishop, "Second Regiment," 83 ("a musket shot"); Wesley Elmore to "Dear Father and Mother," Camp at Mill Springs, January 23, 1862, Elmore Papers, IHS ("first we New"); Samuel McIlvaine to J. B. Willson, Gen. Zollicoffer's Camp on the Cumber-

land River near Somerset, Pulaski Co., Ky., January 21, 1862, in McIlvaine, *Dim and Flaring Lamps*, 12; Account of Lieutenant Lewis Johnson, Company E, quoted in Shaw, *Tenth Regiment Indiana*, 151; cf. James W. Sligh to "Dear Wife," Pulaski Co., Ky., January 17 [*sic*], 1862, Sligh Letters, MHC, describing his attempt to follow the battle's progress by its sound from the camp of the Michigan engineers, a mile away.

29. Shaw, *Tenth Regiment Indiana*, 139 ("continual 'zip,' 'zip' "); Wesley Elmore to "Dear Father and Mother," Camp at Mill Springs, January 23, 1862, Elmore Papers, IHS ("into an open Field").

30. Kise report, *OR* 7:90 ("regiment of rebels"); Wesley Elmore to "Dear Father and Mother," Camp at Mill Springs, January 23, 1862, Elmore Papers, IHS ("do Some Execution"). Although the intensity of combat often blurred participants' sense of time, accounts of this action show remarkable unanimity that it lasted approximately one hour. See Kise report, *OR* 7:90; McIlvaine, *Dim and Flaring Lamps*, 12; J. C. Thompson to J. W[esley] Thompson, Lebanon, Ky., January 30, 1862, ISL (stating that the 10th Indiana fought for seventy minutes before falling back on the main body of the Union force); Harrison Derrick to "Dear Friend Molly," Camp Mill Springs or Zilicofers fortifications, Wayne Co. Ky., 16 miles from Somersett on the Chamberlan River, January 30, 1862, photocopy, Derrick Letters, IHS; Shaw, *Tenth Regiment Indiana*, 139 ("For an hour and a quarter the regiment fought and no help from the rear"); [William E. Carroll], "Letter from the Tenth Regiment, Camp Opposite Mill Creek, Ky., January 21, 1862," *Lafayette (Ind.) Daily Journal*, January 29, 1862 ("For about an hour our regiment held the entire force in check"); and the account of Lieutenant Lewis Johnson, Company E, quoted in Shaw, *Tenth Regiment Indiana*, 151.

31. Manson report, *OR* 7:84; Speed S. Fry to "My Dear Wife," Zollicoffer's Camp, January 20, 1862, Fry Letter, UC; Report of Col. Speed S. Fry, Zollicoffer's Camp, Wayne County, Ky., January 25, 1862, *OR* 7:87 ("proceed at once").

32. Report of Col. Robert L. McCook, Somerset, January 27, 1862, *OR* 7:93 ("approaching in force"); Report of Col. Horatio Van Cleve, Camp Hamilton, Ky., January 22, 1862, *OR* 7:95; Shanks, *Personal Recollections*, 66 ("Damn you sir").

33. Kise report, *OR* 7:91; Shaw, *Tenth Regiment Indiana*, 139; Harrison Derrick to "Dear Friend Molly," Camp Mill Springs or Zilicofers fortifications, Wayne Co. Ky., 16 miles from Somersett on the Chamberlan River, January 30, 1862, photocopy, Derrick Letters, IHS ("retreat for reinforcements"); McIlvaine, *Dim and Flaring Lamps*, 12 ("from some misunderstanding"); Wesley Elmore to "Dear Father and Mother," Camp at Mill Springs, January 23, 1862, Elmore Papers, IHS; Wolford report, *OR* 7:100. Discovering that Confederates had surrounded the area where his unit's horses were being held, Colonel Wolford ordered the horses cut loose and driven down the Mill Springs road toward the Union rear, where his men were later able to catch them.

34. Kise report, *OR* 7:91; Fry report, *OR* 7:87.

35. Bircher, *Drummer*, 40. See also Bishop, "Second Regiment," 83.

36. Speed S. Fry to "My Dear Wife," Zollicoffer's Camp, January 20, 1862, Fry Letter, UC. After the battle, news of the incident circulated through the army immediately, so that some who were not present nevertheless described the event in great detail. See James W. Sligh to "Dear Wife," Pulaski Co., Ky., January 17 [*sic*], 1862, Sligh Letters,

MHC. Others claimed that Fry's account of Zollicoffer's death was "a great hoax." See the account of Lieutenant Lewis Johnson, Company E, quoted in Shaw, *Tenth Regiment Indiana*, 153. It seems unlikely that Fry would have written such an elaborate fabrication for his wife.

37. Speed S. Fry to "My Dear Wife," Zollicoffer's Camp, January 20, 1862, Fry Letter, UC.

38. Thomas report, *OR* 7:79 ("formed in front"); Wolford report, *OR* 7:100; Kise report, *OR* 7:91. Shaw (*Tenth Regiment Indiana*, 139) interpreted Thomas's comment as an implied criticism of the 10th Indiana, illustrating the extreme sensitivity that veterans like Shaw felt for the reputations of their regiments.

39. The counties of origin were Boone (Companies A, F, and I), Montgomery (B), Clinton (C and K), Benton (D), Tippecanoe (E and H), and Fountain (G), with some of the men of Company D coming from Warren or Tippecanoe County. See Shaw, *Tenth Regiment Indiana*, 53 et. seq. The estimate of kinship within the unit is based on a comparison of surnames in the regimental roster and assumes that men with the same surname and enlisting in the same company on the same day were related. Common surnames such as Brown were not counted for this purpose, nor were men who shared surnames but joined different companies, and no adjustment was made for men who were related but did not share common surnames. The estimate of 20 percent is thus extremely conservative; the actual number of relatives could easily have been twice as great. Shaw, *Tenth Regiment Indiana*, 56–121.

40. Fry report, *OR* 7:87.

41. Manson report, *OR* 7:84; Report of Col. Samuel P. Carter, Somerset, Ky., January 30, 1862, *OR* 7:97.

42. Thomas report, *OR* 7:80; Fry report, *OR* 7:87; Report of Lieut. George H. Harries, *OR* 7:95–96; Bishop, *Story of a Regiment*, 38–39; Bishop, "Second Regiment," 84; McCook report, *OR* 7:93 ("top of the next hill").

43. Van Cleve report, *OR* 7:95; Thomas report, *OR* 7:80; Kelly, "Holding Kentucky," in *B&L* 1:389; Bishop, "Second Regiment," 83; Speed S. Fry to "My Dear Wife," Zollicoffer's Camp, January 20, 1862, Fry Letter, UC; McCook report, *OR* 7:93 ("move by the flank"). The 10th Indiana Regiment, which Thomas had earlier sent to support the left flank of the 4th Kentucky, had by this time moved back to the position it had abandoned earlier in the fight, on the 4th Kentucky's right flank. Kise report, *OR* 7:91. See Griffith, *Battle Tactics*, 63–44, for the "passage of lines" maneuver.

44. Bircher, *Drummer*, 25.

45. McCook report, *OR* 7:93.

46. Bishop, "Second Regiment," 83–84. See also Van Cleve report, *OR* 7:95.

47. Harries report, *OR* 7:96 ("With loud hurrahs"); McCook report, *OR* 7:93–94; Grebner, *"We Were the Ninth,"* 84 ("If it gets too hot"). One wing of the regiment fought under the tactical control of Major Kammerling, the acting lieutenant colonel and interim regimental commander, and the other wing was led by a Captain Joseph, acting major.

48. McCook report, *OR* 7:94 ("broke the enemy's flank"); Thomas report, *OR* 7:80; Kise report, *OR* 7:91 ("a perfect rout").

49. Diary Transcript, January 19, 1862, Small Papers, IHS ("a good whiping"); Account of Lieutenant Lewis Johnson, Company E, quoted in Shaw, *Tenth Regiment Indiana*, 151 ("completely played out"); Thomas report, *OR* 7:80; Fry report, *OR* 7:87; Kise report, *OR* 7:91.

50. Harrison Derrick to "Dear Friend Molly," Camp Mill Springs or Zilicofers fortifications, Wayne Co. Ky., 16 miles from Somersett on the Chamberlan River, January 30, 1862, photocopy, Derrick Letters, IHS; Thomas report, *OR* 7:82 (Union casualties); Crittenden report, *OR* 7:108 (Confederate casualties).

51. Wm. J. Tucker to William Orland Bourne, Dayton, November 30, 1865, LC ("I dont see how"); Piatt, *Thomas*, 124–27; Johnson, "War Memories," in Minnesota Commandery, *Glimpses*, 1:15.

52. Grebner, *"We Were the Ninth,"* 84.

53. Harries report, *OR* 7:96.

54. Austin Van Haun to "Dear Sister," Somersett [*sic*], January 28, 1862, Van Haun Papers, WRHS.

55. Harries report, *OR* 7:96; Thomas report, *OR* 7:80.

56. Kise report, *OR* 7:91.

57. A mark of the personal scale of the battle was the care taken to return the bodies of General Zollicoffer and Lieutenant Bailie Peyton, whose dramatic death in a lone charge against the Union lines was recorded by many observers. See Bishop, "Second Regiment," 84; Waddle, *Three Years*, 8; and Dr. J. L. Laverty to Mr. Franklin Alford, Medical Department 6th Reg. Ind., January 30, 1862, in Skidmore, *Alford Brothers*, 201–3.

CHAPTER 4

1. Buell to Lorenzo Thomas, Louisville, January 27, 1862, *OR* 7:568 ("natural expectation"). For Buell's proposal to invade Tennessee with 120,000 men, see Buell to McClellan, Louisville, January 13, 1862, *OR* 7:548–49; for difficulties in pursuing the enemy into eastern Tennessee, see Buell to Lieutenant-Colonel Colburn, [n.p.], January 27, 1862, *OR* 7:930, and Buell to McClellan, Louisville, February 1, 1862, *OR* 7:931–32.

2. Buell to [Margaret Buell], Louisville, Ky., January 14, 1862, Buell Papers, FC ("want of transportation"); Lincoln to Halleck, Washington, December 31, 1861, *OR* 7:524 ("A simultaneous movement"). For Buell's plan, see Buell to McClellan, Louisville, December 29, 1861 (*OR* 7:520–21), and February 1, 1862 (*OR* 7:931–32).

3. Buell to Halleck, Louisville, January 3, 1862, *OR* 7:528–29. Buell believed that the Confederates had 40,000 men at Bowling Green, 20,000 at Columbus on the Mississippi River, and 20,000 along the line connecting those two points.

4. Buell to McClellan, Louisville, January 13, 1862, *OR* 7:548–49.

5. Mitchel, *Biographical Narrative*, 242 ("It rains, then snows"); Dodge, *Old Second Division*, 108 ("time of deep mud"); Henry H. Seys to "My Dear Wife" [Harriet Seys], n.p., January 25, 1862, Seys Papers, SCWC ("almost impossible to tell"); Diary Type-

script, February 7, 1862, Inskeep Papers, OHS ("round town ball"); Briant, *Sixth Regiment Indiana*, 96–97 ("dreary winter evenings"); Alford H. Sampson to "Dear Mother," Camp Wickliffe, Ky., February 7, 1862, Torah W. Sampson Papers, FC ("washing my face").

6. J. Ross Ingerson to James M. Cole, Camp Wood, January 28, 1862, Cole Papers, ISHL ("old Jollycoffer"). See also Henry H. Seys to "My Dear Wife" [Harriet Seys], n.p., January 25, 1862, Seys Papers, SCWC.

7. Dodge, *Old Second Division*, 110 ("incomparably superior"); Nelson to Capt. J. B. Fry, A.A.G., Head Quarters 4th Division, Camp Wickliffe, Ky., December 28, 1861, NA RG 393.2.843, p. 22. See also Diary Typescript, February 8, 1862, Inskeep Papers, OHS; Kelly, "Holding Kentucky," in *B&L* 1:304; Crofts, *Third Ohio . . . Cavalry*, 20; but cf. Curry, *Four Years in the Saddle*, 29, criticizing Sibley tents. For the number of tents issued, see Dodge, *Old Second Division*, 110; Diary Typescript, May 18, 1862, Inskeep Papers, OHS; De Velling, *Seventeenth [Ohio] Regiment*, 69; and McIlvaine, *Dim and Flaring Lamps*, 61.

8. Frederick Marion to "Dear Sister," Camp near Corinth, Miss., May 11, 1862, Marion Papers, ISHL ("the splendid Springfield rifle"); James Jones to "father and mother," [P]ittsburg [L]anding TN, April 26, 1862, IHS ("splendidest gun").

9. Grant, *Personal Memoirs*, 44. For the types and capabilities of small arms used in the Civil War, see McWhiney and Jamieson, *Attack and Die*, 48–50; Hagerman, *American Civil War*, 16–17; Coggins, *Arms and Equipment of the Civil War*, 26–39; Griffith, *Battle Tactics*, 73–76; and Lord, *They Fought for the Union*, 140–42.

10. Morton to Cameron, April 28, 1861, Indianapolis, *OR*, 3d ser., 1:125 ("of an inferior character"); Dodge, *Old Second Division*, 109–10; Nelson to Capt. J. B. Fry, A.A.G., Head Quarters 4th Division, Camp Wickliffe, Ky., January 12, 1862, NA RG 393.2.843, p. 43. Hagerman (*American Civil War*, 308–9 n) states that American arsenals held 500,000 smoothbore muskets and 89,500 rifled muskets of various kinds in 1861, and that 119,000 of these fell into Confederate hands. For the effort to arm Union volunteers in 1861, see Shannon, *Organization and Administration*, 1:107–26; Meneely, *War Department*, 205–9, 227; and Davis, *Arming the Union*, 38–47.

11. J. H. Gilman, [inspection report], Head Quarters, Dept. of the Ohio, Louisville, December 2, 1861, NA RG 393.1.880.

12. Halleck to Buell, St. Louis, January 30, 1862 (*OR* 7:574), and February 1, 1862 (*OR* 7:576) ("at present not essential"); Buell to Halleck, Louisville, February 3, 1862 (*OR* 7:580), February 5, 1862 (*OR* 7:583) ("admit of diversion"), and February 5, 1862 (*OR* 7:584) ("absolutely require it"). Buell did send Halleck a brigade, which never returned to the Army of the Ohio.

13. Buell to Halleck, Louisville, February 5, 1862, *OR* 7:583 ("progress will be slow"); McClellan to Buell, Washington, February 6, 1862, *OR* 7:586; Halleck to McClellan, St. Louis, February 7, 1862, *OR* 7:591.

14. Buell to McClellan, Louisville, February 6, 1862 (*OR* 7:587–88) ("right in its strategical bearing"), February 7, 1862 (*OR* 7:593) ("change of my line"), February 8, 1862 (*OR* 7:594) ("will not decide").

15. Beatty, *Citizen-Soldier*, 107, 143 ("greatest of living soldiers"); O. M. Mitchel to

"Mr. Coe," Camp Madison, t'other side of Green River, February 12, 1862, Mitchel, *Biographical Narrative*, 245, 248 ("rank entitles me"); Waddle, *Three Years*, 9; Cist, *Army of the Cumberland*, 24.

16. Buell to McClellan, Louisville, February 15, 1862, OR 7:620 ("leaving the way"); Halleck to McClellan, St. Louis, February 15, 1862, 8 P.M., OR 7:617 ("bad strategy"); Halleck to Buell, St. Louis, February 15, 1862, OR 7:621 ("not good strategy"). O. M. Mitchel encouraged Buell to undertake the advance. Mitchel, *Biographical Narrative*, 249–51.

17. Van Zwaluwenburg Memoir, p. 16, SCWC ("could not keep up"); Beatty, *Citizen-Soldier*, 103; Kelly, "Holding Kentucky," in *B&L* 1:304 ("impossible to move"); Bishop, "Second Regiment," 82 ("loaded to their roofs"); Minn. Comm., *Minnesota*, 82, 148; Bircher, *Drummer*, 28.

18. Davidson, *Battery A*, 23; Kellogg "Recollections," p. 24, USAMHI ("Theory alone"). For complaints of inexperienced officers overworking their men, see Tapp and Klotter, *Tuttle*, 57, 64; Bishop, *Story of a Regiment*, 195; Canfield, *21st Regiment Ohio*, 31; and Rogers, *125th Regiment Illinois*, 13–14.

19. Canfield, *21st Regiment Ohio*, 31.

20. For the 10th Indiana vs. 14th Ohio race, see Price Diary, January 23, 1862, USAMHI ("tried to run in"); McIlvaine, *Dim and Flaring Lamps*, 39–40; and Shaw, *Tenth Regiment Indiana*, 162–63. For the 17th Ohio vs. 21st Ohio, see Diary Typescript, February 23, 25, 1862, Inskeep Papers, OHS; see also Bennett, *Ninth Michigan*, 10 (9th Michigan vs. 38th Indiana).

21. For the surrender and occupation of Nashville, see Villard, *Memoirs*, 1:228–29; Dodge, *Old Second Division*, 152; Mitchel, *Biographical Narrative*, 252; Buell, *Statement*, 8; and Beatty, *Citizen-Soldier*, 111.

22. Buell to [Margaret Buell], St. Cloud Hotel, Nashville, February 27, 1862, Buell Papers, FC.

23. Dodge, *Old Second Division*, 161; Bircher, *Drummer*, 31 ("all our spare time"); Diary, April 1, 1862, H. C. Patton Papers, IHS; Hazen, *Narrative*, 20–22 ("very busily engaged"); Grose, *36th Regiment Indiana*, 98–99 ("well pleased").

24. Tapp and Klotter, *Tuttle*, 57, 64; Thomas Jefferson Jordan to Simon Cameron, Gallatin, Tenn., April 20, 1862, Cameron Papers, LC ("no glory here").

25. Dodge, *Old Second Division*, 113–15.

26. Ibid., 158. For Confederate cavalry leader John Hunt Morgan's use of enemy uniforms to deceive the Army of the Ohio, see Report of Capt. John H. Morgan, Murfreesborough, Tenn., March 10, 1862, OR 10(1):6, and Report of Capt. John H. Morgan, Shelbyville, Tenn., March 19, 1862, OR 10(1):31. See also Beatty, *Citizen-Soldier*, 115.

27. J. N. Patton to James Barnett, Athens, Tenn., December 29, 1888, Patton Letter, WRHS. Nelson's own pickets were accidentally attacked by members of the 1st Ohio Cavalry later in the same campaign. See Curry, *Four Years in the Saddle*, 31.

28. Dodge, *Old Second Division*, 160 ("lust for butchery").

29. Mitchel, *Biographical Narrative*, 255–58; Morgan report, OR 10(1):6–7, 31–32; Beatty, *Citizen-Soldier*, 114–15; Frank J. Jones, "Personal Recollections and Experience

of a Soldier During the War of the Rebellion,"in Ohio Commandery, *Sketches*, 6:120 ("damn bad swap").

30. Buell, *Statement*, 8–9; Don Carlos Buell, "Shiloh Reviewed," in *B&L* 1:489. In the 1860s the cost of wagon transportation (not including the initial cost of road construction, which armies often had to do for themselves) was roughly ten times greater than that for rail transportation, which in turn was three times more expensive than water freight. To the extent that price was an accurate gauge of efficiency, moving and supplying troops overland by wagon was thirty times harder than doing so by river. See Hattaway and Jones, *How the North Won*, 202 n.

31. President's War Order No. 3, Washington, March 11, 1862, *OR* 10(2):28; Buell to Halleck, Nashville, March 15, 1862, *OR* 10(2):39; Buell, *Statement*, 9; Halleck to Buell, St. Louis, March 16, 1862, *OR* 10(2):42.

32. Special Orders No. 12, Nashville, March 26, 1862, *OR* 10(2):68; Buell to Brig. Gen. E. Dumont, Nashville, March 20, 1862, *OR* 10(2):54–55; Special Orders No. 1, Nashville, March 28, 1862, *OR* 10(2):76; Buell to Mitchel, Camp near Columbia, Tenn., March 27, 1862, *OR* 10(2):71–72; Buell, *Statement*, 9; Van Horne, *Army of the Cumberland*, 1:99–100; Cist, *Army of the Cumberland*, 29. For pressure to protect Nashville, see Johnson to Stanton, Nashville, March 29, 1862, *OR* 10(2):76; Stanton to Halleck, Washington, March 30, 1862, *OR* 10(2):79; Stanton to Buell, Washington, March 30, 1862 (*OR* 10[2]:81), and March 31, 1862 (*OR* 10[2]:81); Buell to Stanton, Columbia, Tenn., 11 A.M., March 31, 1862, *OR* 10(2):81–82.

33. Buell, *Statement*, 9; Buell, "Shiloh Reviewed," in *B&L* 1:491; Van Horne, *Army of the Cumberland*, 1:100; Buell to Halleck, Nashville, March 23, 1862, *OR* 10(2):60.

34. Curry, *Four Years in the Saddle*, 30 (1st Ohio Cavalry's unsuccessful dash to save the Duck River bridge); Van Horne, *Army of the Cumberland*, 1:100 ("a later period"); De Velling, *Seventeenth [Ohio] Regiment*, 100. Beatty (*Citizen-Soldier*, 234–35) describes the efficiency of the army's bridging capabilities in 1863.

35. Dodge, *Old Second Division*, 167–68; Report of Col. Jacob Ammen, Headquarters Tenth Brigade, April 10, 1862, *OR* 10(1):329–30; Van Horne, *Army of the Cumberland*, 1:102; Villard, *Memoirs*, 1:237–38; Henry Stone, "The Battle of Shiloh," in *Campaigns*, 48–49.

36. Hazen, *Narrative*, 24 ("no need of haste"); Curry, *Four Years in the Saddle*, 32–34. For communications problems between Halleck and Buell, see Halleck to Buell, St. Louis, March 30, 1862 (*OR* 10[2]:79–80), and April 2, 1862 (*OR* 10[2]:86); Van Horne, *Army of the Cumberland*, 1:101, 103–4.

37. Ammen report, *OR* 10(1):330 ("get the glory"); Villard, *Memoirs*, 1:239 ("piece of bravado"); Sipes GAR records, CHS ("Nelson was a tyrant"); Van Horne, *Army of the Cumberland*, 1:101; Grose, *36th Regiment Indiana*, 100–101; Williams Diary Typescript, March 29, 1862, SNMP ("most awful cold"). It is possible that Nelson was eager to march not only because of his impetuosity and lust for glory, but also because he specifically expected a battle to occur at any moment on the far side of the Tennessee River. In the William Nelson Papers at the Filson Club, Louisville, there is a waterproof cloth map dated April 1862 that shows the west bank of the Tennessee River, south of the Shiloh battlefield area. The map may have been drawn after the battle, but if Nelson carried it on

his approach to Savannah it would indicate that he expected his division to be operating on the far side of the river at a time when Buell assumed that Grant's army was still safely east of the river.

38. Curry, *Four Years in the Saddle*, 31; Dodge, *Old Second Division*, 166–68; Briant, *Sixth Regiment Indiana*, 98–99.

39. For the march to Savannah, see Dodge, *Old Second Division*, 173; Villard, *Memoirs*, 1:239–40; Truxhall, *"Respects,"* 70; Van Horne, *Army of the Cumberland*, 1:103; Ammen report, *OR* 10(1):330; Bircher, *Drummer*, 32 ("very near freeze"); Report of Maj. Gen. Don Carlos Buell, Field of Shiloh, April 15, 1862, *OR* 10(1):291; and Fisher, *Staff Officer's Story*, 10.

40. Horace Fisher, of Nelson's staff, recorded the time when he first heard the sound of battle. *Staff Officer's Story*, 10; Fisher, "Memorandum," pp. 1, 3, SNMP. For others in the Army of the Ohio who recalled hearing the sound of fighting from up to thirty miles away, see Ephraim A. Otis, "The Second Day at Shiloh," in *Campaigns*, 175, and the accounts of Buell, Ammen, Villard, Tuttle, Bircher, Curry, Dodge, Truxhall, Jones, and Hosea. The men of the 6th Indiana, thirty-six miles away at daybreak, did not hear the firing until they had been on the road for several hours. See Briant, *Sixth Regiment Indiana*, 82–84.

41. Briant, *Sixth Regiment Indiana*, 101 ("each man grasps"); Lewis Hosea, "The Regular Brigade of the Army of the Cumberland," in Ohio Commandery, *Sketches*, 5:331 ("heard the booming"); Van Zwaluwenburg Memoir, p. 18, SCWC ("how to play ball"); Ambrose Bierce, "What I Saw of Shiloh," *Bierce's Civil War*, 11–12 ("long, deep sighing").

42. Buell report, *OR* 10(1):292; Report of Brig. Gen. Alexander McD. McCook, Field of Shiloh, April 9, 1862, *OR* 10(1):302; Dodge, *Old Second Division*, 174–75; Jones, "Personal Recollections," in Ohio Commandery, *Sketches*, 6:120; Grant, *Personal Memoirs*, 178; Villard, *Memoirs*, 1:242; Report of Brig. Gen. Thomas L. Crittenden, Field of Shiloh, April 15, 1862, *OR* 10(1):354. Ironically, poor communication within the Army of the Ohio was responsible for proximity of the divisions of McCook and Crittenden; Buell had earlier ordered his division commanders to halt and rest at Waynesboro, more than thirty miles short of Savannah, but his orders failed to reach them until they had all passed through the town. Villard, *Memoirs*, 1:240; Van Horne, *Army of the Cumberland*, 1:102–3.

43. Nelson's Fourth Division finished crossing the river by 9:00 P.M., by which time Crittenden's Fifth Division reached Pittsburg Landing from Savannah. Two of the Second Division's three brigades arrived at Savannah by 8:00 P.M. and sailed to Pittsburg Landing later that night; the third did not reach the battlefield until 11:00 A.M. the next day. Report of Brig. Gen. William Nelson, Camp on the Field of Battle, April 10, 1862, *OR* 10(1):324. See also the accounts of Bierce, Ammen, Fisher, Van Horne, Buell, Villard, Stone, Hazen, Crittenden, Dodge, Truxhall, Briant, and the Report of Col. William H. Gibson, Field of Shiloh, April 10, 1862, *OR* 10(1):315.

44. Bierce, "What I Saw of Shiloh," *Bierce's Civil War*, 17 ("this abominable mob"); Villard, *Memoirs*, 1:246 ("panic-stricken, uncontrollable mob"); Ulysses S. Grant, "The Battle of Shiloh," in *B&L* 1:474 ("shot where they lay"). For other descriptions of the

scene, see Louis M. Buford to Charles Buford, Jr., Field of Shiloh, April 21, 1862, Charles Buford Manuscripts, LC; Buell, "Shiloh Reviewed," in *B&L* 1:494; — Reynolds to William Orland Bourne, Sycamore, Va., January 23, 1866, Reynolds Letter, LC; Nelson report, *OR* 10(1):32; Hazen, *Narrative*, 25, 46; Buell report, *OR* 10(1):292; Beatty, *Citizen-Soldier*, 162; Briant, *Sixth Regiment Indiana*, 102; and Grose, *36th Regiment Indiana*, 103 ("Such looks of terror, such confusion is beyond description").

Engle (*Buell*, 226–27) describes the arrival of the Army of the Ohio at Shiloh using similar words. For the original version of this passage, see Gerald J. Prokopowicz, "All for the Regiment: Unit Cohesion and Tactical Stalemate in the Army of the Ohio, 1861–1862" (Ph.D. diss., Harvard University, 1994). Professor Engle has apologized for the unattributed borrowing of the above paragraph.

45. Grose, *36th Regiment Indiana*, 103 (" 'You will see' "); Hosea, "Regular Brigade," in Ohio Commandery, *Sketches*, 5:332 ("dim light of dawn"); Bierce, "What I Saw of Shiloh," *Bierce's Civil War*, 17 ("unholy delight").

46. Jones, "Personal Recollections," in Ohio Commandery, *Sketches*, 6:123 ("threading our way"); Crittenden report, *OR* 10(1):355 ("did not wish my troops"); Nelson report, *OR* 10(1):324 ("permission to open fire"); Villard, *Memoirs*, 1:244–45; Fisher "Memorandum," p. 7, SNMP ("Draw your sabres"). See also Fisher, *Staff Officer's Story*, 13.

47. Dodge, *Old Second Division*, 183 ("Fall in here"); B. Frank Dysart to Dear Brother [Philip Dysart], Camp Shyloah, April 23, 1862, Dysart Family Letter Photocopies, SNMP ("we cared not").

48. Buell, *General Buell on General Sherman and the Battle of Shiloh; or, Pittsburg Landing* (N.Y.?, 1865), reprinted from *New York World*, February 18, 1865, Buell Papers, FC ("did not expect"); Buell report, *OR* 10(1):293 ("entire ignorance"); Buell, "Shiloh Reviewed," in *B&L* 1:518–19, 532 ("to know nothing"); Van Horne, *Army of the Cumberland*, 1:109; Villard, *Memoirs*, 1:246.

49. Hazen, *Narrative*, 25 ("impressed me more"). For how the terrain at Shiloh limited both sides' tactical options, see Frank and Reaves, *"Seeing the Elephant,"* 87–88.

50. Nelson report, *OR* 10(1):324–25; Buell report, *OR* 10(1):293; Villard, *Memoirs*, 1:247; Report of Col. William B. Hazen, In Camp, near Pittsburg Landing, Tenn., April 9, 1862, *OR* 10(1):341; Report of Col. Thomas D. Sedgewick, On the Field of Battle, near Pittsburg Landing, Tenn., April 9, 1862, *OR* 10(1):351; "Your true Griffin" to "Esteemed Friend," On Guard at Nelson's HQ Pittsburg Landing, April 13, 1862, SNMP ("cool as a cucumber").

51. Gibson report, *OR* 10(1):315. Alexander McCook was not the only general in the Army of the Ohio to violate the chain of command at Shiloh. See Report of Brig. Gen. Jeremiah T. Boyle, Battle-field of Shiloh, Tenn., in Camp, April 10, 1862, *OR* 10(1):357–58 (Buell and Crittenden directed regiments and companies of Boyle's brigade); Report of Col. Benjamin C. Grider, n.p., April 8, 1862, *OR* 10(1):358 (Crittenden and Buell gave contradictory orders directly to the 9th Kentucky); Report of Col. Edward H. Hobson, On Battle-field, April 10, 1862, *OR* 10(1):361 (Crittenden gave orders directly to the 13th Kentucky).

52. Crittenden report, *OR* 10(1):355; Buell, "Shiloh Reviewed," in *B&L* 1:532;

Louis M. Buford to Charles Buford, Jr., Field of Shiloh, April 21, 1862, Charles Buford Manuscripts, LC. Buell took chances, too, according to his aide Almon Rockwell, who wrote of "balls whistling all about us" during the battle. Diary, April 7, 1862, Rockwell Collection, LC; see also Nelson report, *OR* 10(1):324–25.

53. Jones, "Personal Recollections," in Ohio Commandery, *Sketches*, 6:123 ("but little knowledge"); Dodge, *Old Second Division*, 187–89; Hosea, "Regular Brigade," in Ohio Commandery, *Sketches*, 5:332 ("ringing speech"); Van Zwaluwenburg Memoir, p. 19, SCWC; Alexander Varian to "Dear Father," Pittsburg Landing, Tenn., April 10, 1862, Varian Papers, WRHS ("have faced anything").

54. Hazen, *Narrative*, 27–31; Report of Col. Walter C. Whitaker, Camp near Iuka, Tishomingo, Miss., June 16, 1862, *OR* 10(1):345–47; Fisher, *Staff Officer's Story*, 15; Nelson report, *OR* 10(1):325.

55. Ammen report, *OR* 10(1):333 ("seen the elephant"). Ammen, like many officers, followed the convention of describing regiments as though they were individuals, writing that the 24th Ohio "behaved well, but does not appear as anxious as the other regiments to get into a fight."

56. Hosea, "Regular Brigade," in Ohio Commandery, *Sketches*, 5:331. For the emotions and motivations of troops entering battle, see Hess, *The Union Soldier in Battle*; McPherson, *For Causes and Comrades* (for troops on both sides); and Frank & Reaves, *"Seeing the Elephant"* (for Shiloh in particular).

57. —— Reynolds to William Orland Bourne, Sycamore, Va., January 23, 1866, Reynolds Letter, LC ("in good spirits"); Sipes GAR records, CHS; Grose, *36th Regiment Indiana*, 103 ("These death scenes"). For other descriptions of the death of Grant's aide, Captain Carson, see Williams Diary Typescript, April 6, 1862, SNMP, and Fisher, "Memorandum," p. 8, SNMP. Men in many other regiments were sobered by the sight of casualties before the battle; see, e.g., Bierce, "What I Saw of Shiloh," *Bierce's Civil War*, 18, Briant, *Sixth Regiment Indiana*, 103; "Your true Griffin" to "Esteemed Friend," On Guard at Nelson's HQ Pittsburg Landing, Tenn., April 13, 1862, SNMP; and Van Zwaluwenburg Memoir, p. 19, SCWC.

58. H. W. Engelbracht, "Some war reminiscences," p. 2, SNMP ("completely wiped out"); Grider report, *OR* 10(1):359 ("very thick growth"); Van Zwaluwenburg Memoir, p. 20, SCWC ("intense nerve strain").

59. Payne, *Thirty-Fourth Regiment of Illinois*, 20 ("a minute or an hour"); Bierce, "What I Saw of Shiloh," *Bierce's Civil War*, 24 ("I can't describe it").

60. Hosea, "Regular Brigade," in Ohio Commandery, *Sketches*, 5:332–33. The sound of battle was the only warning Hosea's unit received of the next rebel attack. "We knew by the increased volume of musketry and artillery fire that the enemy had effected a concentration in our front." For other references to gauging the battle by its sound, including that of the "rebel yell," see Ammen report, *OR* 10(1):335, and Briant, *Sixth Regiment Indiana*, 109.

61. For illustrations of typical regimental flags, see Street, *The Struggle for Tennessee*, 146–47. At Shiloh, Nelson ordered his division's regiments to case their colors because the unfurled flags were getting caught and torn in the overhanging trees. Late on April 7, the Union line nearly opened fire on one of Nelson's brigades as it returned from a

charge, because its regiments could not readily be identified as friend or foe without their flags. Fisher, *Staff Officer's Story*, 15–16.

62. Horrall, *Forty-Second Indiana*, 148 ("as the christian"). Army of the Ohio regiments rallied around their colors a number of times at Shiloh. See, e.g., Dodge, *Old Second Division*, 200 (34th Illinois and 30th Indiana); A. McCook report, *OR* 10(1):304 (Colonel Kirk, commanding Fifth Brigade, used a flag to rally the 34th Illinois); Sedgewick report, *OR* 10(1):352 (the 2nd Kentucky came out of the fight with heavy losses "but with our colors safe").

63. General Orders No. 19, Adjutant General's Office, Washington, February 22, 1862, *OR*, 3d ser., 1:899. In February 1862 the ladies of Louisville made a set of flags commemorating the victory at Logan's Cross Roads, which they presented to the regiments that fought there. Bircher, *Drummer*, 30; McIlvaine, *Dim and Flaring Lamps*, 42–43; Shaw, *Tenth Regiment Indiana*, 163.

64. Report of Lieut. Col. George S. Mygatt, Battle-Field of Pittsburg Landing, Tenn., April 9, 1862, *OR* 10(1):348; Dodge, *Old Second Division*, 200. For other color-bearer losses at Shiloh, see Hazen report, *OR* 10(1):341; Whitaker report, *OR* 10(1):344; and Fyffe report, *OR* 10(1):364.

65. Bierce, "What I Saw of Shiloh," *Bierce's Civil War*, 25–26 (" 'Lie down, there!' "); Hosea, "Regular Brigade," in Ohio Commandery, *Sketches*, 5:334 ("hug the earth"); Report of Capt. Edwin F. Townsend, Battle-field near Pittsburg Landing, Tenn., April 12, 1862, *OR* 10(1):313; Dodge, *Old Second Division*, 199 ("intelligence of the disaster"); A. McCook report, *OR* 10(1):304. See Linderman, *Embattled Courage*, chaps. 3, 4, and Hazen, *Narrative*, 22–23, for the evolution of what was considered acceptable behavior for officers under fire.

66. Report of Brg. Gen. Lovell H. Rousseau, Battle-field of Shiloh, Tenn., April 12, 1862, *OR* 10(1):309 ("without the least confusion"); A. McCook report, *OR* 10(1):304; Payne, *Thirty-Fourth Regiment of Illinois*, 20; Briant, *Sixth Regiment Indiana*, 108.

67. Gibson report, *OR* 10(1):315; Report of Lieut. Col. Albert M. Blackman, Camped on the Battle-field, April 10, 1862, *OR* 10(1):320.

68. Report of Col. August Willich, *OR* 10(1):317–18; Report of Brig. Gen. William T. Sherman, Camp Shiloh, *OR* 10(1):251; Report of Maj. Gen. Lewis Wallace, Pittsburg Landing, Tenn., April 12, 1862, *OR* 10(1):172.

69. Hosea, "Regular Brigade," in Ohio Commandery, *Sketches*, 5:334; Willich report, *OR* 10(1):318; Payne, *Thirty-Fourth Regiment of Illinois*, 21; A. P. Dysart to Philip R. Dysart, Camp Shiloah, April 21, 1862, Dysart Family Letter Photocopies, SNMP ("to our dismay").

70. Van Zwaluwenburg Memoir, p. 20, SCWC. On a larger scale, the 26th Kentucky found itself overlapping the 2nd Kentucky and 13th Ohio and became entangled with the latter. Report of Lieut. Col. Cicero Maxwell, Camp Shiloh, April 9, 1862, *OR* 10(1):368. The men of the 59th Ohio were preparing to fire a volley into what turned out to be Nelson's division on the evening of the sixth when Nelson himself told them not to fire. Anonymous [Memoir of Co. C, 59th Ohio], July 14, 1906, p. 7, SNMP.

71. Organization of the Union forces . . . , *OR* 10(1):108; Van Horne, *Army of the Cumberland*, 1:119.

72. Alexander Varian to "Dear Father," Pittsburg Landing, Tenn., April 10, 1862 ("awful grandeur"), and Varian to "Dear Mary," Camp "Field of Shiloh," April 18, 1862 ("spoke to the Rebels"), Varian Papers, WRHS; Thomas Prickett to "Dearest Matilda" [Matilda Darr], Camp on the battlefield of Shiloh, near Pittsburg Landing, April 18, 1862, Prickett Papers, IHS ("never felt so good"); Briant, *Sixth Regiment Indiana*, 110 ("one universal handshaking").

73. Bickering over blame and credit for events at Shiloh between the two Union field armies began immediately after the battle and continued for decades. Thomas Crittenden's aide-de-camp expressed the view prevalent in the Army of the Ohio when he warned a correspondent not to believe newspaper reports praising Grant: "his share is very small. . . . Grant was badly whipped, and if we hadn't have come to his relief when we did his entire army would have been taken prisoners or driven into the Tennessee River." Louis M. Buford to Charles Buford, Jr., Field of Shiloh, April 21, 1862, Charles Buford Manuscripts, LC. For the conflicting views of the two army commanders, see Grant, "Battle of Shiloh," in *B&L* 1:475–76, and Buell, "Shiloh Reviewed," in *B&L* 1:488, 519–20, 522, 529–36.

74. Torah W. Sampson to "Dear Mother," Pittsburg Landing, Tenn., April 12, 1862, Sampson Papers, FC ("never want to see"); Truxhall, *"Respects,"* 72; Briant, *Sixth Regiment Indiana*, 123; Sipes GAR records, CHS ("Completely Cooled"); B. Frank Dysart to "Dear Brother," Camp Shyloah, April 23, 1862, Dysart Family Letter Photocopies, SNMP ("I never dreamt"). See Frank and Reaves, *"Seeing the Elephant,"* for a detailed analysis of how Union and Confederate soldiers reacted after their baptism of fire at Shiloh.

75. Tapp and Klotter, *Tuttle*, 88 ("shocking and sickening"). For other descriptions and reactions, see Curry, *Four Years in the Saddle*, 38, and Davidson, *Battery A*, 27. Villard, *Memoirs*, 1:251–52, is a careful study of the dead and wounded left on the battlefield.

76. Bircher, *Drummer*, 32 ("unbearable stench"). For looting, see Tapp and Klotter, *Tuttle*, 89–90. In contrast to those who saw the battlefield only after the fight, men who participated in it seemed to have been hardened to the horror. A member of the 15th Ohio, for example, recalled seeing hideous sights but also noted that "we soon became accustomed to them." — Reynolds to William Orland Bourne, Sycamore, Virginia, January 23, 1866, Reynolds Letter, LC. See also Briant, *Sixth Regiment Indiana*, 125–26 (Briant had charge of his unit's burial detail).

77. Grant, "Battle of Shiloh," in *B&L* 1:485–86.

CHAPTER 5

1. Haynie, *Nineteenth Illinois*, 34. In his memoirs, Haynie used the term "Army of the Cumberland," the name by which the Army of the Ohio would be known in 1863. Inconsistent nomenclature proved to be a small but persistent obstacle to the development of army identity and pride. In 1889 Buell responded to a letter from a veteran by closing, "and I wish you every good fortune; as a soldier of the Army of the Ohio, or

Cumberland, by which ever name it may be called, deserves." Buell to Isaiah Riatt, Louisville, February 2, 1889, Buell Papers, FC.

2. George W. Landrum to Obed J. Wilson, Signal Camp, 3d Div., Shelbyville, Tenn., April 9, 1862, Landrum Papers, WRHS ("Don't you think"). For optimism in the spring of 1862, see also Peter L. Hornbeck to [Isaac] Bush, Murfreesboro, Tenn., May 1, 1862, Hornbeck Letters, LL; Jim T. Blankenship to "Dear Livie," Pittsburg Landing, Tenn., April 18, 1862, Blankenship Letter Typescript, SNMP ("opinion is that the rebellion is made at an end judging from many defeats they have met with"); B. Frank Dysart to "Dear Brother," Camp Shyloah, April 23, 1862, Dysart Family Letter Photocopies, SNMP ("If the Eastern army only gains victory I think our South will not be longer than the 1st of Sept."); Wayne Alford to Mr. Franklin Alford, Camp 9 miles from Corinth, Miss., May 4, 1862, in Skidmore, *Alford Brothers*, 279; Woodcock, *Southern Boy*, 72–73; Ephraim A. Otis, "Recollections of the Kentucky Campaign of 1862," in *Campaigns*, 227; and Van Horne, *Army of the Cumberland*, 1:127.

3. For institutional pride in the Army of the Ohio, see Frank and Reaves, *"Seeing the Elephant."* The authors studied the letters, diaries, and memoirs of more than three hundred soldiers who fought at Shiloh and found that members of the Army of the Ohio more frequently referred to the confidence they felt in their regiments as a result of their training than did members of Grant's Army of the Tennessee or Johnston's Confederates.

4. Buell to [Margaret Buell], Battlefield near Pittsburg, Tenn., April 9, 1862, Buell Papers, FC ("saved the army," "let the world"); Buell to [Margaret Buell], Camp 10 miles from Corinth, Miss., May 2, 1862, Buell Papers, FC ("false ungrateful and boastful"). For Buell's version of Shiloh, see, e.g., his articles in *B&L* and Buell, *General Buell on General Sherman and the Battle of Shiloh; or, Pittsburg Landing* (N.Y.?; 1865), reprinted from *New York World*, February 18, 1865, Buell Papers, FC.

5. Special Field Orders No. 31, Pittsburg Landing, Tenn., April 28, 1862, *OR* 10(2):138–39. Because Halleck commanded the Department of the Mississippi, the combined armies were properly styled the "Army of the Mississippi," but this name was not officially used. Welcher, *Union Army*, 2:175. Much to Buell's displeasure, Halleck also ordered the transfer of two divisions out of Buell's command, those of Thomas and a general to be named later. Special Field Orders No. 351, Pittsburg Landing, April 30, 1862, *OR* 10(2):144–45; Buell to Halleck, Headquarters Army of the Ohio, April 30, *OR* 10(2):144.

6. Buck to "My Dear Sister," [Helen A. Buck], Hamburgh, Tenn., April 28, 1862, Buck Papers, BHC ("Our army extends"); Hough, *Soldier in the West*, 64 ("nothing in this country"). For the strength of Halleck's force, see the abstracts of returns of the three armies, April 30, 1862, *OR* 10(2):146–54. There was no uniform system of brigade drill as late as January 1863. See, e.g., Scribner, *How Soldiers Were Made*, 113; Spaulding, "Military Memoirs," p. 15, Spaulding Papers, MHC; and Horrall, *Forty-Second Indiana*, 126–27.

7. Shaw, *Tenth Regiment Indiana*, 166 ("Most of our time"), 167 ("mules that fell off"); Hosea, "Regular Brigade," in Ohio Commandery, *Sketches*, 5:335; Briant, *Sixth Regiment Indiana*, 130–31.

8. See, e.g., Hartpence, *Fifty-First Indiana*, 46, and Herr, *Nine Campaigns*, 96–97. Buell took a certain amount of pleasure in Halleck's difficulties, gloating that the press, which had criticized Buell "for moving slowly with an immense army," could "see now that others made no better progress." Buell to [Margaret Buell], Camp 9 miles from Corinth, Miss., May 5, 1862, Buell Papers, FC. Buell considered the secret Confederate evacuation of Corinth "a very good *joke*" on Halleck and Pope. Buell to [Margaret Buell], Corinth, June 2, 1862, Buell Papers, FC.

9. Don Carlos Buell, "Operations in North Alabama," in *B&L* 2:701–8; Buell to Halleck, Nashville, March 14, *OR* 10(2):38; Buell to Mitchel, Camp near Columbia, March 27, *OR* 10(2):71–72; Halleck to Stanton, Pittsburg Landing, Tenn., April 16, 1862, *OR* 10(2):108; Mitchel, *Biographical Narrative*, 276–87; Waddle, *Three Years*, 12–15; Van Horne, *Army of the Cumberland*, 130–32.

10. See Mitchel to Stanton, Huntsville, April 17, 1862, *OR* 10(2):111. Similar messages followed on April 24, 25, and 27; also May 1, 4 (three times), 5, 6, 8, 9, 10, 13, 19, 22, and 31. Mitchel's self-promotion paid off, as Stanton reported to him that "Your spirited operations afford great satisfaction to the President." Stanton to Mitchel, War Department, May 1, 1862, *OR* 10(2):156.

11. The "Great Locomotive Chase" and its aftermath are described by one of the participants in Rev. William Pittenger, "The Locomotive Chase in Georgia," in *B&L* 2:709–16; see also Van Horne, *Army of the Cumberland*, 136–38. For Mitchel's cotton operations, see Mitchel to Stanton, Huntsville, May 13, 1862, *OR* 10(2):188; Mitchel to Stanton, Washington, July 19, 1862, *OR* 10(2):291–93; and Testimony of Col. Francis Darr, Cincinnati, March 24, 1863, *OR* 16(1):616–17. Examples of Mitchel's dramatic requests for help include Mitchel to Stanton, Huntsville, April 24, 1862, *OR* 10(2):124, and Mitchel to Buell, Huntsville, April 27, [1862], *OR* 10(2):133–34.

12. Although Buell and Halleck blamed Mitchel for destroying the Tennessee River bridges, Buell's orders show that he at least shared the responsibility. See Halleck to Stanton, Corinth, Miss., May 31, 1862, *OR* 10(1):668; Mitchel, *Biographical Narrative*, 330–31. Cf. Buell to Mitchel, Field of Shiloh, April 19, 1862, *OR* 10(2):114; Mitchel to Salmon P. Chase, Huntsville, April 21, 1862, *OR* 10(2):115; and Buell to Mitchel, Field of Shiloh, April 23, 1862, *OR* 10(2):118.

13. Buell, "Operations in North Alabama," in *B&L* 2:707 ("in an ostentatious way"). For Mitchel's attempts to remove his division from Buell's authority, see Mitchel to Stanton, Huntsville, May 22, 1862, *OR* 10(2):209; Mitchel to Buell, Camp Taylor, May 24, 1862, *OR* 10(2):212; and Buell to Halleck, Huntsville, July 12, 1862, *OR* 16(2):128. For more sympathetic views of Mitchel's performance, see C. H. Gatch, "General O. M. Mitchel and His Brilliant March into the Heart of the Southern Confederacy," in Iowa Commandery, Military Order of the Loyal Legion of the United States, *War Sketches and Incidents*, 2:110–28; and William Vocke, "The Military Achievements of Major-General O. McKnight Mitchel," in Commandery of the State of Illinois, Military Order of the Loyal Legion of the United States, *Military Essays and Recollections*, 4:83–121.

14. Special Field Orders, No. 90, Corinth, Miss., June 10, 1862, *OR* 10(2):288.

15. Halleck to Buell, Headquarters, May 31, 1862 (*OR* 10[2]:232–33), and Halleck to

Buell, Corinth, Miss., June 7, 1862 (*OR* 10[2]:267–68), June 9, 1862 (*OR* 10[2]:280–81), and June 11, 1862 (*OR* 16[2]:9).

16. Villard, *Memoirs*, 1:288; Buell, *Statement*, 12; Buell, "Perryville," in *B&L* 3:35; Buell to Mitchel, Field of Shiloh, April 23, 1862, *OR* 10(2):118 ("proper line of communication"); Testimony of General [A. M.] McCook, Nashville, December 10, 1862, *OR* 16(1):104 ("have taken 50,000"); Buell to Halleck, Huntsville, July 13, 1862, *OR* 16(2):127 ("useless as a channel"). The Army of the Ohio never received any useful amount of supplies over the Memphis & Charleston road.

17. Briant, *Sixth Regiment Indiana*, 138.

18. Darr testimony, *OR* 16(1):602–3. Darr was the chief commissary officer of the Army of the Ohio.

19. Villard, *Memoirs*, 1:289; Testimony of Col. J. B. Fry, April 25, 1863, *OR* 16(1):705–6; Darr testimony, *OR* 16(1):610; Testimony of Col. W. P. Innes, Nashville, December 24, 1862, *OR* 16(1):247–49; Van Horne, *Army of the Cumberland*, 142–45.

20. Halleck to Buell, Corinth, Miss., June 30, 1862, *OR* 16(2):75.

21. Otis, "Kentucky Campaign," in *Campaigns*, 7:232 ("holiday soldiering"); Halleck to Buell, Corinth, Miss., June 6, 1862, *OR* 10(2):264–65; Th. J. Wood to Col. J. B. Fry, Near Bear Creek Bridge, June 7, 1862, *OR* 10(2):268. Halleck refused to accept the findings of a military commission that blamed the railroad repairs for Buell's failure to capture Chattanooga quickly. See Indorsement, H. W. Halleck, Washington, May 29, 1863, *OR* 16(1):12. It is unclear why Halleck insisted that Buell trace his communications to Memphis. The Jominian theories of military science in which Halleck was steeped emphasized the geometrical relationships of lines of supply and advance; a supply line parallel rather than perpendicular to the front was directly contrary to such teaching. Perhaps the Swiss theoretician's influence on Civil War leaders, even the pedantic "Old Brains" Halleck, may have been less pervasive than traditionally assumed.

22. Report of Brig. Gen. James S. Negley, Shelbyville, Tenn., June 12, 1862, *OR* 10(1):920; Mitchel to Buell, Huntsville, June 8, 1862, *OR* 10(2):275; Mitchel, *Biographical Narrative*, 334; Testimony of James B. McElwee, Cincinnati, April 7, 1863, *OR* 16(1):671–72; Van Horne, *Army of the Cumberland*, 1:132; Edward Ferguson, "The Army of the Cumberland Under Buell," in Wisconsin Commandery, *War Papers*, 1:426.

23. Buell, *Statement*, 15 ("conceal the object"); Buell, "Perryville," in *B&L* 3:35.

24. For enforcement of this policy, see, e.g., James B. Fry to Brigadier-General Crittenden, Camp near Florence, [Ala.], June 23, 1862, *OR* 16(2):53–54, and Horrall, *Forty-Second Indiana*, 114, 127. Buell repeatedly defended his "conciliatory" policy before the commission that investigated his conduct of the 1862 campaign. See, e.g., Buell, *Statement*, 48–49, and *OR* 16(1):228, 350–51, 480–83, 496–505, 540–42, 635, 679. The commission concluded that Buell was following government policy and could not be censured. Grimsley, *The Hard Hand of War*, analyzes the evolution of this policy.

25. In February 1862 Turchin's soldiers had burned a number of houses in Bowling Green, Ky. Beatty, *Citizen-Soldier*, 107.

26. Horrall, *Forty-Second Indiana*, 128 ("shuts mine eyes"). See also Waddle, *Three Years*, 17, and Diary, May 7, 1862, H. C. Patton Papers, IHS. For official reports of the incident, see General Orders No. 39, In Camp, Huntsville, August 6, 1862, *OR*

16(2):273–78; Mitchel to General George S. Hunter, Huntsville, May 24, 1862, *OR* 10(2):212–13; and Mitchel to Col. J. B. Fry, Camp Taylor, Huntsville, June 30, 1862, *OR* 16(2):80.

27. Mitchel to General George S. Hunter, Huntsville, May 24, *OR* 10(2):212–13. For Turchin's court-martial, see Special Orders No. 90, Huntsville, July 2, 1862, *OR* 16(2):92; Special Orders No. 93, Huntsville, July 5, 1862, *OR* 16(2):99; Court-martial records, August 13, 1862, Mihalotzy Papers, ISHL; and Testimony of Col. Marc Mundy, Cincinnati, March 27, 1863, *OR* 16(1):637. For officer resignations, see Jos. R. Scott to Col. J. B. Fry, Bridgeport, July 5, 1862, *OR* 16(2):98; J. B. Turchin to Col. J. B. Fry, Bridgeport, July 5, 1862, *OR* 16(2):98; and George W. Landrum to Mrs. Obed J. Wilson, Battle Creek, Marion County, Tenn., July 7, 1862, Landrum Papers, WRHS.

28. General Orders No. 39, In Camp, Huntsville, August 6, 1862, *OR* 16(2):278; Warner, *Generals in Blue*, 511; Yates to Lincoln, Springfield, August 29, 1862, and Lincoln to Yates (endorsement), September 5, 1862, TLM; Buell to Stanton, Huntsville, July 5, 1862, *OR* 16(2):71 ("entirely unfit").

29. For soldiers' favorable opinions of Mitchel, see Diary, May 1, 1862, H. C. Patton Papers, IHS ("is the man"), and Waddle, *Three Years*, 12–19. For negative opinions, see Henry H. Seys to "Dear Wife," Huntsville, July 23, 1862, Seys Papers, SCWC, and George W. Landrum to Mrs. Obed J. Wilson, Battle Creek, Marion Co., Tenn., July 7, 1862, Landrum Papers, WRHS.

30. Landrum to Wilson, June 24, 1862, Landrum Papers, WRHS ("star on your shoulder," "lunatic"); J. C. Kelton to Buell, Corinth, Miss., July 2, 1862, *OR* 16(2):92; Buell to [C. W. Johnson], Airdrie [Paradise, Ky.], September 20, 1887, pp. 25–26, Buell Papers, FC; Warner, *Generals in Blue*, 327.

31. Mundy testimony, *OR* 16(1):637 ("embittered them"); Shaw, *Tenth Regiment Indiana*, 185–86 ("prejudiced the men"); Beatty, *Citizen-Soldier*, 152 ("my good fellows"); Jos. Sturge Johnston to ——, [near Reynold's Station], August 16, 1862, Johnston Papers, CHS ("kid-glove policy"); Beatty, *Citizen-Soldier*, 172 ("cold, smooth-toned, silent"). For Turchin's popularity, see Johnston to ——, Camp Anderson, October 14, 1861, and Johnston to ——, Pittsburg Landing, Tenn., March 31, 1862, Johnston Papers, CHS.

32. Lincoln to Orville H. Browning, Washington, September 22, 1861, "private and confidential," *AL* 4:532 ("a whole company"); *New York Times*, December 17, 1861, p. 3, col. 3 ("no Abolition crusade"); Testimony of General Rousseau, Louisville, January 21, 1863, *OR* 16(1):351; [A. M.] McCook testimony, *OR* 16(1):107 ("the Abolition press").

33. Finn Diary Photocopy, May 28, 1862, USAMHI ("were no abolitionists"); Kirkpatrick, *Experiences*, 10 ("was not received"); Funk, *Hoosier Regiment*, 30. See also Joyce, *A Checkered Life*, 74 (men of the 24th Kentucky objected to the Emancipation Proclamation); John A. Bross to [Mrs. John A. Bross], on the march [near Louisville], October 4, 1862, Bross Letters, Private Collection (Kentuckians considered the Emancipation Proclamation worse than 30,000 rebels).

34. Rousseau testimony, *OR* 16(1):351 ("have their negroes"); Buell to Colonel Harker, Huntsville, August 10, 1862, *OR* 16(2):303; ——, Aide-de-camp and Assisting

Adjutant General to Brigadier General McCook, Camp near Florence, Ala., June 21, 1862, *OR* 16(2):44. It is unusual to find an anonymous order in the Official Records but understandable why no one would wish to be associated with this.

35. Beatty, *Citizen-Soldier*, 84; Scribner, *How Soldiers Were Made*, 131–32; Horrall, *Forty-Second Indiana*, 133; George W. Landrum to Mrs. Obed J. Wilson, Battle Creek, Tenn., July 15, 1862, Landrum Papers, WRHS, and earlier letters.

36. Dodge, *Old Second Division*, 329 ("growing radicalism"). For Buell's order, see General Order No. 79, Head Quarters 3rd Division, Camp Andrew Jackson, Tenn., March 11, 1862, NA RG 393.1.880. For incidents of resistance to the recapture of fugitive slaves, see Charles W. Carr to Sarah [Carr], October 10, 1862, Carr Papers, CHS; Canfield, *21st Regiment Ohio*, 50; John A. Bross to [Mrs. John A. Bross], on the march [near Louisville], October 4, 1862, Bross Letters, Private Collection; Beatty, *Citizen-Soldier*, 117–18; Bennett, *Ninth Michigan*, 11–12; M[arcus] Mundy to Lincoln, Louisville, November 27, 1862, in Holzer, *The Lincoln Mailbag*, 77–78; and Tourgée, *Story of a Thousand*, 105. See also Th. J. Wood to Col. J. B. Fry, Head Quarters 6th Division, Army of the Ohio, Decherd, Tenn., August 4, 1862, with annotations, NA RG 393.1.880.

37. George W. Landrum to Mrs. Obed J. Wilson, Battle Creek, Marion Co., Tenn., July 15, 1862, Landrum Papers, WRHS ("wish we had"); Connolly, *Three Years*, 17 ("active earnest leader"). Landrum's notion of an ideal leader was "more such as Hunter, Butler, Pope and Seigel.[*sic*] With such, the war would soon be ended." This seems likely enough, although the result would probably not have been what Landrum had in mind.

38. Grant, "Battle of Shiloh," in *B&L* 1:482.

39. Buell to [William F.] Smith, Louisville, October 28, 1887, Buell Papers, FC.

40. See, e.g., General Orders No. 32, In Camp, Huntsville, July 21, 1862, *OR* 16(1):793–94, and General Orders No. 37, In Camp, Huntsville, August 1, 1862, *OR* 16(1):820.

41. Special Field Orders, No. 162, Corinth, Miss., July 16, 1862, *OR* 16(2):167–68.

42. General Orders No. 50, Louisville, October 30, 1862, *OR* 16(2):654.

43. Williams, *Lincoln and His Generals*, 48 ("charm or glamor"); [A. M.] McCook testimony, *OR* 16(1):124 ("have frequently felt"); Fry testimony, *OR* 16(1):222; Finn Diary Photocopy, June 28, 1862 (Buell made no remarks in response to a serenade by Finn's band); Buell to [Margaret Buell], Camp [near Corinth, Miss.], May 5, 1862, Buell Papers, FC; Johnson, "War Memories," in Minnesota Commandery, *Glimpses*, 14. Shanks (*Personal Recollections*, 339) observed: "It was the fault of the Western armies that too little attention was paid to the moral sentiments of the men, and that in the Eastern Army the thoroughly-taught sentiment of devotion to the cause was permitted to partially degenerate into love of the leader."

44. Mitchel, *Biographical Narrative*, 224 ("address the general"); Mitchel to Halleck, Huntsville, June 7, 1862, *OR* 10(2):271 ("my entire division"); Anderson to Thomas, Louisville, September 17, 1861, *OR* 4:260 ("the same condition"); Buell to McClellan, Louisville, November 27, 1861 (*OR* 7:450–52) ("greatly in need"), and December 8, 1861 (*OR* 7:482) ("greatly in want").

45. Halleck to Buell, Corinth, Miss., June 12, 1862, *OR* 16(2):15 ("absorbed by the Army"); George W. Landrum to Mrs. Obed J. Wilson, Camp Jefferson, Ky., January 23, 1862, Landrum Papers, WRHS ("leaving my company").

46. Arthur deWint to William Seward, Fishkill Landing, [N.Y.], April 21, 1860 [1861], Cameron Papers, LC ("a staff appointment"); McIlvaine, *Dim and Flaring Lamps*, 67–72.

47. General Orders No. 12, Adjutant General's Office, Washington, February 6, 1862, *OR*, 3d ser., 1:882–83; Buell to McClellan, Louisville, January 13, 1862, *OR* 7:549 ("I need more").

48. Diary Typescript, February 17, May 16, 1862, Inskeep Papers, OHS; Dodge, *Old Second Division*, 114; George W. Landrum to Mrs. Obed J. Wilson, Camp of the 2nd Ohio, Huntsville, May 13, 1862, Landrum Papers, WRHS ("won't use them"); Jesse Merrill to Samuel T. Cushing, Hdqrs. Signal Corps, District of the Ohio, April 24, 1862, *OR* 10(2):295 (Merrill was the chief signal officer of the Army of the Ohio). The idea of a signal corps was so new that when Lieutenant Landrum was assigned to it, he had no idea what to expect: "I do not fully understand the duties. . . . It is a brand new corps just forming." Landrum to Wilson, January 23, 1862, WRHS. Mitchel's hostility toward his signal troops possibly arose out of pique at their instructor's refusal to teach him the code on the grounds that he lacked the proper security clearance. See Landrum to Wilson, February 6, 1862, WRHS.

49. See Landrum to Wilson, July 7, 1862, Landrum Papers, WRHS; Testimony of Capt. Jesse Merrill, February 26, 1863, *OR* 16(1):505–7.

50. Buell to Halleck, Huntsville, July 11, 1862, *OR* 16(2):122–23; James B. Fry to Colonel Thomas Swords, Huntsville, June 29, 1862 (*OR* 16[2]:73), and June 30, 1862 (*OR* 16[2]:78–79); J. D. Bingham to Col. J. B. Fry, Nashville, July 7, 1862, *OR* 16(2):100–101; Darr testimony, *OR* 16(1):602–6.

51. James B. Fry to Captain Greene, Tuscumbia, June 14, 1862, *OR* 16(2):23; Buell to Mitchel, Huntsville, Headquarters, June 19, 1862, *OR* 16(2):39; James B. Fry to Captain Greene, Camp near Florence, Ala., June 23, 1862, *OR* 16(2):54; James B. Fry to Captain Bingham, Huntsville, June 29, 1862, *OR* 16(2):73 ("We expected 150,000"). See also Darr testimony, *OR* 16(1):603; James B. Fry to Colonel Thomas Swords, Huntsville, July 1, 1862, *OR* 16(2):85; and T. L. Crittenden to Buell, Camp near Athens, July 1, 1862, *OR* 16(2):85 ("There is no forage at Athens. . . . I am out of forage").

52. James B. Fry to Captain Bright, Commissary of Subsistence, Camp near Florence, Ala., June 17, 1862, *OR* 16(2):34–35; James B. Fry to Major Sidell, Huntsville, August 17, 1862, *OR* 16(2):357; James B. Fry to Captain Nigh, quartermaster, Camp near Florence, June 16, 1862, *OR* 16(2):32 ("will not answer"); Heath Diary, transcripts printed in *Vevay Reveille-Enterprise*, March 21, 1946, Heath Papers, LC ("Aaway down South").

53. Report of Col. John H. Morgan, Knoxville, July 30, 1862, *OR* 16(1):770; Lincoln to Halleck, War Department, July 13, 1862, *OR* 16(1):738 ("having a stampede").

54. Stanton to General J. T. Boyle, Washington, May 27, 1862, *OR* 10(2):218; General Orders No. 62, Adjutant General's Office, Washington, June 8, 1862, *OR* 10(2):278; Stanton to Buell, Washington, June 9, 1862, *OR* 10(2):285; Testimony of General J. T.

Boyle, Cincinnati, January 29, 1863, *OR* 16(1):377; Boyle to Stanton, Louisville, July 13, 1862, *OR* 16(1):736.

55. Report of Brig. Gen. T. T. Crittenden, *OR* 16(1):794–95; Bennett, *Ninth Michigan*, 8. Other sources, among them the official reports of Buell and Colonel Duffield, Minn. Comm., *Minnesota*, 151–52, and Andrews, "Surrender of the Third Regiment," in Minnesota Commandery, *Glimpses* 1: 347–48, include a small unit of Kentucky cavalry as part of the garrison.

56. Wm. W. Duffield to Captain O. D. Greene, Head Quarters 23d Brigade, Murfreesboro, Tenn., April 11, 1862, NA RG 393.1.880; J. G. Parkhurst to Colonel James B. Fry, Head Quarters 9th Regt. Mich Inf., Murfreesboro, May 9, 1862, NA RG 393.1.880; Bennett, *Ninth Michigan*, 13–14; John C. Love to "Dear Parents," Murfreesboro, July 20, 1862, Love Papers, MHC.

57. Report of Col. William W. Duffield, Murfreesboro, Tenn., *OR* 16(1):801 ("lack of discipline"); Findings of a Court of Inquiry, General Orders No. 4, Hdqrs. Dept. of the Cumberland, January 24, 1863, *OR* 16(1):797; Bennett, *Ninth Michigan*, 10–11, 13; "M L P" to "My Dear Mrs. Starr," Coldwater, [Michigan], July 27, 1862, and Parkhurst to "My Dear Helen," Murfreesboro, July 3, 1862, both in Parkhurst Papers, MHC; Dorus M. Fox to Col J. B. Fry, Head Quarters 9th Regt Mich Vol, Tullahoma, Tenn., August 15, 1862, NA RG 393.1.880.

58. Minn. Comm., *Minnesota*, 152 ("somewhat remarkable"); Duffield report, *OR* 16(1):801; Bennett, *Ninth Michigan*, 12; Crittenden report, *OR* 16(1):794; Findings of a Court of Inquiry, January 24, 1863, *OR* 16(1):797.

59. John C. Love to "Dear Parents," Murfreesboro, Tenn., July 20, 1862, Love Papers, MHC ("a wild tornado"); Duffield report, *OR* 16(1):803 ("very painful"); Bennett, *Ninth Michigan*, 14–15; Peter L. Hornbeck to Isaac Bush, Murfreesboro, July 29, 1862, Hornbeck Letters, LL; John Gibson Parkhurst to "My Dear Helen," McMinnville, [Tenn.], July 15, 1862, Parkhurst Papers, MHC; Crittenden report, *OR* 16(1):795; Findings of a Court of Inquiry, January 24, 1863, *OR* 16(1):797; Report of Lieut. Col. John G. Parkhurst, *OR* 16(1):804.

60. Report of Brig. Gen. N. B. Forrest, Knoxville, July 22, 1862, *OR* 16(1):810.

61. Report of Col. Henry C. Lester, *OR* 16(1):807–8; Report of Capt. John M. Hewett, *OR* 16(1):799; Parkhurst report, *OR* 16(1):805–6; Duffield report, *OR* 16(1):803; John Robertson, *Michigan in the War*, 296–97 (the 9th Michigan lost 13 killed and 78 wounded); John Gibson Parkhurst to "My Dear Helen," McMinnville, July 15, 1862, Parkhurst Papers, MHC (the 9th Michigan lost 12 killed, 50–70 wounded, and 150 captured); Crittenden report, *OR* 16(1):795–96; Andrews, "Surrender of the Third Regiment," in Minnesota Commandery, *Glimpses* 1:349–52.

62. Lester report, *OR* 16(1):808; Minn. Comm., *Minnesota*, 152–5; Crittenden report, *OR* 16(1):796; Andrews, "Surrender of the Third Regiment," in Minnesota Commandery, *Glimpses*, 1:349–52. Captain Andrews was one of those who voted to fight.

63. Benjamin F. Wells to "Dearest Melissa," Bowling Green, Ky., July 22, 1862, Wells Letters, MHC.

64. Bennett, *Ninth Michigan*, 18 ("cursing Col. Lester"); "M L P" to "My Dear Mrs.

Starr," Coldwater, [Michigan], July 27, 1862, Parkhurst Papers, MHC; Peter L. Horn-beck to Isaac Bush, Murfreesboro, Tenn., July 29, 1862, Hornbeck Letters, LL; Henry Stone, "The Operations of General Buell in Kentucky and Tennessee in 1862," in *Campaigns*, 263 ("pusillanimous colonel").

65. Beatty, *Citizen-Soldier*, 124 ("insane effort"); Briant, *Sixth Regiment Indiana*, 143–44; Bennett, *Ninth Michigan*, 9; [Nevin], "Regimental History," LC, September 3, 1862. See Interrogatories, Capt. James St. C. Morton, *OR* 16(1):721–22, for the number and sites of the stockades that Buell authorized. For Morgan's August raids, see various official reports at *OR* 16(1):843–57 (Gallatin), 862–70 (Clarksville), and 871–82 (Harts-ville); for their effects, see Testimony of Major Sidell, December 25, 1862, *OR* 16(1):252–57, and Villard, *Memoirs*, 1:295.

66. Frederick Marion to "Dear Sister," Camp on Elk River, August 17, 1862, Marion Papers, ISHL; Otis, "Kentucky Campaign," in *Campaigns*, 233–34; Report of Maj. Gen. George H. Thomas, Decherd, Tenn., August 7, 1862, *OR* 16(1):839; Report of Col. Ferdinand Van Derveer, Camp near Winchester, Tenn., August 9, 1862, *OR* 16(1):840–41; Villard, *Memoirs*, 1:300. See Testimony of Col. E. M. McCook, January 16, 1863, *OR* 16(1):329, for reference to other "unofficial" executions of guerrillas.

67. Report of Maj. Gen. D. C. Buell, Huntsville, August 9, 1862, *OR* 16(1):838; General Orders No. 32, Headquarters Army of the Ohio, July 21, 1862, *OR* 16(1):793 ("neglect of duty"); Dorus M. Fox to Col J. B. Fry, Head Quarters 9th Regt Mich Vol, Tullahoma, Tenn., August 15, 1862, NA RG 393.1.880 ("lost enough property"); Ben-nett, *Ninth Michigan*, 9. The court of inquiry that met in December 1862 at General T. T. Crittenden's request cleared his name and the reputation of the 9th Michigan and placed full blame on Colonel Lester, who had been dismissed from the service on December 1, 1862.

68. Stone, "Operations of General Buell," in *Campaigns*, 264 ("a fatal blow").

CHAPTER 6

1. Buell, "Perryville," in *B&L* 3:36 ("thousand other details"); Buell, *Statement*, 17. For more pessimistic evaluations of the raid's effects on the Army of the Ohio, see Bennett, *Ninth Michigan*, 17; Testimony of General Thomas L. Crittenden, February 27, 1863, *OR* 16(1):516; Villard, *Memoirs*, 1:292–93; Dodge, *Old Second Division*, 284; and Van Horne, *Army of the Cumberland*, 1:147.

2. Villard, *Memoirs*, 1:332 ("degree of readiness"); Van Horne, *Army of the Cumberland*, 144.

3. Consolidated Morning Report of the District of the Ohio, August 1, 1862, *OR* 16(2):246–47.

4. Pursuant to General Orders No. 69, Washington, August 28, 1861 (*OR*, 3d ser., 1:461), volunteer regiments were responsible for recruiting their own replacements.

5. Tourgée, *Story of a Thousand*, 21–22, 24 ("glory or adventure"). See also Richards, *Letters*, 4. When conscription began later in 1862, the demarcation of regimental districts

was used to coerce communities into producing volunteers, since incomplete regiments were to be filled by drafts from their assigned areas.

6. James G. Theaker to "Dear Brother" [John Theaker], Camp Dennison, [Ohio], August 25, 1862, in Theaker, *Through One Man's Eyes*, 4.

7. Marshall Diary, September 7, 1862 ("these noble institutions"), September 13, 1862 ("as hard as any"), LC; Tobias Charles Miller to "My Dear Brother & Sister," Louisville, September 25, 1862, Miller Papers, CHS ("Hard Bread, Bacon"); John Daniel Shank to "Dear Farther and mother and sisters," Camp Mitchell, September 15, 1862, in Hunter, *One Flag*, 23 ("I may be killed"); Thomas J. Frazee to "Dear Parents, etc.," Camp Jaquess near Louisville, August 31, 1862, Frazee Papers, ISHL ("as good a regament").

8. Silas Curtis Stevens to E. P. Stevens, South Fork, N.C., August 31, 1903, Stevens Papers, CHS ("good machine soldiers"); Rowell, *Yankee Artillerymen*, 35–36; Hinman, *Si Klegg*, 44; Theaker to "Dear Brother" [John Theaker], Camp Dennison, Ohio, September 3, 1862, in Theaker, *Through One Man's Eyes*, 5. For officer appointments in July 1862 regiments, see Connolly, *Three Years*, 13–14; Dodge, *Seventy-Fifth Illinois Infantry*, 24, 28; James S. Blodgett to Newton Bateman, September 7, 1862, Bateman Papers, ISHL; Ross Diary, August 13, 1862, ISHL; Diary Transcript, August 14, 1862, Howe Papers, IHS; Diary, August 29, 1862, Tilford Papers, FC; and Gross Diary, pp. 75–78, WRHS. Some units already in the field still conducted elections to determine whom to recommend to their state governments for promotion. See Tapp and Klotter, *Tuttle*, 110–11.

9. Levi Adolphus Ross to "My Dear Father," Louisville, September 16, 1862, Ross Family Papers, ISHL ("in utter contempt"); Van Zwaluwenburg Memoir, p. 18, SCWC ("we never knew").

10. John Pierson to "Dear Wife," Camp 3 Miles South [of] Nashville, September 12, 1862, Pierson Papers, SCWC ("Strengthen the Army"); Buell, "Perryville," in *B&L* 3:33 ("waste of time").

11. See Buell to Boyle, Huntsville, August 16, 1862, *OR* 16(2):353; Halleck to Buell, War Department, August 12, 1862, *OR* 16(2):314; Boyle testimony, *OR* 16(1):371–72. Indiana sent eleven regiments and three artillery batteries; Ohio sent at least sixteen infantry regiments. Terrell, *Indiana*, 195; Reid, *Ohio in the War*, 2 passim.

12. Buell to Nelson, Huntsville, August 17, 1862, *OR* 16(2):357; Buell, "Perryville," in *B&L* 3:43 ("always solicitous"); Buell, *Statement*, 20 ("energy and ability"); Nelson to Buell, Nashville, July 19, 1862, *OR* 16(2):183 ("lost his senses"); Minn. Comm., *Minnesota*, 157 ("been their fault"); Bennett, *Ninth Michigan*, 19.

13. Buell to Boyle, Huntsville, August 17, 1862, *OR* 16(2):358; General Orders No. 112, Washington, August 19, 1862, *OR* 16(2):375; Halleck to Buell, Washington, August 20, 1862, *OR* 16(2):375 ("continue the general direction").

14. Nelson to Halleck, Louisville, August 23, 1862, *OR* 16(2):394 ("one hour before"); General Orders No. 3, Louisville, August 24, 1862, *OR* 16(2):416; Halleck to Wright, Washington, August 30, 1862, *OR* 16(2):456. See also Boyle testimony, *OR* 16(1):377, 383.

15. Nelson to Wright, Richmond, August 27, 1862, *OR* 16(2):435–36. For Nelson's

criticism of Manson and Cruft, see Circular, Headquarters 4 Division, near Athens, Ala., July 1, 1862, Nelson Papers, CHS; J. Mills Kendrick, Asst. Adjutant-General to Nelson, Headquarters 4 Division, McMinnville, Tenn., August 16, 1862, Kendrick Papers, CHS; [orders], Headquarters, 4 Division, Murfreesboro, Tenn., July 30, 1862, Nelson Papers, CHS.

16. Nelson to Wright, Richmond, August 27, 1862, *OR* 16(2):435.

17. Winters, *50th Ohio*, 9; Tourgée, *Story of a Thousand*, 9; Alden F. Brooks to ——, n.p., August 1, 1912, Brooks Letter, Regimental Papers, container 23, folder 3, WRHS; Reid, *Ohio in the War*, 2:260 ("not been drilled"); Report of Brig. Gen. Charles Cruft, In the Field, near Louisville, September 5, 1862, *OR* 16(1):919; Byron D. Paddock to John S. Andrews, Camp Swords, Ky., August 18, 1862, Ness Collection, folder 21, MHC; Byron D. Paddock to "Dear Hattie," Louisville, August 14, 1862, Paddock Letter, USAMHI ("perform their part").

18. James W. Bingham to "Dear Mother," Bowling Green, Ky., September 7, 1862, Bingham Letters, MHC ("you ought *not*"); Cruft report, *OR* 16(1):919 ("almost entire ignorance").

19. Report of Maj. Gen. William Nelson, Lexington, Ky., August 31, 1862, *OR* 16(1):908; Report of Brig. Gen. Mahlon D. Manson, Indianapolis, September 10, 1862, *OR* 16(1):911; Stone, "Operations of General Buell," in *Campaigns*, 267 ("only just brigaded").

20. Manson report, *OR* 16(1):912; Reports of J. B. Armstrong (5:412–13), Lieutenant-Colonel Harman J. Korff, Cincinnati, September 5, 1862 (5:413–14), Jim R. S. Cox, "Indianapolis 'Journal' Account" (5:415–19), and "Telmah," "Another Account" (5:419–22), in Moore, *Rebellion Record*; Van Horne, *Army of the Cumberland*, 1:181–82. For modern accounts of the battle, see Lambert, *When the Ripe Pears Fell*, and McDonough, *War in Kentucky*, chap. 5.

21. Return of Casualties in the Union forces, *OR* 16(1):909; Table of Casualties, battle of Richmond, Ky., August 30, *OR* 16(1):936.

22. Manson report, *OR* 16(1):914–15; Cruft report, *OR* 16(1):918 ("collection of citizens"); Boyle to Halleck, Louisville, August 31, 1862, *OR* 16(2):466; Boyle to President Lincoln, Louisville, August 31, 1862, *OR* 16(2):465.

23. John Patton Memoir, 2:33–34, LC ("not been sufficiently drilled"); Shanks, *Personal Recollections*, 345 ("without knowing or caring").

24. Buell, "Perryville," in *B&L* 3:40 ("a superior force"); Halleck to Buell, Washington, August 8, 1862, *OR* 16(2):286; Buell, *Statement*, 20–21; Buell to Grant, Huntsville, August 12, 1862, *OR* 16(2):315–16; Van Horne, *Army of the Cumberland*, 1:155; George A. Bruce, "General Buell's Campaign Against Chattanooga," in *Mississippi*, 129. Bruce notes that Buell was preoccupied with minutia during the campaign, issuing over four hundred orders and dispatches in August 1862, including one describing an elaborate and impractical code for communicating by colored signal rockets, a copy of which is preserved in the Buell Papers, FC.

25. Buell to Halleck, Decherd, Tenn., via Corinth, Miss., August 24, 1862, *OR* 16(2):406–7; Buell, *Statement*, pp. 20, 24–30; Buell, "Perryville," in *B&L* 3:40; Van Horne, *Army of the Cumberland*, 1:158; General Orders, Decherd, August 30, 1862, *OR*

16(2):454–55. For the actual strength of Bragg's army, see Field Return Abstract, August 27, 1862, OR 16(2):784.

26. Testimony of General Thomas J. Wood, December 17, 1862, OR 16(1):173–74; Testimony of George H. Thomas, December 18, 1862, OR 16(1):182–83, 188–92, 202–3; Testimony of General J. B. Steedman, Nashville, December 13, 1862, OR 16(1):134 ("Don Carlos won't do"); cf. A. McD. McCook testimony, OR 16(1):88 ("possibly could be"); Crittenden testimony, OR 16(1):522. See also Villard, Memoirs, 1:297–98.

27. Steedman testimony, OR 16(1):135; Shaw, Tenth Regiment Indiana, 184; Fry testimony, OR 16(1):221–22.

28. Halleck to Buell, Washington, August 18, 1862, OR 16(2):360 ("great is the dissatisfaction"); Buell to Halleck, Huntsville, August 18, 1862, OR 16(2):360; Halleck to Buell, Washington, September 2, 1862, OR 16(2):471 ("March where you please"); Deposition of Andrew Johnson, Military Governor of Tennessee, OR 16(1):697–98; Buell, Statement, 49; Thomas testimony, OR 16(1):192; Moody, A Life's Retrospect, 264–67. There was no love lost between Johnson, who had long complained that Buell was neglecting his military needs, and Buell, who considered Johnson's unsolicited views on military strategy "absurd." See Buell to Halleck, Buell's Headquarters, April 26, 1862, OR 10(2):129.

29. Arza Bartholomew, Jr. to [Frances Bartholomew], Camp near Louisville, September 27, 1862, "Civil War Letters of Arza Bartholomew, Jr.: Co. G, 21st Michigan Infantry, Enlisted Aug. 14, 1862, Died at Murfreesboro, Tenn., May 8, 1863, Written to his Wife Frances," comp. George C. Christman, Bartholomew Letters Typescript, SRNB ("light as snow"); Diary Typescript, September 25, 1862, Biddle Papers, BHC ("Dust so bad"); Horrall, Forty-Second Indiana, 138; Briant, Sixth Regiment Indiana, 148; W. R. Claspill to "Dear Friend Harry," Camp near Nashville, November 9, 1862, ISHL ("dryest and dustiest"); Penfield GAR records, CHS ("hot dusty, days").

30. Horrall, Forty-Second Indiana, 138, 145 ("no unusual thing"); Penfield GAR records, CHS; Waddle, Three Years, 9; Freeman, "Eighteenth U.S. Infantry," in Minnesota Commandery, Glimpses 3:120 ("in great mouthfuls"); Kansas, 1(2):104.

31. Patterson, William Elwood Patterson, 10–15, 15 ("played out entirely"); Mallory, "Not in a Useless Cause," p. 27, WRHS; Kirkpatrick, Experiences, 12 ("nothing but flour"); Kansas, 1(2):105; Diary Transcript, September 20, 1862, Inskeep Papers, OHS; Villard, Memoirs, 1:305; Herr, Nine Campaigns, 105 ("glad when I got thar"); Briant, Sixth Regiment Indiana, 147; Diary, September 15, 1862, Tilford Papers, FC; Gates, Rough Side of War, 23–26; Waddle, Three Years, 26–27; Mundy testimony, OR 16(1):641 ("most terrible march").

32. Buell, "Perryville," in B&L 3:41–42. For chaos in the command system affecting Munfordville, see Deposition of General H. G. Wright, OR 16(1):692–93; Testimony of Col. John T. Wilder, December 20, 1862, OR 16(1):205, 212, 214; and Stone, "Operations of General Buell," in Campaigns, 7:276.

33. The garrison at Munfordville was commanded by Colonel John T. Wilder, a volunteer officer who was unsure of the protocol of surrendering to an overwhelming force. He took the unusual step of asking the advice of Confederate General Simon Bolivar Buckner, who gave him a tour of the besieging forces, which left him convinced

that he could not resist any further. See Wilder testimony, *OR* 16(1):209–10, and Harrison, "Battle of Munfordville."

34. Bragg later explained that after the surrender of Munfordville, his army was so low on provisions and (he believed) so heavily outnumbered by the Army of the Ohio that he could not risk a battle. He also thought that the Army of the Ohio could bypass Munfordville to the west by using the roads through Brownsville or Morgantown to reach Louisville. Reports of General Braxton Bragg, Headquarters Army of Tennessee, May 20, 1863, *OR* 16(1):1090.

35. *Kansas*, 1(2):107 ("no regularity"); Morris Fitch to "Dear Folks," Louisville, September 25, 1862, Fitch Letter, Ness Collection, folder 21, MHC ("all fooling aside"); John Easton to [George] Stolz, Camp at Crab Orchard, Ky., October 17, 1862, ACFWHS ("suffering and privation"); George F. Alverson to "Dear Father," Louisville, September 26, 1862, Alverson Letter, USAMHI ("the damdest time"); Webster Diary Transcript, September 26, 1862, USAMHI ("intolerably sore").

36. Shaw, *Tenth Regiment Indiana*, 185 ("desire of the army"); John Easton to [George] Stolz, Camp at Crab Orchard, Ky., October 17, 1862, ACFWHS ("Deep were the curses"); Lathrop, *Fifty-Ninth Regiment Illinois*, 155 ("never have held bran"). See also Fry testimony, *OR* 16(1):218, 223; Testimony of Col. A. D. Streight, Nashville, December 14, 1862, *OR* 16(1):148–49; Testimony of Col. Lewis D. Campbell, Cincinnati, December 4, 1862, *OR* 16(1):79; Tapp and Klotter, *Tuttle*, 122; Gates, *Rough Side of War*, 27–28; Herr, *Nine Campaigns*, 107; Waddle, *Three Years*, 26; and Dodge, *Old Second Division*, 327–28.

37. John Easton to [George] Stolz, Camp at Crab Orchard, Ky., October 17, 1862, ACFWHS ("from the major General"); Diary Transcript, September 22, 1862, Small Papers, IHS ("Buell is a coward"); Tapp and Klotter, *Tuttle*, 125 ("traitor, tyrant, fool"); Charles D. Kerr, "An Episode in the Kentucky Campaign of Generals Buell and Bragg," in Minnesota Commandery, *Glimpses*, 4:270 ("depose General Buell"); R. Delavan Mussey to Joseph R. Barrett, Louisville, September 30, 1862, Mussey Letters, UC ("the truth is that"); Dodge, *Old Second Division*, 338. For Tuttle's promotion, see *Report of the Adjutant General of the State of Kentucky*, 1:616–17. At subsequent hearings, Buell's defenders claimed that the army was not demoralized but gave very evasive or qualified answers to direct questions on the point. See Crittenden testimony, *OR* 16(1):554; Rousseau testimony, *OR* 16(1):354; and Mundy testimony, *OR* 16(1):644.

38. Hosea, "Regular Brigade," in Ohio Commandery, *Sketches*, 5:337 ("raggedest, dirtiest, lousiest"); John A. Bross to [Mrs. John A. Bross], Camp near Louisville, September 29, 1862, Bross Letters, Private Collection; Buell, *Statement*, 35 ("perfectly raw, undisciplined"); Woodcock, *Southern Boy*, 99–100 ("very easy to discern"); Lathrop, *Fifty-Ninth Regiment Illinois*, 155; William H. Bradbury to "My Dearest Wife," Louisville, September 26, 1862, LC ("being mostly green"). For the prevalence of what was called "French leave" (unauthorized absence from the ranks) in late September 1862, see Darr testimony *OR*, 16(1):612; Testimony of Maj. [J. M.] Wright, Cincinnati, April 6, 1863, *OR* 16(1):663–64; Testimony of Col. J. B. Fry, [April 25, 1863], *OR* 16(1):714; Lathrop, *Fifty-Ninth Regiment Illinois*, 155, Kellogg "Recollections," p. 33, USAMHI; and Shaw,

Tenth Regiment Indiana, 170. Waddle (*Three Years*, 28) mentions other pleasures that soldiers found in Louisville.

39. Rogers, *125th Regiment Illinois*, 15; Winters, *50th Ohio*, 14; James Vernor to "Dear Mother," Jeffersonville, Ind., [September 25, 1862], Vernor Family Collection, BHC.

40. Herr, *Nine Campaigns*, 107 ("conduct of General Buell"). See also Patterson, *William Elwood Patterson*, 15.

41. Gates, *Rough Side of War*, 15 ("dirty, ragged division"), 29.

42. Boyle testimony, *OR* 16(1):372; Stone, "Operations of General Buell," in *Campaigns*, 278.

43. Levi Adolphus Ross to "My Dear Father," Louisville, September 16, 1862, Ross Family Papers, ISHL ("rapidly becoming initiated"). See also Ross Diary, September 1862, ISHL; Diary Typescript, note to entries for September 1862, Howe Papers, IHS (the 79th Indiana was "kept pretty busy in drilling"); Silas Curtis Stevens to E. P. Stevens, South Fork, N.C., May 25, 1903, Stevens Papers, CHS (the Chicago Board of Trade Battery drills frequently); Godard Diary, September 8, 1862, SRNB (the 89th Illinois drills eight hours per day); Gardner Diary, September 8, 1862, Barnett Papers, container 2, folder 17, WRHS (Battery E, 1st Ohio Artillery, drilled three times each day).

44. John Patton Memoir, 4:76–77, LC ("never spent an hour"); Reece, *Illinois*, 6:416 ("hardly an attempt"). See also Congleton Diary, October 7, 1862, LC; Rousseau testimony, *OR* 16(1):348, 350, 358–59.

45. Buell, *Statement*, 35; Otis, "Kentucky Campaign," in *Campaigns*, 244; Brown, Murphy, and Putney, *Behind the Guns*, 25; Gates, *Rough Side of War*, 29; Morris Fitch to "Dear Folks," Louisville, September 25, 1862, Fitch Letter, Ness Collection, MHC ("many green regts"); Shaw, *Tenth Regiment Indiana*, 170 ("had wisely decided"); Waddle, *Three Years*, 28; Herr, *Nine Campaigns*, 110 ("sandwiched in between"). For nascent brigade spirit, see Hough, *Soldier in the West*, 63 ("Our Brigade consists of the very first troops that went into Kentucky. . . . We have a reputation"), and Bishop, "Second Regiment," 80.

46. Special Orders No. 158, Louisville, September 29, 1862, *OR* 16(2):558–59; Buell, "Perryville," in *B&L* 3:45. For descriptions of the provocation of Davis and the murder of Nelson, see J. B. Fry, "Killed By a Brother Soldier," quoted in J. Montgomery Wright, "Notes of a Staff-Officer at Perryville," in *B&L* 3:60; Lathrop, *Fifty-Ninth Regiment Illinois*, 157–59; Wright, "A Glimpse of Perryville," 129–30; James Vernor to "Dear Brother," near Jeffersonville, Ind., [September 30, 1862], Vernor Family Collection, BHC; Diary, September 29, 1862, Tilford Papers, FC; "S" to "Dear Laura," Jeffersonville, Ind., September 20 [*sic*], 1862, Ness Collection, folder 21, MHC; and Buell to Halleck, Floyds Fork, Ky., October 3, 1862, *OR* 16(2):566–67. A good secondary account, which argues that Davis deliberately sought to provoke Nelson into a duel but lost his composure and committed murder instead, is Jenkins, "A Shooting at the Galt House."

47. Stone, "Operations of General Buell," in *Campaigns*, 279; Marshall, *Twenty-Second Regiment Indiana*, 23 ("course he pursued"); Day Elmore to "Dear Father & Mother," Camp Louisville, September 29, 1862, Elmore Papers, CHS ("got the wrong man");

John A. Bross to [Mrs. John A. Bross], Camp near Louisville, September 29, 1862, Bross Letters, Private Collection ("Almost every body"); "S" to "Dear Laura," Jeffersonville, Ind., September 20 [sic], 1862, Ness Collection, folder 21, MHC; Tourgée, *Story of a Thousand*, 105; Diary Typescript, September 29, 1862, Howe Papers, IHS ("soldiers and citizens"); Bennett, *Ninth Michigan*, 19 ("instead of mourning"). See also Spaulding, "Military Memoirs," p. 8, Spaulding Papers, MHC; James W. Bingham to "Dear Mother," Louisville, September 29, 1862, Bingham Letters, MHC.

48. Thomas Prickett to [Matilda Darr], Louisville, September 30, 1862, Prickett Papers, IHS ("rough old customer"); Otis, "Kentucky Campaign," in *Campaigns*, 245–47 ("not wholly unexpected"); Stone, "Operations of General Buell," in *Campaigns*, 279; Waddle, *Three Years*, 29; Ross Diary, September 30, 1862, ISHL ("unwhipped of justice"); Diary, September 29, 1862, Tilford Papers, FC ("considered a great tyrant"); Culver, *"Your Affectionate Husband,"* 9 ("heard no one").

49. Buell to Halleck, Floyd's Fork, Ky., October 3, 1862, OR 16(2):566–67. Since no formal charges were brought against Davis within the time that he could be held without being charged (Buell being distracted by the Battle of Perryville and its aftermath), Davis was released from military arrest on October 13. The army remained so short of experienced generals that he was returned to division command in November. State criminal proceedings against Davis were delayed during his military service (in which he rose to corps command level) and eventually dropped. See Jenkins, "A Shooting at the Galt House," 115–18. Jenkins debunks various conspiracy theories that accuse Governor Morton and other politicians of protecting Davis; for these, see Tapp, "The Assassination of General Nelson."

50. General Orders No. —, Hdqrs. Department of the Ohio, Louisville, September 1, 1862, OR 16(2):987 (appointing Gilbert); Wright deposition, OR 16(1):693; Boyle testimony, OR 16(1):375–76; Stone, "Operations of General Buell," in *Campaigns*, 272; F. B. James, "Perryville and the Kentucky Campaign of 1862," in Ohio Commandery, *Sketches*, 5:161 ("under a bushel"); Comment by General Buell, Testimony of Capt. George S. Roper, Nashville, December 27, 1862, OR 16(1):285 ("his rank entitled him"); Steedman testimony, OR 16(1):136; Bishop, *Story of a Regiment*, 70. For Gilbert's explanation of his promotion, see Gilbert, "Bragg's Invasion of Kentucky," 221–22.

51. Col. J. C. McKibben to Halleck, Louisville, September 29, 1862, OR 16(2):554; Hazen, *Narrative*, 54; Thomas to Halleck, Louisville, September 29, 1862, OR 16(2):555; J. J. Crittenden, Garrett Davis, R. Mallory, and G. W. Dunlap to His Excellency the President, Louisville, September 29, 1862, OR 16(2):557–58; Halleck to Buell and Thomas, Washington, September 29, 1862, OR 16(2):555; Otis, "Kentucky Campaign," in *Campaigns*, 249 ("source of regret"); R. Delavan Mussey to Joseph R. Barrett, Louisville, September 30, 1862, Mussey Letters, UC; Shaw, *Tenth Regiment Indiana*, 169; Nathaniel S. Shaler, "The Kentucky Campaign of 1862," in *Campaigns*, 215.

52. Special Orders No. 159, Louisville, September 30, 1862, OR 16(2):560.

53. Frederick Marion to "Dear Sister," Nashville, September 12, 1862, Marion Papers, ISHL ("pulled out his revolver").

54. The Seventh Division, under George W. Morgan, remained trapped at Cumberland Gap. The army's forces around Nashville, including two brigades sent from Grant's

army, constituted the Eighth Division under the command of Brigadier General James Negley.

55. See Sheridan, *Personal Memoirs*, 1:126–35, 190 ("Buell's good intentions").

56. Herr, *Nine Campaigns*, 110 ("very best of spirits").

57. Shanks, *Personal Recollections*, 247. An early commentator on Buell's record, George A. Bruce, called him "one of the most intellectual officers of the old army" but also "the victim of infinite and useless details." Bruce, "Buell's Campaign Against Chattanooga," in *Mississippi*, 147.

CHAPTER 7

1. J. M. Wright testimony, *OR* 16(1):665 (without the Twelfth Division, made up entirely of new regiments and not assigned to a corps, Buell had 66,000 men); Herr, *Nine Campaigns*, 110 ("a gaudy picture").

2. Buell to Halleck, Mount Washington, Ky., October 3, 1862, *OR* 16(2):566; Buell to Major-General Wright, Bardstown, Ky., October 5, 1862, *OR* 16(2):575; Buell, "Perryville," in *B&L* 3:47; James B. Fry to Thomas, [n.p.], October 5, 1862, 1 A.M. and 11 P.M., *OR* 16(2):576; James B. Fry to McCook, [n.p.], October 6, 1862, 11:30 P.M., *OR* 16(2):578–79. Dodge (*Old Second Division*, 345–53) describes the advance of the Second Division toward Frankfort.

3. For the wagon train of the Army of the Ohio, see Lewis Zahm to Col. J. B. Fry, Salt River, [Ky.], October 3, 1862, *OR* 16(2):567–68; James M. Sligh to "Dear Mother," HQ 1 Mich. Eng., October 7, 1862, Sligh Letters, MHC; and Dodge, *Old Second Division*, 357. For corps columns, see Lucius Wood to [Addie Wood], Camp near Perryville, Ky., October 14, 1862, Wood Letters, E. G. Wood Family Papers, folder 3, WRHS; Sheridan, *Personal Memoirs*, 1:193; McCook testimony, *OR* 16(1):89; and A. McD. McCook to Thomas, Bloomfield, Ky., October 5, 1862, *OR* 16(2):575 ("blissful ignorance").

4. General Orders No. 46a, Louisville, September 27, 1862, *OR* 16(2):552 ("few necessary articles"); Buell, "Perryville," in *B&L* 3:45; McCook testimony, *OR* 16(1):89; Diary Typescript, October 1, 1862, Inskeep Papers, OHS; John A. Bross to [Mrs. John A. Bross], Camp near Lancaster, Ky., October 15, 1862, Bross Letters, Private Collection; Shaw, *Tenth Regiment Indiana*, 169 ("travelling light").

5. Shaw, *Tenth Regiment Indiana*, 170 ("all kinds of trumpery").

6. Nelson to Wright, Richmond, August 27, 1862, *OR* 16(2):435; Jerome Carpenter, *Rochester Chronicle*, September 25, 1862, in Overmyer, *Stupendous Effort*, 28.

7. Congleton Diary, October 8, 1862, LC ("pack peddler"); Marshall Diary, October 4, 1862, LC ("thrown away a portion"); Rogers, *125th Regiment Illinois*, 28; Patterson, *William Elwood Patterson*, 16.

8. Patterson, *William Elwood Patterson*, 16 ("about played out"); Morris, *Eighty-First Indiana*, 15 ("completely worn out"); Wright testimony, *OR* 16(1):655 ("great number of stragglers"); Darr testimony, *OR* 16(1):613 ("usual close order"). See also Fry testimony, *OR* 16(1):714, and Crittenden testimony, *OR* 16(1):524.

9. A. McD. McCook to Thomas, Floyd's Fork, Bardstown Road, [Ky.], October 2,

1862, *OR* 16(2):565 ("cannot be helped"); Ross Diary, October 7, 1862, ISHL ("mules, hog and goose"). See also Marshall Diary, October 4, 1862, LC; Herr, *Nine Campaigns*, 112; Diary, Hempstead Papers, MHC, p. 81; Wright, "Staff-Officer at Perryville," in *B&L* 3:60; Morris, *Eighty-First Indiana*, 15; Lucius Wood to "Dear Father Mother and Sister," Camp near Bloomfield, Ky., October 5, 1862, Wood Letters, E. G. Wood Family Papers, folder 3, WRHS; Stone, "Operations of General Buell," in *Campaigns*, 7:281; Rogers, *125th Regiment Illinois*, 35; Winters, *50th Ohio*, 15. Jerome Carpenter (*Rochester Chronicle*, September 25, 1862, in Overmyer, *Stupendous Effort*, 28) includes a detailed description of how the stone turnpikes of Kentucky were "pulverized . . . [to] a superfine dust, from one-half inch to two inches deep."

10. Marshall Diary, October 8, 1862, LC ("dryer and hotter"); Lucius Wood to "Dear Father Mother and Sister," Camp near Bloomfield, Ky., October 5, 1862, folder 3, E. G. Wood Family Papers, WRHS ("hot & heavy"); Shaw, *Tenth Regiment Indiana*, 171–72 ("dress parade at midnight").

11. Buell, "Perryville," in *B&L* 3:47; Buell, *Statement*, 37–38; Herr, *Nine Campaigns*, 112; James B. Fry to Thomas, [n.p.], October 7, 1862, 7 P.M., *OR* 16(2):580–81; James B. Fry to McCook, [n.p.], October 8, [1862], 4 A.M., *OR* 16(2):587–88.

12. Thomas to Buell, Hayesville, October 7, 1862, 6 P.M., *OR* 16(2):580; Thomas to Buell, Rolling Fork, Ky., October 8, 1862, 3 A.M., *OR* 16(2):587; Report of Maj. Gen. Alexander McD. McCook, Camp, near Crab Orchard, Ky., October 18, 1862, *OR* 16(1):1038; Report of Brig. Gen. Lovell H. Rousseau, In the Field, October 17, 1862, *OR* 16(1):1045.

13. Wright, "Staff-Officer at Perryville," in *B&L* 3:60 ("eagerly awaited for"); Buell, *Statement*, 37 ("no longer anticipated").

14. Cf. Stone, "Operations of General Buell," in *Campaigns*, 281, and Arrian, *Campaigns of Alexander*, bk. 6, sec. 26. This was the third time in a year that Buell had been thrown from his horse; see Chapter 4.

15. Diary Typescript, October 8, 1862, Connelly Papers, IHS; William P. White, quoted in Herr, *Nine Campaigns*, 459 ("an awful time"); Gates, *Rough Side of War*, 29 ("for every cupful"); Herr, *Nine Campaigns*, 112 ("most execrable water").

16. Rogers, *125th Regiment Illinois*, 35. Veterans recognized that the order to remove their knapsacks in preparation for battle was not issued lightly, because once soldiers set down their belongings, they rarely saw them again. Griffith (*Battle Tactics*, 161) discusses the general significance of orders to remove packs. Many Army of the Ohio soldiers wrote of dropping (and often losing) their packs as part of the experience of battle. See, e.g., Anonymous [Memoir of Co. C, 59th Ohio], July 14, 1906, p. 7, SNMP ("I remember piling my knapsack by a small tree with a lot of others [at Shiloh] and it may be there yet as I have never seen it to this day"); Edward F. Dutcher, "Officer's Certificate of Disability," December 13, 1887, photocopy, Dutcher Papers, SRNB; Glezen "Civil War Diary," p. 4, ISL; Diary Typescript, October 8, 1862, Howe Papers, IHS; Winters, *50th Ohio*, 19; and Morris, *Eighty-First Indiana*, 16.

17. Sheridan, *Personal Memoirs*, 1:194; Report of Maj. Gen. Charles C. Gilbert, Near Crab Orchard, Ky., October 18, 1862, *OR* 16(1):1072; Report of Brig. Gen. Philip H. Sheridan, Camp on the Rolling Fork, October 23, 1862, *OR* 16(1):1081–82; Report of

Col. Daniel McCook, Battle-field Chaplin Hills, October 9, 1862, *OR* 16(1):1083–84; Report of Col. William C. Kise, Camp near Crab Orchard, October 10, 1862, *OR* 16(1):1074; Diary Transcript, October 8, 1862, Small Papers, IHS; Shaw, *Tenth Regiment Indiana*, 173 ("spirited confab"); Report of Lieut. Col. Daniel D. T. Cowen, Battle-field near Perryville, Ky., October 9, 1862, *OR* 16(1):1085–86 (52nd Ohio); Work Diary Transcript, October 8, 1862, USAMHI. At this time and throughout the rest of the day Sheridan's men received support from the 2nd Michigan Cavalry and 9th Pennsylvania Cavalry, occupying the ground between Gilbert's and McCook's corps. See Diary, October 8, 1862, Hempstead Papers, MHC, and "Y.S.," "Cincinnati *Gazette* Account," Battle-Field of Perryville, October 9, 1862, in Moore, *Rebellion Record*, 5:527–28.

18. Artillery units in the Army of the Ohio tended to be known by the names of their commanders. Captain Loomis's unit was also called the "Coldwater Artillery," based on its origins as a prewar militia unit from Coldwater, Mich. See Dyer, *Compendium*, 3:1276.

19. Sheridan, *Personal Memoirs*, 1:196; A. McCook report, *OR* 16(1):1039; Rousseau report, *OR* 16(1):1044.

20. Rousseau report, *OR* 16(1):1045 ("suffering intensely"); [Chandler], "5th Indiana Battery," pp. 20–21, SRNB; Report of Captain Peter Simonson, Camp near Harrodsburg, Ky., October 12, 1862, *OR* 16(1):1055; Alfred Pirtle to "Dear Ma," HQ 3 Div Ordnance Dept., Camp Sane, Tyree Springs, Tenn., December 2, 1861, Pirtle Papers, FC ("staves and sponges").

21. A. McD. McCook testimony, *OR* 16(1):90; Buell, "Perryville," in *B&L* 3:47; Buell report, *OR* 16(1):1025 ("somewhat expected an attack"); Wright, "Staff-Officer at Perryville," in *B&L* 3:60 ("going serenely away"). For the audibility of artillery at Buell's headquarters, see Testimony of Capt. J. H. Gilman, Nashville, December 24, 1862, *OR* 16(1):245–46; Testimony of Capt. O. A. Mack, Nashville, December 26, 1862, *OR* 16(1):275–76; and Roper testimony, *OR* 16(1):284.

22. Roper testimony, *OR* 16(1):284 ("heavy and furious"); Otis, "Kentucky Campaign," in *Campaigns*, 251; Buell report, *OR* 16(1):1025 ("any serious engagement"); Shaler, "Kentucky Campaign of 1862," in *Campaigns*, 217 ("an idle way").

23. Buell report, *OR* 16(1):1025 ("difficult to credit").

24. A. McCook report, *OR* 16(1):1039–40; Rousseau report, *OR* 16(1):1045; Horrall, *Forty-Second Indiana*, 150.

25. Report of Col. Leonard A. Harris, [n.p., n.d.], *OR* 16(1):1049; A. McCook report, *OR* 16(1):1039 ("advance a body"); Rousseau report, *OR* 16(1):1045; A. McCook testimony, *OR* 16(1):90 ("that's my water").

26. Diary, October 8, 1862, Montgomery Papers, LC; A. McCook report, *OR* 16(1):1040; Rousseau report, *OR* 16(1):1045.

27. Testimony of Col. W. H. Lytle, Cincinnati, December 2, 1862, *OR* 16(1):70; James M. Sligh to "Dear Father," HQ 1 Mich Regt, October 17, 1862, Sligh Letters, MHC; Simonson report, *OR* 16(1):1056; [Chandler], "5th Indiana Battery," p. 22, SRNB ("first real fight"); Henry M. Kendall, "The Battle of Perryville," DC Commandery, *War Papers*, 3:381 ("a more terrible fight"); Report of Col. Joseph W. Frizell, In the Field, October 10, 1862, *OR* 16(1):1053; Harris report, *OR* 16(1):1049.

28. Horrall, *Forty-Second Indiana*, 150–52 ("first intimation we had"), 273; William R.

Stuckey to [Helen Stuckey], Camp on the march, October 19, [1862], Stuckey Papers, IHS ("no place to stop"); Kirkpatrick, *Experiences*, 13–16.

29. Beatty, *Citizen-Soldier*, 178, 182 ("on the colors"); Dodge, *Seventy-Fifth Illinois*, 42; "Y.S.," "Cincinnati *Gazette* Account," Battle-Field of Perryville, October 9, 1862, in Moore, *Rebellion Record*, 5:530–31.

30. Report of Col. John Beatty, [n.p., n.d.], *OR* 16(1):1057–58; Report of Col. George Humphrey, Camp near Harrodsburg, Ky., October 12, 1862, *OR* 16(1):1057; Speed, Kelly, and Pirtle, *Union Regiments of Kentucky*, 428; Lytle testimony, *OR* 16(1):70; "Y.S.," "Cincinnati *Gazette* Account," Battle-Field of Perryville, October 9, 1862, in Moore, *Rebellion Record*, 5:530–31.

31. Report of Col. Alfred R. Chapin, Chaplin Hills, Ky., October 11, 1862, *OR* 16(1):1055 ("no military science"); Report of Col. Benjamin F. Scribner, Near Harrodsburg, Ky., October 13, 1862, *OR* 16(1):1052; Harris report, *OR* 16(1):1050.

32. Scribner, *How Soldiers Were Made*, 259–60 ("sort of moral gravitation").

33. Shanks, *Personal Recollections*, 339–41 ("next to impossible").

34. Rousseau report, *OR* 16(1):1047 ("closer in a moment"); Harris report, *OR* 16(1):1050–51.

35. Return of Casualties in the Union forces . . . , *OR* 16(1):1033; Scribner report, *OR* 16(1):1052; Report of Lieut. Ellis E. Kennon, Near Crab Orchard, Ky., *OR* 16(1):1067.

36. Harris report, *OR* 16(1):1049.

37. A. McCook report, *OR* 16(1):1040; Rousseau report, *OR* 16(1):1046–47.

38. Alden F. Brooks to ——, n.p., August 1, 1912, Brooks Letter, Regimental Papers, container 23, folder 3, WRHS ("the night before"); A. McD. McCook testimony, Nashville, December 8, 1862, *OR* 16(1):90 ("could not march"); Report of Capt. Percival P. Oldershaw, In Camp near Crab Orchard, Ky., October 15, 1862, *OR* 16(1):1059.

39. See Tourgée, *Story of a Thousand*, 132, and Telephone conversation with Kurt Holman, Superintendent, Perryville State Historic Site, April 12, 1994.

40. Report of Capt. William P. Anderson, [n.p.], October 10, 1862, *OR* 16(1):1062–63.

41. Report of Col. James Monroe, Chaplin River, October 11, 1862, Tuttle Papers, WRHS; Silas M. Shepard to [William Orland Bourne], n.p., n.d., Shepard Letter, LC; William A. Pepper to "My Dear Sister," Danville, Ky., October 16, "Civil War Writings of William Allen Pepper," [ed.] Arnold Kent Kilen, transcript, Pepper Papers, ISHL.

42. Report of Col. Albert S. Hall, Perryville Battle-field, Ky., October 10, 1862, *OR* 16(1):1065; Tourgée, *Story of a Thousand*, 119–21; Anderson report, *OR* 16(1):1063; Alden F. Brooks to ——, n.p., August 1, 1912, Brooks Letter, Regimental Papers, container 23, folder 3, WRHS ("made a mistake").

43. Josiah Ayre Diary, October 8, 1862, quoted in Kentucky Department of Parks, *Perryville Battlefield State Historic Site* (Frankfort: N.p., n.d.).

44. Oldershaw report, *OR* 16(1):1060–61 ("perfectly unmanned"); Wright, "Staff-Officer at Perryville," in *B&L* 3:61; Connolly, *Three Years*, 21; William A. Pepper to "My Dear Sister," Danville, Ky., October 16, "Civil War Writings of William Allen Pepper," [ed.] Arnold Kent Kilen, transcript," Pepper Papers, ISHL; Hall report, *OR* 16(1):1065; Tourgée, *Story of a Thousand*, 102–3, 124. Brigade Adjutant William Anderson described

the behavior of some officers on this part of the battlefield as "disgraceful," but Albion Tourgée wrote an impassioned defense of the conduct of the 105th Ohio and 123rd Illinois, based in part on the high casualties the units suffered and the reports of their Confederate opponents. Anderson report, *OR* 16(1):1063; Tourgée, *Story of a Thousand*, 130–36.

45. Oldershaw report, *OR* 16(1):1060; Anderson report, *OR* 16(1):1063.

46. Taylor, "The Battle of Perryville," 276 ("less than an hour"), 277 ("whirling the rammer"); Tourgée, *Story of a Thousand*, 124–27 ("wholly dissipated"); Shanks, *Personal Recollections*, 137; Connolly, *Three Years*, 21–22.

47. Oldershaw report, *OR* 16(1):1059; Kennon report, *OR* 16(1):1066–68 ("want of discipline"); Report of Col. W. P. Reid, Near Perryville, Ky., October 9, 1862, Tuttle Papers, WRHS; Reid, *Ohio in the War*, 2:620.

48. Connolly, *Three Years*, 25; Report of Lieut. Col. Silas A. Strickland, Camp near Perryville, October 10, 1862, *OR* 16(1):1069; Kennon report, *OR* 16(1):1066–68; Oldershaw report, *OR* 16(1):1060–62 ("behind a stump"); Winters, *50th Ohio*, 20 ("very mild indeed"); A. McCook report, *OR* 16(1):1040–41.

49. [Nevin] "Regimental History," p. 3, LC ("last four miles"); Report of Col. John C. Starkweather, On Battle-Field, October 11, 1862, *OR* 16(1):1155.

50. Wilberforce Nevin to "My Dear Mother," In Camp at Crab Orchard, Ky., October 16, 1862, Nevin Letterbook, LC.

51. Charles W. Carr to Sarah [Carr], October 10, 1862, Carr Papers, CHS; Rousseau report, *OR* 16(1):1046; Starkweather report, *OR* 16(1):1156 ("disorder and confusion").

52. Report of Brig. Gen. Robert B. Mitchell, Goodnight Spring, Ky., October 9, 1862, *OR* 16(1):1078; Rousseau report, *OR* 16(1):1047; Herr, *Nine Campaigns*, 114–15; Report of Col. Michael Gooding, Danville, Ky., October 14, 1862, *OR* 16(1):1080; Diary, October 8, 1862, Howlett Papers, ISHL; Dodge, *Seventy-Fifth Illinois*, 44–47.

53. Buell report, *OR* 16(1):1031 ("no sound of musketry"); Buell, "Perryville," in *B&L* 3:48; Otis, "Kentucky Campaign," in *Campaigns*, 250; Gilman testimony, *OR* 16(1):245–46; Mack testimony, *OR* 16(1):275–76; Wright, "Staff-Officer at Perryville," in *B&L* 3:61; Charles C. Gilbert, "On the Field of Perryville," in *B&L* 3:57. See Boatner, *Civil War Dictionary*, q.v. "acoustic shadow."

54. Wright, "Staff-Officer at Perryville," in *B&L* 3:61.

55. For the vulnerability of the Confederate position at Perryville, see Joseph Wheeler, "Bragg's Invasion of Kentucky," in *B&L* 3:15.

56. Farmer Memoir, p. 270, LL ("perforated"). For accounts of Rousseau's inspirational presence at Perryville, see, e.g., Horrall, *Forty-Second Indiana*, 151, and James M. Sligh to "Dear Father," HQ 1 Mich Regt, October 17, 1862, Sligh Letters, MHC.

57. Rousseau report, *OR* 16(1):1047 ("could not look"); Tourgée, *Story of a Thousand*, 119, 124.

58. A. McCook report, *OR* 16(1):1040. The aide whom McCook sent to Sheridan was Captain Lewis Hosea of the 16th U.S.

59. Merrill testimony, *OR* 16(1):507–9, 511; Roper testimony, *OR* 16(1):284; James, "Perryville," in Ohio Commandery, *Sketches*, 5:155; Don Carlos Buell, "Battle of Perryville," manuscript, p. 2, Buell Papers, FC.

60. Buell, "Perryville," in *B&L* 3:49; Buell report, *OR* 16(1):1031 ("aid or control"); A. McCook report, *OR* 16(1):1040 ("safety of my corps").

61. For modern criticism of Sheridan for failing to report the fate of First Corps to Buell, see, e.g., The General [pseud.], "The General's Tour Guide: The Battle of Perryville," *Blue and Gray* 1 (October–November 1983): 21–44.

62. Ross Diary, October 8, 1862, ISHL ("reserve the fire"; "a terrible ordeal"); John H. Sackett to "Dear Brother," Dry River, Ky., October 16, 1862, Sackett Papers, ISHL ("hardly hold them"); Edwin H. Benton to "My Dear Father," Nashville, November 13, 1862, Benton Letter, MHC ("where is ye?"); [Newlin], *[The Preacher Regiment:]*, 100–101 ("good execution"); Peter Weyhrich to Dietrich C. Smith, Camp Near Nashville, December 1, 1862, Smith Collection, ISHL; Thomas Frazee to "Dear Parents," [n.p.], October 13, 1862, Frazee Papers, ISHL; Day Elmore to "Dear Father," Camp on Rolling Fork, Ky., October 25, 1862, Elmore Papers, CHS.

63. Ross Diary, October 8, 1862, ISHL ("grape, Canester and death"). See also Brown, Murphy, and Putney, *Behind the Guns*, 29–31, and Aten, *Eighty-Fifth Regiment, Illinois*, 33.

64. Silas L. Parker to "Dear Father, Mother and Sister," Camp near Crab Orchard, Ky., October 16, 1862, Ness Collection, MHC.

65. Sheridan, *Personal Memoirs*, 1:198 ("next to impossible"); Steedman testimony, *OR* 16(1):132 ("his own use"); Shaw, *Tenth Regiment Indiana*, 173. See also Herr, *Nine Campaigns*, 459.

66. Gilbert report, *OR* 16(1):1072 ("upon the point"); Gilbert, "On the Field of Perryville," in *B&L* 3:58 ("the astounding news"). Before he met Gilbert, Captain Fisher encountered General Schoepf bringing two brigades of Gilbert's reserve toward the front. Perhaps infused with Gilbert's spirit of blind obedience and resistance to initiative, Schoepf declined to take responsibility for diverting the brigades to McCook's hard-pressed front and, instead, directed Fisher to see Gilbert.

67. Gilbert, "On the Field of Perryville," in *B&L* 3:58–59 ("promptness and intelligence"); Gilbert report, *OR* 16(1):1073; Wright, "Staff-Officer at Perryville," in *B&L* 3:61; *Kansas*, 1(2):109 ("like an eggshell"). Wright claimed that Schoepf actually sent two brigades; if so, only one arrived in time to do any fighting.

68. Widney Diary Typescript, October 8, 1862, SRNB.

69. Levi Adolphus Ross to "My Dear Father," Louisville, September 16, 1862, Ross Family Papers, ISHL ("majority of our officers").

EPILOGUE

1. Return of casualties in the Union forces . . . , October 8, 1862, *OR* 16(1):1033–36. Hafendorfer (*Perryville*, 452–53) notes that the actual casualties suffered were probably greater than the number officially reported.

2. [Chandler], "5th Indiana Battery," p. 23, SRNB ("done our best"); Lucius Wood to [Addie Wood], Camp near Perryville, October 14, 1862, folder 3, E. G. Wood Family Papers, WRHS ("ready to respond"); John A. Bross to "My Dear Father," In Camp near

Nashville, November 14, 1862, Bross Letters, Private Collection ("like a spirited horse"). Wood and the other members of the 121st Ohio were keenly aware that their regiment had not acquired a good reputation at Perryville and went into action at Chickamauga in September 1863 crying "Wipe out Perryville!" Reid, *Ohio in the War*, 2:621.

3. Ross Diary, October 8, 1862, ISHL ("coolly indifferent"); Connolly, *Three Years*, 25 ("without his help"); Lucius Wood to "Dear Parents and Sister," Perryville, October 31, 1862, folder 3, Wood Family Papers, WRHS; Van Zwaluwenburg Memoir, p. 25, SCWC; Culver, *"Your Affectionate Husband,"* 24; Diary Typescript, October 8, 1862, Connelly Papers, IHS;; Gates, *Rough Side of War*, 31; Kirkpatrick, *Experiences*, 17; Shaw, *Tenth Regiment Indiana*, 186 ("never would fight"); Solon Marks, "Experiences with the Ninth Brigade, Rousseau's Brigade, Army of Ohio," in Wisconsin Commandery, *War Papers*, 2:109 ("some one blundered").

4. Shaw, *Tenth Regiment Indiana*, 174; Rogers, *125th Regiment Illinois*, 39; Levi Adolphus Ross to "My Dear Father," New Market, Ky., October 26, 1862, Ross Family Papers, ISHL; Connolly, *Three Years*, 27; Thaddeus A. Minshall to "Dear Friend," Camp on Rolling Fork . . . , October 24, 1862, Minshall Papers, FC ("big lump fish"); Eugene Lyford Letter Photocopies, SRNB ("an old granny"); Hight and Stormont, *Fifty-Eighth Regiment of Indiana*, 102; Stone, "Operations of General Buell," in *Campaigns*, 285 ("an indifferent spectator"); R. Delavan Mussey to Joseph R. Barrett, Near Crab Orchard, Ky., October 16, 1862, Mussey Letters, UC ("in our grasp"); Kendall, "Battle of Perryville," in DC Commandery, *War Papers*, 3:384–85; A. McD. McCook testimony, *OR* 16(1):124; Fry testimony, *OR* 16(1):221; David Tod to Stanton, Columbus, Ohio, October 30, 1862, *OR* 16(2):652 ("With one voice").

5. Halleck to Rosecrans, Washington, October [24], 1862, *OR* 16(2):640 ("army of operations"); Buell to Halleck, Louisville, October 29, 1862, 11:30 A.M., *OR* 16(2):651 ("the papers report"); Briant, *Sixth Regiment Indiana*, 159 ("Buell's official head").

6. [Chandler], "5th Indiana Battery," SRNB, p. 27 ("army was electrified"); Ross Diary, November 10, 1862, ISHL ("Great joy in camp"); Beatty, *Citizen-Soldier*, 189 ("unpopular as Buell"); Diary, November 3, 1862, H. C. Patton Papers, IHS ("shout after shout"); Jos. Sturge Johnston to ———, [near Reynold's Station], November 16, 1862, Johnston Papers, CHS ("such general satisfaction"). See also Otis, "Kentucky Campaign," in *Campaigns*, 253.

7. General Orders No. 8, Hdqrs. Fourteenth Army Corps, Department of the Cumberland, Louisville, November 5, 1862, *OR* 20.2:11.

8. [Fitch], *Annals*, 302–19.

9. Gates, *Rough Side of War*, 33; Godard Diary, December 20, 23, 1862, SRNB; Widney Diary Typescript, December 19, 1862, SRNB; Blakely Diary Typescript, December 4, 11, 19, 1862, SRNB; Diary, November 1862, Cole Papers, ISHL.

10. Cozzens, *No Better Place to Die*, is the standard modern account of the battle.

11. Briant, *Sixth Regiment Indiana*, 160.

12. After the Battle of Missionary Ridge, the army spent the winter of 1863–64 in Chattanooga, preparing for the advance on Atlanta. The three corps of the old Army of the Ohio had been reorganized into two (numbered IV and XIV), after Hooker's XI and XII Corps were officially transferred into the army in September 1863. Hooker's troops

were consolidated into XX Corps in April 1864, and it was with three corps (IV, XIV, and XX) that the Army of the Cumberland under Thomas entered the Atlanta campaign. Sherman, who succeeded Grant as commander of Union troops in the West, led the Army of the Cumberland, the Army of the Tennessee (under James B. McPherson), and a new Army of the Ohio (under John Schofield) to victory at Atlanta. The Army of the Cumberland ceased to exist after Sherman divided it up in November 1864, sending one corps with Thomas north to defeat John Bell Hood's quixotic attempt to capture Nashville and taking the other two with him on the "March to the Sea."

Bibliography

PRIMARY SOURCES

Manuscripts

Allen County Fort Wayne Historical Society, Fort Wayne
   John Easton Letter
Burton Historical Collection, Detroit Public Library, Detroit
   James Biddle Papers
   Henry A. Buck Papers
   James Vernor Letters, Vernor Family Collection
Chicago Historical Society, Chicago
   D. F. Bremner, "The Early History of Company E" and "History of the Cairo
      Expedition," William H. Christian Collection
   Charles W. Carr Papers
   Day Elmore Papers, Civil War Collection
   Joseph Sturges Johnston Papers
   John Mills Kendrick Papers
   Tobias Charles Miller Papers
   William Nelson Papers
   Leonard R. Norton Application Records, Grand Army of the Republic of Chicago
      Papers
   Lewis R. Penfield Application Records, Grand Army of the Republic of Chicago Papers
   Levi H. Sipes Application Records, Grand Army of the Republic of Chicago Papers
   Silas Curtis Stevens Papers
Filson Club Historical Society, Louisville
   Jeremiah T. Boyle Letter, Miscellaneous Collection
   Don Carlos Buell Papers
   Johnson W. Culp Papers
   Thaddeus A. Minshall Papers
   William Nelson Papers
   Alfred Pirtle Papers
   Torah W. Sampson Papers, Miscellaneous Collection
   John H. Tilford Papers
Illinois State Historical Library, Springfield
   Newton Bateman Papers, Miscellaneous Collection
   W. R. Claspill Letter, Orlin H. Miner Collection
   James M. Cole Papers
   Thomas J. Frazee Papers

James C. Howlett Papers

Frederick Marion Papers

Geza Mihalotzy Papers

William A. Pepper Papers

Levi Adolphus Ross Letters and Diary Transcript, Ross Family Papers

John H. Sackett Letter, Sackett Papers

Peter Weyhrich Letter, Dietrich C. Smith Collection

Indiana Historical Society, William H. Smith Memorial Library, Indianapolis

Jesse B. Connelly Papers

Harrison Derrick Letters

Wesley Elmore Papers

Lancelot Chapman Ewbank Papers

Joseph C. Haddock "Historical Sketch of the 4th Indiana Battery," Joseph C. Haddock File

Daniel Wait Howe Papers

James Jones Letter

Samuel P. Oyler Letter, Daniel Wait Howe Papers

H. C. Patton Papers

Thomas Prickett Papers

Wm. Jasper Ralph Diary Photocopy and Transcript, Civil War Miscellany Collection

Thomas Small Papers

William Roberts Stuckey Papers

Indiana State Library, Indiana Division, Manuscript Department, Indianapolis

Joseph P. Glezen "Civil War Diary" and "History of 80th Regiment" (microfilm)

J. C. Thompson Letter

Library of Congress, Washington, D.C.

William H. Bradbury Letter, Miscellaneous Manuscripts Collection

Louis M. Buford Letters, Charles Buford Manuscripts, Miscellaneous Manuscripts Collection

Simon Cameron Papers

James A. Congleton Diary, Miscellaneous Manuscripts Collection

Charles Wesley Heath Papers, Miscellaneous Manuscripts Collection

John Wesley Marshall Diary Transcript, John Wesley Marshall Collection

James H. Montgomery Papers, Miscellaneous Manuscripts Collection

Wilberforce Nevin Letterbook and "Regimental History," Francis B. Sayre Collection

John Patton Memoir, 27 vols.

[ ] Reynolds Letter, William Orland Bourne Collection

Almon F. Rockwell Papers

Silas M. Shepard Letter, William Orland Bourne Collection

Wm. J. Tucker Letter, William Orland Bourne Collection

Lilly Library, University of Indiana, Bloomington

James Coulter Papers, Indiana History Manuscripts Collection

Eli P. Farmer Memoir

James Hill Papers

Peter L. Hornbeck Letters, Bement Collection

Leroy S. Mayfield Papers, Indian History Manuscripts Collection

The Lincoln Museum, Fort Wayne
    George W. Squier Letters
    Richard Yates Letter, Lincoln Manuscripts Collection
Michigan Historical Collections, Bentley Library, University of Michigan, Ann Arbor
    Amos W. Abbott Papers
    Edwin H. Benton Letter, J. M. Bagley Collection
    James W. Bingham Letters, Kingsley Scott Bingham Collection
    Benjamin Bordner Letters, Nina L. Ness Collection of Civil War Manuscripts
    Morris Fitch Letter, Nina L. Ness Collection of Civil War Manuscripts
    Henry Mortimer Hempstead Papers
    John C. Love Papers
    Byron D. Paddock Letter, Nina L. Ness Collection of Civil War Manuscripts
    Silas L. Parker Letter, Nina L. Ness Collection of Civil War Manuscripts
    John Gibson Parkhurst Papers
    James W. Sligh Letters, Sligh Family Collection
    Oliver Lyman Spaulding Papers
    Benjamin F. Wells Letters, Wells Family Collection
National Archives, Washington, D.C.
    Record Group 393, parts 1 and 2
Ohio Historical Society, Columbus
    Ephraim S. Holloway Papers
    William F. Hunter, Jr., Papers
    John D. Inskeep Papers
Private Collection
    John A. Bross Letters
Schoff Civil War Collection, William L. Clements Library, University of Michigan, Ann
        Arbor
    John Pierson Papers
    Henry H. Seys Papers
    Jacob Van Zwaluwenburg Diary and Memoir
Shiloh National Military Park, Tennessee
    Anonymous [Memoir of Company C, 59th Ohio], 59th Ohio File
    Jim T. Blankenship Letter Typescript
    Dysart Family Letter Photocopies, 34th Illinois File
    H. W. Engelbracht, "Some war reminiscences of H. W. Engelbracht," trans. E. H.
        Engelbracht, 2nd Kentucky File
    Horace N. Fisher, "Memorandum of Sept. 5, 1904: Buell's Army at Shiloh, Apr. 6 and 7,
        1862" (photocopy)
    Maurice J. Williams Diary Typescript, 36th Indiana File
    "Your true Griffin" to "Esteemed Friend," 6th Ohio File (photocopy)
Stones River National Battlefield, Murfreesboro, Tennessee
    Arza Bartholomew, Jr., Letters Typescript, 21st Michigan File
    Alpheus Miles Blakely Diary Typescript, 74th Illinois File
    [Daniel Chandler], "5th Indiana Battery," 5th Indiana Battery File (photocopy)
    Edward F. Dutcher Papers, 74th Illinois File
    Frederick W. Godard Diary, 89th Illinois File (photocopy)

Eugene Lyford Letters, 88th Illinois File (photocopies)

Lyman S. Widney Diary Typescript, 34th Illinois File

U.S. Army Military History Institute, Civil War Miscellaneous Collection, Carlisle Barracks, Pennsylvania

George F. Alverson Letter

Sylvanus Bartlett Diary Typescript, in William H. Bartlett, "Aunt and the Soldier Boys," Graham Family Papers

Daniel Finn Diary Photocopy

Edgar Romeyn Kellogg, "Recollections of Civil War Service with the Sixteenth United States Infantry"

John C. McClurkin Memoir

Byron D. Paddock Letter

James A. Price Diary

Joseph Sims Letter

Jackson E. Webster Diary Transcript

Julius Birney Work Diary Transcript

Frederick H. Young "Biographical Sketch"

University of Chicago, Chicago

Speed S. Fry Letter, Butler-Gunsaulus Collection

R. Delavan Mussey Letters, Lincoln Miscellaneous Manuscripts Collection

Western Reserve Historical Society, Cleveland

Alden F. Brooks Letter, Regimental Papers

Philander B. Gardner Diary, James Barnett Papers

William L. Gross Diary

George W. Landrum Papers

Silas S. Mallory, "Not in a Useless Cause: The Journal of Events During My Career as a Soldier in the Union Army, Including a Short Synopsis of My Early Life," ed. William F. Mallory, Jr., 1969, Silas S. Mallory Papers

J. N. Patton Letter, James Barnett Papers

William Ransom Tuttle Papers

Austin Van Haun Papers

Alexander Varian Papers

Aquila Wiley Papers

Lucius Wood Letter, E. G. Wood Family Collection

Federal and State Publications

Buell, Don Carlos. *Statement of Major General Buell, in Review of the Evidence before the Military Commission, Appointed by the War Department, in November, 1862.* N.p., n.d.

Minnesota Board of Commissioners. *Minnesota in the Civil and Indian Wars, 1861–1865.* St. Paul: Pioneer Press Co., 1890.

Reece, J. N. *Report of the Adjutant General of the State of Illinois.* 9 vols. Springfield: Phillips Bros., 1900.

Report of the Adjutant General of the State of Kansas, 1861–'65, Volume 1 (Reprinted by authority). Topeka: Kansas State Printing Co., 1896.

Report of the Adjutant General of the State of Kentucky. Vol. 1, *1861–1866.* Frankfort: Kentucky Yeoman Office, 1866.

Robertson, John, comp. *Michigan in the War.* Rev. ed. Lansing: W. S. George & Co., 1882.

Terrell, W. H. H. *Indiana in the War of the Rebellion.* 1869. Reprint, Indiana Historical Collections, vol. 41. N.p.: Indiana Historical Bureau, 1960.

U.S. Bureau of the Census. *Historical Statistics of the United States: Colonial Times to 1970.* Bicentennial ed. 2 vols. Washington, D.C.: GPO, 1975.

U.S. War Department. *The War of the Rebellion: A Compilation of the Official Records of the Union and Confederate Armies.* 128 vols. Washington, D.C.: GPO, 1880–1901.

Published Diaries, Personal Papers, and Memoirs

Basler, Roy P., ed., Marion Dolores Pratt and Lloyd A. Dunlap, asst. eds. *The Collected Works of Abraham Lincoln.* 9 vols. New Brunswick, N.J.: Rutgers University Press, 1953–55.

Beatty, John. *The Citizen-Soldier; or, Memoirs of a Volunteer.* Cincinnati: Wilstach, Baldwin & Co., 1879.

Bierce, Ambrose. *Ambrose Bierce's Civil War.* Ed. William McCann. Washington, D.C.: Regnery Gateway, 1956.

Bircher, William. *A Drummer Boy's Diary: Comprising Four Years of Service with the Second Regiment Minnesota Veteran Volunteers, 1861 to 1865.* St. Paul: St. Paul Book & Stationery Co., 1889.

Blackburn, Theodore W. *Letters from the Front: A Union "Preacher" Regiment (74th Ohio) in the Civil War.* Dayton: Morningside Press, 1981.

Blegen, Theodore C., ed. *The Civil War Letters of Colonel Hans Christian Heg.* Northfield, Minn.: Norwegian-American Historical Association, 1936.

Chamberlain, Dick, and Judy Chamberlain. *Civil War Letters of an Ohio Soldier: S. O. Chamberlain and the 49th Ohio Volunteer Infantry.* Flournoy, Calif.: Walker Lithograph, Inc., 1990.

Connolly, James A. *Three Years in the Army of the Cumberland.* Ed. Paul M. Angle. Bloomington: Indiana University Press, 1959.

Culver, Joseph Franklin. *"Your Affectionate Husband, J. F. Culver": Letters Written during the Civil War.* Ed. Leslie W. Dunlap. Iowa City: Friends of the University of Iowa Libraries, 1978.

Doubleday, Abner. *Reminiscences of Forts Sumter and Moultrie in 1860–'61.* New York: Harper & Brothers, 1876.

Fisher, Horace Cecil. *A Staff Officer's Story: The Personal Experiences of Colonel Horace Newton Fisher in the Civil War.* Boston: Todd, 1960.

Gates, Arnold, ed. *The Rough Side of War: The Civil War Journal of Chesley A. Mosman, 1st Lieutenant, Company D, 59th Illinois Volunteer Infantry Regiment.* Garden City, N.Y.: Basin Publishing Co., 1987.

Grant, Ulysses S. *Personal Memoirs of U. S. Grant.* Ed. E. B. Long. New York: Da Capo Press, 1982.

Hazen, W[illiam] B. *A Narrative of Military Service.* Boston: Ticknor & Co., 1885.

Herr, George W. *Nine Campaigns in Nine States: Episodes of the Civil War. . . .* San Francisco: Bancroft Co., 1890.

Hough, Alfred Lacey. *Soldier in the West: The Civil War Letters of Alfred Lacey Hough.* Ed. Robert G. Athearn. Philadelphia: University of Pennsylvania Press, 1957.

Hunter, Edna Shank. *One Flag One Country and Thirteen Greenbacks a Month: Letters from a Civil War Private and His Colonel.* San Diego: Hunter Publications, 1980.

Johnson, Robert U., and Clarence C. Buel, eds. *Battles and Leaders of the Civil War.* 1884–88. 4 vols. Reprint, New York: Castle Books, 1956.

Joyce, Alexander. *A Checkered Life.* Chicago: S. P. Rounds, Jr., 1883.

Kirkpatrick, George Morgan. *The Experiences of a Private Soldier of the Civil War.* N.d. Reprint, N.p.: The Hoosier Bookshop, 1973.

McIlvaine, Samuel. *By the Dim and Flaring Lamps: The Civil War Diaries of Samuel McIlvaine.* Ed. Clayton E. Cramer. Monroe, N.Y.: Library Research Association, 1990.

Moody, Granville. *A Life's Retrospect: Autobiography of Rev. Granville Moody, D.D. (Brigadier General by Brevet).* Ed. Sylvester Weeks. Cincinnati: Cranston & Stowe, 1890.

Patterson, Lowell Wayne, ed. *Campaigns of the 38th Regiment of the Illinois Volunteer Infantry, Company K, 1861–1862: The Diary of William Elwood Patterson.* Bowie, Md.: Heritage Books, Inc., 1992.

Richards, Henry. *Letters of Captain Henry Richards of the Ninety-Third Ohio Infantry.* Cincinnati: Wrightson & Co., 1883.

Scribner, B[enjamin] F. *How Soldiers Were Made; or, The War As I Saw It, Under Buell, Rosecrans, Thomas, Grant and Sherman.* New Albany, Ind., 1887.

Shanks, William F. G. *Personal Recollections of Distinguished Generals.* New York: Harper & Bros., 1866.

Sheridan, Philip H. *Personal Memoirs of P. H. Sheridan.* 2 vols. New York: Charles L. Webster, 1888.

Sherman, William T. *Personal Memoirs of Gen. W. T. Sherman.* 2 vols. New York: Charles L. Webster, 1890.

Skidmore, Richard S., ed. *The Alford Brothers: "We All Must Dye Sooner or Later."* Hanover, Ind.: Nugget Publishers, 1995.

Tapp, Hambleton, and James C. Klotter, eds. *The Union, the Civil War and John W. Tuttle: A Kentucky Captain's Account.* Frankfort: Kentucky Historical Society, 1980.

Taylor, Robert B. "The Battle of Perryville, October 8, 1862: As Described in the Diary of Captain Robert B. Taylor." Ed. Hambleton Tapp. *Register of the Kentucky Historical Society* 60 (October 1962): 255–92.

Theaker, James G., annot. Paul E. Rieger. *Through One Man's Eyes: The Civil War Experiences of a Belmont County Volunteer.* Mt. Vernon, Ohio: Printing Arts Press, 1974.

Truxhall, Aida Craig. *"Respects to All": Letters of Two Pennsylvania Boys in the War of the Rebellion.* Pittsburgh: University of Pittsburgh, 1962.

Villard, Henry. *Memoirs of Henry Villard: Journalist and Financier, 1835–1900.* 2 vols. Boston: Houghton, Mifflin & Co., 1904.

Waddle, Angus L. *Three Years with the Armies of the Ohio and the Cumberland.* Chillicothe, Ohio: Scioto Gazette Book & Job Office, 1889.

Winters, Erastus. *In the 50th Ohio Serving Uncle Sam.* N.p., n.d.

Woodcock, Marcus. *A Southern Boy in Blue: The Memoir of Marcus Woodcock, 9th Kentucky Infantry (U.S.A.).* Ed. Kenneth W. Noe. Knoxville: University of Tennessee Press, 1996.

Regimental Histories

Aten, Henry J. *History of the Eighty-Fifth Regiment, Illinois Volunteer Infantry.* Hiawatha, Kans., 1901.

Bennett, Charles W. *Historical Sketches of the Ninth Michigan Infantry (General Thomas' Headquarters Guards) with an Account of the Battle of Murfreesboro, Tennessee, Sunday, July 13, 1862: Four Years Campaigning in the Army of the Cumberland.* Coldwater, Mich.: Daily Courier Print, 1913.

Bennett, Lyman G., and William M. Haigh. *History of the Thirty-Sixth Regiment Illinois Volunteers, During the War of the Rebellion.* Aurora, Ill.: Knickerbocker & Hodder, 1876.

Bishop, Judson W. "Narrative of the Second Regiment." In Minnesota Board of Commissioners, *Minnesota in the Civil and Indian Wars, 1861–1865.* St. Paul: Pioneer Press Co., 1890.

———. *The Story of a Regiment: Being a Narrative of the Service of the Second Regiment, Minnesota Veteran Volunteer Infantry, in the Civil War of 1861–1865.* St. Paul: N.p., 1890.

Briant, C. C. *History of the Sixth Regiment Indiana Volunteer Infantry, of both the Three Months' and Three Years' Services.* Indianapolis: Wm. B. Burford, 1891.

Brown, Thaddeus C. S., Samuel J. Murphy, and Wm. G. Putney. *Behind the Guns: The History of Battery I, 2nd Regiment Illinois Light Artillery.* Ed. Clyde C. Walton. Carbondale: Southern Illinois University Press, 1965.

Canfield, Silas S. *History of the 21st Regiment Ohio Volunteer Infantry, in the War of the Rebellion.* Toledo: Vrooman, Anderson & Bateman, 1893.

Crofts, Thomas. *History of the Service of the Third Ohio Veteran Volunteer Cavalry in the War for the Preservation of the Union from 1861–1865.* Toledo: Stoneman Press, 1910.

Curry, William Leontes. *Four Years in the Saddle: History of the First Regiment, Ohio Volunteer Cavalry.* Columbus: Champlin, 1898.

Davidson, Henry Martin. *History of Battery A, First Regiment of Ohio Vol. Light Artillery.* Milwaukee: Daily Wisconsin Steam Printing House, 1865.

De Velling, Charles T. *History of the Seventeenth Regiment, First Brigade, Fourteenth Corps, Army of the Cumberland: War of the Rebellion.* Zanesville, Ohio: E. R. Sullivan, 1889.

Dodge, William Sumner. *A Waif of the War; or, The History of the Old Seventy-Five Illinois Infantry, Embracing the Entire Campaigns of the Army of the Cumberland.* Chicago: Church & Goodman, 1866.

Floyd, David Bittle. *History of the Seventy-Fifth Regiment of Indiana Infantry Volunteers: Its Organization, Campaigns, and Battles (1862–65).* Philadelphia: Lutheran Publication Society, 1893.

Funk, Arville L. *A Hoosier Regiment in Dixie: A History of the Thirty-eighth Indiana Volunteer Infantry Regiment.* Chicago: Adams Press, 1978.

Grebner, Constantin. *"We Were the Ninth": A History of the Ninth Regiment, Ohio Volunteer Infantry April 17, 1861 to June 7, 1864.* Trans. Frederic Trautmann. 1897. Reprint, Kent, Ohio: Kent State University Press, 1987.

Grose, William. *The Story of the Marches, Battles, and Incidents of the 36th Regiment Indiana Volunteer Infantry.* New Castle, Ind.: Courier Co. Press, 1891.

Hartpence, William R. *History of the Fifty-First Indiana Veteran Volunteer Infantry: A Narrative of its Organization, Marches, Battles and Other Experiences in Camp and Prison; from 1861 to 1866.* Cincinnati: Robert Clarke Co., 1894.

Haynie, Henry J. *The Nineteenth Illinois: A Memoir of a Regiment of Volunteer Infantry Famous in the Civil War of Fifty Years Ago for its Drill, Bravery and Distinguished Services.* Chicago: M. A. Donahue & Co., 1912.

Hight, John J., and Gilbert R. Stormont. *History of the Fifty-Eighth Regiment of Indiana Volunteer Infantry: Its Organization, Campaigns and Battles from 1861 to 1865.* Princeton, [Ind.]: Press of the Clarion, 1895.

Horrall, S[pillard] F. *History of the Forty-Second Indiana Volunteer Infantry.* Chicago: Donohue & Henneberry, 1892.

Lathrop, David. *The History of the Fifty-Ninth Regiment Illinois Volunteers.* Indianapolis: Hall & Hutchinson, 1865.

Marshall, R. V. *An Historical Sketch of the Twenty-Second Regiment Indiana Volunteers: From Its Organization to the Close of the War, Its Battles, Its Marches, and Its Hardships, Its Brave Officers and Its Honored Dead.* Madison, Ind.: Courier Co., [1885].

Morris, George W. *History of the Eighty-First Regiment of Indiana Volunteer Infantry in the Great War of the Rebellion, 1861 to 1865.* Louisville, Ky.: Franklin Printing Co., 1901.

[Newlin, W. H.]. *[The Preacher Regiment:] A History of the Seventy-Third Regiment of Illinois Infantry Volunteers: Its Services and Experiences in Camp, on the March, on the Picket and Skirmish Lines, and in Many Battles of the War, 1861–65.* N.p., 1890.

Overmyer, Jack K. *A Stupendous Effort: The 87th Indiana in the War of the Rebellion.* Bloomington: Indiana University Press, 1997.

Payne, Edwin W. *History of the Thirty-Fourth Regiment of Illinois Volunteer Infantry: September 7, 1861, July 12, 1865.* Clinton, Iowa: Allen Printing Co., 1903.

Perry, Henry Fales. *History of the Thirty-Eighth Regiment Indiana Volunteer Infantry: One of the Three Hundred Fighting Regiments of the Union Army in the War of the Rebellion.* Palo Alto, Calif.: F. A. Stuart, 1906.

Rogers, Robert M. *The 125th Regiment Illinois Volunteer Infantry: Attention Battalion!* Champaign, Ill.: Gazette Steam Print, 1882.

Rowell, John W. *Yankee Artillerymen: Through the Civil War with Eli Lilly's Indiana Battery.* Knoxville: University of Tennessee Press, 1975.

———. *Yankee Cavalrymen: Through the Civil War with the Ninth Pennsylvania Cavalry.* Knoxville: University of Tennessee Press, 1971.

Shaw, James Birney. *History of the Tenth Regiment Indiana Volunteer Infantry: Three Months and Three Years Organizations.* Lafayette, Ind., 1912.

Speed, Thomas, R. M. Kelly, and Alfred Pirtle. *The Union Regiments of Kentucky: Published under the Auspices of the Union Soldiers and Sailors Monument Association.* Louisville: Courier-Journal Job Printing Co., 1897.

Sutherland, Glenn W. *Five Days to Glory.* South Brunswick, N.J.: A. S. Barnes & Co., 1970.

Tourgée, Albion W[inegar]. *The Story of a Thousand: Being a History of the 105th Ohio Volunteer Infantry, in the War for the Union from August 21, 1862 to June 6, 1865.* Buffalo: S. McGerald & Son, 1896.

Other Published Primary Sources

Casey, Silas. *Infantry Tactics, for the Instruction, Exercise, and Maneuvers of the Soldier, a Company, Line of Skirmishers, Battalion, Brigade, or Corps d'Armee.* 3 vols. 1862. Reprint (3 vols. in 1), Dayton, Ohio: Morningside House, Inc., 1985.

Cist, Henry M. *The Army of the Cumberland.* Vol. 8 of *Campaigns of the Civil War,* 1882. Reprint, New York: Jack Brussel, n.d.

Commandery of the District of Columbia, Military Order of the Loyal Legion of the United

States. *War Papers.* 4 vols. 1887–1918. Reprint, Wilmington, N.C.: Broadfoot
    Publishing Co., 1993.

Commandery of the State of Illinois, Military Order of the Loyal Legion of the United
    States. *Military Essays and Recollections: Papers Read Before the Commandery of the State of
    Illinois, Military Order of the Loyal Legion of the United States.* 8 vols. 1891–1923. Reprint,
    Wilmington, N.C.: Broadfoot Publishing Co., 1992–93.

Commandery of the State of Wisconsin Military Order of the Loyal Legion of the United
    States. *War Papers: Being Papers Read Before the Commandery of the State of Wisconsin
    Military Order of the Loyal Legion of the United States.* 4 vols. 1891–1914. Reprint,
    Wilmington, N.C.: Broadfoot Publishing Co., 1993.

Dodge, William Sumner. *History of the Old Second Division, Army of the Cumberland:
    Commanders: M'Cook, Sill, and Johnson.* Chicago: Church & Goodman, 1864.

Duke, Basil W. *A History of Morgan's Cavalry.* Ed. Cecil Fletcher Holland. Bloomington:
    Indiana University Press, 1960.

[Fitch, John]. "An Officer." *Annals of the Army of the Cumberland: Comprising Biographies
    Descriptions of Departments, Accounts of Expenditions, Skirmishes, and Battles . . .*
    Philadelphia: J. B. Lippincott & Co., 1863.

Fry, James B. *Operations of the Army Under Buell: From June 10th to October 30th, 1862, and the
    "Buell Commission."* New York: D. Van Nostrand, 1884.

Gilbert, C[harles] C. "Bragg's Invasion of Kentucky." *Southern Bivouac* 1 (September 1885):
    217–22.

Hinman, Wilbur F. *Corporal Si Klegg and His "Pard": How They Lived and Talked, and What
    They Did and Suffered, While Fighting for the Flag.* Cleveland: Williams Publishing Co.,
    1887.

——. *The Story of the Sherman Brigade: The Camp, the March, the Bivouac, the Battle; and How
    "The Boys" Lived and Died during Four Years of Active Field Service.* Alliance, Ohio: The
    author, 1897.

Holzer, Harold, ed. *The Lincoln Mailbag: America Writes to the President, 1861–1865.*
    Carbondale: Southern Illinois University Press, 1998.

Iowa Commandery, Military Order of the Loyal Legion of the United States. *War Sketches
    and Incidents: As Related by the Companions of the Iowa Commandery Military Order of the
    Loyal Legion of the United States.* 2 vols. 1893–98. Reprint, Wilmington, N.C.:
    Broadfoot Publishing Co., 1994.

Military History Society of Massachusetts. *Campaigns in Kentucky and Tennessee, including the
    Battle of Chickamauga, 1862–1864: Papers of the Military Historical Society of Massachusetts.*
    Vol. 7. Boston: Military History Society of Massachusetts, 1908.

——. *The Mississippi Valley, Tennessee, Georgia, Alabama, 1861–1864: Papers of the Military
    Historical Society of Massachusetts.* Vol. 8. Boston: Military History Society of
    Massachusetts, 1910. Reprint, Wilmington, N.C.: Broadfoot Publishing Co., 1989.

Minnesota Commandery of the Military Order of the Loyal Legion of the United States.
    *Glimpses of the Nation's Struggle: Papers Read Before the Minnesota Commandery of the
    Military Order of the Loyal Legion of the United States.* 6 vols. 1887–1909. Reprint,
    Wilmington, N.C.: Broadfoot Publishing Co., 1992.

Mitchel, F. A. *Ormsby Macknight Mitchel: Astronomer and General: A Biographical Narrative.*
    Boston: Houghton, Mifflin & Co., 1887.

Moore, Frank, ed. *The Rebellion Record: A Diary of American Events, with Documents,*

Narratives, Illustrative Incidents, Poetry, etc. 11 vols. New York: G. P. Putnam's Sons, 1861–63; D. Van Nostrand Co., 1864–68.

Nicolay, John G. *The Outbreak of Rebellion*. Vol. 1 of *Campaigns of the Civil War*, 1881. Reprint, New York: Jack Brussel, n.d.

Ohio Commandery of the Military Order of the Loyal Legion of the United States. *Sketches of War History, 1861–1865: Papers Read Before the Ohio Commandery of the Military Order of the Loyal Legion of the United States.* . . . 9 vols. 1888–1916. Reprint, Wilmington, N.C.: Broadfoot Publishing Co., 1991–93.

Piatt, Donn, and Henry Van Ness Boynton. *General George H. Thomas: A Critical Biography*. Cincinnati: Robert Clarke & Co., 1893.

PONTIAC [pseud.]. "Affairs in Kentucky." *New York Times*, December 25, 1861, 3.

Reid, Whitelaw. *Ohio in the War: Her Statesmen, Her Generals, and Soldiers*. 2 vols. Cncinnati: Moore, Wilstach, & Baldwin, 1868.

Stevenson, Daniel. "General Nelson, Kentucky, and Lincoln Guns." *Magazine of American History* 10 (August 1883): 115–39.

Van Horne, Thomas B. *History of the Army of the Cumberland: Its Organization, Campaigns, and Battles, Written at the Request of Major-General George H. Thomas*. 3 vols. Cincinnati: Robert Clarke & Co., 1875.

——. *The Life of Major-General George H. Thomas*. New York: Charles Scribner's Sons, 1882.

Wright, J[ohn] M. "A Glimpse of Perryville." *Southern Bivouac* 1 (August 1885): 129–34.

SECONDARY SOURCES

Anderson, Fred. *A People's Army: Massachusetts Soldiers and Society in the Seven Years' War*. New York: W. W. Norton & Co., 1984.

Boatner, Mark Mayo, III. *The Civil War Dictionary*. Rev. ed. New York: David McKay Co., 1988.

Burton, William L. "Ethnic Regiments in the Civil War: The Illinois Experience." In *1980 Selected Papers in Illinois History*, 31–40. Springfield: Illinois State Historical Society, 1982.

——. *Melting Pot Soldiers: The Union's Ethnic Regiments*. Ames: Iowa State University Press, 1988.

Clary, David A., and Joseph W. A. Whitehorne. *The Inspectors General of the United States Army, 1777–1903*. Washington, D.C.: GPO, 1987.

Cleaves, Freeman. *Rock of Chickamauga: The Life of General George H. Thomas*. Norman: University of Oklahoma Press, 1948.

Coggins, Jack. *Arms and Equipment of the Civil War*. New York: Fairfax Press, 1962.

Cozzens, Peter. *No Better Place to Die: The Battle of Stones River*. Urbana: University of Illinois Press, 1990.

Current, Richard N. *Lincoln's Loyalists: Union Soldiers from the Confederacy*. Boston: Northeastern University Press, 1992

Davis, Carl L. *Arming the Union: Small Arms in the Civil War*. Port Washington, N.Y.: Kennikat Press, 1973.

Dyer, Frederick H. *A Compendium of the War of the Rebellion*. New York: Thomas Yoseloff, 1959.

Engle, Stephen D. *Don Carlos Buell: Most Promising of All*. Chapel Hill: University of North Carolina Press, 1999.

Frank, Joseph Allan, and George A. Reaves. *"Seeing the Elephant": Raw Recruits at the Battle of Shiloh*. Contributions in Military Studies, No. 88. New York: Greenwood Press, 1989.

Fratt, Steve. "American Civil War Tactics: The Theory of W. J. Hardee and the Experience of E. C. Bennett." *Indiana Military History Journal* 10 (January 1985): 4–17.

Griffith, Paddy. *Rally Once Again*. N.p.: Crowood Press, 1987. Reprinted as *Battle Tactics of the Civil War*. New Haven: Yale University Press, 1989.

Grimsley, Mark. *The Hard Hand of War: Union Military Policy toward Southern Civilians, 1861–1865*. New York: Cambridge University Press, 1995.

Hafendorfer, Kenneth A. *Perryville: Battle for Kentucky*. 2d ed. Louisville: KH Press, 1991.

Hagerman, Edward. *The American Civil War and the Origins of Modern Warfare: Ideas, Organization, and Field Command*. Bloomington: Indiana University Press, 1988.

Harrison, Lowell H. "The Battle of Munfordville." *Civil War Times Illustrated* 13 (June 1974): 4–9, 45–47.

Hattaway, Herman, and Archer Jones. *How the North Won: A Military History of the Civil War*. Urbana: University of Illinois Press, 1983.

Hess, Earl J. *The Union Soldier in Battle: Enduring the Ordeal of Combat*. Lawrence: University Press of Kansas, 1997.

Hicks, John D. "The Organization of the Volunteer Army in 1861 with Special Reference to Minnesota." *Minnesota Historical Bulletin* (February 1918): 324–68.

Hughes, Susan Lyons. *Camp Dick Robinson: Holding Kentucky for the Union in 1861*. N.p.: Kentucky Historical Society, 1990.

Humes, Thomas William. *The Loyal Mountaineers of Tennessee*. Knoxville: Ogden Bros. & Co., 1888.

Jenkins, Kirk C. "A Shooting at the Galt House: The Death of General William Nelson." *Civil War History* 43 (June 1997): 101–18.

Lambert, D. Warren. *When the Ripe Pears Fell: The Battle of Richmond, Kentucky*. Richmond, Ky.: Madison County Historical Society, 1995.

Liddell Hart, Basil. *History of the Second World War*. 2 vols. New York: Capricorn Books, 1971.

Linderman, Gerald F. *Embattled Courage: The Experience of Combat in the American Civil War*. New York: Macmillan, 1987.

Long, E. B. *The Civil War Day by Day: An Almanac*. Garden City, N.Y.: Doubleday, 1971.

Lonn, Ella. *Foreigners in the Union Army and Navy*. N.p.: Louisiana State University Press, 1957. Reprint, New York: Greenwood Press, 1969.

Lord, Francis A. *They Fought for the Union*. New York: Bonanza Books, 1960.

McDonough, James Lee. *War in Kentucky: From Shiloh to Perryville*. Knoxville: University of Tennessee Press, 1994.

McKinney, Francis F. *Education in Violence: The Life of George H. Thomas and the History of the Army of the Cumberland*. Detroit: Wayne State University Press, 1967. Reprint, Chicago: Americana House, Inc., 1991.

McMurry, Richard M. *Two Great Rebel Armies*. Chapel Hill: University of North Carolina Press, 1989.

McPherson, James M. *For Causes and Comrades*. New York: Oxford University Press, 1997.

McWhiney, Grady, and Perry D. Jamieson. *Attack and Die: Civil War Military Tactics and the Southern Heritage*. University, Ala.: University of Alabama Press, 1982.

Meneely, A. Howard. *The War Department, 1861: A Study in Mobilization and Administration*. New York: Columbia University Press, 1928.

Mitchell, Reid. *Civil War Soldiers: Their Expectations and Their Experiences*. New York: Viking, 1988.

——. *The Vacant Chair: The Northern Soldier Leaves Home*. New York: Oxford University Press, 1993.

Robertson, James I., Jr. *Soldiers Blue and Gray*. Columbia: University of South Carolina Press, 1988.

Royster, Charles. *The Destructive War: William Tecumseh Sherman, Stonewall Jackson, and the Americans*. New York: Alfred A. Knopf, 1991.

Shannon, Fred Albert. *The Organization and Administration of the Union Army, 1861–1865*. 2 vols. Cleveland: Arthur H. Clark Co., 1928.

Street, James, Jr. *The Struggle for Tennessee*. Alexandria, Va.: Time-Life Books, 1985.

Tapp, Hambleton. "The Assassination of General Nelson, September 29, 1862, and Its Ramifications." *Filson Club History Quarterly* 19 (October 1945): 195–207.

Warner, Ezra J. *Generals in Blue: Lives of the Union Commanders*. N.p.: Louisiana State University Press, 1964.

Weigley, Russell F. *The Age of Battles: The Quest for Decisive Warfare from Breitenfeld to Waterloo*. Bloomington: Indiana University Press, 1991.

Welcher, Frank J. *The Union Army, 1861–1865: Organization and Operations*. Vol. 2, *The Western Theater*. Bloomington: Indiana University Press, 1993.

Wiley, Bell Irvin. *The Life of Billy Yank: The Common Soldier of the Union*. Baton Rouge: Louisiana State University Press, 1952.

Williams, T. Harry. *Lincoln and His Generals*. 1952. Reprint, Westbrook, Conn.: Greenwood Press, 1981.

Woodworth, Steven E. " 'The Indeterminate Quantities': Jefferson Davis, Leonidas Polk, and the End of Kentucky Neutrality, September 1861." *Civil War History* 38 (December 1992): 289–97.

Index

Army of the Tennessee, 83, 114, 157, 189; at
  Shiloh, 101–2, 109
Army of the West, 115
Artillery, types of, 88
Athens, Ala., 119, 121, 129; sack of, 122–23
Ayres, Josiah, 174

Balaclava, Battle of, 6
Ball's Bluff, Battle of, 59
Bartholomew, Arza, Jr., 147
Bartlett, Sylvanus, 54
Bates, Joshua, 25
Battles: indecisiveness of, 2–4, 111, 188,
  193 (n. 5); traditional accounts of, 3;
  technology-based explanations of, 3–4,
  193–94 (n. 6)
Beatty, John, 42, 124, 133, 187; on Buell's
  civilian policy, 123; at Perryville, 170, 172,
  179
Beauregard, P. G. T., 39
Bennett, Charles, 154
Benton, Edwin, 181
Biddle, James, 147
Bierce, Ambrose: at Shiloh, 99, 100, 105–6,
  107, 109
Bingham, James W., 142
Bircher, William, 76, 99, 111
Bishop, Judson W., 18, 19, 28; on importance of drill, 47; at Logan's Cross Roads,
  70–71
Bordner, Benjamin, 40
Bowling Green, Ky.: as strategic objective,
  84, 88–89
Boyle, Jeremiah, 140, 157; commands Elev-
  enth Brigade, 41; commands Kentucky
  troops, 140; commands Louisville gar-
  rison, 141, 143; impressed with Buell, 152
Bragg, Braxton, 3, 136–37, 144, 185, 186,
  187, 188; invades Kentucky, 145; and race
  to Louisville, 147, 148, 149; and Perryville
  campaign, 159, 160, 162, 163, 179, 183,
  185
Bramlette, Thomas, 29, 33, 93; as drillmaster,
  51; and disease, 63–64
Briant, C. C., 85, 98, 119, 187, 188; at
  Shiloh, 99, 110
Brigades: cohesion of, 5, 40, 47, 153, 170,
  172, 175; organization of, 38–39; leaders

of, 40–41, 81, 179; training of, 54, 187;
  reorganization of, 152–53
—First, 41, 42, 54; at Perryville, 183
—Second, 41; at Logan's Cross Roads, 69–
  70, 75, 78, 81
—Third, 41; at Logan's Cross Roads, 69, 73,
  81
—Fourth, 41, 140; at Shiloh, 103, 104, 108
—Fifth, 40; at Shiloh, 108
—Sixth, 40, 44, 45, 54–55, 58, 61
—Seventh, 41
—Eighth, 41, 122–23
—Ninth, 40; at Perryville, 166–67, 170–71,
  173
—Tenth, 41
—Eleventh, 41
—Twelfth (East Tennessee), 41, 65, 69, 84; at
  Logan's Cross Roads, 75–76, 78, 81
—Thirteenth, 41
—Fourteenth: at Shiloh, 103
—Fifteenth, 41
—Seventeenth: at Perryville, 166, 168, 170–
  72, 176, 180
—Nineteenth, 93; at Shiloh, 104
—Twenty-second: at Shiloh, 104
—Twenty-third: at Murfreesboro, 130–31
—Twenty-eighth: at Perryville, 163, 166,
  172, 175, 176–78, 180
—Thirtieth: at Perryville, 177–78, 180, 183
—Thirty-third: at Perryville, 167, 173–74,
  177, 180
—Thirty-fourth: at Perryville, 172–73, 175–
  76
—Thirty-sixth: at Perryville, 164
Brooks, Alden F., 173
Bross, John, 7, 9, 153, 185
Browning, Orville, 11
Bruce, Sanders D., 104
Buchanan, James, 35
Buck, Henry A., 25, 115
Buckner, Simon Bolivar, 14, 15
Buell, Don Carlos, 9, 13, 21, 44, 49, 50, 132,
  142, 159, 201 (n. 3); commands Army of
  the Ohio, 17, 22, 35; prewar record, 35; es-
  timates enemy strength, 36, 144; organizes
  brigades, 38–41; requests more officers, 40,
  127–28; organizes divisions, 41–45; and
  slavery, 45, 124–25; soldiers' confidence in,

ville & Nashville, 16, 55; Kentucky Central, 43; Memphis & Charleston, 95, 113, 117, 118–19, 129; Central Alabama, 120

Randall, Alexander, 11

Regiments: soldiers' loyalty to, 4–6, 17, 28, 92, 115, 131, 139, 143–44, 201 (n. 71); state origins of, 10, 18, 28, 107, 137–38; officer selection for, 30–32, 56, 200 (nn. 62, 64); names of, 32; integrity of, 34, 140, 152; training of, 47–53; cohesion of, 75, 79, 101, 104, 107, 168, 171–72, 174–76, 177, 187; recruitment of new, 137–38; insularity of, 144, 177

Reid, Whitelaw, 22

Richmond, Ky., Battle of, 1, 142–44, 145, 153, 155, 171; casualties at, 143

Rifled muskets: effect of, 3, 60; availability of, 4, 36–37, 87–88; types of, 87

Rockcastle Hills, skirmish at, 54, 68

Rosecrans, William, 5, 67, 186; commands Army of the Ohio, 186; commands XIV Army Corps, 187; reorganizes army, 187; compared with Buell, 187, 188; at Chickamauga, 188

Ross, Levi, 152, 154, 162, 187; at Perryville, 181–82

Rousseau, Lovell, 14, 144; raises regiments, 12; commands Fourth Brigade, 41; at Shiloh, 103, 108, 110; and slavery, 123, 124; commands Third Division, 156; at Perryville, 163, 164–65, 166–68, 171, 172, 178, 179, 180

Rowlett's Station, action at, 6, 54–55, 60, 62, 79, 108; casualties at, 58; psychological effects of, 59–60, 79, 110, 113

Sackett, John, 181

Sampson, Alford, 85, 100

Sampson, Torah, 110

Schoepf, Albin, 54, 68; commands First Brigade, 41; in Logan's Cross Roads campaign, 69; enmity toward Buell, 145, 156; commands First Division, 156; at Perryville, 180–81, 183, 240 (n. 66)

Scott, Winfield, 10, 11, 13, 14, 36, 51

Scribner, Benjamin, 47, 51, 54; opinion of Rowlett's Station, 59–60; at Perryville, 170–71, 172

Seward, William, 11

Shank, John Daniel, 138

Shanks, W. F. G., 36, 46, 158, 171

Shaw, James, 71, 117, 123, 149, 153, 160–61, 186

Sheridan, Philip: commands Eleventh Division, 157; at Perryville, 164, 180, 181–83

Sherman, William Tecumseh, 14, 27, 29, 36, 41, 42, 44; commands Army of the Ohio, 15; sanity questioned, 15–16; relieved of command, 17; political acceptability of, 45; opinion of troops, 46; commands Army of the Tennessee, 189

Shiloh, Battle of, 6, 83, 114, 117, 139, 156, 173, 174, 189; sound of fighting at, 99, 106, 178; Grant's army routed at, 100–101, 216–17 (n. 44); terrain at, 102, 103, 105; casualties at, 105, 107, 109, 110, 111; friendly fire at, 109; victory at, 109–10, 111; psychological effects of, 110–11, 113; credit for victory at, 114–15, 220 (n. 73)

Shortle, George, 71

Shortle, Samuel, 71

Sill, Joshua W.: commands Ninth Brigade, 40; commands Second Division, 156

Simonson, Peter, 168, 170

Sipes, Levi H., 110

Small, Thomas, 78, 150

Smith, William F., 125

Smith, William Sooy: commands Fourteenth Brigade, 103; at Shiloh, 103; commands Fourth Division, 157

Sommerly, Rufus, 21

Squier, George W., 64

Stanton, Edwin, 95, 117, 122, 123, 130

Starkweather, John C.: commands Twenty-eighth Brigade, 163; at Perryville, 163, 166, 167, 175, 176–77

Stevens, Silas, 139

Stone, Henry, 133, 186

Stones River, Battle of, 178, 187, 188

Strickland, Silas A., 176

Stuckey, William, 168

Tactics, 49–51, 54; manuals of, 51; at Rowlett's Station, 57, 60; at Logan's Cross Roads, 71, 73, 75, 76–77, 79, 81; at Shiloh,

Sixth Division, 86; and slaves, 125; dis-
agrees with Buell, 145
Woodcock, Marcus, 18, 64, 151
Woodruff, W. E., 12, 13
Wright, Horatio G., 145, 148; commands
Department of the Ohio, 141; promotes
Gilbert, 155
Wright, J. M., 161, 163, 178

Xenophon, 149

Yates, Richard, 30

Zollicoffer, Felix K., 62, 67, 68–69, 74, 75,
178
Zouaves, 51, 53